A COMPLETE GUIDE TO

BED & BREAKFASTS, GUESTHOUSES & INNS OF MISSOURI

Other Books in the
Show Me Missouri Series:

A COMPLETE GUIDE TO

BED & BREAKFASTS, GUESTHOUSES & INNS OF MISSOURI

By
Harry Hagen

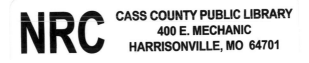

Pebble Publishing, Inc.
P.O. Box 2, Rocheport, Missouri 65279

Other Books By Harry M. Hagen

The Complete Missouri Travel Guide
Misselhorn's Pencil Sketches of St. Louis
Misselhorn's Pencil Sketches of Missouri
A Guide to Ste. Genevieve
Adventures in St. Louis
Saint Louis: A Portrait of the Past
This is Our St. Louis

1999-2001 Edition
ISBN 1-891708-04-X 14.95

Pebble Publishing, Inc., P.O. Box 2, Rocheport, MO 65279
Phone: (800) 576-7322 • Fax: (573) 698-3108
E-mail: pebble@showmestate.com

Printed by Walsworth Publishing, Marceline, Missouri, USA

For my wife Leona and my family

My sincere thanks to Jamie McIlroy of Clarksville, Mo., Jim Peters of Washington, Mo., Ann Day of Belleville, Ill., Anna Kirchner of Ste. Genevieve, Mo., Carole Keyes of Defiance, Mo., and Martin Bellmann of Jamestown, Mo., for the beautiful pen and ink sketches of the homes found in this guide and for the fine watercolors on the covers.

A special thanks to Carol Keyes of Defiance for three of the watercolors on the covers and a very special thanks to Jamie McIlroy for more than 10 years of a wonderful relationship—more than 200 pen and ink drawings and ten watercolors including four for this edition. I could not have done these books without her help.

This guide is arranged first by region, then by the city or town in that region, then by the accommodations listed alphabetically in that city or town. If the accommodation is not in a city or town, it will be listed under the nearest one. To find a specific B & B, guesthouse or inn, please use the Index of Inns at the back of this guide. The various regions of Missouri are listed in the Table of Contents as are the cities and towns within the region.

CONTENTS

INTRODUCTION

Bed and breakfast, guesthouse or inn, no matter what you call them, the idea is the same. A place where travelers are treated like welcome guests, not just room numbers. It is a concept that has been around Europe and Great Britain for many years: a private home where travelers rented an extra bedroom, were given breakfast the next morning, then went on their way.

This concept became popular in the United States during the late 1970's (although "tourist homes" had been around since the 1930's). They appeared mainly along the east and west coasts and have long been the discerning traveler's choice. Gradually moving inland, today, they can be found in every State in the Union. Missouri is no exception. There are over two hundred places listed in this guide, which does not include many smaller homes which use a reservation service only.

With this publication I have endeavored to list, with descriptive text, most of the accommodations which will appeal to persons seeking out that special place. Whether you are a business traveler tired of the hotel/motel scene, a couple on a romantic getaway, a family looking for something a little different or a vacationer longing for a few days of peaceful solitude you will find it here.

Each listing is an adventure. It can be a guest house or an inn overlooking the Missouri River at Washington; an historic home in the heart of Missouri River wine country in Hermann; or an antique filled house in historic Arrow Rock, Lexington or Ironton; a farm house with vistas of fields and forests at Bourbon, Marthasville, New Haven or Clarksville. You can find huge Victorian houses all around the State in such towns as Hannibal, Carthage, Marshfield, New Franklin or St. James. Great Mansions are to be found not only in St. Louis or Kansas City, but also in Springfield, St. Joseph, Gallatin, and Independence. In the last few years romantic getaways have become popular at places like New Florence, Ozark, Branson, Louisiana and Gerald.

Missouri's inns grace the countryside in every region. You are never far away from some quaint place tucked away in picturesque river towns, in Ozark valleys or nestled in rolling hills. Historic towns such as Ste. Genevieve, Jamesport, Bethel, Rocheport, Cape Girardeau, Fulton, St. Charles, Independence and Weston beckon those with a love for history.

Half the fun of staying at a bed and breakfast is discovering Missouri along the way. Many of the State's back roads are dotted with fine antique shops, great family restaurants and fantastic views you won't soon forget.

Throughout this guide (and listed in the index) we have mentioned some special restaurants we think you will enjoy. They could be housed in a particularly notable building, have an interesting history or possess a certain ambiance. You may not recognize the name of the restaurant or even the name of the town, but if you decide to try an entrée at one of these special eateries, you won't be disappointed.

An opportunity to stay at a B & B, guesthouse or inn can greatly enrich a travel experience. Each home has its own special qualities. Not surprisingly, inns are often a reflection of the style and personality of the innkeeper(s). Even so, all of the hosts have one thing in common. They enjoy having people share their home. You will find them ready to spend a relaxing evening exchanging ideas or chat about local history with new-found friends over breakfast. This, after all, may be one of the most appealing feature of being a guest at a B & B.

Expect the unexpected. You may find fresh cut flowers in your room, perhaps a glass of wine with cheese, fresh fruit or a cup of coffee or tea in the evening. There may be a mint or cookie on your pillow at night. Many hosts go to great lengths to provide those special touches that make a stay memorable. Often guests are invited to use the living room, den or a sitting area which are provisioned with books, games, magazines, or perhaps a television set.

Reservations are usually required and are certainly a must at popular vacation spots in the height of the season. When making your reservation you can check in advance about whether smoking is permitted, pets are allowed, baths are shared (and with how many) and the availability of accommodations for children. Be sure to ask what the rates are and what they include. What are the breakfast hours? Is it continental or full? What are check in and check out times? Are credit cards accepted? Make your Reservations early and confirm with a deposit. Should your plans change and you cancel well in advance, your deposit will be refunded. If you do not have a reservation, call ahead before going to any B & B, guesthouse or inn.

There are some host families who do not wish to be listed in any guide, and would rather have their guest go through an RSO (Reservation Service Office). At present, there are several such services available in Missouri. I highly recommend the following services based on both my personal knowledge and comments made by hosts and proprietors.

Ozark Mountain Country Reservation Service, P.O. Box 295, Branson, 65616. (417) 334-4720 or for reservations call toll free 1 (800) 695-1546. Operated and owned by Kay Cameron, her service covers over fifty homes in the southwestern part of the State. Many are located in the Branson area, but Springfield and other towns are included.

Kay is one of my favorite people. She not only has shown me the locations of various inns, but lets me know when a new one opens in her area. She has always invited me to stay as her guest whenever I have been out her way. I can tell you first hand, she is a great person.

Kansas City Bed and Breakfast Service, P.O. Box 14781, Lenexa, Kansas 66215. (913) 888-3638. Eddi (Edwina) Munroe covers Kansas City and several outlying areas.

If you wish to send me information on an area you wish to visit and the accommodations you need, I will gladly put you in touch with the proper people. You may write in care of Pebble Publishing, Inc., P.O. Box 2, Rocheport, Missouri 65279.

Every effort has been made to provide information as accurately and completely as possible. Any comments you would like to make on this guide will be appreciated. Please send them to the address listed above.

I cannot think of a home I would not be pleased to go back to again. I have enjoyed making friends with the gracious people whose warmth and friendliness make their bed and breakfast, guesthouse or inn so special.

I hope you will find this revised and updated 1999–2001 edition a valuable addition to your travel library.

Thank you,

Harry M. Hagen

1999-2001
Edition

Section One

OZARK MOUNTAIN REGION

Brighton
Eden B & B

Branson Area
Aunt Sadie's
Barger House
Bird's Eye View
Branson Hotel
Branson House
Brass Swan
Cameron's Crag

Cedar View
Cinnamon Hill
Crystal Cove
Emory Creek
Gaines Landing
Grandpa's Farm
Historic Kite
  House

Josie's Getaway
Lakeshore
Martindale
Rhapsody Inn
Red Bud Cove
Thurman House

Carthage
Grand Avenue
Leggett House

Fordland
Red Oak Inn

Marionville
White Squirrel

Nevada
Red Horse Inn

Springfield
Virginian Rose
Walnut Street Inn

Marshfield
Dickey House

Ozark
Dear's Rest

Zanoni
Zanoni Mill Inn

Rockbridge
Rainbow Trout

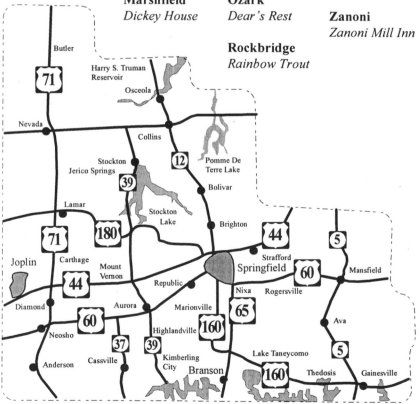

H istory, great natural beauty and plenty of water are the keys to the Ozark Mountain Region's popularity for hundreds of thousands of tourists every year.

Branson and the nearby communities have more than twenty B & Bs listed. Nestled in the tree-covered hills near Missouri's southern border, just outside of Branson, is Silver Dollar City where the pioneer handicrafts of the last century are preserved. Visitors wandering the City's shady street may see a blacksmith at work, taste candy just minutes after watching it made or see dozens of other "crafts in action." Even more crafts are in evidence each fall when the National Festival of Craftsmen is held here.

Also here is the Shepherd of the Hills Farm, overlooking some of the Ozark's most breathtaking scenery. It is the site of an outdoor theatre where the Shepherd's tale is told nightly. Here, Harold Bell Wright lived while writing "the Shepherd of the Hills." Thousands come each year to see a large local cast unfold the story of Ozark frontier life.

Another unique feature of the area is the School of the Ozarks, where students work part-time in several self-sustaining student industries on campus. Here the Ralph Foster Museum is housed with thousands of interesting items.

History becomes scenery at the seven rustic gristmills in the vicinity. The Zanoni Mill Inn offers lodging and at Rockbridge is the Rainbow Trout Ranch B & B. This region is dotted with many caves offering a look at Missouri's "inside" story. One of them, Fantastic Caverns, just north of Springfield, is the only cave in the State that has riding tours through the underground. Eden B & B is located north of Springfield at Brighton.

Enhancing all this natural beauty are four man-mad attractions; Table Rock, Bull Shoals, Taneycomo and Norfolk Lakes. The fishing is excellent, ranging from cold-water trout to an old Missouri favorite, bass.

The backwoods charm of the Ozark Mountain Region takes on a more cosmopolitan air farther north in its two major cities of Joplin and Springfield. As the two largest metropolitan locales in southern Missouri, their color and excitement complement the charms of their natural surroundings.

Joplin started as a mining camp in the nineteenth century. Lead deposits gave the town its life, but when the lead began to run out, Joplin turned to commerce above ground. Today, Joplin is a growing city of modern shopping malls, parks and plentiful recreation opportunities.

Springfield, the "Queen City of the Ozarks," is one of the fastest growing cities in southern Missouri. Located (as is Joplin) on the Interstate 44, Springfield is a crossroads of commerce and travel. The city's fine recreational facilities, plus its central location in southwest Missouri, make it a popular stop for visitors. There are many fine antique shops throughout the city as well as first class restaurants. Virginian Rose B & B and the Walnut Street Inn are nice places to stay in Springfield.

Seventeen miles east of Springfield, just off Interstate 44 is the town of Marshfield, where the Dickey House Mansion B & B is located.

South of Springfield on the way to Table Rock Lake is Nixa on Rt. 160 with the Wooden Horse Inn and on Rt. 65 is Ozark where Dear's Rest B & B can be found.

The tranquility of Wilson's Creek National Battlefield, just southwest of Springfield is in marked contrast to the thunder of battle that echoed there during the Civil War. Farther west, at Carthage, another crucial Civil War Battle occurred. Today Carthage is the site of the world's largest gray marble quarry. Marble from this quarry was used in the construction of Missouri's State Capitol building. The Leggett House B & B and Grand Avenue Inn are located here.

Several famous Missourians are honored in the Ozark Mountain Region. At. Lamar, former President Harry S. Truman's birthplace is now a State Historic Shrine. The George Washington Carver National Monument, near Diamond, honors this scientist's discoveries and contributions. The home of Laura Ingalls Wilder, a famous children's author, is preserved near Mansfield.

Moving toward the central part of the State, the hills of the Ozark Mountains Regions slowly change. Several rivers, including the Osage and the Niangua have played a part in shaping the countryside here. Deep valleys, river bluffs and even prairie lands are now mixed with gently rolling hills.

Rich in historical background, this was the last stronghold of the Osage Indians who for 300 years lived along the river that bears their name. Gone now, their span of Missouri history is remembered at several of the area's museums and in private collections of relics.

In later year, during the Civil War, this region was bitterly contested by both sides. The bloody battles and raids that characterized the civil War experiences are memorialized at the bushwhacker Museum in Nevada. The Red Horse Inn is in Nevada.

The development of this area has been dominated by its rivers. First, it was the Indians living nomadic lives along the rivers edge. When the earliest settlers came to western Missouri, the rivers were their highways for commerce and travel. Today, the rivers are valued for the recreational opportunities they provide.

Two Corps of Engineers lakes, fed by the rivers, insure continued growth as a recreational center. Pomme de Terre, well stocked with bass and muskie, has the largest walleye population of any lake in the State. It is a natural for fishermen and other water sport enthusiasts.

Stockton Lake, the State's newest, has been stocked with northern pike in addition to many other hard-fighting game fish.

Several other lakes and rivers in this part of the State have numerous spots for family outings. At Bennett Spring State Park, a natural spring with cold, rapidly flowing water is a haven for trout and an attraction for anglers.

Each year more and more vacationers seeking an escape from the city are finding the clear waters and the green hills of the Ozarks a satisfying choice.

BRANSON

Since its beginning as a store and post office founded by Reuben Branson in 1881, Branson has been one of the significant towns in the Ozark Mountain Region.

Located on the banks of beautiful Lake Taneycomo, Branson has become one of the premier resort towns attracting over five million visitors a year. For years it has been known as the "Trout Capital of the Ozarks" with Bull Shoals and Table Rock lakes just a few miles away. But it is the influx of Country Music stars that has Branson stealing the thunder from Nashville and attracting the cream of country Music talent. So successful has Branson become that during the past few years both country and contemporary singers not known for a country bent have built their own theaters to entertain year round. Wayne Newton, John Davidson, Andy Williams, the Osmond Family, Glen Campbell, Kenny Rogers, Boxcar Willie, Shoji Tabuchi, Roy Clark and Mel Tillis to name a few. In fact, the theater section of Branson is aptly called 76 Country Boulevard.

What started the Country Music influx, was the success of local music groups, the growing popularity of Silver Dollar City, the famous Shepherd of the Hills drama, great fishing and of course the very beautiful setting in the Ozark hills.

The Silver Dollar City theme park portrays life in the Ozarks of the 1880's. You can enjoy a visit to Mutton Hollow Craft Village. Walk down the shady streets lined with majestic oaks where dozens of shopkeepers ply their trade. Faithfully recreating the crafts of a century ago, the glass blower forms fragile pieces before your eyes. The candy maker pulls taffy, the wood carver chisels on native woods, the potter creates beautiful pieces on his wheel, and the broom maker can make a custom broom for your fireplace as it was done over 100 years ago.

Water rides, a children's petting zoo and elaborate climbing playground, performances by costumed dancers, string and washboard bands, numerous restaurants with varied fare, clean restrooms, a parking lot shuttle and evening performances of Country Music are some of the features that have made this an annual must for many tourists.

Not to be missed is the evening drama presented by 80 local actors at the Shepherd of the Hills farm. It is ranked as one of the best attended outdoor dramas in America. During the day you can also take a tour of the farm that carries you back in time to relive the times and legends of the hill people. You will see many of the places written about in the book by Harold Bell Wright on which the play is based.

Located at Point Lookout, just south of Branson is the School of the Ozarks. Over 1,200 students earn their way through college at one of the 65 workstations. When possible, students work at jobs that give them practical experience in their field of interest. Visitors are welcome. While there you can tour Edward's Mill, which features a 14-foot water wheel. Or visit the Williams Memorial Chapel and the Ralph Foster Museum, accurately dubbed "The Smithsonian of the Ozarks" for its outstanding exhibits depicting the heritage of this region.

Ozark talent is everywhere. In addition to big name stars you can hear great country music by local favorites: the Bald Knobbers, The Foggy River Boys, The Plummer Family and the Presleys.

A variety of activities are available here: water skiing, float trips, square dancing, horseback riding, golf, tennis, museums, caves, boating, seaplane rides, and swimming.

Near Branson are the towns of Hollister, Forsythe, Kimberling City, and Lampe; all with nice shops and restaurants. Hollister is just a mile south of Branson on the opposite side of Lake Taneycomo, which was created in 1931 when the White River was dammed. The center of town is a series of Tudor style buildings along Downing Street. It is listed on the National Register of Historical Places.

Towering bluffs, secluded timbered coves, ridges and hollows of the Ozark Mountains along with miles of free, calm, crystal clear waters will excite any nature lover. Abundant wildlife includes deer, wild turkey, mink, waterfowl, songbirds and the bald eagle.

The beauty of redbud and dogwood in spring, the lush green of summer, the brilliant fall colors and mild winters make this area worthwhile in any season.

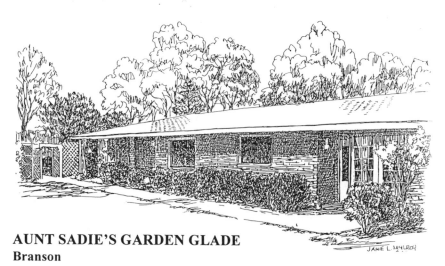

JANIE L. MCILROY

AUNT SADIE'S GARDEN GLADE
Branson

An atmosphere that is quiet, serene and peaceful aptly describes Aunt Sadie's. It sets in the midst of a wooded glade with large trees, wild flowers and birds. The house is a long, low brick ranch style. The owners, Linda and Dick Hovell, have their livings quarters at one end of the premises. The guests have use of the parlor, dining room and large outside deck. You can play the piano in the entry foyer if you like.

A large living room/dining room is carpeted in rose. There is an upholstered sofa and love seat with bright floral pattern, a pair of rose colored upholstered rockers, glass top coffee and end table with unusual lamps. A large picture window overlooks the screened-in porch and a deck. The porch has wicker seating, a table and television and lots of plants. Off the porch, the deck also has wicker seating and an umbrella table and chairs.

The dining area is furnished with a large French Provincial table and eight cane-back chairs, a china cupboard and server. A small corner cupboard holds a collection of pitchers.

Linda serves a full country breakfast in the dining room. Juice, fresh fruit in season, fresh pastries and French bread pudding with strawberry sauce. Entrees might be an egg dish with two meat dishes, biscuit and gravy or her "breakfast in a bag," for those who must depart early.

On check-in there is hot cider or hot chocolate in colder months lemonade or iced tea in summer along with some kind of pastry. Fresh flowers and candy are placed in the rooms and there is wine or a non-alcoholic beverage for honeymooners or those celebrating anniversaries.

A cozy two-bedroom cottage is in a secluded part of the grounds. Rooms are fully carpeted and have ceiling fans. There is a very nice bathroom. There is also a refrigerator, microwave, and a coffeemaker. There is a nice front porch with a white wicker sofa and chairs, and a wrought iron end table.

One bedroom is furnished with a full-size, antique white iron, ornate bed with a floral bedspread and matching valances at the window. An antique oak dresser and a day bed complete the room.

The other room has a full-size maple bed, wash stand used as a night table, a wardrobe and a television set on a wrought iron sewing machine base which makes a table with a pair of splitback chairs.

Linda and Dick have just completed two more cottages for guests, which are also very private. They are carpeted wall-to-wall, have a deck, a gas fireplace and a private bath. Among the furnishings are a king-size white iron bed, a color television and a 2-person whirlpool and hot tub. In a small area there is a refrigerator, microwave and coffeemaker. Breakfasts are served at the main house.

AUNT SADIE'S: 163 Fountain, Branson, 65616. (417) 335-4063. For reservations 1 (800) 944-4250. Four cottages with private baths. Easy access to attractions. Open all year. No pets. Restricted smoking. Children welcome. Dick and Linda Hovell, innkeepers.

DIRECTIONS: Call for directions.

BARGER HOUSE BED & BREAKFAST
Branson

L ocated on the waterfront of Lake Taneycomo is a charming version of one of America's most famous dwellings, the circa 1683 Parson-Capen House in Topsfield, Massachusetts. Ralph Barger, the new owner, has retained all the ambience, comfort and friendliness I found here on my last visit.

Guests are invited to use all living quarters of the house. An entry hall leads to the keeping room that has a brick floor with area rugs and a cozy native stone fireplace. A French door opens onto the 54-foot deck that has a great view of the lake. It's a perfect spot for the 35-foot swimming pool and hot tub which guests are invited to use. If you have a boat, you may use the private boat dock and slip. You may want to fish from the dock. It's almost guaranteed you will catch some nice trout. The tackle's furnished, so's the bait.

The carpeted dining room is wallpapered in a light blue print design above a chair rail. There is an oak china cupboard, buffet, large table and chairs for six. A server holds a silver tea set. A large brass chandelier hangs over the table.

Ralph prepares and serves breakfast – and what a breakfast it is! About 8 a.m. juice, coffee and fresh fruit is served on the deck. Around 9 a.m. in the dining room there is ham, bacon, sausage or pork chops with biscuits and gravy, chipped beef on toast or his signature entrée, cream cheese stuffed French toast. He also serves grilled KC strip steaks, or pork chops, with eggs to order, potatoes, and toasted French bread, a popular western breakfast idea he brought with him from Nevada.

The carpeted library and meeting room is extremely large and is furnished with upholstered love seats, a pair of wing back chairs, a Victorian arm chair, a sofa table and a drawer table. A large bookcase on either side of a native stone fireplace holds books and other nice things. I don't want to forget a great Old World globe and a ceramic chess set. Pull back dark green swag drapes are on the French doors leading to the deck.

Two accommodations are on the second floor. One is wallpapered in a small burgundy print and furnished with a "Thomasville Museum" bedroom set consisting of an oak queen-size four poster bed with matching dresser, two night tables with glass lamps and a pair of white upholstered chairs. Ralph has added a unique feature. He has opened up a former walk in closet, installed French doors and a balcony for a pristine view of the lake, the pool and downtown Branson. The alcove has two chairs and an antique coffee table for enjoying the coffee and snacks that Ralph always provides.

The Blue Suite is a two-room suite with a queen bed and nightstand, a Boston rocker, and a dresser with an antique hand painted glass lamp. At the foot of the bed is a beautiful cedar chest that Ralph says is a "near" antique because he made it in high school many years ago. The other room has a double trundle bed to accommodate children, a cable TV, sofa, chair and coffee table. Each accommodation has a large carpeted bath with tub, shower and double vanity.

The Honeymoon Suite is on a lower level. A private staircase from the deck or a private parking space next to the Suite may be used if you wish. The bedroom has a queen-size, dark cherry four poster bed, an antique walnut marble top dresser and table and two Victorian chairs. A brass swag lamp hanging over a cherry nightstand adds to the ambience. An adjoining room has a plush sofa with coffee table, an oak table and chairs for private dining, and a refrigerator and TV/VCR. Also, the perfect thing for honeymoon couples—a beautiful heart shaped whirlpool tub surrounded by candles and silk magnolias.

BARGER HOUSE B & B: 621 Lakeshore Drive, Branson, 65616. (417) 335-2134 or 1 (800) 266-2134. Website: http://www.natins.com/branson/lodging/bargerhouse. A Bed and Breakfast close to everything in Branson: Silver Dollar City, Shepherd of the Hills Farm, Stone Hill Winery, theaters, restaurants and shopping. Three factory merchant outlets are within easy driving distance. Smoking outside only. Children welcome. Ask about bringing pets (cat in residence, not in guest's rooms or dining area). Open year round. Ralph Barger, Innkeeper.

DIRECTIONS: Please call for reservations and directions.

BIRD'S EYE VIEW BED & BREAKFAST
Branson/Point Lookout

K ay and Glen Cameron built this house about five years ago for Kay's mother, Hazel Binion. By all means you should get to know Hazel and her cat Annie. She is a really neat lady. Hazel occupies the upper portion of the house while the guest section is on the lower level. A huge deck wraps around the half-octagon with a large hot tub overlooking Lake Taneycomo and in the distance, Branson. The Bird's Eye View is particularly beautiful at night with thousands of lights flickering. I remember when there were no more than two hundred in the whole town!

The guest area is half of an Octagon. The outside walls consist of framed glass walls and full-view glass doors. The entire space is open, but set up with four distinct areas. There is a completely furnished kitchen with full-size refrigerator and range. Kay furnishes microwave pop corn and of course the microwave. Regular, decaffeinated and flavored coffees and teas are also provided. The dining room area has a round table and four rush seated chairs. In the center is the sitting area with an upholstered love seat that faces an entertainment center. A television, VCR, and several dozen movies are waiting for you. There is also a table, floor lamp and a rattan swivel rocker. Binoculars are furnished to enjoy the spectacular view. Remember to look down for the birds because they are usually flying far below you.

The sleeping area is at the back of the room opposite the kitchen. It contains a king-size bed topped with a ruffled half-canopy. A round night table covered with a ruffled skirt is topped with crocheted lace. This table holds a reading lamp and an alarm clock if you want to set it. An antique wardrobe that has been in Kay's family for at least three generations holds extra pillows and bedding. The suite is fully carpeted and the two sets of glass doors and long windows have vertical blinds. Kay has lots of craft items, floral arrangements, pictures, plants and of course birds throughout.

There is a large private bath with twin vanities, shower stall and a whirlpool bath. I've stayed here on several occasions and the whirlpool was great!

Breakfast may be delivered to the suite or a hearty breakfast is served in the dining area next door, overlooking the lake.

As the Bird's Eye View is just three miles from Branson, you have the best of both worlds. You are secluded and can enjoy the peace and quiet along with a great panoramic view for miles. However, you are only five minutes away from Highway 76 and the heart of Branson for shops, musical entertainment, restaurants and sight-seeing.

BIRD'S EYE VIEW B & B: P.O. Box 526, Point Lookout, 65726. (417) 336-6551 or 1 (800) 933-8529 for reservations. A large suite with private deck and hot tub. No pets. No small children. Smoking on deck. Open all year. Visa, Mastercard and Discover accepted. Website for a digital reality view of Lake Taneycomo and the suite: http://birds-eyeview.com. Kay and Glen Cameron, hosts.

DIRECTIONS: From Branson, take US 65 south two miles to Route V. Turn right on V and proceed about 1 ½ mile. Turn right on V-1 or Acacia Club Road for ½ mile. Home is on the right. Always call first.

BRANSON HOTEL BED & BREAKFAST INN
Branson

The Branson Town Company built this historical landmark in 1903 with the coming of the first railroad to go through town, namely the St. Louis Iron Mountain & Southern Railroad. The hotel, which overlooks the town, was a meeting place for important people in Branson's history. Harold Bell Wright, well-known author, stayed here while writing his novel *The Shepherd of the Hills*. The historic building remained in operation as a hotel until 1979, then was a restaurant for a number of years. When Jim and Teri Murguia purchased the building, they renovated it and opened it again as a hotel bed and breakfast.

For the second year in a row Branson Hotel Bed & Breakfast Inn has been selected to receive AAA's four-diamond motel rating for "significantly exceeding requirements for appearance, quality of operation and customer service."

Just to the right of the entrance hall is a guest parlor with plenty of seating and reading lamps. Great paintings are on the walls. A bookcase holds Teri's pottery collection. All of the woodwork in the entry hall and parlor is original, even the old-time transoms. Just off the parlor is a bright and airy dining room with two walls of floor to ceiling small paned windows. There is a mission style huntboard and a huge dining table, that seats eighteen guests with bentwood chairs.

A fine breakfast is served at eight-thirty and is not to be missed. Teri serves the meal family style and prepares everything. It could be quiche, casseroles, strata, eggs benedict, or corn pancakes with fresh blueberries. There are always hot homemade muffins, coffeecake, fresh fruit, juice, jams, jellies and coffee or tea.

Guests may choose from eight guestrooms all with private baths, ceiling fans, television, telephone, bathrobes and other bath amenities.

On the first floor are two guestrooms. The Celebration Room has salmon walls, wall-to-wall carpeting and lace curtains. There is a king-size high back bed and matching dresser. Antique tables are used as night stands and an antique lamp table is set between a pair of wing back chairs.

The Rose Room has a queen-size oak high back bed, a pair of floral design upholstered wing chairs, antique oak dresser, antique chest and night tables with lamps.

On the second floor a hall entrance leads to a large verandah with Adirondack chairs. A perfect place to watch the Branson activities.

The Wicker Room has a queen-size white iron bed, two wicker armchairs, table and reading lamp, an antique chest and night table.

The Duck Club Room is decorated with duck prints and decoys, wallpaper in burgundy and white duck pattern and burgundy print drapes. It has a dark oak queen-size four poster bed, a pair of wicker armchairs, an empire style dresser and an antique table.

The Vintage Room is furnished with a queen-size oak highback bed, an antique pegged dresser, and a pair of wing chairs.

A queen-size oak sleigh bed and dresser, pair of wing chairs, tables and brass lamps are in the Fox's Den. The room has dark green carpeting, fox hunt patterned drapes and coordinated wall prints. I like this room!

In the English Garden Room is a queen-size brass and iron bed, two floral print armchair, an antique night table and dresser. Light green carpet, lace curtains, prints and pictures decorate the room.

The Honeymoon Room has a king-size bed with New England fish net canopy, floral bed linens, two wing chairs, antique dresser, night tables and lamps.

BRANSON HOTEL B & B INN: 214 W. Main St., Branson, 65616. (417) 335-6104. Open March through December. AAA four stars. Eight guestrooms with private baths. A/C, parking, free local calls. No children or pets. Smoking on verandah. Teri Murguia, innkeeper.

DIRECTIONS: From north or south on Hwy. 65 take Hwy. 76 east into old Branson. Proceed along Main Street (76) to Hotel.

BRANSON HOUSE
Branson

On a hillside setting amid quaint, romantic country flower gardens, tall, old oak trees which are surrounded by rock walls of native field stone, Branson House is ideal for honeymooners, family reunions or vacations. The house overlooks the town of Branson and the bluffs of Lake Taneycomo.

Early 1900's charm in this authentic country home is evident in each of the six guestrooms, all with private baths and central air-conditioning.

A huge, comfortable, homey parlor has a stone fireplace with built-in bookcases and dark beamed ceilings. The carpeted room has several seating arrangements with chairs and antique tables. The walls are decorated with many pictures and prints. There are plenty of art books, magazines and games. A wall unit houses a television.

The dining room also has dark beamed ceilings and a built-in server and dish cupboard. A brass chandelier hangs over the large reproduction mission oak table with fourteen matching chairs. The living room carpeting carries through to this room.

Breakfast is served either in the dining room or the large front porch, weather permitting. On the porch stone planters hold geraniums and other plants and shrubs. The huge yard is shaded by many large trees and there is a great, old stone wall around the property.

A full gourmet breakfast is served by the owner, Sylvia Voyce, consisting of either caramel crème French toast, egg strata or a spicy egg boat full of good things—or similar menu. Juice, a fruit platter, homemade apple raisin muffins, coffeecake and coffee, tea or milk, or a similar menu.

Complimentary sherry is served in the late afternoon.

Guests may choose from six guestrooms, all with private baths. Guest phones are provided with free local calls.

The Tapestry Room on the second floor is furnished with a king-size, cherry four poster rise bed, an upholstered sofa and antique English commode.

The second floor guestrooms include the Honeymoon Room with a king-size country pine poster bed. The room has a large area carpet, upholstered sofa and conversation group.

The French Balcony Room has a French door leading onto a small balcony with a private stairway as your entrance and exit. It is furnished with a queen-size, ornate iron bed and a pair of wing chairs. There is also a dressing room with a vanity and bench.

The Potpourri Room has a full-size antique iron bed, a pair of wing chairs and lamp table, and a small antique chest.

The Marigold Room is decorated in pale yellow with French linens on the twin iron beds. It also has table lamps, an old oak chest and gold Queen Anne chairs.

On the first floor, the Flower Garden Room has a queen-size antique oak reproduction bed, an oak chest, an antique wicker rocker, a wicker chair and two wicker tables.

BRANSON HOUSE: 120 Fourth Street, Branson, 65616. (417) 334-0959. Open all year. A six-guestroom B & B within walking distance to shops, restaurants and antique shops. Children over 8 years old welcome. No pets. Smoking on patio or porch. Off street parking. Three diamond, AAA Mobile Guide recommended, as seen in "Southern Living" magazine and "New York Times." Member of National Bed & Breakfast Inns Association. Sylvia Voyce, hostess/innkeeper.

DIRECTIONS: Take Hwy. 65 south from Springfield to Hwy. 76 exit. Proceed east on 76 three blocks to Fourth Street. Left on Fourth to house.

BRASS SWAN BED & BREAKFAST
Branson

In a quiet, serene, wooded location with a wonderful view of Lake Taneycomo, Dick and Gigi's Brass Swan B & B is an elegant contemporary home with everything to make your stay a memorable one. And the best part is that it's only 1 ½ miles to the Grand Palace and other 76 Country Boulevard attractions.

A tiled foyer leads to a large carpeted living room. The first thing I noticed in this tastefully furnished home was the stone fireplace. It looked like the perfect place to sit and sip hot apple cider on a cool evening. There is an upholstered sofa and arm chairs, a pair of Chippendale wing back chairs, and a rocker. The glass top end tables have brass lamps. An open section off the living room has a grandfather clock, an electric organ and a curio cabinet. A dining spot also just off the living room is furnished with a large oak table and six matching splitback chairs. There is also a small antique desk, an antique cupboard and a bishop's bench.

An open staircase leads from the living room to a lower level where you will find a nice gathering place with a large stone fireplace. Facing it is a sofa with matching rocker recliners, a pair of upholstered chairs, oak end tables, drop-leaf coffee table and a television. There is also a glass top table surrounded with four upholstered chairs, an old coke box and a pinball machine where you can try your luck. There are lots of games and a stereo. Another part of the room holds a refrigerator, microwave and an exercise machine for guests' use. Popcorn and soda are always available. A separate room with a hot tub is reserved for the Taneycomo Room. From this level a door opens out onto a patio.

Each of the four spacious guestrooms offer a private bath, sitting area, remote control cable TV/VCR, AM/FM clock radio, and ceiling fans. The walls are done in light colors with floral papered borders. The bed linens, drapes or curtains match and the carpeting is all wall-to-wall.

Two guestrooms are on the lower level. The Taneycomo Room is furnished with a queen-size four poster bed, matching bedside table and chest, a cheval mirror, tables and a pair of glider chairs. A door leads to a covered porch with seating. (And, don't forget the hot tub).

Also on this level, the Americana Room has a queen-size tester bed, which has a very unusual tester. The pair of glider chairs with upholstered backs and seats is really comfortable. There is a dresser, a bed bench, combination floor lamp and table and a round table with a floral china lamp. A door opens to a private covered porch with a hot tub and seating.

There are two guestrooms on the main level. The Branson Room is a large room with a king-size bed and wicker headboard. Furnishings include a love seat and two chairs in wicker. There is a pair of bedside tables, armoire, and a coffee table. It also has a whirlpool, fireplace, and a private entrance.

The second room is the Grand Room with a king-size bed, sleeper sofa, a pair of two drawer night tables with glass lamps, triples dresser base under the window, an upholstered rocker, brass floor lamp and a glass and brass coffee table. There is also a whirlpool with a double-headed shower

Gigi serves a hearty family style breakfast which is different each day. Juices fresh fruit, homemade bread, croissants, muffins, jams and jellies, coffee or tea. Her entrees include omelets, quiche or her famous "Brass Swan Surprise." I'm positive you will like this place.

BRASS SWAN B & B: 202 River Bend Rd., HCR Box 2368-Z, Branson, 65616. (417) 334-6873 or 1 (800) 280-6873 for reservations. An elegant four-guestroom home with all the amenities. Open year round. Children over 13 welcome. No Pets. Smoking on decks. Dick and Gigi House, innkeepers.

DIRECTIONS: 1 ½ miles from Hwy. 76 off Fall Creek Rd. on the west side of Taneycomo acres. Call for specific directions.

CAMERON'S CRAG
Branson

Each time I have visited the Branson area, I have stayed at Kay and Glen Cameron's home. Kay owns and operates the Ozark Mountain Country B & B Reservation Service. Her husband, Glen, is a dean at the College of the Ozarks. The first time I met these two nice people, I felt right at home with them, and I still do.

Their home is a long, low, ranch style, perched high on a bluff, just south of Branson. It is away from all the traffic and noise of this tourist town. The outstanding feature of the house is the 140 foot-long deck in the back of the place. It has a spectacular view of the countryside for miles around. Lake Taneycomo makes a large bend far below. The large farm just across the lake belongs to the College of the Ozarks. At night, the lights of Branson can be seen in the distance. There are several groupings of wrought iron furniture on the deck. It is a perfect place to have your breakfast or even a carry-out lunch or dinner from a nearby restaurant.

Entering the house, you are in the large entry hall that has a stone floor and skylights, and a piano against the stone wall. The area is decorated with many house plants. A sofa is in front of the window. The hall leads into the living room furnished with comfortable sofas and chairs. You are more than welcome to use the cable television. During the cold days, a fire is kept going in the fireplace.

At the end of the living room is a dining area, which also leads onto the deck. Breakfast is usually served in this room unless weather cooperates for serving on the deck. Kay uses a Blue Willow design china.

For breakfast, Kay offers a choice of entrees, letting you select it in a most unusual way. She publishes several cookbooks, so you can select three breakfasts, from the huge selection in her cookbooks, and Kay will prepare one of the three for you. With the entrees, she serves fresh fruit, tea or milk and a special blend of coffee made up just for Ozark Mountain Country Bed & Breakfasts or, Cameron's coffee from Hayward, Wisconsin.

There are two guestrooms available, each with a TV/VCR with remote control along with a movie library. There is also a small refrigerator and a microwave, which Kay furnishes for her rooms.

The Around the World Suite has a king-size wicker headboard, a round table with lamp, a pair of wicker arm chairs, two night stands with reading lamps. A private bath has a tub and shower. The suite has a private entrance from the deck where you have your own private hot tub, wrought iron table and chairs. The suite is decorated with curios collected from around the world.

The Highland Rose suite has a private entrance. The furnishings include a king-size bed, upholstered bench at the foot of the bed, a love seat that reclines, a wicker etagere, a pair of wicker chairs, a rattan glass top table and lamp table and coffee bar. A wall of windows with a glass door opens into a room with sunken hot tub and a tile floor.

If you wish, Kay will explain about the Branson area spots to visit as well as good restaurants and shops. Kay coordinates a reservation service with over one hundred host homes for other parts of the Ozark Mountain area. She will be happy to handle your reservations if you are continuing your trip after you leave Branson.

CAMERON'S CRAG: Box 295, Branson, 65615. (417) 335-8134 or 1 (800) 933-8529 for reservations. Website: http://www.bbonline.com/mo/cameron/ and also camerons.crag.com. Open all year. A two bedroom B & B home overlooking Lake Taneycomo. No children under five. No smoking except on the deck. No pets. Visa, Mastercard and Discover accepted. Glen and Kay Cameron, hosts.

DIRECTIONS: From Branson, take Hwy. 65 south just two miles to Rt. V. Turn right on V and proceed about ½ mile. Right on V-1 or Acacia club Road for ½ mile. Sign on the end of the garage. Always call first.

CEDAR VIEW COTTAGE
Branson

Near the end of a quiet country lane surrounded by large pine trees is a nice contemporary "A" frame private cottage. Don't let the appearance fool you for it is much larger than it looks, although still very cozy. It would make a great romantic getaway- as you have the entire house to yourself and complete privacy. It would also be just right for a family or two couples vacationing together.

Upon entering, the hall leads to a great room with a full kitchen that is furnished with everything you need from glassware to pots and pans. It also includes a coffeemaker, coffee, microwave oven and a dishwasher. There is a small dining area with a table and four chairs.

The area overlooking the lake is carpeted wall to wall in a light color. Floor to ceiling windows are 14 feet high and a ceiling fan keeps the air moving. It is furnished with an upholstered sofa and matching wing chair, Queen Anne style end and coffee tables, an antique rocker, iron floor lamp and a color television. Large floral patterned table lamps allow plenty of light for reading. A bentwood ice cream table and chair set is great for early morning coffee. A rock faced gas log fireplace has been added.

Glass doors open onto a deck, which has a magnificent view of Lake Taneycomo. There is a Barbecue grill for your use and a four-person hot tub. A round table with umbrella and chairs is an ideal place to sip a drink and watch the sun go down.

Also on the first level is one of the two bedrooms. It is fully carpeted and pecan paneled. It has a queen-size spindle headboard and a table with table lamp. The one bathroom with tub and shower is on the main floor.

A staircase in the living room leads to a fully carpeted loft bedroom with a balcony rail overlooking the living room. It is furnished with a queen-size bed with floral bed linens, a bedside table with a reading lamp.

CEDAR VIEW COTTAGE: P.O. Box 295, Branson, 65616. (417) 335-3502. For information and reservations call (417) 339-2493. Open all year. No pets. Children over 12 are welcome. The cottage is not designed for small children. A two guestroom "A" frame with one bath. About six miles from downtown Branson. Great shopping and restaurants. Member – Ozark Mountain Country B & B Reservation Service. John Brown, owner.

DIRECTIONS: From the north, Exit Hwy. 65 on Business 65; come on through town. Cross Lake Taneycomo; at the end of the bridge, turn left on Hwy. 76. Continue east on 76 for about two miles. Turn left on "T" Hwy. for another two and a half miles. Turn right into Taneycomo Woods on T-32 (Taneycomo Road). Continue on T-32 for about a mile until you see the lake ahead. Turn left on T-32-A (Pomme de Terre Road). Continue for about one and a half miles curving around the lake. Cedar View Cottage is the second place on the right. Look for #1722 and the Cedar View Cottage sign in front of the white "A" frame cottage.

Jamie McIlroy ©94

CINNAMON HILL BED & BREAKFAST
Branson area/Kimberling City

Nestled in the mountains surrounding Table Rock Lake, Maurice and Shirley De Vrient's Cinnamon Hill B & B is away from the noise and traffic, yet less than thirty minutes from all of the attractions.

This California Mission style stucco bungalow has four guestrooms, a common area and two decks. Maurice and Shirley's quarters are secluded from the main living area of the house for further privacy.

On entering you are in a blue carpeted living room. Furnishings include a floral sofa, a pair of upholstered rockers, a Sheraton style writing desk, mahogany end tables, an upholstered armchair and a mahogany coffee table. The walls are white with a floral border at the ceiling.

A dining el has an oak table with eight Windsor chairs and an antique gateleg table. A crystal chandelier hangs over the table.

A covered deck has wrought iron tables and chairs and breakfast may be taken here if you wish. A lower deck has plenty of seating overlooking the nearby woods. There are lots of birds and small animals to watch.

There are four guestrooms all with private entrance, private bath, ceiling fan and television.

The Mulberry Room is furnished with two antique reproduction full-size, high back, carved oak beds with floral coverlets, three reproduction antique end tables with lamps, a coffee table, a pair of chairs and an antique three drawer chest with rope pattern legs. Shades and curtains are at the windows.

The Cinnamon Room has reproduction high back, carved oak twin beds with floral coverlets, an antique serpentine French washstand with towel bar, an antique barley twist leg lamp table and a pair of ladder back chairs.

The Rose Room has a queen-size poster headboard with a floral coverlet, a matching chest and night stand with reading lamps, a small floral settee and a cheval mirror.

The Magnolia Room is furnished with a depression era wardrobe, a queen-size antique maple bed, a cedar chest, and a most unusual cottage dressing table and stool. An antique straight back spindle chair with a primitive rawhide seat adds a nice touch.

A staircase leads to a lower level and a carpeted common room. It has a wicker love seat and chair, table, bookcase with books, and a server with a coffeemaker. It is wallpapered in a floral print. There's a lot of nice craftwork, painting and collectibles displayed.

Shirley serves her guests a full breakfast: juice, fresh fruit in season, homemade pastry and muffins, as well as homemade jams and jellies, cinnamon coffee cake and coffee or tea. Her entrée menu varies. She has either an egg casserole with bacon or sausage, scrambled eggs and bacon, waffles, and biscuits and gravy. You won't go away hungry.

I really enjoyed my visit with Maurice and Shirley. You will too!

CINNAMON HILL B & B: 24 Wildwood Lane, Kimberling City, 65686. (417) 739-5727 or 1 (800) 925-1556 for reservations. Open all year. Well-behaved children welcome. No pets. Smoking on decks. Within thirty minutes of most attractions, golf course and marina. Four guestrooms with private baths and common area. Maurice and Shirley De Vrient, innkeepers.

DIRECTIONS: From Highway 76, take Highway 13 south to Kimberling City. At the Bank of Kimberling, turn right onto Wildwood Lane to #24.

CRYSTAL COVE BED & BREAKFAST
Branson

C rystal Cove sets on ten acres of woods and hills with frontage on Table Rock Lake. There are walking trails where you can spot all kinds of birds and wildlife, swimming, and a pontoon boat for a scenic ride on the lake. The area around the main cabin and the guest cabin are landscaped with a rock garden, a bridge and a waterfall that cascades down to a fish pond, bordered with flowers, water plants and rocks. Two decks overlooking the fishpond have several wrought iron umbrella tables and chairs.

The main cabin is built of logs, as are the guest cabins. It has a beamed vaulted ceiling. Bare shiny wood floors have area rugs. The gathering room has a floor-to-ceiling stone fireplace with upholstered wing chairs in front of it. There is an upholstered sofa, a twig lamp table and lamp, a corner cupboard, TV and a floor lamp. There are neat pictures and live plants.

The dining room has a fireplace with an antique mantle piece, a wrought iron chandelier hangs from the beamed ceiling. The bare wood floors are highly polished. There are three rattan tables with seating for six at each one. They are decorated with floral tablecloths. A red leather, wing back chair is on either side of the fireplace. There is also an antique Victrola, an antique spinning wheel, a library table and an antique hutch, which holds collections. The dining room overlooks the fishpond.

Deborah Offutt, the innkeeper, serves a delicious Ozark Country breakfast starting with juice, fresh fruit or yogurt, muffins and coffee cake. There are several menus that are offered. An egg quiche served with bacon and friend potatoes with onions and green peppers. Eggs Benedict with potatoes. A peach cobbler stuffed French toast (everyone's favorite), blueberry cream cheese French toast or good old bacon, fried eggs and fried potatoes.

From the gathering room, a staircase with a log railing takes you to a second floor guestroom, the Sewing Room. It is furnished with a king-size log bed, an antique armoire, a triple dresser, a wrought iron round table with two ice cream chairs, an antique sewing machine, floor lamp, antique rocker and a bedside table with a reading lamp. Swags are over blinds at the windows. There is a large bath with a walk-in shower and a Jacuzzi. A door opens onto a 40' porch across the cabin. It's furnished with log seating.

Leaving the main cabin, you cross a little rustic bridge over the fishpond, past the deck to one of three log cabins. Two of the cabins have two private suites, each with a private bath and a Jacuzzi. The Anniversary Suite is furnished with a king-size log poster bed, an antique oak dresser, an antique oak wash stand, a night table with lamp, an upholstered open arm chair and an end table. The bath has a Jacuzzi surrounded by stone and a stone floor. The ceilings are beamed. Both cabins have stone fireplaces.

The Honeymoon Suite is furnished with a king-size log canopy bed, an antique wash stand, dresser, a wicker chair, antique washstand, wicker table and a lamp. The vaulted ceilings have beams. Lace curtains are over blinds. A long porch has all kinds of seating. There is also a stove fireplace.

The middle cabin is called the Sports Cabin. It has a king-size log poster bed, an antique dresser, an oak wash stand is used for a night table, an upholstered open arm chair and a TV. The sitting area has a small antique table and two spindle back chairs, an upholstered queen sofa, a wicker chair and table and a corner fireplace. It is decorated with sports memorabilia. The porch has log furniture. There is also a Jacuzzi and a stone fireplace.

The third cabin has two suites. The Train Room has a king-size log bed, an antique dresser, a leather wing chair, a wash stand with a lamp, and end table and lamp and a floor lamp. A model train is above the headboard of the bed. Full of train memorabilia. There is a stone fireplace.

The Music Room is furnished with a king-size log bed, an antique dresser, a circa 1920 Victrola, a leather wing chair, a small marble top table, a log hall tree and an antique night stand with lamp. Again, a long porch across the cabin has plenty of seating. Both rooms have private baths and fireplaces.

Homemade cookies and soda is offered at check-in.

CRYSTAL COVE B & B: HCR 9, Box 1194A, Branson, 65616. (417) 338-2715. Toll free (888) 699-0444. Website: www.crystal.covebranson.com. Open all year. Children welcome. No pets. Please, smoking on porches. Two cabins with two, one-room suites. One two-room suite cabin and a room in the main cabin. Visa, MC and Discovery. Gift certificates. Bob and Deborah Offutt, innkeepers. Sherry Offutt, right hand and greeter (she's good at both).

DIRECTIONS: From Hwy. 65 & 76 – take 76 west five or six miles to Hwy. 376. Left on 376 to Hwy. 265. Right on 265 for 1 ½ mile. Turn left just before Old Southern Inn at 265-10. Go approximately ½ mile. Sign on right.

EMORY CREEK BED & BREAKFAST
Branson

H ere is an inn I know you are going to like! It offers all the elegance of the Victorian era, with the welcome home feeling of the country. Sammy and Beverly Gray Pagna have done a fine job of combining these two elements. Everywhere are touches of a time long gone, when refinement and grandeur were in vogue.

You enter the inn through a large anteroom guarded by a full-size carousel horse. Beverly's gift shop is to one side offering a selection of many unusual and Victorian gifts. The anteroom also leads into a two-story parlor/lobby with a blue plush carpet, which extends over the entire first floor. The marble fireplace is eye catching, as is an early 1800's gold wash mirror. The parlor is furnished with beautiful period pieces including a pair of heavily carved 18th century side chairs and an Empire sofa. In the dining room, a large brass chandelier hangs over a long trestle table and ten bow back Windsor chairs. There is an antique sideboard and a glass front china cabinet. In the nearby tower room and Library, there are three antique table and chairs offering seating for two's, threes, and fours.

Here in the dining rooms you begin your day by being pampered with an elegant, four-course gourmet breakfast. Start with Emory Creek's Sunrise surprise, a blend of orange and lime juice sweetened with Branson's own honey, and spiced with a dash of nutmeg and clove. Entrees would include ham and cheese quiche, egg souffles, strawberry crepes; blueberry stuffed French toast, Eggs Benedict, and more. There are homemade breads, muffins, jams, jellies and honey, with Emory Creek's own designer blend coffee.

Each of the seven guestrooms has their own character. Some are decorated with magnificent mid-19th century pieces, some have fireplaces. Every room has a grand view with ceiling fans and remote television. Each room has an ornate private bath with oversized Jacuzzi and plush terry robes.

On the top floor, the Rose O'Neil is decorated with late 1800 antiques. A white metal four poster bed sets in the tower portion of the room. A high wing back love seat sets in front of the carved cherry wood and marble fireplace.

The Sammy Lane Suite, serves as the Bridal Suite. All done in blues and whites with white wood furniture, and four poster bed draped in white lace and blue roses tied up in gold and white. An extra large bath area has a double-sized Jacuzzi with 6' stained glass window over the tub. There is separate room with shower. Two blue silk wing back chairs are positioned in front of the fireplace and television.

The Truman Suite has a magnificent, heavily-carved four poster bed draped in green silk and gold cord, an 1860 period desk, a marble top table with a Gone With the Wind lamp, and an 1800's burgundy velvet ornately carved couch. The fireplace has a beveled glass mirror above the oak mantle.

The Laura's Room has a 1920's art deco four piece bedroom set that includes a queen-size bed. The floral spread matches the window valance set over lace curtains.

From the parlor, stairs lead down to the Garden Level sitting room with fireplace, TV/VCR and library of movies. Beveled glass doors lead out to a large porch with porch furniture and swing. A few steps further take you to the bridge leading into the gazebo.

Three guestrooms are on this floor including the Dogwood Room, which has a queen-size replica of a burled cherry, carved high back bed with matching chest.

The Garden View Room is furnished with a queen-size brass bed and brass and iron day bed that opens into another queen-size bed. The window valance, bed linens and ceiling border all match.

The Hawthorne Room has brass twin beds for king-size bed, a wicker armoire and night table, and a pair of upholstered chairs.

Beautifully decorated fruit baskets, cheese trays, and Cappuccino and Biscotti trays may be ordered in advance to have waiting for you upon you arrival, as well as long stem roses or other floral arrangements.

EMORY CREEK B & B: 143 Arizona Drive, Branson, 65616. (417) 334-3805 and 1 (800) 362-7404 for reservations. E-Mail address: emorycreekbnb@pcis.net. Website: www.emorycreekbnb.com. Open all year. A delightful seven guestroom inn. Children over 13. No pets. No Smoking. Smoking on porches only. Sammy and Beverly Gray Pagna and Mark Gray, innkeepers.

DIRECTIONS: Located 4.6 miles north of Branson. From Springfield take Hwy. 65. Approximately two miles south of Hwy. 160 you will see an exit sign, "Exit 16, Hwy. F" – Exit. At exit stop sign take a left under the highway to the other side. You will see a sign that reads "East Outer Road" which is the service road. Take another left, go one mile up that road, which is heading back north and you will be at Emory Creek Bed and Breakfast.

GAINES LANDING BED & BREAKFAST
Branson

When Ted and Darlene Barber purchased Gaines Landing Bed & Breakfast, they became owners of a growing list of B & B homes that don't fit the popular concept of "Old" or "Victorian." In fact, far from it. The Barber's B & B is a two level hillside home built of Canadian cedar with brick accents. It is very contemporary in every sense.

You'll find Ted and Darlene a very warm and friendly couple. They make you feel right at home. Guests are given a key to their own private entrance so they can come and go as they please (not too late at night).

The large carpeted living room has a beamed cathedral ceiling. There is a huge see-through fireplace with all kinds of comfy chairs and sofas. The room is decorated with many Southwestern touches in lamps, pottery and paintings from New Mexico.

The gracious dining room is part of the charm here. It too has a beamed cathedral ceiling and a see-through fireplace and is newly carpeted and wallpapered. There is a beautiful contemporary dining table with eight chairs. A very large built-in china cupboard with leaded glass doors hold Darlene's collections, which overflow to three curio cabinets. You can walk out on a deck overlooking an outdoor area, the countryside and the swimming pool.

On the main level is the Poppyfield Suite consisting of a bedroom and living room. It is furnished with a new and beautiful Country Oak queen bed, night stands, armoire and chest of drawers. One wallpapered wall is a field of poppies, decorated in shades of green and rose. The living area continues with a comfy sofa-bed and chair, TV/VCR, coffee and lamp table, and a small refrigerator and coffee pot. There is a large private bath. There is also a private deck with your own hot tub, and an outside entrance.

On the lower level there are two guestrooms. The Rose Garden Room has a king-size canopy bed with miniature rosebuds climbing along the canopy, a daybed, two night tables, a pair of chairs and a dressing table with a mirrored top which opens. It has a private bath with shower. The room is decorated in shades of rose and pink. On the patio there is a large hot tub surrounded with lattice.

The Forget Me Not Room has a king-size bed and a wall of off-white American Country pieces including corner desk, dressing table and hutches displaying collectible plates and books. There are two night tables, comfortable chairs and TV. The room is decorated in shades of blue and rose. The full bath is off the hallway. There is also a large hot tub surrounded by lattice for this room.

Also on the lower level is a guest common area with sofa and chairs for your comfort. There is a sliding glass door opening onto the pool and deck area, as well as TV/VCR, a wet bar, coffee pot, microwave, and a small refrigerator for each room. Darlene keeps soda and popcorn for guests.

Breakfast is a full country fare. It consists of juice, fresh fruit, hot entrees, fresh breads, cinnamon rolls, or home baked goodies, homemade jams and jellies, coffee and tea. Darlene prepares a country breakfast pie containing sausage, eggs, cheese and milk baked in a pie crust, and other yummy entrees. Or you may have pancakes, waffles or oven French toast. It's all good.

GAINES LANDING B & B: 521 West Atlantic Street, Branson, 65616. (417) 334-2280 or 1 (800) 825-3145. Fax: (417) 334-5557. Open all year. Well-behaved children accepted. No pets. Smoking on patio only. Two guestrooms, plus one two room suite in a contemporary setting with all the amenities you would expect of a first rate establishment. Close to everything. Member, Bed & Breakfast Inns of Missouri, Professional Association of Innkeepers International and the Ozark Mountain B & B Reservation Service. E-mail: darlene@tri-lakes.net. Websites: www.bransoninfo.com/gaines and www.gaineslanding.com. Ted and Arlene Barber, innkeepers.

DIRECTIONS: At Branson, exit off Hwy. 65. Take Hwy. 76 east toward downtown Branson. Turn left at the first street, which is Sixth Street. Go one block to Atlantic Street and right into the Gaines Landing driveway. Always call first.

GRANDPA'S FARM BED & BREAKFAST
Branson area/Lampe

Since there is a Gramma's House in this guide, it is only fitting to have a Grampa's too. This farm is an original homestead with a lot of history. The stone portion was built in 1891. The walls, eighteen inches thick, are of hand hewn limestone dug from an old quarry that was nearby. The house rests on a foundation of solid rock. The man who built the place was paid two horses, two cows and a pig.

The old building, now used as a workshop, was once a "drying shed" for storing fruit. An old scythe and cradle found in the attic of the shed is now on display. It was apparently used to harvest the crops in the fields. If you look closely, faint signs of a road still exist out in back where wagons once traveled up to the mountain top. Also, the remains of an old hand dug well may be found in back. The old barn out in front of the house is nearly one hundred years old. It was built with hand hewn notched logs. Near the barn, you can see the remains of a spring house where butter and milk were kept.

The family room in the original part of the house has the old stone walls with some added paneling. It has a fireplace with wood burning insert. A love seat with an Indian design in the upholstery faces the fireplace. At the other end of the room is a second fireplace with a sofa, also with Indian motif, facing it. The walls are filled with colorful Indian art rugs, handmade dolls, and baskets. A television is for guest's use.

The Mother Hen Room has an antique birds-eye maple full-size bed, a matching dresser, and bunk beds for children. A coffeemaker is for your convenience. The walls are paneled and there is a ceiling fan. A private bath has tub and shower. Extra towels, soap, etc. are in the bathroom cabinets along with some toiletries in case you run out or forget to bring something. A Honeymoon Suite has an attached screened-in porch, garden room with spa and private bath. The suite is decorated in Victorian style using peach and ivory coloring. A huge king-size bed, handmade by Grandpa, is graced with soft flowing curtains and lace. There is an upholstered love seat. Windows across the bedroom and garden room offer a lovely view of the woods from this 800 square foot suite. A real bird's nest was saved intact and serves as home for two ornamental lovebirds.

Just a short walk from the main house will take you to the Hillside Hide-a-way, a two bedroom cottage. Each bedroom has its own sitting area. One unit has a two person hot tub and the other a fully equipped kitchenette. Each unit has tables and chairs. Both suites have a skylight and a ladder leading to a loft room for children. Breakfast is served in the main house.

Pat and Keith like to share their living room with their guest. It has hardwood floors and the walls are paneled. It has a piano and an antique organ. A large bookcase has been beautifully handmade.

Breakfast is served at 8 a.m. unless other arrangements have been made. It is served either in the family room or on a large screen-in porch overlooking a natural spring and farm pond. Unless otherwise requested, breakfast will be a "country" one with eggs, sausage, ham or bacon, fruit and juice, homemade jams and jellies, homemade biscuits, an assortment of breads, and coffee or tea.

The "This 'n That Shoppe" is located in the walk out basement. Feel free to browse. Crafts here are taken on consignment from the local artisans and are really quite good.

In the spring, the farm radiates the beauty of the many redbud and dogwood trees. If you are interested in obtaining some redbud seedlings, Pat or Keith will help you dig up your own. Fall visitors may want to pick up black walnuts or persimmons. There are many things you can see and do here. What fun is a farm if the children can't pet the animals? And they love to do it. For the most part the domestic animals on the farm are friendly, but there may be a protective mother so it is best that children be accompanied by an adult.

GRANDPA'S FARM B & B: Rt. 3, Box 476, Lampe, 65681. (417) 779-5106 or 1 (800) 280-5106. Open all year. Children most welcome. Outside smoking only. No pets. A two unit farm home and two suite separate cottage. Located halfway between Branson and Eureka Springs, AK. An ideal place for a few days away from it all. Member Ozark Mountain B & B Reservation Service. Pat and Keith Lamb, owners.

DIRECTIONS: From Branson take Hwy. 76 west to Hwy. 13. Go south on 13 to Hwy. 86. Right on 86 for five miles. Watch for the sign on road. Driveway is on the left. From Hwy. 65, take 65 south to Hwy. 86, west on 86. Watch for their sign. Driveway on the left.

HISTORIC KITE HOUSE BED & BREAKFAST
Branson area (Hollister)

Here is one of the quaintest houses I believe I've ever seen. Built in 1912, of stone and with a red tile roof, it has all the earmarks of a turn-of-the century arts and crafts house. A stone wall three feet high goes across the property, including a cottage next door, which also belongs to Mark and Donel McCauley, the owners of the Kite House.

When Donel introduced me to her husband, I thought to myself what a deep, rich voice he has. Then I found out he is entertainer Mel Tillis' bass singer. They sure are a nice couple and I spent several hours here.

Entering the house from a stone pillared, wraparound porch, you are in a small entryway that has two wicker chairs and a table. The dining room has a built-in cupboard. There is one of the most unusual dining room sets I've come across. The ten-piece early 1900 set consists of a table, six chairs, a server, china cabinet and a buffet, all carved and all with barley twist legs. A brass chandelier, original to the house, hangs over the table.

A great glassed-in sunroom has tongue and grooved knotty pine paneling and a stone fireplace and hearth. Lots of live plants and the way the McCauley's decorated the room makes you feel right at home. It is furnished with a table with sunflowers painted on the top, chairs, an antique opossum belly cabinet, a twig rocker, an armchair and a love seat. An old wooden chicken crate is on a wall and holds all kinds of interesting things. A door opens to a large patio with huge old trees shading it, as well as the front of the house. There is a wrought iron table and chairs, many flowers and shrubs.

The McCauley's cottage next door to the main house is used for their B & B guests. However, breakfast is served in the main house. The cottage was built in 1909 and reflects the workmanship of the times. There are three separate guest areas, each with a private entrance and private spa/whirlpool.

The Honeymoon Suite, on the first floor, has two rooms entered from the back porch. It has a queen-size antique brass bed with a floral spread and pillow shams. There is a Victorian, twist leg parlor table, an antique vanity, wicker bench, and a wicker etagere. There is a fireplace and a whirlpool. The area is carpeted, lace curtains at the window and a small crystal chandelier.

Also on the first floor, the Hillside Suite features its own private patio, with a hot tub, table and chairs and plants. A lattice fence surrounds it. You can also enter the suite through French doors from the patio. One of the guestrooms has a king-size brass and black iron antique bed, a Federal-style upholstered and wood trimmed sofa, a Victorian, walnut marble top parlor table, an antique radio and an oak antique dresser. There is a stone fireplace. The second room has an antique Eastlake full-size bed, an antique Eastlake marble top dresser with glove boxes and candle stands and an antique mirrored armoire. The bath has a claw foot tub and shower.

On the second floor a two room suite, the Hide-Away Suite, has its own entrance from a patio. One room is furnished with a full-size antique ornate, white iron bed, a low boy antique dresser, a mirrored armoire, an oak chest, an antique upholstered fainting couch and a wicker chair. Under a window eave there are several items I have never seen before. One is a salesman's sample of an upholstered Victorian fainting couch and chair, a wicker chair and a wood cook stove. There is also a bear skin rug. The second room is furnished with an antique, full-size brass bed, an oak wash stand, a tapestry covered open arm chair, a foot stool and a cheval mirror. Both rooms have green carpeting. The spa is on the patio. Notice the doll collection.

Donel serves breakfast in the dining room or sunroom. It consists of juice, fresh fruit in season or a fruit parfait, and homemade Danish rolls (which I had to sample). One of her entrees would be baked French toast with fresh strawberries and whipped cream and served with bacon, or maybe a casserole with sausage, eggs, bread, cheese and milk, served with homemade muffins, a fresh fruit plate with cream cheese dip, coffee, tea or milk.

HISTORIC KITE HOUSE B & B: 397 Esplanade, Hollister, 65672. (417) 334-7341. Website: www.kitehouse.com. Open all year. Children welcome. No pets. Outside smoking. Three suites with private baths, private entrances. Donel and Mark McCauley, innkeepers.

DIRECTIONS: From Springfield, take US 65 South, cross over Lake Taneycomo and go to Hwy. 65B. Turn left on 65B and go to Esplanade on your left. Left to Kite House.

JOSIE'S PEACEFUL GETAWAY BED & BREAKFAST
Branson

One feature of Josie's is the great location. It's just down the road from Silver Dollar City, and that will save you fighting traffic on Highway 76.

Bill and JoAnne's contemporary lake front inn is ideal for a group of friends or family, as you can take the entire house, including the little gazebo in the woods overlooking the lake. The main floor, includes a kitchen, dining area, and a large living room with stone wood burning fireplace. It has a covered porch around three sides with plants and flower, wicker and wrought iron furniture and surrounded by large trees. Great place to have breakfast or watch the wildlife. The large two story, rough hewn cedar home blends right in with the countryside. It has beamed cathedral ceilings, paneled walls and is fully carpeted.

The living room has a Victorian divan and love seats. A small round marble table beside the fireplace is used for breakfast, if you wish. The small dining area has a round oak table and chairs, and an antique wash stand.

Also on the main floor is the Blueberry Lace Room with its touches of Victoriana. It has a king-size spindle bed with a down comforter and several antique pieces. The white paneling has hand stenciling of flowers and leaves at the ceiling. There is cable television and a telephone. The room has a private entrance, exclusive use of an outdoor jacuzzi under a covered roof, a private bath with shower, and a small refrigerator.

The staircase of the second floor is carpeted and the walls are paneled. A balcony overlooks the lower level. The Lily of the Valley Room comes with a queen-size brass and iron bed, an antique marble top wash stand, cedar chest, upholstered arm chair, a rocker, a table with a reading lamp, and cable television. The room is carpeted and Josie has chosen dried flower arrangements that compliment the wallpaper. There is a private bath with shower.

This second room is the Wildflower Hide-a-way room which has a tall headboard, queen-size bed, an antique chest, rocking chair, a small oak table with a "Gone With the Wind" lamp, and an antique floor lamp. The room is fully carpeted and has an attractive wallpaper print and pleated roll up blinds.

On the walk out lower level with its own private entrance is the Forget-Me-Not Suite. Perfect for a romantic getaway, the cozy sofa and coffee table face the stone wood-burning fireplace. Other furnishings include a Victorian love seat, wicker table, a 1920's desk, and cable TV/VCR. Seated at the oak table you can overlook the grounds.

The bedroom contains an antique white iron queen-size bed, a small French Provincial three drawer chest, maple cricket chair and a round drum table with a lamp. The room is attractively wallpapered and has lace curtains at the windows.

In the kitchen area are complete cooking facilities. A table and chairs are placed to give a view of the lake. A private bath has a shower and features a double whirlpool and an illuminated stained glass window. In addition is your own private hot tub on the patio.

In good weather enjoy a special breakfast with a panoramic view of Table Rock Lake from the porch. Menus include waffles, quiche, pancakes or perhaps crumbcake with raspberries and cream. I go for the farmer's breakfast: bacon, potatoes, eggs and cheese all baked together. Always homemade bread or cobbler, juice, fresh fruit, coffee or tea. Or for lighter fare, ask Josie about her gourmet continental breakfast.

JOSIE'S BED & BREAKFAST: HCR 1, Box 1104, Branson 65616. (417) 338-2978. Reservations: 1 (800) 289-4125. Open all year. A contemporary, lake front home on the banks of Table Rock Lake. Plenty of fishing, swimming and hiking. Three miles to Silver Dollar City. Smoke-free environment. No pets. Children welcome. Restrictions may apply. Member, Bed & Breakfast Inns of Missouri. Bill and JoAnne Coats, hosts.

DIRECTIONS: From Branson, take Hwy. 76 west to Indian Point Road (five miles – entrance to Silver Dollar City). Turn left and go 3.2 miles. Turn left at the 60 H street sign. Then an immediate right. Proceed ½ mile to Josie's parking lot.

LAKESHORE BED & BREAKFAST
Branson at Indian Point

Just two miles from Silver Dollar City out on Indian Point, Gladys Lemley's Lakeshore Bed & Breakfast is a fine place for a family with children or a party of four or more traveling together, especially if you like fishing and water activities.

The grounds have a gentle slope leading to the lake shore, just one hundred yards away. Fishing and swimming can be enjoyed right off your own private boat dock. If you have your own boat or wish to rent one, a public boat ramp is just a mile from the house. There's also a paddle boat for you to enjoy.

On the first floor, the Blue Room is furnished with a queen-size bed with walnut headboard, matching bed linens and curtains, night table with reading lamp, cable TV/VCR, a refrigerator and a coffee bar. There is a private bath with tub and shower. Guests have access to a parlor with fireplace.

Also on the main floor is the all-new Sunrise Vista Room. Great for honeymoons and anniversaries, it has a queen-size bed with a caned headboard, a matching triple dresser, an upholstered chair, a sofa (double hide-a-bed), cable TV/VCR, refrigerator and coffee bar with coffeemaker and microwave. The room has a private entrance from the deck overlooking the lake and a private bath with shower and whirlpool tub.

On the lower level is the two bedroom Sunset Vista Suite. There is a private entrance from a large covered patio overlooking the lake. It has a picnic table, grill and lawn chairs. In the yard is a glider swing for four. The beautifully decorated suite has a queen-size brass bed in the alcove of the bedroom/sitting room which has a chaise lounge, queen-size hide-a-bed, cable TV/VCR, cedar chest, bookcase, dresser and reading lamps. A fully furnished kitchen has a refrigerator, microwave, dishwasher and a stove. The adjoining room has a queen-size bed, upholstered arm chair, small antique chest, and a lamp stand. This suite can accommodate a party of six.

A full breakfast is served in the Lemley's dining room. Gladys will usually ask you what you would like to have and then prepare it. She also makes homemade whole wheat bread starting by grinding the wheat. Egg dishes with ham, bacon or sausage, pancakes or an egg with cheese casserole are among her offerings.

LAKESHORE BED & BREAKFAST: HCR 1, Box 935, Branson, 65616. (417) 338-3698. 1 (800) 285-9739. A lakeside home with two guestrooms on the first floor and a two bedroom suite on the lower level with private entrance. Good location for avoiding heavy Hwy. 76 traffic. Open all year. Smoking on patio or deck. No pets. Children welcome. Member, Ozark Mountain Country B & B Reservation Service and Bed & Breakfast Inn of Missouri. Gladys Lemley, host.

DIRECTIONS: From Branson, take Hwy. 76 west to Indian Point Road (Silver Dollar City turn off). Turn left and past SDC parking area. Go 1.5 miles. Turn right at large blue and white sign for Still Waters Resort. Follow road through three way stop to lake and turn right. Fifth house on the left. Websites: http://www.bbim.org/lakeshore/lodging/lakeshore and www.bransonnow.com/lodging/lakeshore.

MARTINDALE BED & BREAKFAST
Branson West

The Martindale B & B offers quiet seclusion surrounded by Table Rock Lake. It was designed for your privacy along with a warm friendly atmosphere where you can enjoy the ancient oak trees, birds and flowers.

Your hosts, Lucille and Ellis Martin have been here for five years, and maintain their home flawlessly so their guests can be sure of everything being to your liking. It has been landscaped and a meandering path will lead you down to the lake where you can fish, swim or just relax. If you bring your boat, a put-in ramp is close by.

Entering the house, you are in a tiled entry. Straight ahead brings you to the family room. It has a high vaulted ceiling and a massive wood burning floor-to-ceiling brick fireplace with hearth. A balcony on the second floor overlooks the room. It is furnished with two upholstered sofas, an upholstered wing back chair, a coffee table, TV, a bookcase and books, an upholstered recliner and a sofa end table and lamp. A door opens onto a deck that has a wrought iron table with four chairs and two wrought iron lounges.

There is also a screened-in porch with a brick floor. It is furnished with a wrought iron sofa, end tables and a wrought iron table and chairs. On nice days you can, if you want, have your breakfast out here. I imagine it's very pleasant.

Off the entry, the dining room has a large window with drapes overlooking the front of the house. It is furnished with a pine trestle table, four chairs and two antique chairs, a bench, a pine hutch and a slant front desk. They have nice pieces including a brass fire box.

Upon arrival Lucille offers homemade cookies and coffee or tea, lemonade in summer and hot chocolate in winter.

A staircase from the entry leads to the two guestrooms, each with a view of the lake and wooded area. Each of the guestrooms have private baths with tub and shower combinations, down comforters as Ozark crafted quilts and a TV/VCR, video tapes and a clock radio.

The two guestrooms include the Ozark Heritage Room, furnished with a queen-size mahogany bed, an armoire, a bench at the foot of the bed, a library table with a lamp by the bedside, a dresser and an upholstered love seat, an end table and a dresser. The room is carpeted and has floral balloon curtains at the windows.

The Pleasant Valley Room is also carpeted and contains mahogany queen-size bed with a Waverly spread in a green, blue and burgundy plaid pattern. There is a matching dresser, an armoire and a library table with a lamp. Other pieces include a round table and lamp and a plaid upholstered love seat. A private entrance to a balcony, which separates both rooms and overlooks the great room has an antique sewing machine as a table, an old trunk, an English wash stand and a magazine rack.

As both hosts are native Ozarkians, they offer a full breakfast that is "sumpt'n" special. Start off with orange juice and fresh fruit in season, or a frozen fruit, then have quiche, sausage biscuit and sausage gravy. There's Amish bread, jams and jellies and coffee, tea or milk.

MARTINDALE B & B: P.O. Box 2204, Branson West, 65737. (417) 338-2588. Toll free: (888) 338-2588. Open all year. No pets. Children by arrangement. Smoking on deck or porch. Two guestrooms with private baths. Enjoy total peace and quiet. MC, Visa and Discovery. Lucille and Ellis Martin, innkeepers.

DIRECTIONS: From Branson: Take Hwy. 76 west to Branson West, then south (left) on Hwy. 13 to Hwy. DD. Turn left on DD. Once you're on DD, go 4.5 miles to DD #20 (Sho-me Baseball and several resorts are advertised there). Turn left on DD #20 and go down hill till you reach a "Y" intersection. Turn left to the Splitrail Resort sign. Turn left and proceed to a group of mailboxes on the right. Turn right, go one block – the road veers to the left. Martindale is the middle two-story gray house on the right. Purple Martindale signs are posted at the 1ˢᵗ Splitrail Resort sign, on DD #20 at the mailboxes and at the house. From the south: Take MO-13 to Kimberling City, continue about three miles north to Hwy. DD. Turn right on DD. From the north: If you are on Hwy. 65 about at Springfield, go 13 miles south to Hwy. EE west three miles to U.S. 160. South to Mo. 248, turn west (right) two miles to Mo. 13, then south (left) to Branson West; continue south two miles to Hwy. DD, turn left on DD.

JAMIE L MCILROY E 94

RED BUD COVE BED & BREAKFAST
Branson

R ed Bud Cove was originally built in 1975 as the boat house on the estate of John Miller, a prominent Kansas City banker and business man. The exterior of the boat house and the grounds have been preserved to the extent possible. The interior has been remodeled to serve as a bed and breakfast.

Located on Table Rock Lake, Red Bud Cove is away from the noise and congestion, yet only minutes from area attractions. Owners, Rick and Carol Carpenter, have a pontoon boat that can be rented or you may rent dock space for your own boat. You may also swim, fish or watch the sunset from the lake's edge, or enjoy the year round hot tub facility.

The living room at the main house is open to guests. It has a huge rock fireplace, tongue and groove walls and beamed ceilings. It is furnished with a sofa and love seat, two upholstered chairs and end tables. Area carpets cover the floor. You can look forward to a hearty, full breakfast, which is cooked by Carol and served by Rick. Served in the dining room overlooking Table Rock Lake. (When I was here, the Lake was home to thirty or forty geese). Breakfast includes juice, fresh fruit, homemade banana bread, or muffins with jellies and jams, coffee, tea or milk. The main course could be French toast with sausage or ham rolls; cheese and hash browned potato casserole or an egg souffle. Seating is at three or four tables all with tablecloths and flowers.

The guest suites, each beautifully decorated, include a bedroom, fully equipped kitchenette, living room, dining area and a private bath. Some suites have fireplaces, some have a spa for two. Other amenities are color television, telephone and air conditioning. Suites have private entrances and most have lake front patio or deck.

The Minnesota Suite has two bedrooms and a spa. The living area has a sofa that opens to a queen-size sleeper, oak table, dining table with four chairs. One bedroom has a king-size bed with a maple chest, the other a queen-size bed and a wardrobe.

The Maryland Suite includes a sofa, end and coffee tables, dining table and chairs, a queen-size bed, chest and wardrobe. Bath has tub and shower.

The Pennsylvania suite is a perfect honeymoon suite with both fireplace and spa. There is a sofa, table with reading lamp, oak table and chairs, a king-size bed, night tables and a chest.

The second and third floors have an entry hall. Five suites are off the hall. The Kansas Suite has sofa, coffee and end tables, table and chairs. There is a queen-size bed, pair of chairs, chest and night tables with lamps.

The Indiana suite has a sleeper sofa, glass top maple coffee table, queen-size bed, chest, upholstered chair and a desk with chair.

The California Suite has a fireplace and a spa. The living area has a sofa and wing chair, glass top brass end and coffee tables. The suite has a queen-size bed. The walls are papered in a stripe pattern above the chair rail.

The Missouri Suite is furnished with a king-size bed and a six drawer chest. The living area has a sofa, a small oak ice box end table and wrought iron table and chairs.

The Kentucky Suite has a living room with a magnificent lake view, a full kitchen and a large bedroom with a king-size bed.

RED BUD COVE B & B: 162 Lakewood Drive, (Table Rock Lake Road 65-48), Hollister, 65672. (417) 334-7144. 1(800) 677-5525 for reservations. Open all year. Children welcome. No pets. Smoking on decks or patios. An eight suite B & B in a renovated boat house. Many amenities await you here. Brochures, maps and directions are available for local attractions. Rick and Carol Carpenter, innkeepers.

DIRECTIONS: From Branson take Hwy. 65 south 7 ½ miles. Turn right on Table Rock Lake Road 65-48 (County road 65 – 180) and go 2 ½ miles to the Red Bud Cove B & B. This is a scenic and pleasant drive.

RHAPSODY BED & BREAKFAST INN
Branson

Patti and Duane Scott designed this grand home to accommodate their bed and breakfast inn. Rhapsody Inn offers the peace and serenity of the Ozark Mountains, the elegance of a fine hotel and the quiet of an isolated wilderness home.

The exquisite Victorian interior is graced with rich mahogany wood and wonderful tapestries. The furnishings have been hand picked and represent quality reproductions of classic Victorian furniture.

Double doors from the front porch open into an ante room with a green and white marble floor. In this area, there is a carved breakfront, a pair of upholstered Victorian arm chairs and a large wooden easel with an oil painting.

An extra large drawing room has a 24-foot ceiling. A brick wood burning fireplace holds a brass fire screen. A large wreath is over the mantel, an ornate brass chandelier hangs from the ceiling. Four floor-to-ceiling windows are covered with lace curtains and burgundy swags. Great framed prints and a gilded ornate mirror are on the walls. It is furnished with an upholstered medallion sofa, which faces the fireplace. There is an antique Victrola, a heavily carved plant stand with a large floral arrangement, two high back Victorian chairs and a television. There is also an upholstered Victorian sofa with marble top end tables and marble top coffee table.

The main dining room is in the turret. Window coverings are white lace curtains with burgundy swags. Beige with gold marbling wallpaper, a wide floral border at the ceilings and burgundy placemats set the tone for the six Victorian tables with marble tops and chairs, an antique oak sideboard holds depression glass dinner service. The framed prints on the wall are exceptional.

At the top of the curved staircase, a hall area has a carved mahogany table with carved wall mirror and live plants. Down three steps and you are in a small sitting area, overlooking the drawing room, with a pair of burgundy Victorian parlor chairs and a marble top table with crystal lamp.

Rhapsody Inn features twelve guestrooms, three whirlpool suites and a handicapped accessible guestroom. Each of the guestrooms are furnished with queen-size beds, upholstered chairs, marble top lyre harp tables, armoires and cable television. Each room is decidedly different and individually decorated. They have two pedestal sinks and showers in the bath.

The three suites include the Bridal Suite, located in the turret on the second floor. It is furnished with a queen-size white iron bed with a creme coverlet, a Victorian sofa, a mirrored armoire with television and VCR, a marble top coffee table and two Victorian arm chairs. A pair of bedside table with electrified oil lamps. Also, a marble top lyre harp console table with a bookshelf stereo. There is a Jacuzzi whirlpool tub, separate shower, double pedestal sink, vanity with makeup mirror and small refrigerator. A hunter green sculptured carpet is on the floor. The large windows have creme lace curtains with green swags. Beautiful prints are on the walls.

Daddy's Room, a bit more masculine, has a queen-size mahogany headboard, a pair of navy blue wing back chairs, a marble top coffee table, a mirrored armoire with TV and VCR, a plaid sofa and a marble top lyre harp console table with mini stereo. The bath has a Jacuzzi whirlpool tub and shower and two pedestal sinks, and a small refrigerator.

The Guardian Angel Room is furnished with a queen-size white iron headboard bed, a mirrored armoire, a marble top mahogany coffee table, a lyre base marble top console table with a stereo, a Victorian love seat and a ladies and gent's upholstered Victorian chairs. There is a television and VCR hidden in the armoire. Gilt framed pictures are on the walls. A border with a guardian angel print is at the ceiling. The room is fully carpeted and green swags are over white lace curtains. The bath also has a Jacuzzi whirlpool, corner shower, double pedestal sinks, vanity and a small refrigerator.

A full breakfast is served each morning in the dining room. Consisting of a variety of fruits, fruit gravy, cereal, sausage gravy and biscuits, homemade coffee cake or sweet rolls, jam & honey for your biscuits, coffee, tea, milk and orange juice. Along with the wonderful assortment on the buffet, Patti serves a breakfast special consisting of either Texas Brunch, Scottish Eggs, Blueberry French Bread Pudding, etc. The breakfast special changes daily.

RHAPSODY INN: 296 Blue Meadows Road, Branson, 65616. (417) 335-2442 or (800) 790-3892. Open all year. Twelve guestrooms, three suites and a handicapped accessible guestroom. Outside pool. Children welcome. No pets. Smoking in designated areas only. All major credit cards. Website: www. rhapsodyinn.com. Patti and Duane Scott, innkeepers.

DIRECTIONS: From Springfield, take Hwy. 65 S to Hwy. 76 exit. Turn left onto Hwy. 76 and go to Fall Creek Road. Turn left onto Fall Creek Road and go to Blue Meadows Road (about 3 miles). Turn right and go 200 yards.

THE THURMAN HOUSE BED & BREAKFAST
Branson

Built in 1986, of stone and cedar siding, the Thurman House is a long low ranch house setting on a beautiful landscaped parcel of ground with large trees, shrubs and flower gardens. Patrick and Carolyn Thurman, the owners, have taken the lower level of their house and made it into something special. After going through the guest area, I think they have done just about everything to put their guests' comfort before anything else.

Pat and Carolyn take only one couple or two couples together or a family. They do not take people who are strangers to each other.

The lower level has been more or less divided into several areas. A family area is carpeted wall-to-wall. The walls are cream color and have nice framed pictures and antique quilts on them. It is furnished with an upholstered sofa and a matching armchair, a pair of upholstered recliners, tables and lamps and an ornate oak side board. There is a gas log fireplace for those chilly mornings and evenings, especially in the late fall and early spring. There is also a 52" TV for those football games.

A kitchenette area has a small refrigerator, a microwave oven , an automatic coffeemaker and a small sink. The dining area has an oak oval table with six spindle back oak chairs, an oak chest and an antique treadle sewing machine and an antique double school desk. Pictures and quilts are on the walls.

One of the bedrooms is fully carpeted and has green colored swags over blinds at the window. It is decorated with artificial floral arrangements, pictures and a birdhouse collection. It is furnished with a queen-size bed and an antique full-size poster bed, each covered with antique quilts. There is an antique marble top dresser with glove boxes, a chest and night stand with lamp.

The other bedroom is also carpeted and has blue drapes over blinds at the window. It is furnished with a queen-size bed with a handmade wedding ring quilt on it. It has a large bath with a walk-in shower. There is also a rocking chair. The cream colored walls have pictures and quilts.

From the family area, a glass door opens out onto a large covered patio with a six-person hot tub and a log glider. In a fenced-in area there is an in-ground 14' x 30' swimming pool. There is a glass top umbrella table and six upholstered chairs and two lounges.

At the rear of the house, there is a small cedar log Chapel, that is used for weddings. When I was here, a couple were to be married in just a few hours. The Chapel has four lead glass windows, each with an art metal dogwood flower candle holder. There are seven hand blown oil lamps and a wooden cross with carved dogwood flowers. A pair of log plant stands, a large artificial plant and a small stained glass chandelier. A brick path leads from a small porch through landscaped gardens.

The Thurmans offer a full country breakfast to their guests, served family-style in your suite. Orange juice and fruit of some kind, scrambled eggs, biscuits and gravy. Or, there's homemade blueberry pancakes served with homemade blueberry sauce, bacon, sausage or a country skillet omelet. Always jams and jellies (homemade), coffee, tea or milk.

This is a nice homey place away from the traffic, but close enough to the attractions, restaurants and shops.

THURMAN HOUSE B & B: 888 State Highway F, Branson, 65616. (800) 238-6630. Website: http://home1.gte.net/thrmhse/index.htm. Open all year. Children welcome. No pets. Smoking on patio. Two-bedroom suite with dining and living area. Close to everything. Hot tub and swimming pool. Patrick and Carolyn Thurman, innkeepers.

DIRECTIONS: From Springfield, take Highway 65 south approximately 30 miles to exit 16 (Highway F). At bottom of off ramp turn left and go .4 miles. House is on the right.

OZARK MOUNTAIN COUNTRY B & B RESERVATION
SERVICE • Kay Cameron, Owner • 1 (800) 695-1546

This reservation services lists some of the Ozark area bed and break fasts in this guide. In addition, here are brief descriptions of a few of the B & B homes that are listed with Kay's service.

OMC 102 – Charming log cabin, with a winter lake view from both directions! The one room cabin is equipped with queen-size bed, kitchen, wood-burning parlor stove, and bath with shower. Continental breakfast delivered to serve at your leisure. Smoking outdoors only.

OMC 105 – Contemporary home with spectacular view of Table Rock Lake. This elegant retreat is open all year. Hearty breakfast served in dining room overlooking lake. AC. The largest guest area is a private suite with bath and whirlpool tub, shower, queen-size bedroom/sitting area combination. Two other lakeview guestrooms each with double bed and bath. Common area for guest with coffee bar, small fridge, pool table, aquarium, library, and TV. School age children welcome.

OMC 119 – Contemporary home on mountain overlooking Table Rock Lake. Very hearty breakfast served in dining room overlooking lake. Largest guest area has private entrance, TV, AC, wood burning fireplace, king-size bed, sleeper sofa, private bath, private hot tub on covered deck. Another room has queen-size bed and private bath with shower. Open all year. Children over eight welcome. Smoking outdoors only.

OMC 126 – On Indian Point one mile to Silver Dollar City. Contemporary home with limited, winter lake view. Swimming pool! Parlor for guest use with wood burning fireplace, cable TV/VCR. Bountiful breakfast! Three guestrooms each with cable TV and private bath. Largest guest area is a private suite with indoor hot tub in sun room and electric fireplace. Sliding glass doors separate this room from bedroom area with king-size water bed and antique furnishings. Another room has a queen-size bed and private hot tub on a private deck. Smallest room, and least expensive, has a full-size bed.

OMC 150 – Private two bedroom cottage, about one mile from Silver Dollar City! The larger bedroom has two full-size beds and access to a hall bath with tub and shower. The other bedroom has a queen-size bed and adjoins a spacious bath with a whirlpool tub. There is a comfortably furnished living room, TV, and a fully equipped kitchen for self-service. There is screened porch off the kitchen and the private patio is equipped with a grill. Way in the distance is a view of Table Rock Dam and the lake. Smoking permitted.

OMC 166 – Two log cabins, about two miles from Branson, each with whirlpool bath, wood burning fireplace, full kitchen for self-service, queen-size bed and TV. The newer, larger, and more expensive cabin also has an extra bedroom and bath.

OMC 173 - New lakeside home offering four guestrooms each with a lakeview bedroom, either a king or queen-size bed and private bath. Spacious lakeview deck. Breakfast is delivered to the private guest area. Smoking outdoors only.

OMC 174 – A large two-story Victorian replica with swimming pool, breakfast buffet, exercise room, spa room with large whirlpool, big-screen TV with over 500 movies available for guests. The spacious guestrooms have TV, a private bath with tub/shower. Several of the larger rooms have two queen-size beds.

OMC 180 – Is a charming traditional-style home close to Branson's attractions. The private, two bedroom, upstairs suite is exclusively reserved for one group, comfortable for up to four. One bedroom has a king-size bed, the other a full. Each room has a TV. Children are welcome. The bath has a tub/shower. A hearty breakfast is served each morning in the dining room on the first floor. The front porch has a private hot tub complete with privacy curtains.

OMC 181 – Private lakeside cottage with a private hot tub on the covered breezeway with a TV! The two room cottage includes a king-size bed and bath. The lake view great room has kitchen and living area with a sleeper sofa. Can comfortably accommodate five. Smoking outdoors only.

OMC 184 – Private two room suite added to a turn-of-the-century bungalow with private entrance, queen-size bed, private bath with tub/shower. The spacious living area includes comfortable furnishings, TV, a parlor stove, dining area where a hearty breakfast is served. The courtyard adjoining the suite has a private hot tub. Smoking outdoors only.

OMC 187 – A charming cottage in a wooded valley close to Branson West. The modified A-frame cottage is fully equipped with a living room area with comfortable furnishings, TV/VCR, gas fireplace, full kitchenette, dining area, queen-size bed in bedroom area, bath, air conditioning, and even a washer and dryer. A special breakfast will be delivered to your cottage each morning. On a secluded, shady deck is a large hot tub. Smoking only outdoors.

OZARK MOUNTAIN COUNTRY B & B RESERVATION SERVICE: Website: www.ozarkbedand breakfast.com.

CAMERON'S CRAG: Websites: www.camerons-crag.com and www.bbonline.com/mo/cameron. E-mail: mgcameron@aol.com.

EDEN BED & BREAKFAST
Brighton

Eden B & B is a 478-acre estate sitting in a secluded valley surrounded by rolling, tree covered hills. Two large springs flow through the yard forming a sex-foot-deep pool. Jackie told me that Indians, as well as passengers on the old Butterfield Stage Coach Line, stopped to refresh themselves at the springs. Evidence of the old road can still be seen as it cuts through the woods.

The owners, Iran and Jackie Cohen, feel Eden is a very special place that would be ideal as a retreat for nature lovers, honeymooners, or just for those seeking a relaxing getaway. There are a variety of domestic animals to pet and feed: Arabian horses, burros, ducks and geese. You may want to walk in the meadow, hike through the woods, fish, or just sun yourself on the deck.

A one-room stone cottage, which is now used as a guest house, and an old spring house are the only remaining buildings from the old farmstead. The cottage was enlarged and a fireplace added. A kitchen area is equipped with cooking utensils, dishes, microwave and a hot plate. There is a sink and an under the counter refrigerator.

The sleeping area has a handmade hickory double bed and a dresser. The living room is furnished with an early American sofa, wicker rocker, table and chairs and a small television. The sofa could be used to sleep a third person. The cottage has a private bath, of course. There is no central heat in the cottage, but the fireplace has a heatolator and there is plenty of cut wood. With several small heaters placed about the cottage, and an electric blanket, there is more than enough warmth for cooler nights. The cottage is air conditioned and there is a deluxe hot tub.

Jackie delivers your breakfast to the cottage. Your choice of either Swedish pancakes and juice or a meat and cheese souffle, fresh fruit, and homemade bread or muffins with jam or jelly. Coffee or tea. Upon your arrival, complimentary wine is offered and in the evening there is a choice of fruit or cookies.

EDEN BED & BREAKFAST: 1694 E. 552nd Road, Brighton, 65617. (417) 267-2820. Open all year. A one-room stone cottage with fully equipped kitchen. Children welcome. Small pets allowed. Smoking permitted. Close to all Springfield attractions. Member, Ozark Mountain Country B & B Reservation Service. Iran and Jackie Cohen, hosts.

DIRECTIONS: Call for reservations and specific directions.

CARTHAGE

High on the south bank of the winding Spring River is the beautiful city of Carthage. It lies in a region where western prairie and Ozark highland meet. The area was part of the territory held by the Osage Indians. Laid out in 1842 as the seat of Jasper County, it is centered in a county of considerable mineral wealth and good farmland.

In July 1861, Carthage was the scene of the second major engagement of the Civil War in Missouri. In 1864, the city was burned to the ground by Southern guerrillas. After the war, a lead and zinc mining boom in Joplin brought the town a share of prosperity. In the 1880s, when the marble quarries were opened, the economic base in Carthage became firmly established. Carthage Marble, with it s magnificent color and hardness, is known worldwide. Among the buildings using this stone is the Missouri State Capitol.

In the late nineteenth century, Carthage was known throughout the nation as the home of the notorious Belle Starr. She was an excellent rider and pistol shot who rode with Quantrill's bushwhackers.

The Jasper County Museum has display cases scattered throughout the first floor of the courthouse. There are several types of collections including a display of local rock and minerals, a variety of Indian artifacts and Civil War relics including uniforms, swords and guns. The mural "Forged in Fire" by well-known artist Lowell Davis can be seen in the courthouse.

Carthage is also the home of the Precious Moments Chapel nestled among the dogwood trees just outside the city. The murals, stained glass windows, sculptures, and carvings all feature the Precious Moments figures. It is certainly one of the most inspirational settings in the area.

GRAND AVENUE BED & BREAKFAST
Carthage

Indicative of many of the homes in Carthage, the Grand Avenue Bed and Breakfast is a late-Victorian mansion that boasts four stained glass windows and generous appointments. Jeanne and Michael Goolsby, the new owners and hosts, have continued the tradition of guest comfort.

Entering from the large, wraparound front porch, the hallway features a gas lamp made of stained glass, oak paneling and a beautiful carved sweeping oak staircase. At the landing there's a stained glass window.

To the left of the front hall is the sitting room, featuring a round five foot diameter stained glass window with beveled glass set in the center. In the center of the room are twin silk oriental rugs, surrounded by a love seat and wingback chairs. The fireplace, set on an angle, features a hearth of Victorian tile and is topped by a beveled mirror in a gilded frame.

Adjoining the sitting room is the dining room. A large antique oak dining table with eight chairs is used for guests' meals. Over the mission table used as a sideboard is a cheery stained glass window that features a number of prisms that fill the room with rainbows of color on sunny days.

Opposite the sitting room on the other side of the front hall is the library. This room features a unique six register miniature upright piano and a bookcase stocked with some of the owners' favorite works. Above the piano is a semicircular stained glass window on top of a four foot square window of beveled glass. Also present is a lending library filled with video tapes.

The stairway leads to the upstairs hallway. Opposite the top of the stair is a wash stand with a wheat pattern carved in the front. Next to the wash stand is an antique love seat upholstered in white brocade. Three guestrooms open off the hallway, with a smaller hallway leading to the back of the house.

All of the guestrooms feature coffee service, private bathrooms with recently updated fixtures. A third person can be accommodated in most rooms.

The Laura Ingalls Wilder room is located on the first floor. Named for the famous Missouri author, this room features a king-size bed, decorative fireplace, and large bathroom including Jacuzzi tub. The walls are covered with a floral print wallpaper. An antique dresser and a variety of lace linens and antique knick-knacks complete the décor.

On the second floor, the Mark Twain Room features a queen-size four-poster bed and antique dresser. This room also has a private bathroom. The E.B. White Room adjoins Twain with a door between them. The two rooms may be rented as a suite, with a queen-size bed and twin-size bed in White, allowing for up to five people in the suite. E.B. White is not rented except as a suite with Twain.

Across the hall the Louisa May Alcott Room features a floral print wall paper, private bathroom with shower, and bay windows overlooking the brick driveway and neighbors' gardens. The room is furnished with a two-front dresser sporting a large mirror of beveled glass, several chairs, and a queen-size bed with walnut headboard. A ceiling fan is located over the bed.

The Charles Dickens Room is located down the back hallway on the second floor. Once, the "maid's bedroom," this cozy and quiet room has a view overlooking the pool and backyard. A full-size iron bed with beautiful quilt featuring an arcing pattern sits near the center of the room. There is a private bathroom with shower.

Breakfast begins with a yogurt, fruit and granola cup. Michael and Jeanne are known for their culinary talents, with main entrees including heart-shaped waffles, multi-grain pancakes, cheese blintzes, omelets, orange-nutmeg French toast, and a sausage egg and cheese casserole. Muffins, biscuits, scones, sausage patties, bacon, and fresh fruit are among the items that are used to complete the meal. Juice, coffee, tea, and soft drinks are served.

Recently Michael and Jeanne also have begun offering dinner to guests. Entrees include apple-smoke chicken breast, grilled pork tenderloin, and grilled steaks (weekends only). Each meal is accompanied by rice, steamed vegetables, and choice of beverage.

Starting in 1999 a series of murder-mystery weekends will be held at Grand Avenue. There is also a new romantic getaway package being offered that includes dinner at a local restaurant famous for its French cuisine, flowers in the room, and other complimentary perks. Central heat and air, ceiling fans, and an outdoor pool are available for guests' comfort.

GRAND AVENUE B & B: 1615 Grand Avenue, Carthage, 64836. (417) 358-7265. A five bedroom home in the historic district close to Precious Moments Chapel, Carthage State Park and Powell Museum. Open all year. No smoking or pets. Well-behaved children welcome. Jeanne and Michael Goolsby, hosts.

DIRECTIONS: Call for specific directions.

LEGGETT HOUSE BED & BREAKFAST
Carthage

This twenty-two room Carthage stone Victorian house was built in 1889-1901 as the home of industrial pioneer J.P. Leggett. He was also the mayor of Carthage from 1906-1912. This home provides a glimpse of the gracious living enjoyed during the turn of the century. It is also a fine example of classical revival architecture and superb craftsmanship. The property occupies two landscaped acres with seventeen varieties of trees among the many plantings. A large porch goes across the front. Breakfast may be taken either on the porch, on the patio, or in the dining room. A full country breakfast is served. Coffee and tea are always available.

Owners, Michael and Bonnie Melvin like to share their entire home. In fact, while Bonnie prepares breakfast, she likes to chat with the guests. Notice the warming oven over the radiator in the kitchen.

A large entry hall has a huge staircase, all of quarter-sawn oak, as are the beamed ceilings and the carved mantle piece over the fireplace. The woodwork will certainly attract your attention. The floor has an oriental carpet and furnishings include an antique settee and side chair.

The front parlor has the original gas and electric light fixtures. It is furnished with an Victorian style antique sofa and side chairs, an antique marble top table, and other chairs surrounding a fireplace.

The family room also has a fireplace. Furnishings include antique sofa, chairs, and gate leg game table, books and games for your enjoyment.

As in other well built, stately homes of the era, the dining room is paneled from the chair rail down and has Victorian patterned wallpaper above. A plate rail around the room holds antique plates. The room has a large walnut dining table with eight chairs, an antique buffet and an oriental carpet, and a fireplace. Above the table hangs the original lead glass chandelier. Through a carved arch, a small, sunny solarium with tile floors has an original Carthage marble fountain. Chairs are placed in front of a large oval window.

Four guest bedrooms are located on the second floor off the upstairs hall which has a leaded cut glass window, an oriental carpet, and is decorated with small antiques.

The White Room has Queen Ann style bed, dresser, pair of chairs, and an oriental rug. The private bath has the original marble shower.

The Bird's-eye Maple Room has a double bed, chest, vanity and a pair of antique chairs.

The Oak Room features twin Jenny Lind beds, antique wash stand, pair of chairs and an oriental carpet.

The Cherry Room has Victorian style high back carved bed, dresser, and an antique sofa. These three bedrooms share a large bathroom.

A wide hall leads to the fifth bedroom. The Pine Room has a double Eastlake bed, and antique dresser. A sink, installed when the house was built, is made of marble with French cabriola legs. This room ha s a private bath and opens to a small screened-in porch.

All of the bedrooms are wallpapered, have lace curtains and have walls decorated with prints and paintings.

The third floor ballroom level has one private bedroom and large room furnished with two full-size beds, a cozy sitting room, and oak billiard table. There is also a bathroom with claw foot tub and shower. This is ideal for family or group guests.

LEGGETT HOUSE B & B: 1106 Grand Avenue, Carthage, 64836. (417) 358-0683. A fine five room B & B in the historic district. Close to Precious Moments Chapel, Civil War Museum, and Powers Museum. Well mannered children welcome. No pets. Visa, Mastercard accepted. Michael and Bonnie Melvin, hosts.

DIRECTIONS: Call Bonnie or Michael for specific directions.

RED OAK INN
Fordland

Carol Alberty fell in love with her father's barn when she was a child. The enormous structure was an enchanting place, which served as her playhouse, while the nearby pastures and woods were her playground. When her father retired, Carol and her husband, Larry, purchased the old barn and surrounding land, which was originally farmed by her grandparents. Now, years later, Carol's childhood playhouse has become home for the Albertys and their children.

The loft floor is now the wainscoting in the upstairs hall, the original barn doors are used for the bedroom doors, and treasured keepsakes from both Larry's and Carol's families have been integrated into the décor.

As you enter the house there is a sitting room that has a sofa and matching wing chair, a rocking chair with upholstered cushions, an antique rocker, two lamp table with lamps, an arm chair and a glass top coffee table. On the floor is an area rug with an Indian motif. Lots of small and interesting nostalgic objects are displayed about the room.

To the right of the sitting room is the sunroom with floor to ceiling windows overlooking meadows and woodlands. There are four sets of tables and chairs, with red checkered tablecloths. Brass sconces are on the walls, which are papered in an ivy print. Breakfast is served here during the summer months.

When the weather is chilly, the warmth of a crackling fire draws guests to the keeping room. Here breakfast is served at a long harvest table. The ceiling and walls are boxcar siding. There are open beams and original posts. A corner wood burning fireplace has a round table and chairs in front of it, along with a love seat and club chairs.

Breakfast consists of juice, fresh fruit, Canadian bacon, scrambled eggs, and biscuits with gravy. There are pancakes or French toast with sausage. Always on hand is homemade bread, jams, jellies, coffee and tea.

Guests may choose from six distinctively decorated rooms, each with a private bath. A first floor guestroom was planned for those not wishing to use stairs. The full-size short four poster Schroll bed is covered with a blue comforter. There is a ball and claw foot chest, and a rocking chair. The room has pale blue gray walls with a pheasant print border at chair rail height and blue checked curtains.

On the third floor is a charmingly furnished sitting area decorated in a Southwestern motif. A quiet spot for reading or doing puzzles. Off the wide hallway on the second floor are five guestrooms. The first on the right is the Cousin Betty Room, which has a queen-size four poster, a wicker love set, chair and a rattan table. Walls are off-white accented with pink and white stripe wallpaper trimmed with a wide floral border.

The second room on the right, Sister Louise, is furnished with a queen-size four poster, wrought iron bed, an antique bonnet chest, a Martha Washington arm chair, and a round lamp table.

The first bedroom on the left, Aunt's Secret Garden Room, has a king-size poster headboard, a Queen Anne chair, a mission oak table and an old treadle sewing machine, night tables and lamps.

The fourth guestroom, called the Friendship Room also has a king-size bed. The room uses soft yellow tones and is wallpapered with a country mural scene.

The fifth room is the Schwartz Room with a four-poster with feather mattress. There is a window seat and a fireplace. French doors go onto a deck. Spiral stairs lead down to the yard.

RED OAK INN B & B: 1046 Red Oak Road, Fordland, 65652. (417) 767-2444. Open all year. Five guestrooms with private baths. Children over eight welcome. No pets. Smoking on porches. Near Wilson Creek Battlefield, Amish Store, Laura Ingalls Wilder home, and Branson. Carol and Larry Alberty, hosts.

DIRECTIONS: From Springfield, take Hwy. 60 east 16 miles to Hwy. U. Turn left on Red Oak Road, and go one mile.

WHITE SQUIRREL HOLLOW BED & BREAKFAST
Marionville

I never knew there was a white squirrel until I heard about White Squirrel Hollow. Clint Wise and I were seated in the dining room while he was telling me the history of the house. As we looked out the window, Clint pointed out several of the squirrels that were running up and down a large tree by the house. And sure enough they are white!

As Clint related to me, the house was built in 1896 by one of the Ozarks' first families. It took over seven years to complete this two and one half story Queen Anne style Victorian home. All of the original beaded woodwork is still in the house. The inlaid hardwood floors, doorway and spandrels are original to the house.

In the entry hall, the unusual spindles on the staircase repeat a different design at every fifth spindle. The entire home has been restored to its original splendor. Furnished with period pieces, it has beautiful stained glass windows and wallpapers which are authentic replicas of Victorian patterns imported from Paris.

The carpeted parlor has a hand carved fireplace and features a large stained glass window. The sofa and chairs are from the early 1920s. Guests can watch television here if they wish.

There is a music room with an antique baby grand piano and 600 volumes of old books which were found in the attic. The painted floor has stenciled designs.

The dining room has redwood and walnut inlaid floors. It also has the original hand blown crystal chandelier. The room has a ten piece matched dining suite. Breakfast is served here or in the warm country kitchen, where guests can chat with Clint as he prepares your meal. One wall of the kitchen is covered with a striking mural depicting an old mill and stream.

You are served a country style breakfast at White Squirrel Hollow. It is typical of many bed and breakfast offerings here in Ozark country. Ham, bacon, or sausage with eggs, juice or fruit, biscuits or breads with jams and jellies and coffee, tea or milk.

A second floor hall room has a wicker settee, two chairs and a table. Currier and Ives prints are on the walls. Five guestrooms are off the hall.

Newlyweds, second honeymooners and romantics will find the Honeymoon Suite to their liking. A four poster bed with a lace canopy is part of the three-piece bedroom set. There is an antique tapestry on the wall, a Persian carpet on the floor and an antique wicker chair. The original chandelier is still here. The room has a private screened in balcony and a private bath.

The Gold Coast Room, with its panoramic view, is reminiscent of the 1849 "gold rush days." The room is spacious, sunny and has a small sitting area. An old quilt covers the poster bed, which is part of a five-piece set dating from the 1920s. The original brass chandelier still hangs from the ceiling. The room has a shared bath.

The Elizabethan Room with its Tate Gallery prints and flocked wallpaper, has a satin canopy covered bed which is part of an English bedroom suite. There are paintings and prints on the walls pertaining to England. This room has a shared bath.

Turkish Corners has a double bed with a tented canopy over it. Two large antique tower lamps are set at each side of the footboard. There is a beautiful crocheted bedspread. This room also has its original chandelier and an oriental carpet. The room has a shared bath.

The Wild West Room has a high back bed with an antique quilt, upholstered chairs and many small items relating to the Old West. It has a private bath.

WHITE SQUIRREL HOLLOW B & B: 203 Mill Street, P.O. Box 412, Marionville, 65705. (417) 463-7626. A five guestroom B & B inn. Close to Springfield, Joplin and the Branson area. Open all year. Preteens welcome. No pets. Smoking in designated areas, but please no pipes or cigars. Clint Wise, innkeeper.

DIRECTIONS: From I-44 go south from Springfield on Hwy. 60. Exit right on Hwy. 14 to County Road ZZ. Left on ZZ to Mill Street and turn right.

DICKEY HOUSE BED & BREAKFAST
Marshfield

The Dickey House is a gracious Greek Revival mansion built at the turn of the century by Samuel Dickey, a prominent prosecuting attorney. It remained in the Dickey family until 1970. From the first glimpse of this beautiful white mansion with it's three foot diameter columns and intricate woodwork on the widow's walk above the beveled glass front entrance, you will feel transported back to an era that has long since passed.

The entry hall has white Greek pillars leading into rooms on both side of the hall. A great staircase leads to the second floor guestrooms. White woodwork highlights the shining floors and area carpeting.

To the left of the entry hall is a parlor with an oriental carpet placed in front of the huge fireplace. A wonderful circa 1880 baroque style leather sofa with ornately caved wood trim and two matching chairs are the centerpieces of the room. The room also contains a carved inlaid coffee table, two lighted display cabinets displaying the owners antique glass collection, several pieces of unusual artwork and carvings in addition to many items from the owner's travels to the Orient. The room has two crystal chandeliers, floral drapes and large plants.

To the right of the entry hall is the dining room. A single pedestal table and six Victorian chairs rest on an oriental carpet. A magnificent carved walnut cupboard, four Hepplewhite side chairs and a drop leaf table are part of the furnishings. Many plates depicting birds and butterflies decorate the walls. There is an oriental display cabinet in the corner filled with unusual carvings.

There is a smaller more intimate parlor off the main parlor. This parlor has a TV/VCR, which the guests are encouraged to use.

Three guestrooms are off the second floor hall, each with a private bath. They are tastefully filled with antiques and reproductions and offer a variety of distinctive touches that let you know you are a welcome guest. There is also a small exercise room off the hall for the guest's use.

The Heritage Room features a fireplace and a large screened balcony. It is furnished with a queen-size four poster rice bed with a canopy, a highboy, a Victorian loveseat and matching chair. The walls are in a plum color wallpaper and the floral bed covers match the drapes.

The Fontaine Room shares the screened balcony with the Heritage Room. This is a charming Victorian style room with a fireplace, a circa 1890 queen-size half tester bed, a pair of Eastlake side chairs, an oak dresser and a marble top Eastlake bedside table with an English wedding lamp. The room is decorated with blue lace curtains, area carpets and floral wallpaper.

The Springtime Room is cheerfully furnished in a floral motif. It has an antique four poster bed and a 1920's chest and vanity. The pale green walls have a dark green border. There are throw rugs on the floor.

There are three private suites on the grounds. All suites have a private bath with shower, a double Jacuzzi, fireplace, TV/VCR, coffee maker and CD player. Each is supplied with a romantic CD, flavored coffees and teas, candy and soda.

Two of the suites are in one cottage. The Garden Suite is furnished with an unusual king-size brass bed. It is carpeted wall to wall and has a marvelous crewel pattered wallpaper above a chair rail. It has a private bath with shower.

The Queen Anne Suite has a large walnut four-poster queen-size bed and is decorated in slightly feminine Victorian style with a chair rail and yellow floral print wallpaper. There is a heart shaped mirror on the wall of the Jacuzzi.

The Carriage House Suite is in a separate building on the property. It is decorated in soft, warm colors of cream, fern green and bronze. It has a queen-size white and brass iron bed with a quarter canopy over the headboard. The Carriage House also has a sofa that opens to a queen-size bed.

A full gourmet breakfast is served. It includes assorted juices, fresh fruit, and gourmet entrée. Here are homemade breads, jams and jellies, imported coffees and select teas.

The grounds of The Dickey House are park-like and beautifully landscaped, just the place to relax and take a nap or read a book. There is also an aviary with turtledoves and finches. The Dickey House is AAA four diamond rated, and is the only so rated Bed and Breakfast in the state of Missouri.

DICKEY HOUSE B & B, LTD.: 331 South Clay Street, Marshfield, 65706. (417) 468-3000. Open all year. Three guestrooms and three private suites. Children over 12 are welcome. No pets. Smoking only permitted outside or on the porches. Lawrence and Michaelene Stevens, innkeepers.

DIRECTIONS: From I-44, exit at Hwy. 38 (exit 100) Marshfield. Take 38 east for 1½ miles to Clay Street. Right on Clay to The Dickey House.

RED HORSE INN
Nevada

This house was built in 1904 and is located just a block south of the town-square. It was completely renovated in 1990 and is now the home of Pat and Karen Chambers and their two sons, Eric and Brian. The house is constructed in the Prairie style of architecture. There is a large country front porch and an expansive wraparound deck on the back of the house complete with a large hot tub!

The carpeted living room is furnished with a sofa, two large, overstuffed side chairs and a glider/rocker. Guests are invited to make themselves comfortable and join the family enjoying the big screen TV with home theater sound system.

The recently refinished dining room has stucco walls and a plate rail that holds a number of antiques and collectibles. Among the dining room furnishings is a nine foot long harvest table with spindle back chairs. An antique oak "Dough Boy" is one of the other beautiful pieces in this room.

The first floor guestroom is the Griffons Room. It's furnished with a queen-size bed, a child's dresser from the early 1800's, and desk. This room displays a number of mementos from the Nevada Griffons, the town's very successful summer collegiate baseball team.

There are four guestrooms on the second floor. The Cherry Room is furnished with a queen-size bed and a hide-a-bed love seat that folds out for a very comfortable night's sleep for a third person. A turn of the century Gentleman's Closet is the featured piece of furniture here. As in all the rooms, there is a ceiling fan. The Cherry Room has a private bath with shower and also cable television.

In the Brass Room you'll find a queen and full-size beds with brass headboards. There's a rocker, washstand and a circa 1840's dresser. The Brass Room has a private bath with "bubble" tub. There is a private door leading to small private deck with a staircase leading to the deck below. There is also cable TV in the Brass Room.

The Iron Room offers antique queen and full-size beds with handmade quilts (which you'll find in every room). An antique table is used for a side table in the quarter bath and there is an antique dresser as well. This room shares the large full bath on the second floor with the Bushwhacker Room.

The Bushwhacker Room has a queen-size bed, an antique dresser with mirror and side table. The large shared bath is just outside the door.

In the kitchen Pat has refinished an old time ice cream table and Karen has made cushions for the two matching parlor chairs. There's a wrought iron table and chairs on the deck just through the kitchen doors and you'll be able to relax in a set of wicker furniture on the deck just outside the dining room.

The deck is handicap-accessible and both the kitchen and dining room have French doors.

Karen's mouth-watering breakfasts don't allow anyone to leave the table hungry! Guests are treated to a breakfast entrée, breakfast meat, fruit, breads or pastries, coffee, juice and milk.

RED HORSE INN: 217 S. Main, Nevada, 64772. (417) 667-7796 or 1 (800) 245-3685. E-mail address: rhibandb@hotmail.com. Open all year. Three rooms with private bath, and two rooms share a large bath. Children are welcome. Smoking permitted on the deck and porch. The Red Horse Inn is a Chambers Hospitality Inc. property. Pat and Karen Chambers, innkeepers.

DIRECTIONS: Located between Kansas City and Joplin on both 71 and 54 highways.

DEAR'S REST BED & BREAKFAST
Ozark

If ever you have an urge to find a hide-a-way from the hustle and bustle, even for a day or two, drive down to the beautiful Ozarks and stay a while with Allan and Linda Schilter at their Dear's Rest Bed & Breakfast.

This rustic cedar sided, post and beam home was crafted by local Amish builders. It is hidden away where you can unwind in the natural beauty and peaceful solitude of the wooded hills of the Ozarks. Here you can enjoy the singing of the birds and unexpected visits from resident wildlife: deer, turkey, raccoons, flying squirrels and so forth. You can hike the old farm roads or just sit and relax on the deck while you soak in the hot tub. Be sure to take a walk along Bull Creek. It is one of the last remaining crystal clear, spring fed creeks in southwest Missouri.

Horizontal, cedar tongue and groove planking is used throughout the house. The living room with its twenty-foot ceilings and open beams, a great stone fireplace and pine floors make this a room of great warmth and comfort. A lot of family antiques were used to furnish the house. An antique secretary bookcase, a leather rocker recliner, two upholstered chairs and ottoman, an oak side table and a pair of floral overstuffed wing chairs are part of the furnishings. Allan's collection of antique toys from his childhood are displayed on the rafters. White imported lace curtains are on the bay window as they are throughout the house. Paintings and handcrafted art decorate the walls. There is also a TV/VCR.

The first floor guestroom has a full-size iron bed and a small chest as part of the furniture. Throw rugs are on the polished pine floors. There is an heirloom handmade quilt decorating one wall, giving an Amish look and feel to the room. There is a large bath and shower.

From the living room, stairs go up to a loft where a second guestroom is located. It has sloping ceilings and a balcony that overlooks the dining area. It is furnished with a full-size antique bed, a dresser, a child's rocking chair, a wicker chair, end tables with reading lamps, an old wooden bench and a display of family heirloom quilts.

The dining area has a tiled floor, one wall of paned windows and a sliding door to the deck. There is an antique round oak table with four oak bow back Windsor chairs, a high chair and a long hand crafted table made by Linda's grandfather.

The deck has a hot tub, a wrought iron table and chairs and a table with benches. The deck is shaded by large trees with the woods just a stones throw away. It is a lovely spot to have your breakfast, weather permitting. It is also a fine spot for bird watching. Linda and Allan love the wild birds and there are many bird feeders to attract them.

Start your day here in Ozark country with a real country breakfast. Linda serves a frozen fruit cup that her guests named "Morning Delight." that is very good. I know because I tried it. Then try scrambled eggs with sausage, biscuits and gravy or waffles, or eggs and bacon. There are always jams, jellies and honey and coffee or tea.

The town of Ozark is absolutely crammed with antique shops and other small stores. The Ozark Village Days are held in June. The Ozarks' Antique Fair in May and the Ozarks' Crafts and Festival in October. They're all worth the trip.

DEAR'S REST B & B: 1408 Capp Hill Ranch Road, Ozark, 65721. (417) 581-3839 or 1(800) 588-2262 for reservations. E-mail: info@dearsrest.com. Open all year. A two guestroom (one in the loft) country home built by the Amish. Absolute privacy. Nestled among the trees accessible to pristine Bull Creek. A great place to enjoy nature. Children welcome. No pets. No smoking. For more information visit their Website: http://www.dearsrest.com. Allan and Linda Schilter, innkeepers.

DIRECTIONS: From Hwy. 65 at Springfield, take Hwy. 65 south to Hwy. 14. Turn left (east) on 14 to Hwy. W. Turn right on W and go seven miles to Logan Ridge Road which is just an extension of W (state maintenance ends here). Go two miles on Logan Ridge to Capp Hill Ranch Road. Turn left to Dear's Rest Drive. Linda and Allan have posted signs along the road.

RAINBOW TROUT RANCH
Rockbridge

Because I am a nostalgic soul and wonder about the past, the little village of Rockbridge holds a great deal of interest for me. In the early 1800s, settlers built a small community at the junction of the Bryant and Spring Creeks. It became known as Rockbridge but was burned to the ground during the Civil War. About 1868, the mill was built and once again a community grew. It, too, was called Rockbridge. Due to the mill's importance, the town became a gathering place. During the years of prosperity, a large, two story general store, a bank, a church, and a blacksmith shop were built. For over one hundred and twenty years, Rockbridge Mill has stood on the bank of Spring Creek.

It is a quiet, secluded place. A place to get away from it all for a brief time. Today the old mill and the peaceful little village are still here. The mill, general store, bank and church which served the hill people so long ago have been restored and now provide the perfect setting for a few delightful vacation days.

I first met Lile and Edith Amyx, the owners of Rainbow Trout Ranch, in 1980 when I was writing a book entitled, The Complete Missouri Travel Guide. I stopped in to see the mill. After chatting with Edith and Lile for some time she offered me lunch. "The trout," she said, "is a specialty." She gave me a quizzical look when I said, "I'd like it fried." Later she told me, "Next time you come down, I will fix it for you properly. . .broiled."

A restaurant and lounge area are housed in the two story general store that replaced the original one that burned down in 1986. Its is most comfortable with a large fireplace, sofas, chairs and a television. The restaurant has a relaxed, homey atmosphere. Plants hang in the windows and the walls are nicely decorated. All three meals are served here, but are not included in the room rates. One item on the menu that you don't see too often is "pressure fried" chicken. In all my travels, I have found only a handful of restaurants that offer chicken prepared this way. A gift and antique shop has various fishing supplies along with lots of great gift ideas.

The accommodations are fairly new, consisting of several groups of brick buildings. The guestrooms all have two double beds, table and chairs and a private bath with shower. The walls are paneled and have wooden shutters on the windows. Local art is displayed on the walls. These buildings were built a short distance away from the original old buildings, and in such a way that they did not detract from the peaceful setting of the town, which is all tucked away in a picturesque valley about six hundred feet wide.

Two of the older buildings are now used for guests. The White House is a large farm house with six guestrooms and three baths and will accommodate 16 people. Another farm house, the Red House, has four guestrooms, two baths and will accommodate eight people.

If you don't care to spend your time fishing, visit the Rockbridge Gun Club, or the Rockbridge Grist Mill Club, where they serve appetizers and mixed drinks in the old grist mill. There is also a lot to see in the area. First of all, you have a thousand acres of countryside to explore and two miles of a clear, fast flowing stream. There are three sections of Mark Twain National Forest nearby. Norfolk and Bull Shoals Lakes are a half hour south. Fifty five miles west, in the Branson area, there is something for everyone. North of Rockbridge, in Mansfield, is the Laura Ingalls Wilder Home and Museum where she wrote her Little House children's books.

RAINBOW TROUT RANCH: P.O. Box 100, Rockbridge, 65741. (417) 679-3619. Enjoy a fresh and different approach to a few days of relaxation in a timeless world of yesterday. Open from March 1 to November 30. Children welcome. Smoking permitted. Reservations well in advance a must. The Amyx Family, owners.

DIRECTIONS: From I-44 at Rolla, go south on Hwy. 63 to Hwy. 60. West on Hwy. 60 about 10 miles to Mountain Grove. South from Mountain Grove on Rt. 95 about thirty five miles to County Road N. Right (north) on N for two miles. From anywhere in Missouri, take Hwy. 60 to Mountain Grove and follow as above.

SPRINGFIELD

The first attempt at establishing a permanent settlement in the Springfield area was made by one Thomas Patterson. In 1821 he brought his family up the James River and purchased a land claim. The next year, 500 Delaware Indians arrived and claimed the government had given them southwestern Missouri for their reservation. One of the white settlers went to St. Louis to find out which claim was correct. The Indians were upheld, and it is said that a Delaware and Kickapoo village was built near the present site of Springfield. The area was soon abandoned by the settlers except for James Wilson who moved in with the Indians, marrying several of their women. When the Delaware left the area, Wilson sent his Indian wives with them, returned to St. Louis to buy farm implements and married a white woman. He returned to the Springfield area to develop a farm on the creek which now bears his name.

White settlers began a slow migration back into the area when, in 1830, the government began moving all Indian tribes westward. In 1829, John Campbell and his brother, Madison, came to southern Missouri to verify reports about the Ozark country. They came north to the site of Springfield, then known as Kickapoo Prairie, and staked a claim by carving their names on a tree near a spring about 1200 feet northeast of the present public square. The site they had selected was well chosen as the spring was excellent and there were important early trails nearby. Within a few months, a small settlement grew up.

In 1833 when Greene County was organized, John Campbell was made county clerk and the county seat was established in his log cabin home. In 1835, Campbell deeded 50 acres to the county for a town site between what is now Campbell and Jefferson, Pershing and Mill Streets. The origin of the town's name is uncertain, but some say Campbell picked the name because there was a field on a hill with a spring under it. In 1838, the town was incorporated and in 1847, it received its charter.

Springfield's population was predominantly in favor of the south when the Civil War broke out. The town was made a military objective for both the Union and Confederate forces during the war. In the Battle of Wilson's Creek, fought 11 miles south of town on August 10, 1861, the Confederate army won the victory. They held Springfield until driven out in 1862 by Union forces, who retained possession of the town until the end of the war.

Springfield grew slowly at first. But, located at the intersection of the area's two most important roads, when the westward migration began, Springfield's expansion was quite rapid. When the Ozark highlands were developed as a recreational area in the 1930's, Springfield became an important center of business and social life. Today, Springfield is Missouri's third largest city and a gateway to Ozark Mountain Country. Historic homes, fascinating museums, caves, forest and lakes make Springfield "the Ozarks' way to get away."

The Springfield Art Museum displays collections of American and European paintings, sculptures, drawings, photographs, prints and decorated arts of the 18th, 19th and 20th centuries. You can also view the arts of the American Indian and Oceanic and Pre-Columbian cultures.

Springfield's Symphony Orchestra has performed for over 40 years. Featuring local musicians as well as guest performances by some of the nation's finest musicians, the Springfield Symphony is not to be missed.

The Battle of Wilson's Creek was probably the most significant battle fought in Missouri. There is a self guided loop drive with a stop at the interpretive shelter at Blood Hill battle site. The audio-visual program explains not only the battle itself, but the events leading up to it as well as the part it played in keeping Missouri in the Union.

Just north of Springfield on Highway 13 is one of Missouri's largest caves, Fantastic Caverns. A jeep drawn tram takes you on a 45 minute tour into a wonderland of beauty and mystery. The caverns are millions of years old and truly one of the Ozarks gems.

The Dickerson Park Zoo has the largest collection of bald eagles in the United States. Other highlights are the African Lion display and the Spotted Leopard exhibit.

While you are in Springfield be sure to visit *Traders Market* located at 1845 E. Sunshine. (417) 889-1145. This is one of the finest shopping galleries I've visited. Over 15,000 sq. ft. of exceptional merchandise offered by over 50 shopkeepers. Browse amid original oil paintings, limited edition prints, watercolors, custom furniture, fine jewelry, imported lace, and exquisite porcelains. There are bird house, teddy bears, brass and pewter, glassware and children's things. A charming European style café offers beautifully served luncheon entrees, extraordinary desserts, exotic coffees and imported teas. Be sure to check out the extensive selection of gourmet food times from around the world.

VIRGINIA ROSE BED & BREAKFAST
Springfield

In 1921, one J.F. Botts came to Springfield from northern Missouri to look for a farm. He found this 1906 farm house with ten acres, purchased it, and moved his family of six here in a Model T Ford. Three generations of the Botts family have lived here.

The house and the original red barn have a unique setting on a tree covered acre in the midst of modern Springfield. The old barn is still there and so is the original well house. Large oak trees surround the house.

Purchased by Jack and Virginia Buck for use as a bed and breakfast, they have used a period décor and furnishings. Upon arrival, guests are invited to browse through their home and join them in the parlor to sip a cup of Earl Grey tea or Snickerdoodle coffee. For relaxation or rainy day fun, there are games and puzzles, a TV/VCR or the piano which you are welcome to play.

The parlor is furnished with a sofa, upholstered swivel rocker, an antique cupboard holding Virginia's ruby red cut glass, an early 1900's table, coffee table and two antique sectional bookcases. The room is carpeted and has drapes over lace curtains at the window.

The dining room has a Queen Anne round table and four ladderback chairs, an old sewing machine and an antique Hoosier cabinet. An antique cupboard holds the rose patterned china which Virginia has collected over the years. She uses this lovely service to serve breakfast to guests.

Speaking of breakfast, guests are served hearty homemade fare which may vary from a ham and egg strata with a fruit cup in a lemon and orange sauce to baked French toast with nuts and brown sugar served with a breakfast meat, juice or fruit. There are always homemade blueberry muffins or cinnamon rolls, jams and jellies, coffee and tea.

On the first floor, the carpeted Brittany Rose Room, named for a granddaughter, features a circa 1915 three piece mahogany bedroom set consisting of a queen-size four poster bed, a chest and vanity. There is also a Windsor chair and bookcase. The walls are covered with an old fashioned rose patterned wallpaper. A large private bath has the original sink and claw foot tub with shower.

The Virginia Rose, a large airy room, has a new five piece oak bedroom set: a queen-size bed, double dresser, wardrobe, and two night tables with reading lamps. There is also an upholstered chair. Blue floral wallpaper, Battenburg accents, white café curtains, blue carpeting, an antique dresser set and a quilt rack with quilts help decorate the room.

The Ella Rose Room, named for Virginia's grandmother, is furnished with a 1920's cottage bedroom set. There is a full-size bed, chest and a vanity. An antique plant stand is used as a night table and there is a vintage library table. A colorful braided rug is on the floor and the walls are papered in a light blue and coral floral print. Robes are furnished for the private bath with shower across the hall.

The Rambling Rose Suite consists of two bedrooms with a connecting door. One is wallpapered in a small rose print paper. Blue drapes have tiny roses. It has a queen-size bed with a handmade quilt, chest, a pair of white wicker chairs, a white wicker table and an antique trunk. The room is decorated with dried wreath and floral arrangements. The adjoining room is under the eaves. The original floors are painted white and have area rugs. It is furnished with a Jenny Lind full-size bed covered with a handmade quilt, an antique library table, small chest, wardrobe, cedar chest and bedside tables. There is also a Jenny Lind trundle bed with a rose comforter. The suite has a private bath with shower.

VIRGINIA ROSE B & B: 317 E. Glenwood, Springfield, 65807. (417) 883-0693. 1(800) 345-1412. E-mail: vrosebb@mocom.net. Open all year. A three guestroom and two bedroom suite home. Children welcome. No pets. No smoking inside. Jack and Virginia Buck, innkeepers.

DIRECTIONS: From I-44, exit on Hwy. 65 south. Proceed to Sunshine Street and exit to right (west). Take Sunshine to Campbell. Turn left and go one mile south to Glenwood and turn left to Virginia Rose B & B.

WALNUT STREET INN
Springfield

Near the hub of Springfield's center city business district, the Walnut Street Inn is a charming pocket of gracious turn-of-the-century living where you can step back in time and capture the warmth and elegance of this Queen Anne Victorian home. The rambling two and a half story house was built in 1894 and has been occupied by several of Springfield's prominent families. It is listed on the Register of Historic Places.

Twenty ornate, iron Corinthian columns with whimsical designs, a hallmark of Victorian architecture, line the wide, wraparound front porch and smaller side porch. A large first floor deck and upper floor balconies overlook the country style yard that is graced with flowering trees and bushes, including 85-year-old redbuds, a 150-year-old linden tree, and seasonal flower beds that bloom almost all year round.

Leaded glass borders each side of the French doors leading into an entry hall. To the right is a large parlor. A circa 1861 box rosewood grand piano is framed by leaded glass windows. Gather around the fireplace with other guests and enjoy fresh coffee or a glass of wine while visiting, playing games, reading and relaxing.

The dining room is a relaxing place to meet others over your delicious breakfasts. The individually painted chairs, each with a different country motif, are taken from the wallpaper above the paneled wainscoting around the room.

One of the memorable parts of your stay will be the breakfasts. Sausage strudel, Belgian waffles, cream filled French toast, all served on china with crystal and linens will greet you each morning in an atmosphere of home-style hospitality.

An ornately carved oak staircase leads to the second floor "gathering room." Guests may relax on lovely wing chairs and sofa comfortable arranged around another fireplace. A game table and chairs provide a good place to play cards, work puzzles, or muse over the plans for the day.

Three guestrooms are on this floor. Each one has a distinctive and individual décor and is furnished with period antiques and reproductions which compliment the overall impression of Victorian elegance. There are two additional guestrooms on the third floor. The private carriage house to the south of the main house has four gorgeous suites. The Cottage Inn two doors from the main house offers a more country feel. Featured as a designer's Showcase Home, the rooms at Walnut Street Inn are exceptional in their decor and attention to detail. Each room has a private bath, some with original porcelain antique fixtures. They all include special touches such as antique pictures, lace curtains and every amenity one would expect of a fine, urban home.

Walnut Street Inn has fourteen beautiful guestrooms in three historic houses that will cause you to want to "try them all" with future stays at the inn. Small family gatherings at the inn become memories for a lifetime.

WALNUT STREET INN: 900 East Walnut Street, Springfield, 65806. (417) 864-6346, Reservations 1(800) 593-6346 or Fax: (417) 864-6184. Visit the inn's web page at: www.pcis.net/walnutstinn or e-mail them at: Walnutstinn@pcis.net. Open all year, closed Christmas and Thanksgiving. Children with well behaved parents welcome. Smoking on porches only. Gary and Paula Blankenship, innkeepers. Resident dog – Georgia.

DIRECTIONS FROM I-44: Exit 82-A for U.S. Hwy. 65 south. Go 2.8 miles to Chestnut Expressway. Go right (west) for three miles to Sherman Avenue. Turn left (south) and go four blocks (.6 mile) until you see the Inn on your left. Park behind the main house.

ZANONI MILL INN
Zanoni

People driving by Zanoni Mill Inn sometimes turn in the drive and ask the owners if they can see the house. And no wonder, for it is nearly an exact duplicate of the Southfork Ranch from the former "Dallas" television series. You almost expect to see J.R. or Bobby Ewing come by. You won't. And much as they would like to accommodate visitors, this is an 1800 acre working ranch and the owners haven't the time to be tour guides.

Milling began at Zanoni Mill, located on the spring fed Pine Creek, during the Civil War days. Today the mill is closed, but it is still a tourist attraction. It has a rare overshot water wheel. It was last in operation in 1951.

In 1980 David and Mary Morrison built their house just in back of the old mill. It faces a large lake where geese and ducks make their home. A gravel road circles the lake and house. David farms and raises cattle. Mary helps him and also has a large garden which she tends.

The house is something to behold. As you come in, a large entry hall is fronted by a wide staircase leading to the second floor. The wall of the staircase is paneled to the chair rail. Above that, a mirror follows the contour of the winding stairs.

On the first floor, at one end of the house, is a huge room with paneled cathedral ceilings and a skylight. This room has an 18 by 38 foot heated swimming pool. All around the sides are rattan and wrought iron lawn furniture. There are many plants and flowers. In addition to the use of the pool, guests can relax afterward in front of the large stone fireplace.

There is a knotty pine paneled recreation room which has a pool table, ping pong table, exercise equipment, and a television for use of the guests.

In keeping with the rest of the house, the bedrooms are large and airy. All are carpeted and tastefully decorated. One room has a queen-size four poster bed, matching dresser and chest and chairs. It has a view of the old red barn. Another guestroom has a double bed, dresser, night tables, upholstered rocker and wrought iron table and chairs. These two rooms share a large, carpeted bath with tub and shower.

The third bedroom is extra large. It has a queen-size bed, chaise lounge, wardrobe and the usual table and chairs. It opens onto a balcony overlooking the lake and beautiful hills. It has a private carpeted bath with tub and shower. A fourth guestroom has a queen-size bed with built-in doors, mirror and a reading lamp in the headboard. There is a desk and a game table among the furnishings. It has a private bath with shower.

Breakfast is served in either the pool area or the kitchen, and Mary serves a great meal. The Morrisons raise all their own meat, have their own eggs fresh from their chickens, and in season, vegetables from their garden so you are assured a fresh breakfast. Guests make their selection the night before from a menu that includes eggs and a meat, or fluffy pancakes with sausage. There are biscuits and gravy, fresh juice, fresh fruit in season, homemade cinnamon rolls, toast, jam and jelly, and coffee, tea or milk.

There is a lot to keep you busy here. If you wish, after breakfast, you can take a stroll on one of the trails that run through the property. You can easily spot wildlife and many species of birds. It's an ideal place for jogging, and then there is fishing in the lake, visiting the old mill or swimming in the pool. If none of this interest you, just relax and enjoy the fresh country air.

ZANONI MILL INN: HC 78, Box 1010, Zanoni, 65784. (417) 679-4050 and (877) 679-4050. E-mail: zanonibb@ozcool.com. Four guestrooms in a luxurious home on 1800 acres. Close to several of the historic mills. Just 60 miles from Branson. Open all year. Closed holidays. No children. No pets. No smoking. Member, Ozark Mountain Country B & B Reservation Service. David and Mary Morrison, innkeepers.

DIRECTIONS: From Hwy. 160 at Gainesville, go west two miles to State Road 181. North on Hwy. 181 approximately 12 miles. The house is on the left.

Section Two

BIG SPRINGS REGION

Bourbon
Greer Hollow Farm B & B
Meramec Farm B & B

Eminence
Cedar Stone B & B
Faulkenberry's B & B
Old Blue House B & B

Ironton
Green Roof Inn

Potosi
Bust Inn B & B

Rolla
Miner Indulgence B & B

St. James
Ferrigno B & B
Painted Lady B & B
Rosati Winery B & B

Salem
Whitmire Guesthouse

Steelville
Frisco House B & B
Parkview Inn

Sullivan
Wildflower Inn

Thayer
Carr House B & B

West Plains
Pinebrook Lodge

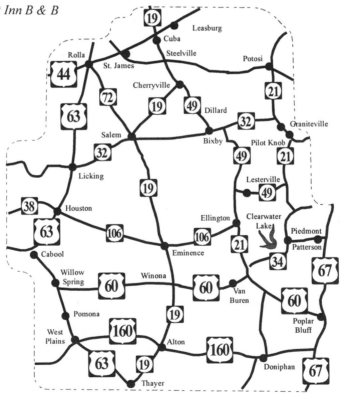

Springs, rivers, hills and forests, all blending to create spectacular scenery, give the Big Springs Region its special character. If you like hiking, try it here in five state parks and large sections of the Mark Twain national forest. If you like water, pick any of the region's springs, rivers or lakes for swimming, canoeing or fishing. If you like unspoiled beauty, there are miles of winding roads with fantastic views. If free flowing rivers, pioneer history and hill country charm appeal to you, it can certainly be found here in the Big Springs region.

With all of south central Missouri's natural wonders, one site ranks as it's premier attraction – Big Springs. Located near Van Buren, Big Spring's underground streams burst to the surface through a single opening, creating America's largest spring. The crystal clear flow, averaging 277 million gallons a day, at times has risen as high as 846 million gallons.

South from Van Buren is Skyline Scenic Drive. If you are in the vicinity, it is too good to pass up. As with other scenic drives in the state, spring and fall are the best times to travel these back roads. But, at any time the beauty of the region is evident.

Big Spring is the heart of the Ozark National Scenic Rivers; a region that boasts of more than 60 major springs. For an impressive sampling of Missouri's natural treasures, spend some time exploring the riverways. Highways and back roads will take you to many of the well-known sites, but the best way to see it all is via an old Missouri favorite, a float trip.

By canoe or flat-bottomed john boat, you can float 134 miles of the Current and Jacks Fork rivers, preserved here in their natural state. Bring your own boat or rent a boat and equipment from one of the many outfitters along the rivers. Either way, you'll never forget a float through Ozark forest, along limestone bluffs and past old homesteads.

Whether you choose the Current and Jacks Fork or other area rivers, such as the Eleven Point, Black, Big Piney or Meramec, you'll find the Ozark countryside beautiful any time of year. If you enjoy tranquility and solitude, try floating either during the week or off-season. An added advantage of off-season floating is the higher water levels in late fall, winter and spring.

For more information on the Ozark National Scenic Rivers contact the National Park Service headquarters in Van Buren.

Just west of Big Springs is one of several Mark Twain National Forest tracts, ideal for hiking. Continuing west from Big Spring to the region's southwest corner, the town of West Plains offers a wealth of community events and shows off it's history and art at the Harlin Museum. The Pinebrook Lodge is located in West Plains. Near Thayer and the state line is Grand Gulf State Park with its intriguing "Little Grand Canyon," which is actually a huge collapsed cave with the remaining section of the cave roof forming a spectacular stone bridge. Carr House B & B is located here.

North of Thayer on Hwy. 19, just west of Winona on Hwy. 60 is Mountain View. Back on Hwy. 19 west of Eminence is Alley Spring, the seventh largest spring in Missouri, which forms a picture-book setting for a favorite with photographers, the Old Red Mill. Bed and breakfasts in Eminence are Cedar Stone Lodge, Faulkenberry's B & B and The Old Blue House.

Going north on Hwy. 19 takes you through the only stand of virgin pine forest left in the state, up to Salem where you'll find Whitmire Guest House. Taking Hwy. 119 southwest of Salem for 21 miles will bring you to Montauk State Park. The seven clear, cold springs in the park form the headwaters of the Current River. Regular stockings from the rainbow trout hatchery provide excellent fishing.

If you head northeast from Big Spring, you'll find Clearwater, the state's most picturesque lake rimmed with stately oaks and hickory forest, steep shorelines and high bluffs. The lake offers boating, swimming, water-skiing and fishing for crappie and catfish.

To see the northern half of the region, start at Rolla, the area's largest town. It has something for everyone. A small-scale version of England's Stonehenge may be found at the University of Missouri campus along with a mineral museum. Rolla also has an antique car museum at Memoryville, U.S.A., an historic log cabin and blockhouse jail in the downtown area and much more. Miner Indulgence B & B is located in Rolla.

Just east is Meramec Spring Park at St. James. Stop off and fish for trout or photograph the towering old iron furnaces that bear silent witness to the region's mining traditions. Ferrigno B & B, Painted Lady B & B and Rosati Winery B & B are at St. James. Not far from here, near Potosi and Viburnum, you can drive through the world's largest lead mining district. The Bust Inn B & B is at Potosi.

Continue on the region's northern edge and you'll pass seven area vineyards and wineries that are open for free tours. They are Ferrigno Vineyards, Reis Winery, Heinrichshaus Vineyards, Mount Pleasant Vineyards, Rosati Winery, St. James Winery and Peaceful Bend Vineyards.

Descend into one of Missouri's most popular caves and enjoy a tour of Onondaga. Then head for Washington State Park to view the famous petroglyphs. The park also has hiking trails and a dining lodge. Meramec Farm B & B is just a few miles from Onondaga in Bourbon, as is Greer Hollow Farm B & B and Wildflower Inn.

Steelville, south of Cuba on Hwy. 19, is the float capitol of America. An easy drive from St. Louis, rubber tube rafting on the Meramac River offers great family fun at a modest price. The town features a revitalized downtown area with lots of antique shops, kids trout fishing, a country music show and Ozark friendliness. The Frisco House B & B and Parkview B & B are in Steelville.

Next, head south to the scenic Arcadia Valley. On your way, stop near Graniteville for a look at Elephant Rocks State Park. Set amid the greenery of the Ozarks, the red granite boulders will amaze you. This state park also features Missouri's first National Recreation trail. It has been designed to provide access to the wonders of nature for the visually handicapped. The mile long "Braille Trail" has 22 Braille-English signs describing the formations and their history.

Near Ironton, the Fort Davidson State Historic Site is a reminder of an 1864 Civil War battle. Cannon ball scars from the Battle of Pilot Knob can be seen today on the walls of the Iron County Courthouse. Built in 1858, it served as both a barracks and a hospital. St. Paul's Episcopal Church, listed on the National Register of Historic Places, is a fine example of a gothic-style church. The green Roof B & B is here in Ironton.

Four miles southwest of Arcadia on Hwys. 21 and 72, the road climbs to the highest peaks in the Ozarks. From here the view of Arcadia Valley, surrounded by seven peaks, is unbroken for twenty-five miles. Following a mountain ledge bordered by a granite guard-wall, the winding curves descend into Big Creek Valley through Royal Gorge, a shut-in with perpendicular walls rising more than one hundred feet above the roadbed. Just to the west is Missouri's highest point, Taum Sauk Mountain rising to a height of 1,772 feet.

At nearby Proffit Mountain, is the 55 acre mountain top reservoir constructed by Union Electric for power generation. There is a free visitors center and museum.

A short drive west is another favorite spot for tourist, Johnson's Shut-Ins. The spectacular rocks and rushing waters are well worth your time. There is also the 2,386 acres of forestlands for hiking, camping and picnicking.

When you've completed your circuit of the Big Springs Region, with its pine-covered hills, crystalline rivers, rustic mills and scenic highways, you'll understand the special appeal of south-central Missouri.

GREER HOLLOW FARM BED & BREAKFAST
Bourbon

When the original home on this farm burned down in 1930, the owners built this large, one room log cabin across a creek from the burned out one. It was built just as you see it today. When Bill and Phyllis Dixon purchased the cabin in 1979, they also obtained the 160-acre tree farm. They renovated the cabin and built onto it a New England style salt box house, which is accurate in every sense. They furnished it with New England antiques and purchased exact replications.

You enter the house and are in an entry hall that has wide plank floors covered with an oriental carpet. The woodwork is painted colonial grey and green, as is the cove moulding. It is furnished with an antique work table, an antique hanging cupboard and an antique chimney cupboard.

The beamed living room and keeping room is a combination. An upholstered sofa sits in front of a large, brick Rumford fireplace. Some of the furnishings include a circa 1840 walnut corner cupboard, a New England one-drawer blanket chest, an antique immigrant's trunk, an upholstered arm chair and a high boy. The wide plank floors have an area rug.

The other portion of this area has an old-time butchering table, an antique drop leaf table, an upholstered wing back chair, a wrought iron floor lamp and a circa 1840 linen press. There is also a long table with four rush-seated chairs and a red wicker rocking chair and loveseat. Definitely not from early New England is the television.

The dining/kitchen area is furnished with a Welsh dresser, a walnut tressle table with six Windsor style chairs, a painted New England cupboard, a wrought iron floor lamp, a wrought iron candle stand, a small table and an upholstered arm chair. A small table and live plants are in a twenty-five paned bay window. A twelve arm iron chandelier is over the table. The area has on display a grandfather clock, yarn winder, a spinning wheel and other early American pieces along with some very nice framed prints.

Greer Hollow Farm offers guests an upstairs bedroom and a private bath with a tub and shower. And, it's a pleasure to climb the wide stairs and see how Phyllis has decorated the landing. There are antique trunks, a shelf clock, antique candlesticks, a hanging cupboard, an antique dry sink with the original blue paint on it and a small bench. A circa 1879 samples, splint baskets and crocks fit right in with the beaded pine paneling. At the top of the stairs, Grandpa's room with its wide pine floors and six over six panel windows is furnished with a full-size bed with hand made quilts. A small library table as a nightstand has a brass lamp. There is an antique chest on chest, an upholstered armchair, floor lamp and a small twig table. The woodwork is grey, the walls are off white. It's decorated with dried florals.

The thirty by thirty-foot log cabin is entered either from its own entrance or through the keeping area. I fell in love with this large room with its beamed ceilings, wood burning fireplace, wide pine floors and log walls. In the setting area there is an upholstered sofa with a wrought iron lamp behind it. A table and reading lamp, a small bench for a coffee table and a cottage type table with a television. Decoys and oil lamps are on the mantelpiece.

In an alcove, there is a full-size iron bed, an antique jelly cupboard, and a rush seat ladder back chair.

In one corner, a fully equipped kitchen has a table and four ladder back chairs, a wood burning stove and an unusual pie safe.

Upstairs, under the eaves, a guestroom is furnished with a maple full-size rope bed with handmade quilts, two tables with lamps and a baby crib. The eight over eight paned windows have drapes made out of quilts. There's beaded paneled walls. A private entrance leads to a porch.

Phyllis' full breakfast consists of juice, fresh fruit in season, a fresh egg dish with bacon or sausage, muffins, bagels or homemade bread, jams and jellies. Or whole wheat pancakes with bacon or sausage. Always coffee, tea or milk. With advance reservations and at an additional cost, Phyllis will prepare a great dinner and serve it to you by the fireplace. Either fish or chicken, pasta with olive oil and fresh herbs, homegrown tomatoes, lettuce and other vegetables, homemade bread and desserts.

Phyllis also serves refreshments on arrival. I am absolutely positive you are going to like this place, and Phyllis too!

GREER HOLLOW FARM B & B: Star Route 82A, Bourbon, 65441. (573) 732-4979. One guestroom with private bath and a great log cabin. Open all year. Children welcome. No pets. Smoking on porches. Phyllis Dixon, innkeeper.

DIRECTIONS: Call for information and directions.

MERAMEC FARM BED & BOARD
Bourbon

Here is a great chance to experience living on the land. This 470-acre working cattle ranch, with a quaint old farm house, is open to guests. Your hosts, Carol Springer and David Curtis, represent the sixth generation of their family to farm this place. In 1811, Carol's great, great, great, grandfather settled here. This was the first farm deeded in the county in 1823. The present farm house was built in 1883 by Carol's great grandfather, and 100 years later, Carol became the owner.

Carol and David offer their guests the use of the whole house. You enter from a large screened-in porch that has rocking chairs and a glider, an ideal place to sit and relax. The living room has a fireplace, while the parlor/bedroom has original beaded wainscoting, built-in bookcases and a wood burning stove.

Lodging includes breakfast and dinner served family style. Most of the food served is raised on the farm. A huge breakfast included two kinds of baked breads and pastries, omelets or quiches for larger groups, fresh sausage, ham or bacon, potatoes, a casserole with eggs and cheese, juice, fruit salad and coffee or tea.

This century-old house offers one upstairs guestroom. It is a small room with an antique, full-size brass bed. Three windows over look a vista of forest and fields as far as you can see.

An air-conditioned guest cabin built from the farm's cedar trees is just far enough away from the main house to give you plenty of privacy. The cabin has a full kitchen, living area and screened-in porch. The two guestrooms and loft can sleep eight people.

Both children and adults will enjoy the farm activities: gathering eggs, feeding cattle, exploring the old farm buildings including a hay loft, seeing the farm animals and having picnics. A country lane, right in front of the house, is ideal for a moonlit stroll. Here peace and quiet prevail, broken only by the howl of the coyote or a screech owl's call.

Meramec Farm is for outdoor enthusiasts. The setting of wild country and river offers great recreation. In summer, canoeing, swimming and spelunking are cooling diversions. Canoes and horses are available for rental nearby. Crisp, fall weather and bright foliage inspire hikes, orchard visits, and bicycling. Winter is fine for cross-country skiing, ice skating, and watching birds feed as you sit by the fireplace. When spring blooms across the farm, wildflower walks, fishing and picnics are in order. It's a great place to be.

In addition, the owners of Meramec Farm B & B invite you and your horse to ride with them. You'll ride along the Meramec River bottoms, through rolling fields and then to the tops of rugged wooded hills. You can choose a ride that combines leisure with challenge. They will manage all of the details. Home cooked meals with the resident rancher are part of each trip. To insure a quality riding experience, rides are limited to ten persons. If you have a larger group, special arrangements can be made.

A visit to Meramec Farm wouldn't be complete without the popular "cow tour." Guests ride on hay into the herds to see and feed the cattle. "Bale jumping" is a rural sport which appeals to all ages. Have your child's picture taken on the back of a cow!

MERAMEC FARM BED & BOARD: 208 Thickety Ford Road, Bourbon, 65441. (573) 732-4765. A two guestroom farm house plus secluded two bedroom and loft cabin. Open all year. Children welcome. No pets. No smoking in house. E-mail: mfarmbnb@fidnet.com. Website: www.wine-mo.com/meramec/html. Carol Springer and David Curtis, hosts.

DIRECTIONS: From I-44 to Bourbon. Exit on Rt. N and go nine miles to Meramec River. Cross river and go ¼ mile and turn left on Thickety Road (gravel). Continue ½ mile to first drive. Century farm sign.

CEDAR STONE BED & BREAKFAST
Eminence

Cedar Stone B & B is tucked away in Shannon County amid the hills and the Ozark National Scenic Rivers. Built for Carole White in 1992, this fantastic peeled log lodge has two huge porches that give you a wonderful view of the woods and surrounding countryside. The upper porch is covered and is furnished with wicker tables and chairs. It is an ideal spot to enjoy a cup of tea. The lower porch has large wooden rocking chairs.

Entering the lodge from the front porch, you are in a two story living/dining area. A balcony runs around three sides of the second floor. A mammoth stone fireplace has a seating area in front of it. There are two leather chairs, along with a couch, easy chairs, end tables and coffee table all made from heavy planked wood. A large brass chandelier hangs from the log beamed ceiling. The walls are of logs and are very attractively decorated with paintings and other art work.

The dining area is just adjacent to the fireplace, so on chilly days you can enjoy the fire during breakfast. There are a dozen or so large tables, each lighted with quaint oil lamps. Guests can select their own table.

Carol serves a full country breakfast which is varied during your stay. An example would be juice, some type of fruit dish, then either ham, sausage or bacon with eggs, homemade biscuits and gravy, topped off with homemade cinnamon rolls, jelly and jam, coffee, tea or milk.

There are eleven guestrooms at Cedar Stone, each with country furnishings as the focal point and handmade quilts and other decor for finishing touches. Each room has a different decorating scheme. They all have private baths, cable television, ceiling fans and carpeting.

Five guestrooms all with queen-size beds are on the first floor. One has a rattan bed, with a pair of chairs, tables with reading lamps and a chaise lounge. Two walls are of log. There is a display of fishing lures and a mounted game fish.

A second room has a cedar chair rail and is decorated in a Southwest Indian motif. There is a posted headboard bed, a small chest, two rocking chairs and an antique night table with reading lamp.

The next room has wrought iron wall decorations and a log chair rail. The furnishings include an iron headboard, wrought iron tables and chairs and a wrought iron stand with pitcher and bowl set.

The fourth guestroom uses a twig headboard and furnishings include an antique chest and a pair of barrel chairs. The last guestroom on this floor has a tongue and groove pine chair rail, an unusual cutout headboard, an antique marble top wash stand, and an ice cream table and chair set.

A wide staircase leads to the six upstairs guestrooms. At either end of the hallway is a sitting area offering a quiet place to read, visit with other guests or just sit and take in the ambiance of the lodge. One end is furnished with twig and log tables and chairs. The other end has wicker and wrought iron seating. A mounted game head of an elk and a bear rug are on display.

Two queen-size poster headboard beds with a table and lamp between them are in the first room along with an armoire and a cedar cradle. The second room has a circular bed with a quilted headboard, a wash stand and a rush seat rocker. There is a balcony off this room.

In the third room are two queen-size beds with a wicker table and lamp between them, and a wicker armoire with doors and drawers. A queen-size twig bed with a bright red floral spread, two twig chairs and an antique oak armoire is found in the fourth room.

Room five has two king-size beds, a rolltop desk, oak chairs and night stand and a wrought iron coat rack. A white king-size wicker bed and night table, oak chairs and a long wicker table are in the last guestroom. There is also a balcony off this room.

CEDAR STONE LODGE B & B: Box 289, Eminence, 65466. (573) 226-3436 or 226-5656. Open all year. An eleven guestroom lodge all with private baths. Children welcome. Pets can be housed. Smoking on porches. Carole White, innkeeper.

DIRECTIONS: Located one mile south of Eminence on Hwy. 19.

FAULKENBERRY'S BED & BREAKFAST
Eminence

This home was built in 1896 by Missouri State Senator David Bales, and was part of a six hundred acre farm. Paul Faulkenberry, one time Mayor of Eminence, lived here in 1930, and it has been in the Faulkenberry family for seventy years. Paul Faulkenberry's son, Paul, now owns the property and operates Faulkenberry's Bed and Breakfast here. The original acreage is now six acres of native pine trees and wildflowers that surround the house and make a wonderful view from the second floor. A pair of red-tailed hawks nest in one of the trees. There are also numerous song birds and on occasion, you can get a glimpse of deer, wild turkey, and even a rare badger.

When you enter the house, you are in a large L-shaped room with parquet floors covered with fine antique carpets. An unusual mantle piece has a glass door on either side with shelves holding collectibles. The living room area is furnished with a piano, a marble top French square table with four chairs, a large French, mirrored armoire, and an antique chest with a gold-leaf mirror. A small table is between two open arm chairs with upholstered seats and backs, a pair of upholstered arm chairs and an ottoman. A large bookcase has a collection of books on the Lives of Great Artists, and a collection of porcelain, soapstone and vases. A large window in front of the room and another at the rear of the room have floral drapes. The walls are painted in a tangerine color.

The L of the room is the dining area. It is furnished with a French Provincial table and four matching chairs and a four door breakfront. A crystal chandelier hangs over the table. From the dining room, you can step out to an atrium with a brick floor, flower beds and potted and hanging plants. There is a round wrought iron table and chairs. A small library off the dining room has a bookcase full of books and magazines.

A first floor guestroom is off the library. It is carpeted wall to wall in a teal color carpet. The room has a carved French, full-size bed, a chest and matching vanity, a pair of night stands and reading lamps, a pair of upholstered side chairs and a television. The windows are covered with white curtains and floral drapes. Antique prints in antique frames and original oil paintings are on the walls. There is a private bath with shower.

Also, on the first floor, a rather large guestroom, has beige wall-to-wall carpeting, yellow walls and shuttered windows with yellow floral drapes. It is furnished with a full-size bed with a plush comforter, several upholstered chairs, a ladies desk and a dresser. A breakfront holds a collection of antique pieces. There is a large private bath with a tub and shower.

A carpeted staircase from the library leads to the two guestrooms that are under the eaves. One is wallpapered with a green and red floral pattern on three walls white the one is solid green. It is carpeted wall to wall. The windows have floral drapes. It is furnished with a full-size bed and matching chest. An upholstered open arm chair with a cane seat and back and a marble top dresser that has a landscape painting across the front of it. Wall lamps are on each side of the bed.

The second guestroom on this floor has wall-to-wall carpet and floral drapes are over sheer curtains at the windows. There is a full-size bed with floral bed linens, a small, one drawer chest, a television and a pair of night tables with lamps. The two second floor guestrooms share a large private bath with tub and shower.

Breakfast is served in the dining area, or, weather permitting, in the atrium. Paul offers a choice of gourmet coffees, juices, French toast with sausage or bacon and a fruit plate. He might also offer a friatta of eggs, cheese and herbs baked and served in a small iron skillet. Or, there is the traditional breakfast of eggs, sausage gravy and biscuits. Always pastries, coffee, tea or milk. Served on antique linens and dishes.

Upon arrival, Paul offers guests Missouri wines, cheese, crackers and fresh fruit. For special occasions, there are flowers, chocolates and champagne or wine.

FAULKENBERRY'S B & B: 127 Faulkenberry Way, Eminence, 65466. (573) 226-3620. Open all year. A peaceful, relaxing getaway. Four guestrooms, with two private and two shared baths. No pets. Outside smoking. Older children. Paul Faulkenberry Innkeeper.

DIRECTIONS: From I-44, take Cuba exit (208) go south 90 miles to Eminence. From the south, take Hwy 60 to Winona. Then take Hwy 19 north to Eminence.

THE OLD BLUE HOUSE BED & BREAKFAST
Eminence

The old Blue House is over one hundred and thirty years old. Built around the 1860s, at one time or another it has housed a pharmacy, beauty shop, grocery store, children's clothing shop, sporting goods store and a gift shop on the main floor. Upstairs, above this room was the old telephone office which is now a guestroom. Exactly when it was opened or when it closed is anybody's guess, but at the top of the narrow steps is a glass door with a hand painted sign that still reads "Telephone Office."

Each room is filled with antiques and beautiful framed prints are displayed everywhere.

On the entrance side of the home there is a garden with magnolia and maple trees, peonies, lilacs, iris and roses. Up the stairs from the garden takes you to a porch and into the living room where guests are signed in. A door leads to a large gazebo furnished with outdoor furniture.

The Kitchen has a large antique farm table and ladder back chairs. On display is a collection of blue granite ware and old blue bottles line a window ledge. Guests can eat in the kitchen or on the covered porches, which have wrought iron tables and chairs.

Wanda offers a continental breakfast which includes juice, fresh fruit in season, two different tea breads and coffee or tea. However, for a very slight extra charge you can order a full breakfast of sausage and scrambled eggs, biscuits and gravy served up with fruit or juice, tea breads, jams, jellies, coffee, tea or milk.

There are three guestrooms: one on the main floor and two upstairs.

David's Room, named for Wanda's son, is on the main level. French doors open onto a porch. The room has pine floors and the walls are paneled.

This is the room that once was used for a retail shop. It is furnished with a full-size burgundy iron bed, a glider rocker and a love seat to match, an antique gentleman's chest, antique mirrored wardrobe, a six-legged antique table and a drop-leaf desk. It is decorated with live plants and dried floral arrangements. It has a private bath and shower.

The Telephone Room is fully carpeted and has French doors that lead to a porch furnished with a metal table and chairs. It has a full-size, antique iron and brass bed, an antique upholstered rocker, an antique oak high boy with a mirror, an oak antique sideboard with mirror, and an antique drop leaf table and chairs, and a television.

A small room off this room is furnished with an antique four poster twin bed, an antique Victrola and a small roll-top desk. This is ideal for a third person. This room has a television also. A hall leads to a bath with a tub and hand held shower head.

Patricia's Room, named for Wanda's daughter, is furnished with a 1920's bedroom suite consisting of a full-size bed, dresser, and a wardrobe. There is an upholstered glider rocker, an oak slant front desk and an oak wash stand. It is wallpapered with a small floral print pattern below. It is fully carpeted and has a private bath. A door exits onto a large gazebo furnished with Victorian-type iron and cast aluminum furniture.

From the house, it is an easy walk to the Jack's Fork River where you can take a cool dip in summer weather. You may want to check out the craft and antique shops or just relax on one of the porches with a refreshing drink and watch the local Main Street traffic.

Don't miss a trip to the Old Red Mill at Alley Springs. You will also thoroughly enjoy Blue Springs and Round Spring with its cave to explore.

OLD BLUE HOUSE B & B: 109 S. Main Street, P.O. Box 117, Eminence, 65466. (573) 226-3498 or (800) 474-9695. Open all year. A three guestroom home with private baths. No small children. No. Pets. Smoking on porches. Wanda Pummill, innkeeper.

DIRECTIONS: Located at 109 South Main Street in downtown Eminence. From I-44 exit at Cuba and take Hwy. 19 south to Eminence.

GREEN ROOF INN
Ironton

There are over 200 establishments listed in this revised edition of the guide. Green Roof Inn is one of the most remarkable. From the time I first saw this circa 1886 Victorian home, with all of its gingerbread trimmings and care and skill with which June Haefner, the owner has done the decorating, I could hardly believe my eyes.

The wraparound porch has plenty of seating, mostly of wrought iron pieces. Some of these were made by John Haefner and some are antiques. In the front hall is a grandfather clock, a marble top table on a metal base, and a collection of vintage clothing on an old hall coat tree. John laid the marble floor.

To the left through a wrought iron trimmed door, a parlor has a three piece Victorian parlor suite, two large marble top Victorian tables, an organ, and a huge glass-front bookcase holding antique china. There is a tiled corner fireplace and a crystal chandelier. The parlor leads into a large guestroom which has a vintage 1917 bedroom suite that belonged to June's parents. Just a few of the antiques in the room include a wicker chaise lounge, settee, grandfather clock, circa 1880 tall cedar chest, spool cabinet, grafhanola and a china cabinet. The carpeted room has stained glass windows and a corner fireplace.

Another parlor to the right of the hall has a three piece Victorian parlor suite in the original upholstery. There is also an antique German sideboard, a huge wall clock, Victorian chairs, marble top tables, and a glass front cabinet from the St. Louis World's Fair.

The dining room has a huge oak table and chairs, an antique corner cupboard, a china cabinet, a huge carved sideboard, and a baker's rack. John made the plate shelves that go around the walls of the room. There are collections of cut glass, silverware, oil paintings, prints and china.

Guest may request what they want for breakfast, but it should be mentioned in advance. June usually serves oat bran and bran muffins, fruit juice, fruit cup and a casserole of eggs, sour cream, mushrooms and cheese. Breakfast is served on the porch, deck or gazebo when the weather is mild, or in the kitchen in front of an antique wood burning stove.

In the evening, June serves wine with cheese and crackers. She places candy and ice water in the room and turns down your bed. In the morning, she brings you a pot of coffee.

Up the walnut stairway is a large hall lined with period decorations. The hall leads to a balcony, which runs across the front of the house. It has comfortable seating arrangements.

Four guestrooms occupy the second floor. All share a large bath that was installed in 1908. It has a large tub, marble sink, art glass mirrors, and a collection of shaving mugs.

One guestroom has a high-back burled walnut bed, marble top dresser and wash stand, a two door armoire and small antique tables for night stands. There is a collection of vintage ladies clothes displayed.

Another room has an ornate carved bed, marble top dresser and table, a large mirrored armoire, antique ladies desk, and a marble top table with an antique pitcher and bowl set.

The third room has an antique carved walnut bed with railroad caboose lights on either side, a marble top dresser, an armoire, a leather easy chair and a wing chair.

The fourth guestroom has a carved, oak antique bed, oak wardrobe and wash stand, an oak dresser with glove boxes and an oak recliner.

A third floor suite contains two guestrooms, a sitting area and a small covered porch. One bedroom has a 1920's bedroom set, the other has a 1940's maple set. There is a private bath.

GREEN ROOF INN: 102 S. Shepherd, Ironton, 63650. (573) 546-7670. Open all year. No pre-teens. No smoking. June Haefner, innkeeper.

DIRECTIONS: Call for specific directions.

JAMIE L. McILROY©1993

BUST INN BED & BREAKFAST
Potosi

The Bust Inn B & B was built in 1908, just after the turn of the century, by Lucy McGready Bust. Your hostess, Elizabeth Bust is the great granddaughter of Lucy Bust.

By retaining the natural woodwork, the stained glass windows (some original) and fireplace and some of the original lighting fixtures, guests have an opportunity to experience the look and feel of living four generations ago. The Inn offers four guestrooms, two with their own half baths, and two larger rooms with full private baths. One features a romantic jacuzzi for two.

On the main floor guests enjoy the full use of the parlor, sitting room, dining room and a wraparound front porch with porch swing. The entry hall has stained glass windows and a most unusual original oak staircase with sunburst carvings.

To the right of the hallway, the parlor has a corner fireplace with an oak mantel from Sears Roebuck purchased in 1904. The parlor furnishings include a sofa in a floral pattern, an antique Eastlake love seat and matching chair in a pink and blue striped fabric, a platform rocker, an old time Victrola and an antique parlor table. The walls are painted and have a wide floral border at chair rail height. White lace curtains are at the windows. The kerosene hanging lamp is original.

At one time in the past, the room just off the parlor was used as a game room. It is now used as a family room and is furnished with a matching parlor set that has a Victorian overstuffed sofa and a pair of chairs.

A complete breakfast is served in the dining room. There are three tables with tablecloths covered with a lace topping. Coffee and juice are served while the rest of breakfast is being prepared. Then there is fresh fruit in season, homemade breads served with jams and jellies, rhubarb and strawberry coffeecake or orange marmalade muffins. One of the gourmet entrees is a bacon and egg omelet with a spinach and cream cheese filling topped with Hollandaise and served with roasted new potatoes. Another is the smoked ham and broccoli served in a fried pastry cup. And there is always good old bacon and eggs. You have a choice of coffee, tea or milk.

A second floor guestroom is furnished with an antique poster bed, an oak wardrobe with drawers and mirrored door, and an overstuffed sofa. A large blue and white area carpet is on the floor. White walls have a blue papered border, and white lace curtains are at the window. In the room is the jacuzzi for two. There is a private bath.

Another guestroom has a five piece art deco bedroom set from the 1930's. Even the lamps are of the art deco period. There is also a Martha Washington chair. The walls are painted mauve and have a wide floral print border.

A smaller room off the hallway has antique twin beds and an antique table and lamp. An oriental carpet is on the floor. Elizabeth has displayed old photographs of her family on the walls and tables.

The fourth guestroom has a matching three piece antique bedroom set which includes a high back bed, a marble top dresser with candle stands and a washstand that holds an antique three piece pitcher and bowl set. There is a platform rocker, an antique cedar chest and a wooden rocking chair. The room has floral print wallpaper and a green carpet. A private bath has a claw foot tub.

Potosi is centrally located in the heart of Missouri's park land region, rich in natural recreational areas. This region also offers the opportunity to experience an era long past through historical home tour, regional museums and antique shops. You will also find county fairs, festivals and good old-fashioned hospitality.

BUST INN B & B: 612 East High Street, Potosi, 63664. (573) 438-4457. Open all year. A four guestroom Victorian home. Children welcome. No pets. Smoking on porch. Elizabeth Bust, innkeeper.

DIRECTIONS: Potosi is located on Hwy. 8 and Hwy. 21, approximately 75 miles south of St. Louis.

A MINER INDULGENCE BED & BREAKFAST
Rolla

A Miner Indulgence draws its name from the 130-year history of the Missouri School of Mines and Metallurgy, now the University of Missouri-Rolla. Innkeepers Ron and Barbara Kohser have strong ties to the university as a result of Ron's 25 years on the faculty as a professor of metallurgical engineering. The house itself is a 30-year-old brick colonial home located on a small wooded bluff with the scenic view of local farmlands. To the rear of the property is a ridge that served as an encampment for up to 12,000 Union troops stationed in Rolla during the Civil War.

The most striking feature upon entering the home is a beautiful sweeping oak staircase. The foyer alcove is decorated with antiques, which include an old National cash register, an oak Singer sewing machine and a coat rack.

To the left, the living room is furnished with a blend of new and antique pieces. A sofa and two rockers, one antique, provide comfortable seating. Some of the interesting accent antiques include a 1920s St. Louis Post Dispatch newsboys cart, a steamer trunk, a curved-front secretary desk, a corn sheller, old school desk, and an antique tool box which has been turned into a coffee table with wood tools as accessories. A walnut grandmother's clock, built by the owner's grandfather, stands in one corner. Completing the décor is a display of Rockwell collectible plates and framed prints.

Breakfast is served on the 1880-vintage birch drop leaf table in the dining room, to the right. The leaded glass doors of an antique china cabinet proudly display a set of vintage Noritake china. Additional furnishings include an oak spinning wheel, antique high chair that folds into a stroller, candle-stand, an old sewing machine table that holds a silver coffee/tea service, and a collection of demitasse cups and saucers. Lace curtains at the windows, Victorian-style wallpaper, and live plants complete the décor.

Guests are free to relax and enjoy television in the family room, which also contains several unusual antiques. A blue and white enamel 1923 vintage Universal gas cook stove and complementing kitchenware are most nostalgic, as is the old "possum belly" cupboard. During the winter months, gas logs burn in the fireplace.

Upstairs are the two spacious guestrooms each with their own private bath and sitting area. One room is furnished in an early American style with solid oak reproduction queen-size bed, triple dresser, chest, and bedside tables. The sitting area has an upholstered love seat, coffee table, and small antique rocker. Conversation pieces include an antique invalid's chair, old handmade sled, an antique sewing machine, child's tea service, and engineering and drafting tools. The walls are off-white with a floral border at the ceiling.

The second guestroom is more Victorian in style with an antique, black walnut, full-size bed, wash stand with reading lamp, cheval mirror, and dark walnut library cabinet with a collection of Country Cousin figurines. The sitting area has an upholstered sofa that opens to a queen-size bed and a Queen Anne table and bench. Two reproduction doll buggies and dolls accessorize the room. Both rooms contain walk-in closets and complimentary coffee makers with an assortment of coffees, teas, and hot chocolates.

The landing at the top of the stairs has an antique table and chairs, an antique icebox and an assortment of small antiques. Along the balcony is a library of books on local history and old campus yearbooks. Reinforcing the theme of A Miner Indulgence is a collection of miner figurines. For those who have trouble leaving the office behind this area also provides the convenience of a nearby phone and e-mail access.

While the breakfast menu varies, Barb's full breakfast typically consists of fresh orange juice, fruit cup (fresh in season), an egg dish (scrambled, fried, or omelet), and waffles, French toast or pancakes, each with a flavor unique to A Miner Indulgence. Bacon or sausage is served as a side dish and no meal is complete without coffee, tea, or milk. Early morning risers are treated to coffee or tea on the front porch (weather permitting) and are encouraged to enjoy the beautiful Ozark surroundings.

An in-ground heated swimming pool, 8-person hot tub, and four wooded acres compliment the home. Wildlife and many species of birds are often seen. It is peaceful and relaxing here and I know you'll feel at home.

A MINER INDULGENCE B & B: 13750 Martin Spring Drive, P.O. Box 672, Rolla, 65402. (573) 364-0680. Open all year. Well behaved children 12 years or older are welcome. No pets. Smoking outdoors in the pool area. Two rooms with private baths. Barb and Ron Kohser, innkeepers.

DIRECTIONS: From I-44 Exit 184, turn onto the South Outer Road (Martin Spring Drive) and proceed west for 1.5 miles. Look for their sign and private drive on left.

FERRIGNO WINERY BED & BREAKFAST
St. James

In the 1920s Italian Immigrants first came to the St. James region and started growing grapes. In 1976, Dick and Susan Ferrigno took a leap of faith. They bought this property to operate a winery. At the time they lived in St. Louis where Dick was a professor at the university of Missouri, and Susan taught 6th grade.

It took six years to establish their vineyards. In 1982 they opened Ferrigno Vineyards and Winery to the public with nine of their own wines An old dairy barn, built in 1930 was renovated with the first floor used for production. The second floor now has the tasting room and a nice gift shop. Tours of the winery start from here.

When Dick and Susan decided to start a bed and breakfast, the third floor became the guest quarters. At the top of the stairs is a small sitting and reading area with a sofa sleeper, an antique rocking chair and an upholstered rocker.

Up a couple of steps is the bedroom which has a three piece 1940s style waterfall bedroom suite. There are wicker chairs and an antique rocking chair. Handmade scatter rugs are on the floor.

In 1991, Ferrignos built a new home and converted there former home into a guest cottage. The six rooms are divided into two suites, each with a private bath. The Seyval Suite has a bedroom with a double bed, dresser, night tables and seating. The large living room has an old brick fireplace, leaded glass windows and parquet floors with oriental rugs. There is also a queen-size sleeper sofa and chintz covered chairs.

The Vidal Suite has French country-style bedroom furniture. The adjoining sitting room has a piano among the furnishings.

A fully furnished dining room and kitchen and a screened-in porch are shared by the two suites. A group or two families can take the entire house. You are permitted to do your own cooking.

There is a covered wine garden with an old well house, shrubs, large trees and picnic tables. On the upper level there is a covered dining pavilion with a view overlooking the vineyards. This is a perfect spot for a picnic.

Susan prepares a full breakfast with omelets, french toast, bacon, smoked turkey, homemade muffins or sweet rolls, blueberry pancakes, coffee or tea. Naturally, they make their own grape juice. Breakfast is served at the main residence, a few minutes walk away through the vineyards.

A complimentary wine tasting and bottle of wine is offered to guests upon arrival. And sometime during your stay, you can tour the winery and vineyards, fish in the farm pond, enjoy the hammocks or simply watch a gorgeous sunset.

Ferrigno Winery Bed and Breakfast is just a few miles north of St. James and the many antique and craft shops. Meramec Springs Park, fifteen miles away offers trout fishing , a mining museum and a look at the source of the Meramec River. Be sure to ask Dick and Susan about other places to see.

FERRIGNO WINERY B & B: 17301 State Route B, St. James, 65559. (573) 265-7742 or evenings 265-8050. A one bedroom suite in the winery plus two suites in a guest cottage. Open all year. Closed winter holidays. Children welcome. No pets. Smoking on porch. Dick and Susan Ferrigno, hosts.

DIRECTIONS: From I-44, exit at St. James and turn north on Rt. 68. Make first (almost immediate) right turn onto Hwy. B. Go 4.5 miles to winery on left.

PAINTED LADY BED & BREAKFAST
St. James

The home is a full three story Victorian with wrap around veranda and trimmed with gingerbread outside. It's painted with seven colors—cream, shades of blue, copper and a crapapple. The inside is done in rich shades of marble and floral wallpaper on the walls and some ceilings.

As you enter the foyer from the veranda, your eyes will be drawn to the white and oak spindled staircase straight ahead and the balcony above. In the center is a large chandelier suspended from the 20 foot ceiling. To the left is a large parlor with fireplace and carved cherry mantel. The room is furnished with a French sofa, loveseat, antique tea cart, art, floral arrangements and more.

On the right of the foyer is a dining room furnished with a country French dining room set. The table and ladder back chairs set in the turret of the house surrounded with five lace covered windows.

Adjacent to the parlor is the Bridal Suite, named Melanie, for anyone to enjoy. It is a large room with a king canopy bed with lace flowing from its posters. The room also has a wonderful circa 1870 walnut dresser, loveseat, and bedside tables. There is a large private bath with jacuzzi and shower. The patio door opens on to a balcony which connects to a large covered deck with tables and chairs for enjoying the peaceful outdoors.

On the second floor, to the right of the foyer, is the Scarlett room. An ornate white and brass iron queen-size bed sets in the turret with four windows of lace surrounding it. The room has a white loveseat, French dresser, and is wallpapered in ribbons and roses. The large private bath has a tub and shower.

Across the foyer from Scarlett are the Prissy and Bonnie Blue rooms. Prissy has an ornate white iron queen-size bed. Bonnie Blue has a double-size white ornate iron bed. Both rooms are wallpapered on walls and ceilings and have lace curtains on the windows. Both have comfortable chairs and share a bath with a shower or can have a private bath on request.

An extra large room on the lower level is also available. This room is called Rhett. It offers a fireplace, big screen TV with VCR, stereo, and very comfortable seating. The Rhett Room opens to a covered patio with hot tub, tables and chairs, and extra seating to enjoy the lawn, flowers and trees.

Plans include adding another suite adjacent to the Painted Lady, just a few steps away. It will be in the same theme as the Painted Lady with a king-size bed, fireplace, wallpaper and lace, chandeliers, and a jacuzzi for two. It will be very private and perfect for that special occasion.

The Painted Lady also has a two bedroom guest cottage that joins the property. It sets atop a large grassy knoll with a beautiful view. The house sleeps two to six comfortably. It is completely furnished, including TV and in-house phone, full kitchen with all utensils, microwave, stove, and refrigerator. Complimentary coffee and all linens are furnished. Children are welcome at the guest cottage.

The Painted Lady B & B is known for its full country breakfast--fresh fruit dish, juice, combination of muffins, pancakes, waffles, French toast, angel biscuits, egg dishes, breakfast meats, sausage, gravy, etc., and of course, coffee, tea, or milk. Sandy, Wanda and Bee invite you to come share their home and visit their quaint little community with its wonderful wineries, beautiful Meramec Springs, nearby antique shops, canoeing, fishing, golfing and friendly people.

PAINTED LADY B & B: 1127 South Jefferson, (Hwy. 8), St. James, 65559. (573) 265-5008. Open all year. No children. Smoking in designated areas only. Website: http://tigernet.missouri.org/commuity/lodging/painted.html. Also check out the St. James area at http://stjames.k12.mo.us. Sandy and Wanda, innkeepers. Bee Zinn, right hand assistant.

DIRECTIONS: 1.5 miles south of I-44 on Route 68 at St. James. On the right.

ROSATI WINERY BED & BREAKFAST RETREAT
St. James

Set in the heart of Missouri wine country, Rosati Winery enjoys a rich history in the grape and wine business, going back to the 1800s when Italian immigrants found this lush region reminiscent of the vineyards they left behind in Italy. The Winery was built in 1922 by a co-op to allow the grape growers to ship their grapes by train to St. Louis.

Adjacent to the winery, this colonial style house was built in the mid-1920's and reflects the elegance of that era. In 1997, Donna and Marvin Ripplemeyer purchased the winery and extensively renovated the property. However, most of the original winery is still intact, including the Colonial style home that is now Rosati Winery B & B.

Just to the right of the tiled entry hall, there is a common or keeping room. It has a large brick fireplace. It is furnished with a French Provincial sofa, three wood trimmed upholstered chairs, a pair of end tables with reading lamps and a wooden rocking chair. There is a television and a VCR, along with a number of movies. Floral swags are at the windows. The walls have a blue marble design wallpaper above a chair rail and a white on white striped paper below. Pictures, floral arrangement and a large wreath are on the walls.

A dining room has one full wall in lattice work. It is furnished with a Queen Anne style table and four lyre back chairs, an antique ice box, a buffet with an antique Gramma phone and a carved wooden chair with an upholstered seat and back. Bird prints, pictures and a wall clock are part of the decorations.

The guestrooms are on the second floor. The Heritage Room has a king-size bed, an antique chifferobe, an end table with a reading lamp, a Boston rocker, and a lady's desk and chair. It has wall-to-wall hunter green carpeting., blinds and swags at the windows and a floral ceiling border on the white walls. There is a private bath with a tub and shower.

The Carriage Room features equestrian décor, reflective of the innkeepers' love for horses. It is furnished with a king-size bed, night table with lamps, a desk and a rocking chair. A border with a horse décor is at the ceiling. The walls are paneled chair-rail high and papered pale green above. The windows have blinds and swags. A private full bath with tub and shower.

The Rosati Room honors the Italian heritage of the community and has a queen-size white iron bed with a chenille spread, maple end tables and lamps, a desk and a rocker. Pale teal walls have a country scene border at the ceiling. Old photographs are on the walls. The windows have blinds and swags. A private bath has a shower and tub.

The Vineyard Room, overlooking the vineyards, has a queen-size sleigh bed, a secretary desk, night stand, a dresser with an antique mirror and a comfortable chair. The walls have a papered grape motif ceiling border. Pictures reflect Italian heritage. There is a bath with shower.

For those of you who are on a tight schedule, a continental breakfast is available from 7:30 – 8:30 a.m. It consists of fresh fruit in season, pastries, rolls, toast, muffins, hot and cold cereals and coffee, tea, milk or juices. A hot breakfast menu is served from 8:30 – 9:30 a.m. and consists of all of the continental breakfast plus your choice of Belgian waffles, French toast, pancakes or scrambled eggs along with either sausage or bacon.

The Rosati B & B is available for weddings, receptions, parties, meetings, and special dinners. A fax machine and internet access are also available. You might ask about farm and vineyard tours and picnic lunches.

ROSATI WINERY B & B: 22050 State Road KK. St. James, 65559. (573) 265-6880 or (573) 265-6892. Open all year. No pets. Smoking and non-smoking rooms. No children under 12 years of age. Area attractions include river rafting and canoeing, four local wineries, antique and quilt shops. All major credit cards accepted. Donna and Marvin Ripplemeyer, innkeepers.

DIRECTIONS: From I-44 exit at exit 203.

WHITMIRE INN
Salem

Whitmire Inn is a grey shingled cottage built in the 1940s. As it is a non-hosted bed & breakfast—the guests have the entire house to themselves giving them plenty of privacy. It is best utilized with four persons traveling together.

A small entry foyer leads to the carpeted living room. For those chilly nights, a fireplace provides a warm welcome. The room is furnished with a sofa, a love seat as well as two wing chairs, a corner cupboard and several tables and lamps. A nice bay window overlooks the huge old trees on the front lawn.

Off the living room, a sunroom—bright and cheerful—with large windows on three sides, overlooks the side lawn. The room has white wicker furniture with colorful cushions. There is also a plant stand with an attractive live plant. There is a floor lamp, table and another plant stand with a reading lamp—all in green wicker. A perfect spot to sit and read a good book or just to relax.

The dining room has large windows that overlook the side yard. It is furnished with a 1940s walnut dining set that includes a matching buffet.

The kitchen is fully equipped and a breakfast nook is wallpapered in a pink and blue floral print. Everything is provided to assure a comfortable stay. Off the kitchen is a porch leading to the back yard.

The necessary provisions for a continental breakfast are on hand: juice, homemade breads and rolls, fresh fruit in season and dry cereal. You will find jellies, apple butter, and coffee and tea for you to brew and many restaurants close by.

The two guestrooms share a bath that has a tub and shower. One room is furnished with a four poster bed and an antique armoire, a comfortable chair, several tables and lamps and an antique baby cradle. The bed is covered with a white bedspread and a dust ruffle in the 1900's era.

The other room has a five piece bedroom set in bird's-eye maple. This is a very nice set consisting of a full-size bed, dresser, chest and night table. There is also an antique rocking chair. Windows give a view of the landscaped back yard.

Whitmire Inn is right in the heart of the Big Springs Region. It is twenty miles from Montauk State Park with great trout fishing and thirty miles to Meramec State Park. Floating or canoeing on the Currant River is an hour away. There an antique and craft shops nearby.

There is also a fully furnished farm house on the Meramec River surrounded by 60 rolling acres. You can see wild deer and turkey and cows grazing in the fields. It can also be rented by appointment.

WHITMIRE INN: Box 778, Salem, 65560. (573) 729-7221. Open all year. A two bedroom guest house with everything furnished. Children welcome. No pets. Please, no smoking in the house. Charles and Shirley Whitmire, innkeepers.

DIRECTIONS: Salem is located about 30 minutes south of I-44. The town is just south of the convergence of Hwy. 68 and Hwy. 19 and just east of the convergence of Hwy. 32 and Hwy. 72. Please call for reservations and specific directions to the guest house.

FRISCO STREET BED AND BREAKFAST
Steelville

F risco Street is a very large Victorian country home. Painted baby blue with pink trim, it is a striking home with a white picket fence that seems to ramble on and on. The veranda with built in gazebo is a great place to have breakfast, listen to songbirds or watch the train roll by.

The living/dining room combination is a large room. It features a wood-burning fireplace and French doors that open onto a large wraparound porch complete with a porch swing. The living room area is furnished with a floral pattern upholstered camel back sofa, an upholstered French chair, a desk and a 1920's armoire that holds a television and table games. The dining area has a large oak table with four Windsor chairs, a hutch, a small bureau, an antique love seat and a small tripod table with a lamp. The whole area has white woodwork, a chair rail has a solid blue paper below and a floral pattern paper above. It is all carpeted wall-to-wall.

The Lavender and Lace room, on the first floor, is decorated in lavender, lace and morning glories. It is carpeted and has lace curtains at the windows. It is furnished with 1920's carved four poster queen-size bed and a matching vanity. The bed has a green and blue Laura Ashley pattern spread that matches the ceiling border and the upholstery on the antique platform rocker. There is cable television for your enjoyment and a coffee maker for that first cup of morning coffee. There is a private bath with a shower.

On the second floor, the Wildflower Room is bright and sunny with accents in white, blue and yellow. There is a queen-size white wicker bed with a wedding ring pattern quilt, a small chest, a wicker coffee table, a pair of wooden rockers, a wicker lamp table and a small floor lamp. A cozy window seat and balcony overlook the gardens. Three walls have blue and yellow striped and floral wallpaper. The fourth is off-white. The room is carpeted and has lace curtains. A private bathroom has a clawfoot tub with shower.

The Sweet Magnolia Room is richly decorated is forest green, burgundy and navy. It is furnished with a queen-size, black wrought iron four poster bed with a floral spread, a night table on each side with reading lamp, an oak wardrobe dresser, an antique steamer trunk, a television, two black wicker armchairs and a floor lamp. The walls are a camel color with a floral ceiling border and lace curtains at the windows. A door leads to a private balcony that is shaded by a large Northern pine tree. A private bathroom has a walk-in glass shower.

The English Rose Garden Suite is decorated with roses in mind. It features a queen-size four poster white wrought iron canopy featherbed, a pair of white wicker chairs, a small wicker table, a 1920's carved dresser, cable television, bedside tables and reading lamp. A two-person Jacuzzi surrounded by pink ceramic tile is nestled in a corner of the room. A glider beckons on the private balcony. The room is papered in blue and pink roses with Battenburg laced trimmed curtains and live plants.

Complimentary spring water, soda and ice is available at the top of the stairs. Each room is stocked with gourmet coffee and herbal teas. All rooms have fresh flowers and ceiling fans.

Upon arrival, Sandy offers either local wine or juice, iced tea or lemonade with homemade cookies or brownies.

Her special breakfasts include strawberry orange juice or other tempting juices, fresh fruit in season, coffee, tea, cocoa or milk. Entrees may include Italian Strata, Blueberry pancakes, Baked Caramel French Toast or Baked eggs in Mornay Suace. Specialties of the House include Frisco Street Potatoes, Crescent Moon Sweet Rolls and Poached Pears in Blackberry Sauce. Wolferman's English Muffins and honeys and jellies and jams from the Golden Echoes Retirement Center in Steelville round out the menu. You certainly won't go away hungry!

FRISCO STREET B & B: 305 Frisco Street, Steelville, 65565. (573) 775-4247 or 1 (888) 229-4247 for reservations. Open all year. Near Courtois, Huzzah and Meramec Rivers. Meramec Springs Park, Onondaga Cave and Dillard Mill. Antique & specialty stores, and the Greenway Trail within walking distance. Steelville is home to the Meramec Theater and Arlees Linen Factory Outlet. Smoking on balconies or veranda. No pets. Inquire about children. Gift certificates. MC/VISA/Discover and AMEX accepted. Website: www.bbonline.com/mo/frisco/. Sandy and Frank Berrier, owners/ innkeepers.

DIRECTIONS: From I-44, take the Cuba/Owensville exit and turn south on Hwy. 19. Travel 8 miles to Steelville. At the three-way stop, go straight and turn left at Hickory Street. Go over the railroad tracks and turn right on Frisco Street. Third house on the left.

PARKVIEW FARM BED & BREAKFAST
Steelville

One of Steelville's early settlers was Peter Whittenburg, for whom Whittenburg Creek received its name. He built this house in the mid-1800s in a valley overlooking what is now the city park. The large barn with the hay loft is still in use for the animals, including horses that are enjoyed by the owners. The smokehouse, built in 1921, still remains. Extensive remodeling and additions were made in 1996 by the owners, Tom and Jan Weisel, and they opened their B & B in 1997.

Entering the house you are in a "great" great room, with ceilings 15 feet tall! It is carpeted wall-to-wall. Two aquariums will immediately catch your eye. One is a 125-gallon salt water tank. The other is a 75-gallon fresh water tank. The room is furnished with a floral upholstered sofa and love seat arranged in an L-shape. There is a coffee table, an upholstered recliner rocker and an upholstered corner sectional sofa. A piano is in the room and Jan played a few selections. She's very good.

Off the great room, a sitting room has an upholstered sofa and arm chairs. The room has a wood-burning stove and another 75-gallon aquarium.

A dining area has a tile top oak table and six matching chairs, a hutch with mementos of Tom and Jan's trips together in all 50 states, all of Canada's provinces and territories. Jan and Tom like to talk to their guests while breakfast is prepared.

Off the dining area, a sitting area has an upholstered sofa and rockers. A bookcase holds all kinds of books, a VCR with lots of movies, and a stereo with lots of records.

At the top of the oak staircase, a sitting area for guests is fully carpeted with a pale green carpet. It is furnished with a floral upholstered sofa and matching love seat, two end tables with reading lamps, a sofa table and a coffee table. A corner bookcase holds sea shells, dolls and deluxe editions of children's books. A large artificial plant is in one corner.

Two guestrooms are on this floor, one is the Alaska Room. Feel free to browse through the photo albums, postcards and books on Alaska. It is furnished with a matching cherry queen-size bed with a floral spread, a pair of night tables with lamps, a blue upholstered recliner, a corner curio cabinet and a mirrored marble top hat rack. You will enjoy this cozy room where moose and caribou antlers, carvings, and a reindeer hide make it uniquely Alaska. There is a private bath with a skylight in case the Northern Lights travel south.

The Hawaii Room might interest you if you prefer a warmer climate and enjoy viewing your own private aquarium. It is furnished with a queen-size, tall, four-poster bed with a floral spread, a matching triple dresser and chest. There is a rattan glass top table and two rattan chairs. The room is decorated with an authentic grass skirt, leis, a ukulele, shells and other Hawaiian memorabilia. You will find this room light and spacious. Enjoy a piece of fresh fruit at the table in front of the double corner windows as you listen to the songbirds outside. There is a private bath with shower and tub.

On the first floor, in the older portion of the house, the Russian Room boasts a large bay window with a window seat. It is furnished with a four piece matching bedroom suite in Cherry wood, consisting of a queen-size short four-poster bed with a maroon spread, a dressing table, a curio cabinet, an upholstered wing chair and an end table with lamp. It is decorated with handpainted Matrushka (nesting) dolls, musical instruments, pins and boxes as well as flax/linen dolls, embroidered napkins and a beautiful wool throw. The room has a semi-private bath with a shower.

Jan serves what she calls a farmer's country breakfast. Start off with orange juice and fresh fruit. Then a mixture of eggs, sausage, potatoes and cheese cooked in a skillet. Or, banana pancakes or banana waffles. Homemade lemon poppy seed or banana raisin bread, coffee, tea or milk.

Local activities include float trips, Meramec Spring Park, Meramec Country Music Show, fine antique stores and craft shops. I stopped in to see Jan's father, Jim, who is a local woodcarver of shorebird decoys.

PARKVIEW FARM B & B: 117 East Hwy. 8, Steelville, 65565. (573) 775-4196. Open all year. No pets. No smoking. Children over 10 welcome. A three guestroom home in an area full of history. MC/Visa accepted. Main floor is wheelchair accessible. Bicycles, tennis rackets and balls available. Jan and Tom Weisel, innkeepers.

DIRECTIONS: Take I-44 to Cuba, exit 208, go south on Hwy. 19 for 8 miles to Steelville. Approximately 1 mile east of downtown on Hwy. 8. B & B is on the left, just past the new city park.

WILDFLOWER INN BED & BREAKFAST
Sullivan

The Wildflower Inn sits graciously on 42 acres in the foothills of the Ozarks. Surrounded by natural springs and abundant wildlife, the setting is private and relaxing. The sprawling front porch invites you to sit back in an easy rocking chair and experience nature at its finest: Missouri song birds, fields of wildflowers, fresh country air. Soak away the worries of the day in their lovely new spa addition. The B & B has added a one-of-a-kind gazebo and spacious deck right in the middle of Mother Nature. Come and enjoy.

Guests are welcome to sit and visit in the spacious gathering room that has a cathedral ceiling and a Rumford fireplace. A balcony on the second floor overlooks the room. The gathering room is furnished with a sofa and matching love seat, a rocking chair and country end tables with unusual lamps. It is a comfortable place for reading or games or to enjoy the stereo and CD music.

The dining area has knotty pine walls and is furnished with a federal style dining set. There is even a dinner bell.

Breakfast is served either in the dining area or the porch. However, the coffeepot is always perking at sunup for early risers. A complete country breakfast is offered. It includes juice, farm fresh eggs, bacon, ham or sausage, biscuits and gravy. Other main entrees choices include apple quiche, Belgian waffles or western omelets. Added to this are homemade goodies such as orange muffins, English tea ring, coffeecake or fresh baked bread. There is always homemade strawberry jam, coffee, tea and milk.

The inn features two guestrooms on the first floor and two on the second floor. The Buttercup Room on the first floor is a rich yellow pine room that has a high four poster, queen-size bed that has a step stool. The hand-laid hardwood floor is accented by a bedspread of buttercup yellow lilies with matching drapes. There is a private bath with shower.

Also on the first floor, the distinctive Wild Violet Room with its interesting roof line displays a white iron and brass, queen-size bed. It has a pair of wicker rocking chairs, a wicker end table and a television. The draperies and bed linens carry out the theme of romantic violets and heart-shaped leaves. Weathered wood walls add to the decor. There is a private bath.

On the second floor, the Prairie Rose Room is furnished with a queen-size spindle bed. A pair of upholstered rockers, Queen Anne tables and a hall tree are in a sitting area. Matching bed linens and drapes in a print of light and dark pink roses highlight the room. The oversize private bath has a tub and shower.

The focal point of the Queen Anne's Lace Room is a Victorian queen-size bed with beautiful hand-crocheted ivory lace spread. The room is carpeted and wallpapered. There is a television with VCR. The windows look out at the woods which begin just fifteen feet from the house. The room has a 10 by 18 foot private bath and shower.

There are antique shops in nearby Sullivan, St. Clair, Steelville and Eureka. Canoeing or floating on the Meramec River is a favorite pastime. Swimming, fishing, a nature exhibit, hiking trails and a dining lodge are available at Meramec State Park. Don't miss a tour of Fisher's Cave with hand-held lanterns.

WILDFLOWER INN B & B: 2739 Hwy. D, Bourbon, 65441. (573) 468-7975. A four guestroom inn with private baths. Open all year. The inn is available for small receptions, reunions and retreats. Member BBIM. Catering accommodations can be arranged. No facilities for children. No pets. Smoking on porch. Fax: (573) 860-5712. Mary Lou and Jerry Hubble, innkeepers.

DIRECTIONS: Located 3 miles off I-44. Take exit 225 at Sullivan. Turn west on the south service road and then left on Hwy. D. Turn left at the Inn sign after crossing a long concrete bridge.

CARR HOUSE INN
Thayer

For almost one hundred years, this stately old house was stood watch over Chestnut Street in the small town of Thayer. Built in 1906 by William Carr, who was a prominent merchant, this Queen Anne Victorian house looks much like it did when it was first built.

From the moment you step into the foyer with its tall ceilings, parquet floor, and welcoming fireplace, you'll know you've taken a step back in time.

You enter the house off a large, wraparound porch that has wrought iron furniture. The foyer is furnished with a deck, three slat back chairs and a built-in bench. A beautiful brass and etched globe chandelier hangs from the ceiling. The parquet floor is something to admire. Lace curtains are at the windows and a large gilt mirror is on the classic gold flocked papered walls.

Large double doors lead to a 30-foot parlor with a fireplace. Sue Williams, the owner, had all the carpets taken up to reveal the original pine floors. At the front of the room, there are two upholstered sofas, an armoire, a pair of matched upholstered chairs, a lamp table and reading lamp, a floral pattern upholstered wing chair, coffee table and a large antique, glass door bookcase that holds a collection of pottery pieces. At the other end of the room there is a Victorian fainting couch, a pair of slat back chairs, an antique table and an antique mirror. The walls are a dark rose with white woodwork. The windows have lace curtains with drapes over them.

The dining room has white paneling chair rail high with rose painted walls above the rail. A bronze and crystal chandelier hands over a long dining table and six chairs. There is a credenza, an antique server and a plant stand with a large live plant. A corner fireplace is tiled and has a carved mantelpiece. There is a large lace curtained bay window with a cushioned seat. The floors are parquet.

A grand open staircase leading to the guestrooms is of quarter-sawn oak.

A guestroom, 30-feet long, has grey walls, white woodwork and has wall-to-wall Berber carpeting. It is furnished with a queen-size, antique reproduction sleigh bed, a blue upholstered wing chair, a small lamp table, a Martha Washington armchair, a slant front desk and chair, an upholstered arm chair with an Ottoman, an antique spiral leg table and reaching lamp, an upholstered Victorian sofa and a coffee table. Original art is on the walls and lace curtains are at the five windows. A large private bath has a tub with shower.

The second guestroom has a queen-size sleigh bed with a handmade quilt, a wicker rocking chair, a circa 1920s radio cabinet with a television, a night table and lamp and a rattan arm chair. The walls are yellow and the woodwork is white. The room is carpeted wall to wall with Berber carpeting. There is a small brass chandelier with glass globes. It also has a window seat. There is a large private bath with tub and shower.

The two room Victorian Suite is furnished with a pale yellow four poster queen-size bed with crisp bed linens. There is a night table with a reading lamp, an upholstered arm chair, a dressing table, cedar chest, towel rack and a wardrobe. The walls are papered yellow and the woodwork is white. Lace curtains are on the three windows. There is a tiled private bath with a walk-in shower.

The sitting room walls are papered with a yellow and white stripe paper below a chair rail and a colorful floral pattern above. Lace curtains are at the windows. It is furnished with an upholstered love seat, a wicker table and lamp, a wicker chair, a small wrought iron table and a painted coffee table.

Upon arrival, Sue offers cheese and crackers, fruit, cookies, and iced tea or lemonade in the summer and cocoa or hot cider with a cinnamon stick in the winter.

Breakfast is served in the dining room. Sue starts it off with either orange juice or Catawba grape juice. The entree varies and includes an apple cinnamon French toast stuffed with cream cheese and served with a baked apple with cinnamon syrup, and sausage. Or, an egg and three cheese strada served with bacon, sausage or ham. Coffee, tea or milk.

CARR HOUSE INN: 304 Chestnut Street, Thayer, 65791. (417) 264-7771. A three guestroom Victorian home where you can enjoy a romantic stay in the peacefulness of a small town. Open all year. Not suitable for children. No pets. Smoking on porch. E-mail: carrhse@ozarks.com. Sue Williams, innkeeper.

DIRECTIONS: Take U.S. Highway 63 south into Thayer. At traffic light, turn right. At police station, turn left and go up the hill. After passing the Baptist Church, the inn is the first house on the right.

PINEBROOK LODGE BED & BREAKFAST
West Plains

Pinebrook Lodge first opened in 1924 as an elite health resort catering to the wealthy and prestigious. The owners, Robert and Alice-Jean Eckhart, tell me that legend has it that some of the famous people who were guests here in the early days of the lodge included Franklin Roosevelt, Herbert Hoover, Harry Truman and even Al Capone.

This historic property is surrounded by the Mark Twain National Forest, and sits in the midst of a hundred acres of the Eckhart's own property. The grounds abound with pine, oak, cedar, red bud, dogwood and fruit trees. There is a meandering brook in which to cool your toes or just sit and enjoy. There is a four acre lake where you can watch deer or a beaver building their dam. An old original log cabin sits on the shore of the lake.

Entering the lodge, you are in a large keeping room which is 27 by 18 feet. There is a wood burning fireplace, 10-foot beamed ceilings and six large windows. There is a baby grand piano, an upholstered sofa and matching love seat, an early 1900s drop leaf, gateleg table, coffee table and another sofa. The windows have plaid drapes. There are lots of live plants. A door leads to a long porch that runs the entire length of the lodge.

Off the keeping room, the library with its hunter green walls and large bookshelves, is furnished with a red leather chair, an upholstered sofa and matching chair, end tables and lamps, a game table, a television and VCR with movies. A braided rug is on the floor. The room overlooks a patio.

A large dining room has seating for 14 guests at three tables. There is a corner brick fireplace. It is furnished with a piano and a French Provincial china cabinet, buffet and server. On the upper part of the walls is an original painting of a country scene. A door leads to the patio.

A long staircase leads to the second floor guestrooms, all of which have been enlarged and renovated by the Eckharts.

The Dogwood Room and the Federal Room both have queen-size beds, upholstered sofas, antique dressers, and private baths with showers. The Dogwood looks out on the path toward the lake and the Federal faces the second floor porch and the brook across the front meadow.

The Sweet Violet Room has a king-size brass bed, an armoire, a tub shower and plenty of space to relax and watch the birds from the windows that surround three sides of the room.

The Serenity Room is furnished with extra long twin beds, an armoire and a wicker set. It is decorated in soothing florals. This room also has a private bath.

The Country Garden Room looks onto the porch and the brook. It has a queen-size canopy bed, dresser, wardrobe, a Boston rocker and an upholstered chair. There is a large private bath with a tub and shower.

The two rooms of the Cedar Suite share a bath. One room has a full-size antique sleigh bed while the other has a maple full-size bed.

A small sitting room provides access to the second floor porch where you may greet the morning or watch the spectacular sunsets.

A full breakfast is served in the spacious dining room. On warm summer days, breakfast may be served on the secluded patio or on the comfortable front porch. The Eckharts offer fresh fruit in season, a frothy orange drink, French toast stuffed with cream cheese, and orange marmalade and another dish with apricot sauce for a topping and sausage. At times, they serve their Southwest casserole, made with tortillas, corn, cheese, sour cream, served with salsa and guacamole and spicy breakfast pork chops served with fried bananas, a fruit cup and muffins. Coffee, tea or milk.

Pinebrook Lodge is convenient to many activities and attractions that will make your stay in the Ozarks more enjoyable. There are a number of old water mills and springs for your sight-seeing pleasure. Canoe and float trips are just a ten minute drive away. Antique and craft shops are numerous in the area. Plus, if you are a race car fan, the West Plains Motor Speedway is home to many major racing events.

PINEBROOK LODGE B & B: 791 State Route T, Siloam Springs, West Plains, 65775. (417) 257-7769. Open all year. Children welcome. No pets. Outside smoking. A nice place where you can really get next to nature. Robert and Alice-Jean Eckhart, innkeepers.

DIRECTIONS: From Hwy. 63 at Rolla, take 63 south to Hwy. 14. Go west on 14 for 10 miles to Siloam Springs State Route T. Go south on T (it only goes one way) 1.5 miles to Pinebrook Lodge, on the right side of the road between two pillars. Do not go past the paved part of the road or you have gone too far. Go down drive between the pillars.

Section Three

RIVER HERITAGE REGION

Bonne Terre
Victorian Veranda B & B

Cape Girardeau
Neumeyer B & B
Riverwalk B & B

Jackson
Trisha's B & B
White House B & B

De Soto
Arlington Hotel B & B

Kimmswick
Wenom Drake House

Poplar Bluff
The Stuga B & B

Sikeston
Kline House B & B

Ste. Genevieve
Annie's B & B
Creole House B & B
Hurdick House
Inn Ste.Gemme Beauvais
Somewhere in Time B & B
Southern Hotel B & B
Steiger Haus B & B
Steiger Haus
   Downtown B & B

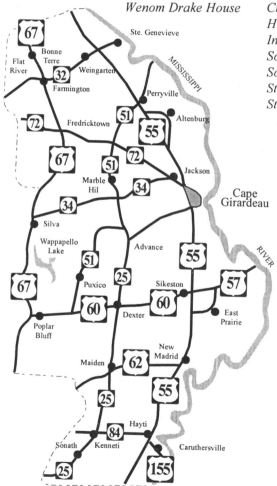

As you travel south from St. Louis on I-55 and U.S. 61 (the old Camino Real), then circle north on U.S. 67, you can experience a variety of cultures and scenery. German, Spanish, and French heritage can be observed. There is a touch of the "Old South" to be found journeying through the rolling countryside of the Ozark Mountain foothills and across the lowlands of the Mississippi River delta.

The best starting place for a trip through the River Heritage Region is at Kimmswick, a mid-century town that stands today much like it did in 1860. Located on the Mississippi River, twenty miles south of St. Louis, the town offers a chance to step back into the less hurried days of the past. Whether you're browsing the antique shops or enjoying the hospitality of the restaurants and inns, you will be surrounded by an enduring town where many of Kimmswick's businesses and residents still occupy the original buildings. Wenom-Drake B & B is located here.

The Mississippi River and mining history lend their special appeal to this diverse area. Both have affected Ste. Genevieve, Missouri's oldest town located just south of Kimmswick. Founded in 1735, the French community was settled by lead miners, farmers, and fur traders. When you visit St. Genevieve, stop first at the information center, then sample its history at the Ste. Genevieve Museum. With this as a background, you'll be ready to tour the homes and businesses dating back to the 1700s with their distinctive architecture. The bed and breakfasts here include Annie's, Creole House, Hurdick House, Inn Ste. Gemme Beauvais, Somewhere in Time, Southern Hotel Inn and Steiger House.

Next head south to Perryville with its many historic sites. The National Shrine of Our Lady of the Miraculous Medal is seated within the historical Church of the Assumption (1827). The St. Mary's Seminary (1827) includes four noted museums. The Faherty House Museum features a circa 1830-90 exterior and interior.

Old Appleton is a quaint 19th century settlement The 160 year-old dam and waterfall here have, for years, been a picturesque setting for artists and shutterbugs. It's an ideal spot for a picnic. The old mill was washed away by the flood waters several years ago, but the little town is certainly worth a visit.

As you continue south, stop for a look at Tower Rock rising 85 feet from the Mississippi River. It was designated a National landmark by President U.S. Grant. Altenburg, Wittenburg and Frohna, all old German settlements, have retained a strong religious heritage since the Saxon Lutherans from Germany immigrated here in 1839.

Further south, Jackson offers a number of attractions. Let the sights and sounds of a ride behind Engine No. 5 of the historic "Iron Mountain Railway" take you away to the glory of the steam train era. The region's only steam train, is a must do for all rail fans and those too young to remember the adventure that accompanied steam train travel. Trisha's B & B and the White House B & B are located in Jackson.

Your river route will bring you to the region's largest city, and one of its most historic, with a tradition dating back to the early 1700s. Cape Girardeau has preserved many reminders of its past. Downtown, you'll admire historic buildings such as the restored Victorian Glenn House (1883), Old St. Vincent Church (1853), a fine example of Gothic Architecture, and the remains of the old Civil Ware fortifications. Neumeyer B & B and River Walk B & B are in Cape Girardeau.

South from Cape, you will see the landscape change from rollercoaster hills to rich farmland. Your route will carry you away from the river, past Charleston with its stately old homes. Here, in the spring, thousands of Azaleas burst into bloom. You will also find Sikeston which is home to Missouri's largest rodeo held each year in August. Kline House B & B is located here.

West from "Cape" you'll find the Bollinger Mill State Historic Site, featuring a covered bridge and a working grist mill. And, at Marble Hill, stop and view the old Massey log house.

You'll return to the river at historic New Madrid. One of history's most violent earthquakes occurred here about 190 years ago. The small river town has known many travelers over its long history. Evidence of the earliest known inhabitants can be seen in the 1,000 year-old Mississippian Indian mound located near the south interchange of I-55 and Highway 61. French and Spanish settlers later came to New Madrid, and in 1789, Revolutionary War Colonel George Morgan established it as the first American settlement west of the Mississippi River. New Madrid's location on the river was of strategic importance to both Union and Confederate forces during the Civil War. Examples of pre-Civil Ware architecture are found at the Hunter-Dawson State Historic Site. The site is restored to a working museum farm of the 1860-80 period.

While you are in the area, visit Big Oak Tree State Park, where you can walk through 1,000 acres of virgin forest including the towering oaks that give the park its name.

To the south is Missouri's bootheel. These lowlands that seem to have more in common with states further south. Bounded on the east by the Mississippi River and on the west by the St. Francois River with drainage canals in between, this is crop country. Cotton, soybeans and peaches are important crops. To explore this country, proceed on I-55 to Hayti, then west on U.S. 85 approximately 15 miles to Route 25. Ten mile north will take you to Route 53 and into Poplar Bluff. There are several interesting local historical museums as well as the Margaret Harwell Art Museum. The Stuga B & B is located here.

U.S. 67 leads north to the 8,600 acre Lake Wappapello. It is one of the state's largest lakes. A different kind of water experience awaits just to the east. The 21,670 acre Mingo National Wildlife Refuge and the adjacent Duck Creek Wildlife Area are the largest area of hardwoods swamp preserve in the State. Don't pass up this beautiful wildlife preserve.

Still heading north, you will return to hill country. Stop off at Millstream Gardens, park-like setting of Ozark forest and scenic stretches of the St. Francis River.

In this part of the region, mining was the key to the area's growth. From Farmington, the largest town in the old lead mining district, to towns such as Leadington and Leadwood, the impact of mining is obvious. At Flat River, you can learn more at the Lead Belt Mineral Museum.

In Bonne Terre be sure to visit the Shepard House located at 11 South Main Street. It was built by Cornish miners in 1865 and is now a museum with displays of artifacts from Bonne Terre Mine as well as furniture depicting life during the early period of Bonne Terre's history. At the nearby Eckert's Orchards, you can pick your own fresh fruit in season. A wonderful Bed and Breakfast, the Victorian Veranda, is located here in Bonne Terre.

There are two state parks in the northern corner of the area. St. Francois State Park has streams, springs and a hiking trail. Hawn State Park typifies the beauty of the scenery found throughout this region.

Just north of Bonne Terre on I-55 the town of De Soto's old De Soto Hotel has been renovated and now houses the Arlington Hotel B & B along with a very nice restaurant.

In the River Heritage Region of Missouri, you'll find historic towns, the mighty Mississippi River, state parks and state historical sites aplenty.

VICTORIAN VERANDA
Bonne Terre

This elegant 1880 Queen Anne style home was built by the St. Joe Lead Mining Company as a place for the company president to stay when he came to Bonne Terre. Later, it was called the St. Joe Club/Boarding House and was used by the company engineers until the mines closed.

In August, 1992, Galen and Karen Forney purchased the 17 room house with the idea of using it as both their home and a bed and breakfast. They opened it as the Victorian Veranda in February of 1995.

The original parlor, now the Gathering Room, has been completely renovated and is used as the guests' living room It has a fireplace, beamed ceiling and two large bay windows. The two sofas are upholstered in a large flowered print that matches the window treatments. A large overstuffed chair is perfect for reading by the fireplace or watching the cable television. A small closet has been turned into a refreshment closet where guests can help themselves to cold beverages. Soft green color wallpaper and a green carpet that covers the floor is all set off with a wide white baseboard.

The large dining room has a beamed ceiling, floral wallpaper above the chair rail and white painted wainscoting. Along with an antique glass front china cabinet, which displays antique wedgewood china, is a large oak dining room table and chairs, an antique cupboard and another oak table with an ongoing puzzle just waiting for the guest to put together.

A full breakfast of fresh fruit, juice, eggs, breakfast meats, homemade muffins or Karen's special stuffed french toast along with freshly ground coffee will help you start your day of antiquing or hiking.

Just off the dining room in what was once the music room, is another parlor with a fireplace and large bay window. An oriental rug is on the beautiful wood floor. The room is furnished with a Victorian style sofa and chairs, lyre end tables and sofa table. There is also a Baldwin grand piano for those music lovers.

The four guestrooms are on the second floor, accessible by a stairway with the original beaded board walls. In the hallway, there is a love seat, table and plenty of books.

Victoria Suite is a romantic room decorated in soft mauves, pale green and floral Victorian décor. It has a queen-size high back Victorian bed, queen-size sofa sleeper, antique dresser, and a wing back chair. The large private bathroom has a thermal massage bath big enough for two.

Sir Drake Room is decorated in rich colors of cream, burgundy and hunter green. A green iron queen-size bed with a hand made quilt awaits you. Victorian accents are showcased throughout the room. The private bathroom has the thermal massage bath for two.

Antique Rose Room is a spacious room of antique yellow and blue floral wallpaper and décor. Relax on the bay window seat overlooking the town's park. This room also has a Victorian queen-size iron bed and the private bathroom is in the dormer with the thermal massage bath for two in the room.

The fourth room available is the Countryside Room with soft colors of apricot and green floral wallpaper and decorated with antique and country accents. There is an oak four poster queen-size bed with quilts, antique dresser and chair. Private bathroom with shower.

Galen and Karen love to show off their home and invite guests to relax on their very large wraparound veranda. Come and sit on the wicker rocking chairs or swing on the porch swing while you sip on a cold glass of lemonade and enjoy the beautiful park in front of the Inn. Near completion will be a large gazebo connecting to the veranda.

VICTORIAN VERANDA B & B: 207 E. School Street, Bonne Terre, 63628. (573) 358-1134 or (800) 343-1134. Four guests rooms all with private bath. Open all year. No Pets. Inquire about children. No smoking. Full breakfast. Galen and Karen Forney, owners and innkeepers.

DIRECTIONS: From St. Louis take I-55 south to Hwy. 67. South on 67 to Bonne Terre exit. Turn right on Hwy. 47, then left on Allen Street. Turn right at Main Street, then an immediate left onto East School Street to the inn.

CAPE GIRARDEAU

T radition says that missionary priests erected a rude cross on the Cape de la Crois (now Gray's Point) south of the city in 1699. About 1720, a French ensign named Girardot (or Girardo), stationed at Kaskaskia for several years, is thought to have settled on "the Cape." You can view this rocky promontory just north of the city on the Cape Drive Parkway. Maps as early as 1765 designate this point on the river as "Cape Girardot" or "Girardeau." Verified history of the area begins about 1786 when Louis Lorimier and a band of Shawnee and Delaware Indians moved across the Mississippi into upper Louisiana, then the Spanish Territory.

The growth of the town was halted abruptly when the United States Land Commission rejected Lorimier's Spanish land title, thus invalidating all titles to lots in the city. In 1815, the county seat was moved to Jackson and Cape Girardeau population declined. In 1836 however, some 25 years after Lorimier's death, the United States recognized his title and the town experienced a rebirth.

During the Civil War, Cape Girardeau was more important as a post to guard communications than as a military objective. Union soldiers occupied the town in July of 1861 erected fortifications at the four approaches to the town by river and road, and repulsed a confederate attack on April 17, 1863. The war affected Cape Girardeau mainly due to the cessation of river traffic and the spoilage of the back country by raiding guerrillas and troops.

Cape Girardeau was first settled by American families from North Carolina, Tennessee and Kentucky. Later the community attracted many German settlers. Both the Southern and German traditions are still in evidence. A few Classic-Revival residences, erected by pioneers who grew rich on frontier trade, remain in the older parts of the town. Elsewhere, houses suggestive of the German influence stand flush with the sidewalks. These are usually one-and-a-half stories, but some are two-story structures with cast iron balconies that break the primness of the unornamented facades.

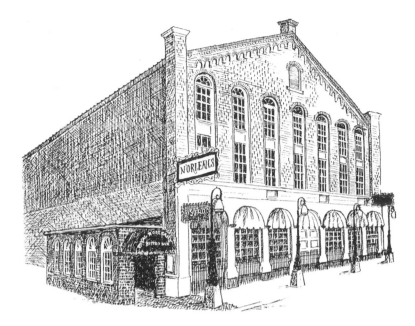

ROYAL N'ORLEANS RESTAURANT
Cape Girardeau

Dining at the Royal N Orleans Restaurant is a 40 year old Cape Girardeau tradition where it is known as the finest restaurant in the area.

Built in 1865 by the Turner Society, a group of Masons purchased the building and named it The Opera House. The stage was located on the second floor while shops were on the first. Over the next one hundred and twenty years it housed many different businesses on the first floor, including the Royal N Orleans Restaurant from 1954 until 1990.

In 1990 a fire almost ended the existence of this historic building, but due to the efforts of area businessman and entrepreneur, Dennis Stockard, it was saved and restored to its present grandeur. Jerri and John Wyman purchased the existing business in October of 1995.

The menu offers such traditional favorites as Chateaubriand for two. They boast of the best steaks in all Missouri. The Oysters Casino, a house specialty and escargot are popular fare as well. Their diverse and excellent menu also includes lamb, pork, chicken and pasta dishes

ROYAL N'ORLEANS RESTAURANT: 300 Broadway Street at the corner of Broadway and Lormier, Cape Girardeau, 63703. (573) 335-8191. Open Monday through Saturday from 5:00 p.m. until 11:00 p.m. Reservations recommended. Nightly specialties and an extensive wine list. John and Jerrianne Wyman, proprietors.

NEUMEYER'S BED & BREAKFAST
Cape Girardeau

Developed at the turn of the century, the bungalow has been called the ideal family home and represents a marked contrast to the Victorian house - more simple, comfortable and informal.

The Neumeyer Bed and breakfast is housed in one the first bungalows erected in Cape Girardeau. Built in 1910 by a well-known local contractor, J.W. Gerhardt, the 3,000 square foot home shows many examples of superior craftsmanship.

The low roof line extends over a spacious verandah that reaches forty feet across the front and around the side of the house. This overhang shelters the porch, giving a feeling of coziness and comfort. When was the last time you sipped a drink while relaxing on a porch swing? Decorated with hanging flower baskets, the porch offers both a great swing and rocking chairs. The gentle amenities of life are still observed here.

Coming in through the four foot wide front door, you sense a return to a bygone era of gracious hospitality. You enter a large living room characterized by original oak paneling, beamed ceiling and plate rails, not to mention the well stocked built-in book shelves. The room, and several others, are illuminated by huge windows topped with many small panes. Upholstered chairs, settees, and rocking chairs make you feel right at home.

At the end of the living room, through a wide-open colonnade, is a comfortable den. Like the rest of the home, it features dark oak beams and paneling, with a wood-burning fireplace. A sofa, two upholstered recliners and a rocking chair allow guests an ideal place to sit and read or chat. A stained glass window brightens the room.

The dining room also has a fireplace along with oak built-in china cabinets, paneling and beams. Your day will begin here with a hearty breakfast prepared by Tom and Terri. They offer bacon and eggs, pancakes, egg casserole, waffles with seasonal fruit and quiches or crepes with either fruit or an egg and meat mixture. Juice, coffee, or tea and homemade breads round out this morning repast.

While retaining its timely charm, the Neumeyer B & B provides modern comfort with central air conditioning, individual heat controls in each room and ceiling fans. Three bedrooms are available for guests on the second floor. Each has its own private bath.

The South Room, decorated in yellow, features a brass queen-size bed, dresser, rocking chair, and a day bed.

The North Room, done in floral peach and earth tone wallpaper, has a queen-size, antique four poster bed and is decorated with Tom's landscape photographs.

The East Room, decorated in rose tones and floral wallpaper, boasts a queen-size antique sleigh bed and a dresser and rocking chair. The private bath is down the hall and bathrobes are provided.

After a long search, Tom and Terri settled on this house because of its warm, open atmosphere. They believe in treating each guest as a long time friend. Refreshments are offered after registering. On special occasions, such as honeymoons or anniversaries, wine or champagne is offered. Tom has a photographic studio business and Terri is a teacher. At the Neumeyer's "The door is always open and the light is in the window."

NEUMEYER'S B & B: 25 S. Lorimier Street, Cape Girardeau, 63703. (573) 335-0449 or toll free (888) 423-5184. A three bedroom B & B host home near the Mississippi riverfront, restaurants, historic homes, churches, museums, antique malls and Southeast Missouri State University. Open all year. No pets. A cat in residence. No smoking bedrooms. Children welcome. Tom and Terri Neumeyer, hosts.

DIRECTIONS: From I-55, take Cape/Jackson exit on Hwy. 61 (Kingshighway) to Independence Street. Drive east on Independence 1.5 miles to Lorimier Street, which is one and a half blocks past city hall. The Neumeyer is the fifth house on the right.

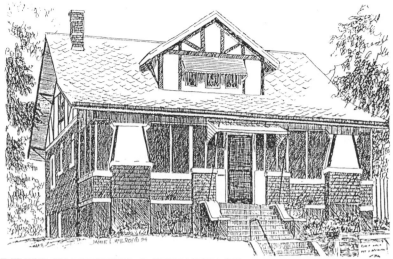

RIVER WALK BED & BREAKFAST
Cape Girardeau

R iver Walk Bed & Breakfast was built around 1923 by the owner of a local lumber company. The house was the longtime residence of father and son doctors in the Ashley family. The house features a rare black marble fireplace in the commons area, hardwood floors, a broad front porch with its own swing, and a patio for entertaining on sunny days. Most unusual are the six original pocket windows, the only working examples of their kind in the city.

Located in a quiet tree-shaded neighborhood, owner and innkeeper, Jeannie Stout offers a home of distinct charm and comfortable accommodations and southern hospitality. Upon arrival, Jeannie offers cake and coffee or tea.

The living room has a fireplace with bookshelves on either side. Lots of books to read here. A sofa faces the fireplace. There is a matching recliner rocker, lamp tables with lamps, an etagere, coffee table and a television. One wall is paneled chair rail high and one is fully paneled.

The dining room has a pecan dining set consisting of table, chairs, a cupboard, an antique hall tree, desk and an etagere. It has an area carpet. A breakfast nook, where Jeannie usually serves breakfast, has a round table and leather chairs. A door opens to the yard and a patio. The yard is nicely landscaped with shrubs, cannas, elephants ears, hanging plants and trees.

Jeannie prepares a full breakfast. There is orange juice or V8, homemade jams and jellies or preserves, coffee and tea. Guests can select early morning coffee, teas and juices from a breakfast bar and enjoy the front porch or the dining room while you wait for breakfast. Jeanne serves a breakfast meat along with an egg dish, pancakes or waffles and her famous sweetbread. She has perfected her biscuit recipe and now guests gobble them up.

There are four guestrooms on the second floor. At the top of the stairs, the Blue Room has a full-size bookcase headboard bed, a 1940's wardrobe, lamp tables and a pair of captains chairs. A quilt rack holds towels and wash cloths. Blue curtains match the bedspread.

The Wedding Room has a large four poster, queen-size bed and a sofa table in golden oak. There is also a pair of open-arm side chairs with upholstered seats.

The Green Room is furnished with a queen-size bed covered with a green spread, an arts and crafts bookcase, a dark pine dresser with mirror, a pair of upholstered chairs and a quilt rack for towels. The room is carpeted and has a wide floral border at the ceiling of the grey walls. The windows have antique lace panels and green side drapes.

The Men's Room is furnished with a single brass bed with a colorful quilt on it. There is a desk and floor lamp, an arts and crafts bookcase, and a night table. It is a cheerful room with red and green drapes, a ships clock, a copper ship's plaque, a brass bedwarmer and an old-time shaving mirror with a shaving mug and brush.

RIVER WALK B & B: 444 Marie, Cape Girardeau, 63703. (573) 334-4611. Open all year. Children welcome. Smoking on porch or patio. No pets. Visa and Mastercard accepted. A four guestroom home with shared bath. Six blocks from downtown and the Mississippi River. Zuma Vanderpoel, Jeannie's mother and right hand at the B & B has recently passed away. There's the recording machine for your messages. Jeannie Stout, innkeeper.

DIRECTIONS: From I-55, turn east on Rt. K exit. Go to William Street and proceed to Sprigg avenue. Left on Sprigg, through two traffic signals and at the second caution light, turn right on Washington. Go one block and turn right on Marie. The third house on the left.

THE ARLINGTON BED & BREAKFAST INN
De Soto

It has taken more than one hundred and thirty years for the Arlington Hotel (first known as the De Soto House when built in the mid-1800s) to appear again in its magnificent state. In those days it was a hotel catering to passengers of the Iron Mountain/Missouri Pacific Railroad that ran past its doors. Now, this grand old dame of great historical value is accommodating visitors once more in the grandiose style of the Victorian lady it once was. It is now known as the Arlington Bed and Breakfast Inn. The owners are Rich and Brenda Jenkins.

I saw this hotel many years ago, and to see it now, it looks like somebody waved a magic wand over it and "presto" what a transformation. Newly painted a bright white with black shutters on all of the windows, the wraparound porches on the first and second floors, shrubs and tall trees, this place looks wonderful.

The original lobby with its marble fireplace has been changed into a recreation room, with a pool table. It has a large antique slant front, secretary bookcase, an upholstered camel back love seat and an upholstered wing back chair.

A common room is furnished with oriental area carpets, an upholstered sofa and wing chair, a desk and a television. This room also has the original marble fireplace.

There are eighteen guestrooms available, with one being on the first floor with a ramp for easy access to a room for the handicapped. All the other seventeen rooms are distinguished by names. Each room is of Victorian vintage décor. All are carpeted and nicely wallpapered and have private baths. Some rooms have an exposed brick wall, most have white lace curtains, crystal or brass chandeliers, framed prints and pictures on the walls. Names of rooms like Lavender and Old Lace, Wine and Roses, Pink Peony, The Conductor's Room are decorated to fit the name. The Jefferson Davis Room, was so named as the Confederate President once spent the night in the hotel.

Wide, carpeted halls on the second and third floors have furnishings where you can make yourself comfortable. Some rooms have twin beds, others have full size beds. Some have armoires, poster beds, rocking chairs, but no two are alike.

Guest rooms are reached by the original staircase of long ago. Off the first floor landing, the Jenkins have a small gift shop.

After a rest-filled night in the guestroom of your choice, join other guests in the Jefferson Davis Room where a delicious breakfast is served in the eloquent style of the 1800s. It is served buffet style and includes juices, scrambled eggs, bacon, sausages and ham. Then there is biscuits and gravy, American or hash brown potatoes, cut fruit, Danish pastry and coffee, tea and milk.

Rich and Brenda also serve lunch and dinner to the general public. It too, is served buffet style. I had lunch the day I visited here, and let me tell you, I didn't go away hungry. They had four different meats (I had pork chop) two hot vegetables, potatoes, gravy, soup, salad and a variety of desserts. Iced tea, lemonade and coffee. They have a Friday and Saturday night special of steak and prime rib.

Catering and banquet facilities for up to 45 persons are available. A nice gift shop is on the stairway landing.

ARLINGTON B & B INN: 207 East Main Street, De Soto, 63020. (636) 337-0043. Open all year. An 18-room historic hotel, all private baths. Some exit to second floor porch. No pets. Children welcome. Designated smoking. E-mail: thearlingtonB & B@joln.net. Rich and Brenda Jenkins, innkeepers with help from their children.

DIRECTIONS: From I-55 exit onto Hwy. 67 south. Go two miles and exit on 110 west (CC). At top of ramp go right five miles to De Soto (Main Street). Left on Main Street and go four stop signs, turn left over train tracks.

TRISHA'S BED & BREAKFAST
Jackson

Built at the turn of the century by the prominent Mueller family of Jackson, this nine room Victorian house has retained all of the amenities it had at the time it was erected. The ornate woodwork and lighting fixtures are two areas which illustrate the beautiful workmanship of ninety plus years ago.

Gus Wischmann, who recently retired, and his wife Trisha, have tastefully decorated the large old home with antiques and locally made arts and crafts. The rooms are spacious and comfortable with sitting areas on both floors provided for guests.

Off the entry hall is the family parlor which guests are invited to use. In a large bay window is a sofa with a blue colonial print and matching curtains at the window. An armoire conceals a television and stereo. A beautiful tiger oak fireplace houses gas logs which add ambiance to the parlor. Two rocking chairs and two upholstered arm chairs provide ample seating.

French doors also lead off the entry hall into a very inviting tea room and small gift shop. Trisha's Tea Room features homemade breads, soups, entrees, desserts and lots of tea. Ideal for special tea parties and other occasions. Trisha recently expanded the gift shop area with unique products.

Breakfast is served in the dining room, furnished as it would have been at the turn-of- the-century with a large oak table with bow-backed chairs, an antique wood burning stove and a Hoosier cabinet. A large area carpet covers the floor. In the bay window is a French sofa and attractive large house plants. You are served on blue and white china, with crystal and silverware.

An important part of the stay here is the morning breakfast. Fresh juice, fruit salad, homemade muffins and rolls, jellies, jams and coffee or tea. A variety of other dishes are also available including quiche, crepes, casseroles, blueberry pancakes, waffles plus some other surprises.

Dinner is offered to guests if requested in advance, usually at the time they make reservations to stay. Trisha serves a variety of dinner entrees.

On the second floor, at the head of the stairs, is a small sitting area with a love seat, wash stand and a refrigerator. The four guestrooms are off the hall. Each one is decorated in accordance with its name.

The front room is called Millicent's Petticoats Room. It has a queen-size four poster bed, a vanity and an interesting private bath. Trisha has a large collection of period petticoats and lingerie displayed here.

The Georgia Belle Peach Room is decorated with peach wallpaper and curtains. A king-size bed has an unusual lattice work headboard. There is an antique love seat and an upholstered French chair. There is a private bath.

Another guestroom, called Lavender Paradise, has a king-size bed. Needless to say it is decorated in Lavender. It is a large bright room furnished with a wicker rocker and night tables. There is a private bath with shower.

The fourth guestroom is named Pink Ice. It is furnished with a 1920s full-size bed and a matching vanity and dresser. There is a shower, lavatory in-room. This room often houses long-term stay guests or students. It also has an outside entrance.

All of the guestrooms have natural wood floors, small antique and decorator pieces, lots of paintings on the walls and are very comfortable.

Two large porches have swings and comfortable seating.

I think you will find Gus and Trisha's home to be very much to your liking. I know they will make you feel at home and will help in any way they can with information and directions to nearby places of interest.

TRISHA'S B & B: 203 Bellview, Jackson, 63755. (573) 243-7427 or (800) 651-0408. A four guestroom Victorian home just ten minutes from Cape Girardeau and close to some of Missouri's most interesting points to visit. Full breakfast included in rate. Dinner served by advance reservation. Open all year. Children over five welcome. No smoking. E-Mail: trisha@igateway.net. Website: www.rosecity.net/trains. Gus and Trisha Wischmann, hosts.

DIRECTIONS: South from St. Louis on I-55 to Jackson. Exit on Hwy. 61 at exit 105. Call for specific directions and a brochure.

WHITEHOUSE BED & BREAKFAST
Jackson

In 1908 Theodore O. Link, the creator of Union Station in St. Louis, designed the unusual house just four blocks from Jackson's train station. Built in the Romanesque style, and featuring fourteen rooms, the house dominates more than three acres of surrounding lawns and woods.

It features a broad wraparound porch, original oak and pine floors and woodwork, pocket doors, fireplace, and a grand archway joining the foyer to the interior of the house.

Owners, Norman and Violet Colyott purchased the house and now have their bed & breakfast here and are delighted to welcome their guests in the manner foreseen by its' designer, blending an appreciation of high style with an informal sense of comfort and convenience.

The huge entry hall has a carved oak staircase and an oak archway with columns leading into the family room. The entryway has a piano and an antique fainting couch. An Oriental carpet is on the floor and a glass and brass chandelier hangs from the ceiling.

A wood burning stove is in the family room, furnished with a pair of sofas, occasional tables, lamps, an upholstered recliner, television and an oak bookcase. Guests are invited to make full use of this room.

There is also a library that contains an antique Murphy bed, a leather chair and sofa and a bookcase with lots of books. An oriental carpet is on the floor.

Oak beams, a chair rail and the original stained glass windows are some of the architectural details in the dining room. A large pedestal oak table and six chairs, a cupboard and a game table rest on the oriental carpet. An original chandelier with blue glass shades hangs from the ceiling.

Violet serves a full breakfast consisting of juice fresh fruit in season, a variety of Danish rolls, jams and jellies, coffee or tea to go along with ham and eggs (any style), American fried potatoes, biscuits and dry cereal.

Four spacious guestrooms with two baths are available. A first floor room is furnished with a four poster carved bed, end tables and reading lamps, a Chippendale circa 1930s chest, a small breakfront and an antique trunk. Lace curtains and floral pull back drapes are at the window. The white walls are decorated with nice paintings.

A second floor guestroom is carpeted and has mini blinds at the window. There is a queen-size bed, night tables and lamps, an antique trunk and a desk. The walls have a blue plaid print wallpaper and nice pictures.

An antique full-size iron bed, an upholstered chair, a wicker table, a full length floor mirror occupy the third room. There is also a bookcase full of enough overstuffed bears, cats and dogs to make any child take notice. There is also a rattan chair, and a table with reading lamp. Lace curtains are at the windows.

A carpeted fourth guestroom has an antique full-size iron bed, an ornate antique night table, a kidney shaped desk with lamp and a large fern stand that holds an antique pitcher and bowl set. The five large windows have lace off-white curtains. The walls are papered in a floral print.

WHITEHOUSE B & B: 802 E. Washington, Jackson, 63775. (573) 243-4329. Open all year. Children welcome. No smoking in house. No pets. A four guestroom B & B with two shared baths. Norman and Violet Colyott, innkeepers.

DIRECTIONS: From I-55 take the Fruitland - Hwy. 61 exit and go right on Hwy. 61. Go two miles to the courthouse and turn left on Main. Go to Bellevue, turn left and go half a block to Washington.

KIMMSWICK

Although I have Kimmswick listed in the River Heritage Region, it is only 20 miles south of St. Louis. Theodore Kimm, a native of Brunswick, Germany, laid out the Town of Kimmswick in 1859. The site he chose had the advantages of both river and railroad transportation and proximity to St. Louis, Following the Civil War, this early German community prospered with new businesses. There was also a beautiful park with recreation resort complete with rides and a dance pavilion. Because of the healthful mineral springs north of the town, Kimmswick served as the summer home for many prominent St. Louisans. It was easy commuting from St. Louis to Kimmswick by train or excursion steamer. In these early years, Kimmswick was an important railroad stop and port for travelers and shipping. But the coming of the automobile changed all that. New highways bypassed the town; trains and boats ceased to stop; and Kimmswick became an almost forgotten place.

Many of the historic buildings were destroyed. It was the loss of these historic buildings that generated the idea of a restoration project. In 1970, several of the old Kimmswick houses were renovated, and more were to follow. Several old log buildings, in danger of being demolished were moved here from other areas and are now restored. Touring Kimmswick doesn't take a lot of time since the tiny town is bounded by just four blocks.

Kimmswick has once again taken back her importance. Because of so much appreciation being given to the town's rich heritage, Kimmswick is now a living museum. The restoration has brought new life to the town but has not changed the town's uniqueness. It is still the same quiet small town contained within the same early boundaries drawn by its founder, Theodore Kimm, in 1859.

Descendants of many early families continue to live in Kimmswick. Today, the old houses and businesses now house shops, restaurants, museums and bed & breakfasts. In them are welcoming shopkeepers, merchants, craft persons and artisans to greet you. The Log Barbagallo House, built in 1850, was moved to Kimmswick and restored to the French style house it had originally been. The Burgess-How House and Museum was the first log building to be moved here. Built in 1840, it had been the home of Edward How and his family.

It is truly remarkable to be able to walk around this town that has stayed virtually the same for over one hundred and thirty-five years. If you ever have the chance to visit here, please don't pass up the opportunity.

If it's antiques you're looking for, try *Grandmother B's Antiques,* located in the circa 1884 Rauschenbach building. Judy Bellchamber's shop carries a complete line of antiques including estate jewelry, prints, dolls and lots of small items. Her specialty is "quality furniture." Judy pointed out a circa 1860 hand carved German sideboard eight feet tall. There was a Queen Anne walnut curio cabinet with two doors and a mirrored back, a walnut spinet desk, a mahogany drop leaf table, an Eastlake Victorian marble top dresser, a circa 1880 turned spindle day bed, a Queen Anne ball and clawfoot mahogany china cabinet, a walnut game table and a 1920's stenciled oak buffet. There were two large display cases full of cut glass, flow blue, stemware, porcelain and unusual items. There was also an eight piece Czechoslovakian cannister set, an oak mantle clock, a walnut shaving stand and several wall shelves. (636) 467-1374.

For gifts a little out of the ordinary, visit the *Pioneer House* at 4th and Market. They specialize in Heritage table and window lace, but there are many things that would make wonderful gifts: copperware, lots of spatterware and crocks, florals, glassware, handmade fringed lamp shades and lamps, unique wood carvings and quite a few antiques. Be sure to visit the Bear's Den. Carol Breihan has a mini-mall at the rear of her Pioneer House Shop. Twenty dealers carry a variety of nice things: books, crafts, pottery, porcelain and quilts. (636) 464-4050.

Just across the street is the *Victorian Heart,* whose motto is "from our heart to yours." Lisa Chrisco and Renee Breihan have a very nice shop here with lots of Battenberg lace, blue delft from Holland, sterling silver rings, Staffordshire teapots from England, cobalt blue glassware, beautifully framed Victorian prints, collectors mini tea sets, bath "Fizzmos" and candles. Between this shop and the Pioneer House, they have the largest selection of imported lace in the area, including lace mantle scarves. (636) 464-9377.

BLUE OWL RESTAURANT & BAKERY
Kimmswick

Back in 1987 when I first tried the Blue Owl Restaurant, customers had to wait in line. Several times since then Mary has expanded the seating capacity, but there is still a waiting line and for good reason!

There is a quaint and charming atmosphere here. You can be sure of warm and friendly service and wonderful meals served on Old English China. And, if you have a mind to try Mary's recipes, there are seven great cookbooks, each featuring something different. I guarantee you won't mind standing in line.

The Blue Owl Restaurant and Bakery is famous for hearty breakfasts, country style lunches and fabulous desserts. Breakfast selections include fluffy biscuits and apple butter, country baked ham, quiche with fresh fruit, and biscuits and gravy. Caramel rolls are served on weekends.

Lunches feature homemade soups, salads, sandwiches, quiches, croissants, and delicious home cooked meals. Savor the aroma of Chicken and Dumplings and Roast Beef with real mashed potatoes served every Sunday. Soups include Cream of Broccoli, Canadian Cheese, Vegetable Beef and the famous White Chile.

The Blue Owl Bakery has homemade pies, assorted specialty cakes such as Death by Chocolate, cheesecakes, pastries, cookies and candies, baked daily and made with only the finest ingredients.

Enjoy outside dining on Ms. Mary's Veranda with live music, year round. Mary and her staff will welcome you and promise an unforgettable dining experience.

BLUE OWL RESTAURANT & BAKERY: Located at Second & Mill Streets, Kimmswick. (636) 464-3128. Open Tuesday through Friday 10:00 a.m. to 3:00 p.m. Saturday and Sunday 10:00 a.m. to 5:00 p.m. Breakfast served 10 a.m. to 11:30 a.m. Closed Monday. Mary Hostetter, owner.

THE OLD HOUSE RESTAURANT
Kimmswick

The first time I saw The Old House Restaurant, it was getting dark. Several inches of snow were on the ground and on an old rail fence. A soft glow from kerosene lamps glimmered through the windows, and the old log house seemed to invite me in. I've been going there regularly ever since. The oldest part of the house was built in 1770, with an addition in 1830.

It served as a trading post in its earlier years, and later as a tavern and stage coach stop. Old plank floors, fireplaces, and the log walls make it a warm and cozy place.

Frank Kasal, his daughters, Marie Hensley and Ellen Wilson and their partner Joann Ehlen, serve lunch and dinner. The menu includes roast prime rib of beef, steaks, catfish and chicken. Chicken and dumplings are served every Wednesday and Sunday. Entrees include dinner salad, or soup of the day, potato, and fresh baked from with honey butter. All of the breads, soups, and desserts are homemade. My favorite is hot apple pie with whiskey sauce.

THE OLD HOUSE RESTAURANT: 2nd and Elm Streets, Kimmswick, 63053. (636) 464-0378. A great country restaurant with lots of ambience. Open for lunch and dinner Tuesday through Sunday from 11:00 a.m. to 8:00 p.m. Closed on Monday.

DIRECTIONS: From St. Louis take I-55 south about 20 miles to Kimmswick exit. Turn left to Hwy. 61 (about 3 blocks). Right on 61 to K (1 block). Take K into Kimmswick.

WENOM-DRAKE HOUSE BED & BREAKFAST
Kimmswick

T he Wenom-Drake House was named for each of its first two owners,
John Wenom and Fred Drake. John Wenom came to America in 1852
from Alsace, France. He was a teenager at the time. He lived with his
family on a farm not far from Kimmswick. When he built this house in 1877,
he was married and had seven children.

In 1918, the descendents of Wenom sold the house to Fred Drake. He
built an addition onto the south side of the house which he opened to overnight
guests. The addition has long since been removed. It is believed that Drake
sold the house in the early 1930s.

Several owners lived in the house following the Drakes. In 1974 the
house was acquired for the purpose of using it as a historic tour home.
Gradually it was redecorated and furnished with antiques, becoming one of
the fine tour houses of Kimmswick.

In 1992, Ken and Abby Peck purchased the Wenom-Drake house, and it
once again became a family home as well as a bed and breakfast.

The parlor floor is covered with a Persian rug and is furnished with a
Victorian love seat and matching chair, a Victorian Wing back love seat, an
Eastlake upholstered platform rocker, an Empire library table and a Queen
Anne wing chair. A game table holds a ceramic chess set. Original artwork is
on the walls which have a Victorian print wallpaper. A small brass chandelier
hangs from the ceiling and drapes are at the windows.

In the dining room there is a highly carved dining table and sideboard, a
1930's cupboard, and an antique maple and burl slant front bookcase, A
reproduction Webster wood stove sits beside an unusual plate warmer cabinet.
An oriental carpet is on the floor and a small chandelier hangs from the

ceiling. The room is papered in a Williamsburg Peacock patterned paper. Abby's mother's game set and a twelve-piece cannister set are on display.

Guests are served a hearty morning meal with many breakfast favorites. After fruit or juice there is bacon or sausage, fresh eggs and grits, pancakes or a baked treat of the day, and coffee, teas and milk. It is served between 7:00 a.m. and 9:00 a.m. in the kitchen or dining room.

Three guestrooms are on the second floor. The Blue Room faces east and provides the early riser with a panoramic sunrise and a view of the village of Kimmswick. It is furnished with an antique Eastlake full-size bed and matching marble top dresser. There is also a slant front desk with ball and claw feet, two oak arm chairs, an Eastlake upholstered platform rocker and a small antique immigrant chest. The room has a private bath with tub and shower.

The Brass Room is light and airy. It has an antique queen-size brass bed with an overhead canopy rail. A hobnail bedspread is quite old. There is an Empire sofa that make a good reading place, an antique wardrobe, a small writing desk, and a unique maple chest that is a family heirloom. There is a good view of the town from this room as well. A private or shared bath has tub and shower.

The Red Room is a bit smaller, but has its own porch overlooking the woods, which are home to many song birds. The room is furnished with an antique, full-size Eastlake bed, a barrister bookshelf, a 1920's low boy dresser, a child's wicker chair and an unusual Mexican ceramic stove. A wooden office chair has a throw made of old neckties. An elegant red glass kerosene chandelier hangs from the ceiling. Small throw rugs are on the original floors. The bath is shared with the Brass Room and is often offered when a family or group is traveling together.

WENOM-DRAKE HOUSE B & B: P.O. Box 1225, Kimmswick, 63053. Corner of Fourth and Beckett. (636) 464-1983. Open all year. A three guestroom historic house with private or shared bath. Children over five welcome. Smoking only on porches. No pets. Ken and Abby Peck, innkeepers.

DIRECTIONS: From I-55, take Kimmswick exit to the east. Proceed to Hwy. 61 and turn right. Go one block to Hwy. K. Left on K to Fourth. House is on the corner of Fourth and Beckett.

THE STUGA BED & BREAKFAST
Poplar Bluff

Beginning in 1850 and until after the turn of the century more than a million Swedish emigrants left their homeland to find a new life in America. Among them were the ancestors of Tonnie and Jim Moss who through the generations perpetuated and passed on the tastes, the interests, the customs and the traditions of their native Sweden. When Tonnie and Jim created their bed & breakfast their Swedish heritage was a prominent factor in its development.

In 1949 Tonnie made her first trip to Sweden traveling with her parents and grandparents. One of her great grandfathers lived in a small house next to the family home in Raneo in the province of Norbotten near the Arctic Circle. The little house was called a Stuga. Years later when Tonnie and Jim opened their bed and breakfast in the little cottage next to their home, The Stuga seemed a perfect name.

The original cottage was built in 1887 and consisted of two rooms at the front, a parlor and a bedroom, with an exterior entrance to each, and a kitchen and porch at the rear. At the turn of the century the kitchen was enlarged and the porch enclosed. Later the kitchen became the dining room and a new kitchen and another bedroom and bath were added while maintaining the architectural style and Scandinavian influence similar to thousands of others like it dotting the prairie landscape of the Upper Midwest.

You can experience a taste of Sweden at The Stuga. The entire house is yours to enjoy and you have that extra bedroom if you are traveling with children, relatives or friends.

The highly polished pine and cypress wood floors throughout The Stuga give it a clean and fresh look and emphasize the predominant use of wood furniture in all the rooms. The parlor with its oak rocking chairs, bench, desk, library table, hat rack and other furnishings all evoke the pure and simple elements of Swedish design. The white walls provide the backdrop for several prints by well-known Swedish artist Carl Larsson showing interior scenes of country homes in Sweden. An extensive library wall contains numerous books on Swedish history, customs, myths, provincial crafts and lots of childrens books and toys.

The dining room walls are of white board and batten with a plate rail that holds Tonnie's collection of colorful Swedish elves called Tomtes, along with Dala horses and other family treasures gathered on trips to Sweden.

One guestroom is furnished with a four piece matching cherry wood bedroom set which includes a full-size four poster bed, a dressing table, a chest and a side table. There is also an old Victrola with a hand crank. The polished cypress floor is covered with multicolored woven throw rugs typical of a tapestry picturing Stockholm, Sweden's capitol city.

The other bedroom is furnished with an 1800's four poster walnut bed, an antique chest in walnut and a night stand. This room also has throw rugs on the polished pine floor.

Your hosts, Tonnie and Jim, serve their guests a traditional Swedish breakfast starting with fresh juice and seasonal fruit, followed by those typically rich Swedish pancakes with hot melted butter, warm syrup, lingonberries, sausage and coffee, tea or milk. Breakfast can be served in the dining room or on the deck surrounded by dogwood, redbud and cedar trees. Guests may also prepare their evening meal in the fully equipped kitchen.

Bicycles stand ready for those inspired to tour the town under their own power. Guests may test their skills at a game of croquet or horseshoes on the back lawn. A nearby park has a measured hiking trail with exercise stations for the hearty.

THE STUGA B & B: 912 Nooney Street, Poplar Bluff, 63901. (573) 785-4085. A two bedroom guest cottage, just off the town's historic brick main street. Open all year. Children welcome. No pets. Smoking on patio or deck. Located just fifteen miles from Wappapello Lake for great fishing, swimming and boating. Tonnie and Jim Moss, innkeepers.

DIRECTIONS: From the north or south take Hwy. 67 into Poplar Bluff. From the east or west take Hwy. 60 to Hwy. 67 and go south to Poplar Bluff. Turn East on Maud, go 9 blocks to N. Main, then left on N. Main and one block to Nooney. Check in at 900 Nooney Street.

KLEIN HOUSE BED & BREAKFAST
Sikeston

You'll like the "at home" feeling of the Klein House. Built at the turn of the century by James and Margaret Klein, it was built using cypress they cut from their farm.

A huge magnolia tree (the largest I've ever seen) shades the wraparound front porch. A porch swing, cushioned green wicker chairs and a table is a good spot for enjoying coffee before breakfast. There's also a swing in the magnolia tree.

The entry hall has a tiled corner fireplace with a beautiful oak carved mantelpiece. The original oak staircase features 174 carved acorns. This is an unusual staircase. The hall has an antique oak parlor table, a library table, and a bookcase. A large gold leaf mirror is on the wall and a small crystal chandelier hangs from the ceiling.

To the right of the entry hall, a parlor is furnished with an upholstered sofa and matching love seat, a round coffee table, a cottage style rocking chair, a round lamp table with a reading lamp and a Queen Anne style desk and chair. For a taste of the old and new, there is a 1930's floor model radio and an entertainment center with a TV/VCR and a stereo with record albums and CDs. A large area carpet is on the floor, lace curtains at the bay windows and nice framed prints are on the white and silver striped papered walls.

Large French doors lead to the dining room. It is furnished with a mahogany double pedestal table and chairs, a large hutch, a Victorian parlor table and a server. An Oriental carpet is on the floor, white lace curtains at the bay window and the walls are papered in a burgundy and tan striped pattern. There are small antique pieces, old kerosene lamps, silver plate and pottery pieces.

A small sitting room at the top of the stairs has a reproduction Victorian loveseat, an antique oval library table that holds a 1920's portable Victrola. The room is filled with stuffed bears of all kinds. It's decorated with quilts, an early lace dress and other interesting items. The original brass chandelier is still here and area rugs are on the floors.

Camille's Room is furnished with an antique queen-size bed, a matching dresser and chest from the 1890s. There is also an upholstered sofa, an upholstered open armchair, a platform rocker, television, night table and a desk and chair. It has mauve wall-to-wall carpeting, white muslin curtains and wallpapered in a black and green design of small flowers. The woodwork is painted white. The large private bath has an antique washstand, a tub and shower.

The Rose Room, bright and sunny, has a queen-size 1930's bed, an antique dresser, antique chiffonier, an upholstered red arm chair, a wicker trunk, oak chest, rocking chair, two night tables with lamps, an oak music cabinet and a television. It is carpeted wall-to-wall with a green sculptured design carpet, has white Battenburg curtains and papered in dark green stripes with flowers and vines.

Upon arrival, guests are served cookies or brownies and lemonade or tea. Breakfast consists of several entrees. Either a cream cheese pastry and a skillet of eggs, bacon, cheese, green peppers, onions and mushrooms baked and served in a small skillet or waffles or pancakes, yogurt with whipped cream, hot fruit compote and coffee or tea.

KLEIN HOUSE B & B: 427 So. Kingshighway, Sikeston, 63801. (800) 884-2112, #69. Website: www.rosecity.net/sikeston/kleinbb/index.html. Open all year. MC and Visa. Smoking on porches. No pets. No children under six years old. Two guestrooms with private baths. Ken & Vicki Rubenacker, innkeepers.

DIRECTIONS: Call for directions.

STE. GENEVIEVE

O f all the French establishments in the Upper Mississippi Valley during the 1700s, none have retained their original character more than
Ste. Genevieve, the oldest permanent settlement in Missouri.

The exact date of the founding of Ste. Genevieve, "*le vieux village de
Ste. Genevieve,*" is not certain, but the year 1735 is generally agreed upon.
The old site was some three miles downstream from the present town, in
what was known as *le grand champ*, the big field. Most of the early settlers
were the French who came first to Canada and then to the Illinois Country.
The town served as a center for the development of the Upper Mississippi
Valley. After the Treaty of Paris in 1763, France ceded to England the lands
east of the Mississippi River. Many of the inhabitants at Kaskaskia fled to St.
Genevieve to avoid being under English rule. Among the early settlers to the
town were Francois Valle, Jean Baptist Valle, Sr., Parfait Dufour, Joseph
Bolduc, Nicholas Janis, and Vital Ste. Gemme Beauvais. Anglo-Americans
started to enter the region in small numbers from the eastern settlements
during the 1790s.

Since the earliest days, St. Genevieve at the *le grand champ* had been
troubled by the flooding of the Mississippi. Some of the residents started
relocating to a more secure spot just a few miles upriver to *les petites cotes*,
the little hills. Then in 1785, the old village of Ste. Genevieve was virtually
destroyed by a devastating floor. For almost two hundred years, that date has
been known as *l'anne des grande eaux*, the year of the great flood.

Many historic homes in St. Genevieve dating back to the 1770s have
been restored and furnished to afford glimpses into the past of the people in
Missouri's oldest settlement. There are seven homes open to the public, as
well as a museum and the old cemetery. The downtown area has been
designated a National Historical District.

The Amoureux House is one of the better landmarks. Built around 1770
by Jean Baptist Ste. Gemme, the house was occupied by Mathurin Amoureux
sometime after 1800. The home was supposedly moved from its original site
on *le grand champ* after the flood of 1785 to its present location. This structure
is the most primitive in Ste. Genevieve and represents one of the most
important examples of Creole houses left standing in the Mississippi Valley.
Next door there is a wonderful little country store furnished with store fixtures
over 100 years old. There is a large selection of quality merchandise including
handmade quilts, dolls, pewter pieces, candles, imported soap, potpourri,
napkins, baskets, hand woven place mats and other craft items.

The Bequette-Ribault House is the more nearly typical of early Ste.
Genevieve houses. It stands on the original site where it was built about the
year 1775 by Jean Baptiste Bequette.

The Bolduc House, built around 1770, was moved to its present site about 1784. It is now regarded as the most authentically restored Creole house in the nation. It has been restored and furnished with accurate detail. There is a stockade fence, frontier kitchen, living quarters, and an 18th century garden.

The Bolduc-LeMeilleur House was built by a grandson-in-law of Louis Bolduc in 1820. It is an interesting example of the combined influences of French and American architecture on local homes.

The Felix Valle House was built in 1818 and was occupied by Felix and Odile Pratte Valle as a residence and also served as the commercial offices for Felix's business interests in furs, lead and iron.

The Green Tree Tavern was built in 1791 by Francois Janis. Much of the hardware, woodwork, doors and mantels are original. After 1800, the house was converted into a tavern and boarding house. The original Green Tree Tavern sign may be seen in the Ste. Genevieve Museum.

The Guilbourd-Valle House was built in 1806 by a pioneer French settler. It is one of the most elegantly furnished museum houses in town. In the attic, a Norman truss and hand-hewn oak beams are secured by wooden pegs. Former slave quarters are on one side of the house.

The memorial cemetery is one of the picturesque sights in town. Many of the settlers who built the houses now named after them are buried here. Some headstones carry birth dates from the early 1700s.

As Missouri's oldest town, Ste. Genevieve is an antique treasure chest. Joel and Beverly Donze's *Odile's Line and Lace Shop*, located at 34 S. Third Street, is a great place to shop or browse and the owners are very pleasant people. The shop features vintage selections such as dresser scarfs, pillow coverings, tablecloths, napkins, exquisite handkerchiefs, collars, and doilies. Since I was here last, Beverly has added some new things to go along with the old. China, brass items, cameos, fans from Spain. Victorian silver and gold enameling, candlesticks and snuffers, frames of every-size and shape, a collection of furry cats and a line of Heritage lace including doilies, runners and mantlescarfs. (573) 883-2675.

Another interesting place to visit is the *Show Me Missouri Shop* located at 73 N. Main Street. It is open seven days a week and features the best of Missouri made products. There is a good selection of wines, Oberle, sausages and cheeses and Baron spices. Homemade jams, jellies and apple butter from Little Cedar Berry Farms, Thompson Farms and Centennial Farms. Plus pure maple syrup from sap tapped from hard maple trees in Ste. Genevieve County. Don't overlook the framed prints and pictures and the various books on Missouri. When I was here, Herb and Norma Fallert, the owners, pointed out some nice antique pieces: a burled knockdown walnut wardrobe, a ladies drop front writing desk, a newly upholstered sofa, a pre-Victorian sofa, a pie safe, an English oak server and an etagere. (573) 883-3096.

There are several restaurants in town that I would recommend. Judy and Rosie Schwartz's *Old Brick House Restaurant* at 3rd and Market is located in the oldest brick building west of the Mississippi River. There is plenty of history here to go along with plenty of good food. The menu features liver knifly, a German dish that is an area specialty. Other menu selections include fried chicken, roast beef, country steak and pork chops all served with vegetables and salad. There is also an all-you-can-eat buffet. (573) 883-2724.

Another good place to dine is Madeline Jett's *Anvil Saloon Restaurant* at 46 S. 3rd Street, right in the middle of the historic district. The building has been either a restaurant or a tavern since 1855 and still retains the original 150 year old bar and back bar. Maggie offers a full service menu. However, you can't go wrong with the great hamburgers with onion rings and don't miss her desserts. Homemade pies include the best coconut pie I ever ate, French apple ala mode and a tasty four layer chocolate pie. (573) 883-7323.

Ste. Genevieve is one of my favorite towns. I have been visiting here for over twenty years. A visit any time of the year is great; however, there are two special weekends. *Jour de Fete,* on the second full weekend in August and the Christmas Walk on the first full weekend in December are certainly worth anybody's time.

CAFÉ STE. GENEVIEVE
Ste. Genevieve

Built at the turn of the century, this building has always been a hotel, although the first floor, at one time housed shops. Now it houses the Café Ste. Genevieve, and had so for many years. Fourteen modernly furnished rooms are on the second floor.

Floor to ceiling windows, all around the first floor café, have lace curtains with green side drapes. A red and green floral carpet covers the floor. Huge brass chandeliers emit a soft glow and the paneled walls hold nicely framed prints. White tablecloths with green napkins and fresh flowers lend intimacy. Whether you are enjoying a full-course dinner or stopping in for lunch, you will find a hearty welcome in the "oldest permanent settlement west of the Mississippi River."

Open for breakfast at 7:30 a.m., you are offered a full menu.

The luncheon menu includes soup, salad and dessert. Sandwiches include Reuben, Corned Beef, and French dip. A daily plate lunch special is also available, as are catfish fillets on Friday.

The evening menu, besides steaks and chicken, offers beef liver, chicken fried cube steak. Pork chops and country ham. Fish entrees include frog legs, catfish, scallops, and a seafood platter. Each is served with a salad, choice of potato, homemade cheese cake and pie is also available.

Café Ste. Genevieve: Main and Merchant Streets. In the heart of the Historical District. May Inman host. Jacque Inman & Jamie Inman will serve you. Monday -Thursday 7:30 a.m. - 9:00 p.m.; Friday & Saturday 7:30 a.m. - 10:00 p.m.; Sunday 7:30 a.m. - 6:00 p.m.

ANNIE'S BED & BREAKFAST
Ste. Genevieve

There are probably more 18th century houses in Ste. Genevieve than in any town in the mid-west. Annie's B & B misses that distinction by just six years. The oldest portion of the house was built in 1805. The framework is hand hewn and held together by wooden pegs. The house rests on a stone sill twenty to thirty inches wide. In the basement there is a cooking fireplace with a beehive baking oven. The house still retains the original floors, and much of the glass in the original six over nine windows is the old handmade lead glass, some of which, bear the names of earlier occupants probably carved in with a diamond.

Off the entry, with an antique pie safe, the parlor has the original fireplace and original beamed ceiling. It is furnished with an upholstered floral camelback sofa, two upholstered wing chairs with a table and lamp between them, an antique, two door cupboard, and an antique table with two chairs. An antique bench is used as a coffee table. The room is decorated with large live plants and small antique pieces.

A real country kitchen has an antique oak claw foot table and four oak chairs that once belonged to Annie's grandmother. A circa 1920 buffet and a corner cupboard are also here. The floors, ceiling and fireplace are all original. A collection of cookware is on display.

A first floor guestroom, The Victorian Room, is decorated in pastel colors with muslin curtains at the windows. It is furnished with a queen-size iron bed, a pine chest and matching dresser, a blanket chest, night stands and an antique rocker. The fireplace is original. A large bath has a clawfoot tub and a walk-in shower.

At the top of the stairs, stenciled wallpaper is above a chair rail of beaded board paneling. One guestroom is on this floor.

On the second floor, The Blue Room is decorated in deep blues. It has a queen-size metal bed, a hard rock maple rocking chair, a wood and metal steamer trunk, and a two-door wardrobe. Ansel Adams framed photographs are on the off-white walls. A sitting room has an upholstered soda, a lamp table, and chair and desk, coffee table and a television. A large modern bath, decorated in soft pastels, has a walk-in shower and a deep, clawfoot tub.

Now, back to that country kitchen! Annie serves breakfast here, offering a full home made, all you can eat meal. There's juice, an in-season fruit cup, an egg dish, potato casserole, breakfast meat, or pancakes, waffles or French toast. Always coffee, tea, milk, homemade bread or muffins.

At 8:30 in the evening, Annie serves her guests either strawberry shortcake, a berry cobbler in fall and winter, pumpkin pie or bread pudding and complimentary wine. On arrival, there is a gift bag of candied popcorn in your room and a hot drink in winter and a cold drink for summer.

In the back of the house, there are flower and vegetable gardens, a patio, and among the trees there is a large magnolia. By the way, this is the oldest surviving frame house in Ste. Genevieve that was built by an American. It has cedar siding trimmed in green and tan.

ANNIE'S B & B: 207 South Main Street, Ste. Genevieve, 63670. (573) 883-2001. Open all year. Non-smoking facility. Sorry no pets. Ask about children. Within walking distance to six historical properties. Annie and Fred Fellion, innkeepers.

DIRECTIONS: At the intersection of St. Mary's Road and South Main Street.

CREOLE HOUSE BED & BREAKFAST
Ste. Genevieve

R oyce and Marge Wilhauk's Creole House graces 2.5 acres in the historic district of Ste. Genevieve. It was patterned after an early French home and overlooks the Grand Champ or big field.

The tile foyer with heirloom grandfather clock and area carpet leads into an open expanse comprising living room, dining room, and library. The living room fireplace, flanked by two green wing chairs, faces a floral love seat and sofa. Near this conversation grouping, marble topped tables hold books about the early French settlement of Ste. Genevieve. An 1850 square grand piano on the far wall holds a collection of archaeological finds, some handed down from Marge's grandfather. Exceptionally nice paintings and two vintage quilts made by Marge's great grandmother grace the walls and complement the plush carpet.

The dining room suite is hand carved oak in a Jacobean design. An eight light brass chandelier hangs over the table from which guests can view Chef Royce preparing the gourmet breakfast. The adjacent library, with another large table and chairs, doubles as extra dining space or can be used for games, puzzles or pouring over the hundreds of books in the well stocked bookcase. The antique post office desk is used at check-in and checkout time.

The Marcel Suite on the first floor is furnished with a queen-size four poster bed and matching end tables with reading lamps. A fireplace in the bedroom glows with warmth on cool nights. The adjoining private sitting room has a love seat, desk and chairs and features a double jacuzzi bath tub, inviting long, relaxing soaks. Cable TV and a private bath with shower completes the setting.

The Antionette Room with its peaches and cream color scheme has a queen-size bed with white coverlet and a misty white netting floating from a circlet of ivy. A pair of wing chairs flank an antique round table with a reading lamp, a love seat invites lounging, while watching the Cable TV. Nice paintings and floral arrangements are part of the decor. French doors lead to a side gallery. The dressing area has two large oval gilt mirrors with a marble top dressing table and sink. In the private bath is a Jacuzzi tub and separate shower.

From the foyer, an enclosed stairway leads to two large suites. The Bequette Suite can sleep four. It has a king-size poster bed, two dressing tables, love seat and tables with reading lamps, and also has two twin beds. The adjoining private sitting room has a fireplace, sofa, lamp tables, drop-leaf table for games or puzzles, a bookcase and cable TV. The spacious private bath has shower and tub.

The Ribeau Room also sleeps four. It is furnished with a pine queen-size sleigh bed and a set of brass twin beds. It also has four comfortable chairs, a dresser, bookcase, a table for games and puzzles and cable TV. The private bath is just across the hall so robes are furnished for guests' convenience.

A generous full gourmet breakfast is served in the dining room. Royce does all the cooking and prepares several elaborate entrees. For instance, Eggs Marcel consists of hard-boiled eggs on toast covered with a seasoned cheese sauce and topped with asparagus spears and a dash of paprika. All entrees are served bacon, ham or sausage or a combination of each and begin with fresh fruit in season and juice.

The South Galerie now overlooks a 16' x 32' heated swimming pool that is enclosed for year-round use. Chairs and tables on the galerie invite guests to enjoy the lush green plants and palms surrounding the pool.

CREOLE HOUSE B & B: 339 St. Mary's Road, Ste. Genevieve, 63670. (573) 883-7171. (800) 275-6041 for reservations. Open all year. During special events a two-day minimum may be required. Smoking only on gallery. Fax available. Royce and Marge Wilhauk, innkeepers.

DIRECTIONS: From Hwy. 61 and 32, take 61 south to St. Mary's Road. (about 1 mile) Turn left on St. Mary's Road and go 1/2 mile to Creole House.

DR. HERTICH HOUSE
Ste. Genevieve

Built in 1850, by Dr. Charles Hertich, this house stands as it was when first built. The house is a white frame with green shutters. (All original) A long porch goes across most of the house. A brick walk leads to a side garden area. A huge tree, well over a hundred years old shades the yard. An old time picket fence is across the front.

There are four spectacular two room suites plus a guestroom. The four suites are all extra large, measuring approximately 19 x 27 each. They are all furnished with a small refrigerator, coffeemaker, blow dryer, fireplace, coffeemaker, and a television. Each of the suites also have a small table and two chairs if you would like to have breakfast in your room. The four suites all have private baths with double jacuzzis.

Entering the house, you are in a long hallway with burgundy wall-to-wall carpeting and up to the staircase. A Queen Anne writing desk and lamp are in the space under the stairs. At the end of the hall the Doctor's Room has blue wall-to-wall carpets, white lace curtains with blue swags are at the windows. The walls are blue grey. It is furnished with a queen-size sleigh bed and a chevall mirror. The private bath has a tub and shower.

To the left of the entry, the Ste. Genevieve Suite is furnished with a white king-size wrought iron tester bed, a chevall mirror, brass floor lamp and a pair of bedside tables with lamps. Two bar stools act as bedside tables with lamps. The room has a jade green sculptured wall-to-wall carpet. Lace curtains with sheer drapes are on the three windows. It is wallpapered in a green and tan pattern. A sitting room has an upholstered Queen Anne style love seat, an end table with a reading lamp and a floor lamp.

To the right of the entry, The Family Ties Suite is furnished with a king-size bed with a burgundy crocheted coverlet. There are also night tables with lamps, a chevall mirror, floor lamp and an upholstered bench. The room is wallpapered in a gold, pink, and green stripe paper. Lace curtains with a valence that matches the bed coverlet are at the windows. A floral patterned wall-to-wall carpet is on the floor and continues into the sitting room, furnished with an upholstered love seat.

When you go up the stairs to the second floor, you walk down a hall to the front of the house. A telephone is on a window seat for guests convenience.

To the left is the Love Notes Suite. It has a king-size brass bed with white bed linens. As in the other guestrooms, there are a pair of bedside tables, each with a glass lamp. A chevall mirror, brass floor lamp and an upholstered bench are part of the furnishings. A burgundy wall-to-wall carpet is on the floor. The walls are wallpapered in a dark burgundy stripe pattern. Lace curtains with swags are at the windows. The sitting room has an upholstered love seat, floor lamp and an end table.

To the right is the Good Sport's Suite. It is furnished with a king-size poster bed with a plaid coverlet, a brass floor lamp, chevall mirror, night tables and an upholstered bench. Plaid drapes matching the bed coverlet are over lace curtains on three windows. The sitting room has an upholstered love seat and an antique table. The suite is decorated with sports memorabilia.

Breakfast is served across the street at the Inn St. Gemme Beauvais between 8 and 10 a.m. However, if you wish, you may have it served to you in your suite. Just let Janet, the innkeeper, know in advance.

Between 2-3 in the afternoon, high tea is served at the inn and between 5-6 in the evening, hor d'oeuvres are served, also at the inn.

DR. HERTICH HOUSE B & B: North Main Street, Ste. Genevieve, 63670. (573) 883-5744. Or, 1 (800) 818-5744 for reservations. Open all year.

INN ST. GEMME BEAUVAIS
Ste. Genevieve

The Inn St. Gemme Beauvais is the oldest continuously operating inn in Missouri and before I knew what a bed and breakfast was, it was one of my favorite places. The long time owners of the inn, Norbert and Frankye Donze, were dear friends and I visited them often. My grandson Nick accompanied me here at least once a month to have "absolutely the best" sherried peach trifle, a specialty made by the innkeeper, Janet Joggerst.

The history of the inn dates back to the 1840s when Felix Rozier purchased property on Main Street and built this three story brick colonial mansion with walls eighteen inches thick. The venerable old house has withstood nature's elements for over 150 years and is as sound as ever.

Entering the front hall from a broad veranda, its roof supported by six tall pillars, you get an immediate sense of tranquility. It is wallpapered in a bright crewel design, which continues up the walls of the original staircase leading to the guestrooms on the second and third floor. The floors are covered with green and white area rugs. A solid green carpet is on the staircase. An ornate four-armed brass chandelier dated 1849 hangs in the entry. Two huge pictures in the hallway were donated by the Donze children in memory of their parents, who have recently passed away.

Just off the hall is the office, which has a six drawer spool cabinet serving as the registration desk. An old post office box holds the room keys.

The first thing you notice about the dining room is the antique, elegant crystal chandelier imported from Florence, Italy. A burning fireplace with a carved marble mantle adds a cozy touch on a wintry day. There are nine tables graced with linens and fresh flowers. By the way, the restaurant is available for private luncheons or dinners for eight or more if reservations are made four days in advance.

A full French breakfast is served from 8 a.m. to 9:30 a.m. Janet prepares breakfast to order, with five entrees to choose from: ham and cheese filled crepes, quiche Lorraine, Belgium waffles with fruit topping, oatmeal pancakes, or the newest treat: stuffed French toast. Choice of fruit juice, coffee or tea, fresh fruit, apple-raisin oatmeal, and a variety of tea breads are also served.

Guest accommodations include suites and two third floor rooms. Just opened, The Carriage House, is something to behold a small building just behind the inn renovated into a beautiful suite. There is a small kitchenette completely furnished including coffee, soda and a welcome basket. The large bath has two walls of exposed brick and two walls are elegantly papered. The highlight is a large Jacuzzi. A large guestroom has wall-to-wall carpeting, two walls of exposed brick and two walls are papered in a floral design. A great gas log corner fireplace, live plants and dried florals, and great framed prints make this a most delightful room. It is furnished with a king-size, carved four poster rice bed, a pair of Georgian style night tables with crystal lamps, a television, and a white upholstered chair on either side of a lamp table. French doors open onto a small privacy fenced patio with wrought iron furniture.

Off the entry hall, The Currier and Ives Suite is furnished with a queen-size antique, Jenny Lind bed, two antique rush seated chairs and a table, and a spool leg vanity. A collection of Currier and Ives plates are on the wall over the bed. A private bath has a tub and shower. A sitting room has an upholstered sofa and love seat, a leather wing chair, antique hall tree, coffee and end tables. Lace curtains with floral swags at the windows overlook Main Street and the inn's newly planted and landscaped garden.

Another available guestroom in the first floor is just down the hall, called "Wings" because of the angelic décor. In this room, a fainting couch opposes the antique secretary, concealing a television in its upper cabinet. The two double beds are graced with matching floral comforters. The navy and gold overtones throughout the room accent the rooms theme. The free standing corner shower has an adjustable massaging showerhead.

At the top of the stairs the Governor's Suite has a sitting room furnished with a plaid sofa and love seat, a Martha Washington arm chair, an antique lamp table with a reading lamp and an entertainment center that holds a television. A burgundy carpet is on the floor. English prints are on the walls. The bedroom is furnished with a pair of identical Eastlake full-size beds covered with handmade quilts. It has a wash stand, built-in bookcases, an antique dresser and a table and chairs. The walls are papered in a green and mauve stripe paper. The private bath has a Jacuzzi, tub and shower.

The Forever Summer Suite is furnished with a king-size bed and white wicker furniture throughout. The walls have a blue and white striped pattern and blue carpet is on the floor. Mini blinds and lace panels are topped with blue and white balloon valances. The bathroom is quite large and a major highlight to this romantic suite. It boasts of a double whirlpool, a free standing shower, and its sink is actually placed inside an antique dresser.

I have stayed several times in the Garden Suite. It's a nice big room that has a queen-size, high back carved bed with a matching dresser, two antique night tables with lamps, an antique writing desk and chair and an antique wash stand. The walls are paneled and painted white below the chair rail and have pink and white striped wallpaper above. Green carpeting is on the floor. A sitting room has a pair of upholstered chairs and a table with reading lamp. There is also a television. The bath has a shower.

The Memories Suite's sitting room is furnished with a large 1920's, three piece sofa with wood trim, a rocking chair and an arm chair done in plaid fabric. A television is tucked away in a 1930's radio cabinet. There is a writing desk and chair. The bedroom has an antique high back bed and a marble top nightstand with reading lamp. The private bath has a shower. Both this suite and the Garden Suite overlook Main Street.

Two cozy guestrooms are under the eaves on the third floor. The Hunter's Glen Room is fully carpeted and has a queen-size bed. The sitting area has a love seat and coffee table, which faces a television set. The wallpaper reflects the room's image with partridge and hunt scenes. The private bath has a shower.

Grandma's Attic has a queen-size bed, a love seat and coffee table in a little cove nearby. There's also a small round table with two antique chairs, a dresser, and an antique treadle sewing machine. The private bath has a shower.

Many years ago, a tavern was located in the cellar, but more recently it has been used for storage. Today it is a nice conference room, and also able to be used as a small hall for parties, showers, and reunions.

Inn St. Gemme Beauvais has received the Three Diamonds Award for outstanding service from AAA. It was also awarded the Golden Star Award for hospitality and service from Innstyle, Inc. The Inn, in return, has given Janet Jaggerst an award for fifteen years of outstanding service.

INN ST. GEMME BEAUVAIS: 78 North Main Street, Ste. Genevieve, 63670. (573) 883-5744 or (800) 818-5744 for reservations. Open all year. An eight guestroom/suites inn located in the heart of the historical district. Children welcome. No pets. No smoking. Mark and Connie Smith, owners. Janet Joggerst, innkeeper.

DIRECTIONS: Take I-55 and exit at Hwy. 32. Go east about 5 miles to Ste. Genevieve. Turn right onto Market St., and left onto Main Street.

SOMEWHERE INN TIME BED & BREAKFAST
Ste. Genevieve

One would think, looking at this house from the street, it is one of the many houses built in Ste. Genevieve between the 1830's and the 1880's. Not so! This two-story award-winning Colonial home was built in the 1920's. It is located in the heart of the Historical District.

Mary Beth and Jim Ferguson, owners and innkeepers are eager to show you their home and the way they have updated everything to coincide with running the inn. The house won the 1996 St. Louis Post Dispatch Interior Design Contest.

The most used room is undoubtedly the large common room, a new addition. One full wall is of floor to ceiling windows. A French door leads to a large deck with plenty of seating. The deck, in turn, overlooks an in-ground swimming pool. A hot tub is off to one side of the yard. There are lots of plants and flowers. A brick wall surrounds the rear of the house for total privacy. Inside the common room, shiny hardwood floors have area carpets. One wall has bookcases and display cases. Two windows with window seats and four windows have lace swags over blinds. Original watercolor paintings are on the walls. The room is furnished with an upholstered rattan sofa, a matching love seat, a matching armchair in a yellow and blue stripe, and a rattan coffee table. Also a 1920's coffee table, two carved Victorian upholstered parlor chairs, a large oak hutch, a tall ice cream table and three chairs and an antique Aeolian Graduola (Victrola).

The entry hall has a breakfront, and church pew and a library table. Aeolian Graduola. A wide staircase leads to the second floor. Off the entry, the dining room has the original plate rail and white woodwork. The walls are green and the windows have swags over mini blinds. The ceiling is paneled. It is furnished with a small drop leaf table and two chairs, a dining table with four oak chairs and four various antique chairs.

A first floor guestroom, the Grand room, is furnished with a queen-size iron and brass bed with a floral bedspread, a short poster twin bed for a third person, a chest and a floor lamp. There is a brick fireplace. The finished, bare floors have area carpets, lace curtains are at the four windows and live plants and pictures decorate the room. A door leads to a large sunroom that has been made into a bathroom. It has an upholstered sofa and a floor lamp. There is a whirlpool tub. Three walls have windows with mini blinds and lace curtains. One wall has a floral design wallpaper and the other three are lavender color.

At the landing going to the second floor, you go up two steps and go to the front of the house to Elise's Room. It has a full-size carved bed, a vanity, a night table and a child's antique rocker. It has wall-to-wall lavender carpet and teal colored walls. Curtains and floral swags are over blinds at the windows. A room-size private bath has a whirlpool tub. It also has an upholstered fainting couch and a barley twist mirror stand. Three windows have lace curtains and floral swags over blinds.

Richard's Room, on the second floor, is furnished with a circa 1900 full-size bed, a matching vanity, a sofa table, television, corner mirror, an end table and lamp and an upholstered, carved chair. It has green wall-to-wall carpet, deep lavender walls and white woodwork. Three windows have lace curtains and swags over blinds.

In the back yard, the original carriage house, now Arthur's Cottage is located next to the swimming pool. It has a private bath with a shower, refrigerator, sink and coffee maker. Decorated in a nautical theme it is furnished with a queen-size wrought iron bed, a plaid upholstered recliner, a 1930's dresser, a barley twist, a cane back open arm chair, a table and lamp for reading and a wardrobe. There is a green print wall-to-wall carpet, café curtains over blinds on two windows and live plants. One wall has a painting of the Grand Hotel on Mackinac Island.

From 5:30 to 6:30 p.m., hors d'oeuvres, wine and soft drinks are served, and at bedtime there is homemade desserts and gourmet coffee. In the morning coffee and breakfast bread is served at 8:00 a.m. before breakfast.

Breakfast consists of juice, fruit and an entrée special: apple lasan and sausage from the famous local meat market or banana and strawberry stuffed French Toast or quiche. Jams and jellies, coffee, tea and milk.

SOMEWHERE INN TIME B & B: 383 Jefferson Street, Ste. Genevieve, 63670. (573) 883-9397. Toll free: 1 (888) 883-9397 for reservations. A three guestroom and cottage with private baths and hot tubs. Mary Beth and Jim Ferguson, innkeepers. Aspiring innkeeper, Jamie Ferguson.

DIRECTIONS: From I-55, take exit 150 (Hwy. 32). Go East (left) on Hwy. 32 about 5 miles. Hwy. 32 becomes 4th St. Stay on 4th St. to Jefferson. Turn right. Inn is on the left.

SOUTHERN HOTEL BED & BREAKFAST INN
Ste. Genevieve

L isted on the National Register of Historic Places, the Southern Hotel was built in 1795. It was opened in 1805 and was soon famous as the finest hotel between St. Louis and Natchez before and during the riverboat era. It was known for its elegant accommodations, fine food, best gambling rooms and other "niceties" of the day. It also had the first pool room west of the Mississippi River.

After years of improper use, the federal style structure was closed in 1980. It stood vacant until 1986 when Mike and Barbara Hankins bought it. They completely renovated the building bringing it back to its original state. It is once again functioning as it did so many years ago.

As you enter the front door, you are in a large hallway with a huge brass chandelier and the original staircase leading to the second floor. A display case contains a large collection of old photos and lots of other memorabilia pertaining to past events and the history of the hotel.

To the left in what was once the saloon in the early days, is now the Salon Room, a place where guests can meet and relax over a glass of wine. It is a most comfortable room with dark green wallpaper above original wainscoting. The wooden ceiling is original as is the fireplace, where on cold days a cozy fire is kept burning. An oriental carpet softens the new floor put down in 1860. Wing chairs are the only new pieces of furniture. The rest of the room is furnished with antiques.

The dining room also retains the original wainscoting. The walls above are papered in a bright crewel design. Antique prints and a plate collection hang on the walls. A double pedestal table and Georgian chairs seat eight guests, while a drop leaf table accommodates eight more.

Breakfast, served in the dining room, consists of juice, croissants with honey butter and jam, fresh fruit, an egg dish in several varieties, and coffee or tea. Barbara grinds all of her own coffee.

A parlor to the right of the entry hall has a fireplace and the original plank floors are covered with an oriental carpet. A five piece antique Victorian parlor set, an antique harmonium (still works), a baby grand piano, an antique library table and an unusual cupboard will catch your eye. A large quilt for guests to sign before it is quilted and hung in a guestroom is an interesting feature. Several have been completed already.

The old billiard room is back, complete with an antique pool table, card table and an old juke box.

There are eight guestrooms at the Southern Hotel. Four are on the second floor and all have private baths and fireplaces. The four rooms on the third floor have dormer windows and private baths. Each room contains a collection of country Victorian antiques and "whimsies."

The Buttons and Bows Room, used as the honeymoon suite, contains a circa 1775 high-back half tester bed, an 1830 carved and burled armoire, an antique fainting couch, an immigrant's chest and a pair of Victorian upholstered chairs. The antique button collection is most unusual.

In the Cabbage Rose Room there is an antique full-size bed that has a highly carved headboard, an antique wardrobe, wash stand and a wishbone dresser. A comfortable sitting area has a three piece Victorian parlor set. Oriental throw rugs are on the floors and there are house plants and pictures as part of the decor.

The Japonisme Room has an oriental motif with an unusual handmade, iron canopy full-size bed. There is a love seat, and antique wardrobe and a great collection of soapstone is on display. An oriental carpet covers the floor.

The Gentlemen's Room has a king-size, pine tester bed that has a lace canopy. There is an antique jelly cupboard, a circa 1820 linen press, an upholstered chair and an antique rocking chair. Area carpets are on the floor.

Twenty-four handmade antique quilts are displayed in the Quilt Room, some of which belonged to Barbara's great, great grandmother. The room is furnished with an antique four poster Lincoln bed, a pair of upholstered chairs and an antique pie safe which holds linens and towels.

Paul's Purple Room has an antique full-size brass bed with ivy patterned bed linens. There are two upholstered chairs, an antique dresser, lamp table and an oriental carpet. Barbara did the complicated stencilling on the walls.

A very unusual room is the Wysockis Room, named after the famous American folk artist. A chest is done in decoupage with his prints and the headboard of the bed has his American Scenes made into a 3-D wooden village. There is also a love seat and an ottoman.

Lulabelle's Room contains dolls and toys, some dating back to Barbara's childhood (not that long ago). An antique bed, a child's wardrobe, a wooden trunk are part of the furnishings. Two rolltop desks, acting as night stands belonged to Barbara and her sister when they were children.

At the rear of the inn is a wonderful garden. People come from all over to walk through it. I know Barbara worked long and hard to get it just the way she wanted it. There are seating arrangements, antique pieces placed at just the right spots and many beautiful flower beds that can all be viewed by taking a stroll on the brick walk around the grounds.

To top all of this off, a summer kitchen was turned into the Southern Hotel Garden Shop. There are all kinds of interesting gifts to be had, including original oil paintings by Dolly DuFour, (isn't that a great name?) who is one of the nicest people I've met in a long time. There are all kinds of garden accessories, imported nut crackers, cookbooks, garden signs on tile and just a lot of great things. Be sure you check this out. It's well worth the time.

SOUTHERN HOTEL B & B INN: 146 South Third Street, Ste. Genevieve, 63670. (573) 883-3493. Open all year. An eight guestroom inn featuring fine accommodations in a 200 year old landmark. Private baths. Near all historic attractions and dining. Right in the heart of town. Mike and Barbara Hankins, innkeepers.

DIRECTIONS: From St. Louis, go south on I-55 approximately 60 miles to Ste. Genevieve. Exit at Hwy. 32. Go Left on Hwy. 32 about 5 miles to town. Hotel is at corner of Third and Market Streets.

STEIGER HAUS BED & BREAKFAST
Ste. Genevieve

Located on what used to be the "old plank road," the Steiger house was built in 1882 by John Steiger, a prosperous farmer. The large brick home, sitting on a 80 acre farm of rolling hills just outside the city limits of Ste. Genevieve, was quite a showplace at the time it was built. Today, it is in the center of town.

The present owner, Rob Beckerman, told me his mother used to buy their milk and cream at this house. Rob, a member of an 11th generation Ste. Genevieve family, has completely renovated this house retaining all its historic character. On the grounds, an old weathered barn now houses a 16 x 35 foot swimming pool. The loft area contains a rest room and a dressing room. A nice patio and garden are just outside the barn.

At least six times a month, Steiger Haus plays host to a murder mystery party. Guests are sent information prior to their arrival. They become suspects once they do arrive. The mystery takes place from one afternoon or evening until the next morning. Sometime during this period, a murder is committed. It is then up to the guests to solve the crime. Dinner and breakfast are included in the mystery package.

Breakfast is served in the dining room that is furnished with an antique dining suite and a bookcase overflowing with Missouri Historical Reviews, an excellent publication on Missouri history. Breakfast consists of either crepes, blackberry pancakes, French toast, or ham, bacon or sausage with eggs prepared as you wish. There is juice and coffee or tea.

There are two suites on the first floor. Anton's Suite is furnished with a high-back oak bed, an antique armoire and an oak dresser. The sitting room has a fireplace and a television. A sofa makes into a full-size bed. There is also an antique desk and a floor lamp. The room has original painted floors. There is a private bath with tub and shower.

The second first floor suite, Rose's Suite, has an antique full-size brass bed and an oak dresser. The sitting room has an antique full-size iron bed and a day bed. There is also a television, and an antique music stand. This room also has a private bath with shower.

A large, bright hallway on the second floor has the original beaded ceilings. Antique prints and pictures are on the walls. Off the hall is Rob's library housing over 2,000 books including many on Missouri history and very heavy on genealogy. Guests are welcome to use the library.

To the left of the staircase, Josephine's Suite has a queen-size bed, an oak chest and an antique desk which was found on Rob's great grandfather's farm. The sitting room has a full-size antique iron bed, a sofa and a television. The suite has a private bath with tub and shower.

The John George's Suite is furnished with a queen-size wrought iron poster bed with a tester, an antique armoire and an upholstered chair. The second room in the suite has a full-size bed, a 1920s sideboard and a television. A private bath with tub and shower separates the two rooms. This suite may be rented to two or four persons traveling together.

Rob also has a small cottage that was built in 1865 and is located on Main Street in Ste. Genevieve's historic district. Called the John Hael Gasthaus, it has a sitting room, dining room, bedroom and bath on the ground floor. An additional bedroom is located on the second floor. The first floor bedroom has a queen-size bed and telephone with free local calls. The dining room contains a coffee maker with all the fixings and small refrigerator. The second floor bedroom has two twins beds. It is furnished with a changing selection of antiques, as most of the furnishings are available for sale to the guests.

STEIGER HAUS B & B: 1021 Market Street, Ste. Genevieve, 63670. (573) 883-5881. E-mail: steiger-haus@msn.com. A century-plus brick farm house a few blocks from the historical section with four suites. Open all year. Children welcome. Smoking only on porches and patio. No pets. Rob Beckerman, owner.

DIRECTIONS: From I-55, exit at Hwy. 32 (exit 150). Go east about four miles to Hwy. 61. Turn left on 61 proceed to Market street. Right on Market to Steiger Haus.

STEIGER HAUS DOWNTOWN BED & BREAKFAST
Ste. Genevieve

The house that sat on this property from the early 1800s, burned down, probably around 1910, leaving only a summer kitchen, which is now part of this house which was built in the 1920's. Rob Beckerman, the owner of the Steiger Haus B & B at 1021 Market, purchased this house. After renovating the property, he has opened it as a bed and breakfast.

Built of brick, the house is fairly large and has a nice porch across the entire front. Shrubs and flowers have been planted and by next year the grounds should be in good shape.

Rob also features murder mystery parties here as he does at his other location. They have become very popular throughout the entire country.

Entering the house, you are in the living room, furnished with a pair of Queen Anne sofas upholstered in a floral tapestry fabric, an upholstered wing chair of the same material, a marble top plant stand, a floor lamp and end tables. The walls are painted in a plum color, offsetting the white woodwork. There is an area carpet on the floor. The windows have white lace curtains with swags. A copper chandelier hangs from the ceiling.

An arched doorway leads to the dining to the dining room which has a green tile fireplace surrounded with an oak mantelpiece. It is furnished with three antiques reproduction double pedestal tables, each with reproduction high back chairs. The walls are painted green and the woodwork white. There is a large bay window with lace curtains and swags.

A staircase in the living room leads to the two second floor suites. The West Suite, with blue walls and gray painted floors, has a full-size iron bed, an antique walnut armoire and a pair of White Wicker chairs. The woodwork has been left natural. Floral drapes are at the windows. A second bedroom is furnished with a queen-size black and gold bed. The walls are painted green. There is a private bath with a tub and shower, The floor is black and white tile. One wall is of exposed brick.

The East Suite features a queen-size wrought iron tester bed, a cushioned rattan and wicker love seat and a rattan table. The second bedroom has a full-size antique iron bed and an upholstered wing chair. The room still has the original paneled ceiling. Both rooms have floral drapes at the windows. The private bath has the original claw foot tub, but a shower has been added.

On the third floor, grandma's Attic Suite, under the eaves has a full-size bed that rests in an alcove and a steamer trunk. Items that you would probably find in a grandma's house are on display. It has a full-size bed. At the front of the suite, overlooking Merchant Street, a small sitting area has a pair of wicker chairs. A private bath with exposed brick walls has a whirlpool bath.

Back on the first floor, the original 1800s summer kitchen has been incorporated with the rest of the house. But still remaining are the original beamed ceilings. It has two guestrooms. Both have queen-size wrought iron beds. One room has the original 12 over 12 paned windows and a very rustic door that opens to a garden. A small sitting area has a pair of upholstered chairs. The private bath has a two person jacuzzi tub. An outside door is a private entrance and also leads to the dining room. The suite also has a door entering into the main house.

Breakfast is served in the dining room and consists of either blackberry pancakes, crepes, French toast or eggs prepared as you want them with ham, sausage or bacon. There is always juice, coffee or tea.

Off the entry, Rob has a small gift shop.

STEIGER HAUS DOWNTOWN B & B: Market Street, Ste. Genevieve, 63670. (573) 883-5881. Open all year. In the downtown section and the middle of the historic area. No smoking. No pets. Rob Beckerman, owner.

DIRECTIONS: From I-55 exit at Highway 32 (Exit 150) Go East about 5 miles, Cross Highway 61 which becomes Fourth Street. Turn right on Merchant Street to Second Street. Turn left and go one block to Market. Turn left to Steiger Haus, Downtown.

Section Four

ST. LOUIS
REGION

A. Lafayette House B & B
  Lehmann House B & B
  Napoleon's Retreat B & B

B. Geandaugh House B & B

C. Fleur de Lis B & B

D. Cheshire Lodge

E. Seven Gables Inn

F. Eastlake Inn

G. Gables B & B

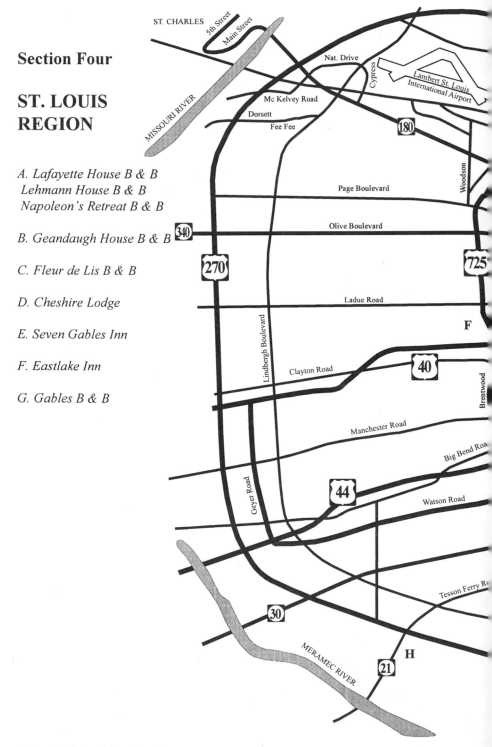

S t. Louis, "Gateway to the West," is a city steeped in tradition. Founded by the French fur traders from New Orleans in 1764, only two years after France ceded Louisiana to Spain, St. Louis slowly grew to be a center of French culture in the Upper Mississippi Valley. From 1770 to 1800, the growing city, whose population was 1,000 in 1800, was the seat of Spain's government for upper Louisiana. However, in 1802 Spain returned the Louisiana Territory to France. The next year the United States bought it. Thus, in 1803 St. Louis became an American city.

A proud heritage has not been forgotten, and the historical landmarks tracing the colorful past are intermingled with soaring new buildings, providing a tasteful blending of the old and the new.

St. Louis is truly a "river city." Nowhere else in the world do two rivers of such magnitude as the Mississippi and the Missouri join. And nowhere else along these two rivers will you find as much on-the-waterfront activity to fill your days and nights with fun.

Many of the city's attractions are on the Mississippi levee within the shadow of the Gateway Arch. The Arch itself, keystone of the Jefferson National Expansion Memorial, has become the fourth most visited attraction in the world. A ride to the top in the special capsule elevators offers a spectacular view of the metropolitan area. Underground, the Museum of Western Expansion is free and open year round.

The cobblestone waterfront has restaurants in old and new riverboats. Visitors walking along the levee may observe the old moorings rings still embedded in weather worn cobblestones once trod upon by hard-working stevedores. Nearby, is historic Laclede's Landing with its nine blocks of shops, restaurants, and night spots housed in restored buildings dating from 1830. The area is one of the downtown's biggest attractions. Other waterfront landmarks are the Old Courthouse, built in 1836, which was the scene of the Dred Scott Trial prior to the Civil War, and the Old Cathedral, dating back to 1834. It is the oldest Cathedral west of the Mississippi River. Both of these places contain fascinating museums and should not be missed.

At Busch Memorial Stadium where the baseball Cardinals play their games, you can tour the St. Louis Hall of Fame, which is located here.

For the history buff, there are numerous landmarks and fully restored homes tracing the city's past from the frontier days through the elegant Victorian period. Easily accessible to the downtown area is the Eugene Field House, home of the children's poet. Other restored homes in the city are the

Campbell, Bissel, DeMenil, Shaw, Hanley, Sappington, and the Taille de Noyer. They reflect the variety of architectural styles that have become a part of St. Louis.

Historic buildings in St. Louis serve as more than just showcases of the past. Beautiful Powell Hall is home of the world renowned St. Louis Symphony. The massive Cathedral of St. Louis, one of the largest churches in the Western Hemisphere, is both a religious center and the site of colorful Byzantine mosaics that draw travelers from all over the world.

Parks and greenery help make a city liveable, and St. Louis has plenty of both. Forest Park, one of America's largest city parks, has bike trails, lakes and many large shade trees to contrast with the city skyline. You can easily fill several days visiting this park. You'll want to spend a day at the Zoo, with 83 acres of award-winning animal habitats. Then there is the Jewel Box floral conservatory and the newly expanded and renovated St. Louis Science Center. Don't miss the Art Museum, originally the art building for the 1904 St. Louis World's Fair. Collections housed here span 5,000 years of culture. The Missouri Historical Society Museum highlights Charles Lindbergh, and includes military and river exhibits. There is also the Municipal Theatre offering 10 weeks of polished outdoor musical productions.

Tower Grove Park with walking paths, a band shell for summer concerts, and picnic pavilions is walking distance from the Missouri Botanical Garden—a National Historic Landmark with more than 70 acres of carefully tended greenery, an indoor rain forest at the Climatron, and American's largest Japanese Garden.

A drawing card for many visitors is the city's many museums. Among them the recently renovated National Museum of Transport, displaying locomotives, buses and other vehicles. There is also the Magic House with hands-on activities for children, and the Wax Museum. At the Jefferson Barracks Historical Park, a former military post dating back to 1826, are two museums as well as several recreation areas.

The home of the world's largest brewer, Anheuser-Busch, is open year round for free tours. Another Busch attraction is Grant's Farm with a game preserve, U.S. Grant's cabin and the famous Clydesdale horses.

Each with their own distinctive flavor, Laclede's Landing, Lafayette Square, the Central West End and Soulard are some of the old neighborhoods that have been restored and now offer shopping, dining and entertainment.

CHESHIRE LODGE
St. Louis

A touch of England in the heart of St. Louis! Cheshire Lodge is a truly remarkable retreat that reflects the rich essence of royal appeal, where you can imagine yourself a privileged guest in a grand Tudor countryside estate.

You enter the world of Old English charm and elegance in the splendid main lobby with the warm glow of the natural fireplace. Like a typical old English hostelry, the Cheshire Lodge is resplendent with rich antiques, detailed dark oak woodwork, brilliant stained glass, and beautiful artwork and tapestries.

The Fox and Hounds Pub, just off the lobby, provides a magical transformation to the exciting days of the chase. Prints of the hunt, winding horns, and the wily fox cast a romantic spell by the soft light of a flickering gaslight and stone hearth. The pubs traditional offerings, such as the half-yard of English beer, spicy sausages, and cheese cellar delights make it a favorite retreat. The drink mixologist, Mark Pollman, has been a friend of mine for over twenty years. I'm sure you will enjoy his unique brand of humor. And for your listening pleasure there is the piano music and vocals of Bill Benson, a fixture here for the last thirty years.

The Lodge's recently redecorated and remodeled guestrooms are graciously appointed with exquisite antiques and authentic, stout period furnishings. Each is distinctively decorated and offers the utmost in comfort and luxury. Rooms of various types and sizes have been designed to accommodate business travelers, vacationers and families.

A typical king studio room contains a king-size bed, wing chairs, a writing desk, a wardrobe which holds a television, and a sofa that opens into a full-size bed. The windows are small leaded glass panes with colorful drapes at them. The floors are carpeted. Each room has a private bath with shower.

There are several king canopy rooms, each with a huge tester bed, wing chairs, desk and television.

The regular double rooms have two queen-size poster beds, wing chairs, desk and television. All of the rooms are fully carpeted and have beautiful antique prints on the walls.

You can even indulge your fantasies and pamper yourself with a romantic getaway in any one of the intimate Fantasy Suites. The Ultimate Bathe Suite, The Captain's Quarters Suite, The Safari Rain Forest Suite, The Treehouse in Sherwood Forest Suite, and The Raj Suite feature jacuzzis. The Rain Forest Suite even has the jacuzzi surrounded by an artificial forest. The Captain's Quarters also has a fireplace. A great way to celebrate any special occasion.

Breakfast is not included in the room rate. However, Monday through Friday, a complimentary Continental breakfast of juice, coffee and Danish is served in the Cock and Bear Room just off the lobby. If you prefer, you may visit the Cheshire's traditional and elegant dining room, which features their famous Buffet Brunch on Sunday mornings.

In the evenings, from Spring to Fall, the large English garden is open and offers appetizers, wine and beer. Guests at the Cheshire can treat themselves to a swim in the beautiful Canterbury Court outdoor pool.

CHESHIRE LODGE: 6300 Clayton Road, St. Louis 63117. (314) 647-7300 or (800) 325-7378. An exceptional 106 room, Old English style inn. Centrally located and just minutes from the Gateway Arch, Union Station, Busch Stadium, St. Louis Zoo and Art Museum. Children Welcome. No pets. Smoking Permitted. Stephan J. Apted, owner. Tony Bon Aoun, manager.

DIRECTIONS: From Downtown St. Louis, take Hwy. 64/40 west and exit at Clayton Road. The Lodge is just one block after this exit. From I-270 take Hwy. 64/40 east to Belleview. Turn left and go to Clayton Road. Right on Clayton Road two blocks to the Lodge.

EASTLAKE INN
St. Louis area/Kirkwood

Kirkwood, one of St. Louis' first suburbs, was mainly a community of large Victorian homes built for the wealthy as country dwellings. The Eastlake Inn is found at the center of the oldest portion of town. Featured in "Better Homes and Gardens Magazine," in 1983, it is a charming two story frame home on a large lot full of huge 100 year old catalpa, dogwood and holly trees. There is a perennial garden and two patios all surrounded by tall hedges. A brick walk leads from the off-street parking to the front door.

The entry hall has a stenciled Williamsburg pattern on an oak hardwood floor and contains an antique treadle sewing machine and an Eastlake mirror. Arches on either side lead to the living room and dining room. A chess set from England sets in front of the east window for guests to enjoy.

The fully carpeted living room has a wood-burning fireplace. It is furnished with an overstuffed love seat, an upholstered recliner rocker, a walnut armoire, an antique Eastlake wash stand and a Victorian love seat. An unusual cabinet holds Lori Murray's collections of dolls and china. There is a very nice hanging wall cupboard which holds additional dolls and a collection of antique bears.

Off the living room, a sunroom offers a quiet place for guests to gather for old-fashioned board games, curl up with a good book or join in conversation with other guests.

In front of a window in the dining room are a 1920s cottage table and two chair set painted in blue. The walls have English paneling to the chair rail, the mantle is walnut, and an oriental rug covers the floor. Furnishings include an oak pedestal table with six matching chairs, a server, a cherry Eastlake china cupboard and an antique jam cupboard. The room is lighted by a chandelier made in Portugal of 1,129 separate pieces. A door opens to a screened-in porch with a pair of wrought iron chairs and a table. A pleasant spot for early coffee, breakfast or just relaxing, weather permitting.

The stairs leading to the second floor are natural wood with a stenciled design on the risers.

On the second floor are three guestrooms decorated with paintings and craft items made by Lori. Each room has a private bath. The Magnolia Room's window overlooks a large magnolia tree, hence the name. The room has an antique Eastlake chest on chest and matching marble top dresser. The queen-size four poster bed is covered by a magnolia pattern bedspread. A wrought iron floor lamp and an upholstered armchair are in a small alcove in front of a window with pink cottage curtains. An Eastlake table serves as a nightstand. There is also an antique school desk and a treadle sewing machine.

Across the hall is the small, cozy Sunset Room. It is furnished with a full-size antique white iron bed, an Eastlake dresser with glove boxes and candle stands and a 1920s upholstered Signoret arm chair and 1920s night stand. The windows, covered with colored striped curtains that match the area rug, get the late evening sun. A natural vine ceiling border circles the room.

The Garden Room at the front of the house overlooks the large yard with garden and patio. It has an antique full-size Eastlake bed with matching dresser, a nightstand and a small antique oil stove used for decoration only. Lace curtains are at the windows. The walls are painted blue and have a border in a colonial design. An Eastlake writing desk is placed at the window overlooking the garden.

Breakfast is served at 8:00 a.m. in the dining room, in the sunroom or in summer on the patio. Lori varies her breakfast entrees, which include ham, and green pepper omelet, scrambled eggs with roasted potatoes, stuffed French toast, whole-wheat pancakes, French toast, souffle, or cheesy breakfast burritos. Breakfast always includes juice, coffee, tea or milk

With advance notice Lori will pick guests up at the Amtrak station in Kirkwood.

EASTLAKE INN: 703 N. Kirkwood Road, Kirkwood, 63122. (314) 965-0066. Open all year. A three guestroom inn with private baths. Close to fine restaurants, antique shops and boutiques. No smoking. No children under 12. No pets. Website: www.eastlakeinn.com. Lori and Dean Murray, innkeepers.

DIRECTIONS: Located on the northwest corner of Kirkwood Road and Jewel Avenue.

FLEUR-DE-LYS INN
St. Louis

This stately Tudor-style home is a haven for both the business traveler and perfect for a romantic getaway. Completely restored, the Fleur-de-Lys Inn is something very special: leaded glass, marble walls, hand-crafted woodwork and other turn-of-the-century architectural treasures.

You enter into the reception hall which is paneled chair rail high with quarter-sawn oak. There is a large, carved breakfront. Carpeted stairs lead to the four second floor guestrooms.

To the right of the entry hall, the front parlor, with its coved ceilings, has a rich burgundy carpet. It is furnished with a slant front secretary bookcase, a grandfather clock and a tripod table. An upholstered camel back sofa and two upholstered arm chairs face a fireplace. A small crystal chandelier hangs from the ceiling. There are silk flower arrangements, plants and framed prints.

A wide doorway from the parlor leads to a great library. An oriental rug is over the wall-to-wall carpeting. There is a tufted leather sofa and two comfortable upholstered wing chairs, a large ottoman and an antique English pub table that holds a chess set. A large cabinet holds a television and an extensive book collection is in the built-in bookcase. A magnificent brass chandelier hangs from the ceiling, blinds are over the two large windows.

Across the hallway, a large dining room with hunter green walls and a crystal chandelier is furnished with a double pedestal table with six Chippendale style chairs and two upholstered chairs. There is a matching breakfast and hunt board and a pair of Queen Anne low boys with brass lamps.

In what would have been a second front parlor, there is now a dining area. It is furnished with a drop leaf table with three Queen Anne chairs and a round table with four lyre-back chairs. There is a fireplace and a large area carpet. On the walls are two large framed prints.

The guestrooms are named in honor of St. Louis' stately parks. Each one is fitted with direct dial telephones, fax and modem lines and cable TV.

The Tower Grove Park Suite is named for the Victorian walking park located just a few blocks from the inn. The suite is 500 square feet and contains an enormous Victorian mansion bed, a matching armoire and a wash stand. There is also a Victorian fainting couch, an upholstered rattan love seat and a Queen Anne writing desk. Designer fabrics in ivory damask are used in window treatments, bed coverings and upholstery. An oriental carpet is on the floor. The huge windows have blinds and swags. A jacuzzi for two and a separate shower are in the suite's bath.

The Forest Park Suite is furnished with a king-size wrought iron bed with green and red bed linens, an antique upholstered Lincoln rocker, an antique wooden steamer trunk, writing table, a pair of night tables with reading lamps and an entertainment center. The suite features a double whirlpool tub.

The Reservoir Park Room is named for the historic park and water tower that it's bay window overlooks. This room features a queen-size, carved four poster plantation bed, a pair of round night tables with reading lamps, a mirrored armoire, a small low boy, an upholstered open arm chair, and a writing desk. It is carpeted wall to wall. Designer bed linens and homey decorations make this a charming room. There is a bath with a shower.

The Botanical Garden Room also overlooks Reservoir Park. In its bay window are two white wicker chairs and a large upholstered pouf ottoman for relaxing. It features a full-size, partially canopied antique walnut bed with a featherbed comforter. An antique chifferobe holds a television. Botanical prints are on the pale yellow walls. The bath has a shower.

Upon arrival, Kathryn serves coffee, tea and homemade cookies. Her breakfast consists of an early buffet of a selection of two juices, fresh fruit in season, homemade granola, yogurt, fresh baked muffins and coffee cappuccino. Then an egg souffle, Belgium waffles or German style pancakes with fresh fruit and a side meat dish.

FLEUR-DE-LYS INN: 35 Russell Blvd., St. Louis, 63104. (314) 773-3500. 1 (888) 969-3500 for reservations. A two suite and two guestroom with private baths. Off street parking. Major credit cards. No smoking except patio, balcony or the cigar porch. No pets. Kathryn Leep and Daniel Sills, innkeepers.

DIRECTIONS: Located in the historic South grand neighborhood at Grand and Russell.

THE GABLES BED & BREAKFAST
St. Louis

Located in "Old Town" of Historic section of Ferguson, the Gables B & B is a seven Gable English Tudor style home that is surrounded by trees and shrubs. An area at the back of the house has a wonderful garden with a fish pond, flowers, bird baths a gazebo, B-B-Q, large trees and other greenery. As John and Claudine DuRall, the owners, walked through the garden with me, I thought how peaceful and relaxing it was.

A shaded walk up steps leads to the front entrance. The living room is carpeted wall to wall in a pale green carpet. It is furnished with a green upholstered Camel back sofa, end tables with lamps, a piano and a broken pediment slant front secretary. There is also a floral upholstered wing chair, an ornate grandfather clock and a pair of Jacobean arm chairs. A fireplace has bookcases on either side of it. Small antiques and mementos of the DuRall's travels will certainly hold your attention. The room has pale green drapes over sheer curtains and the walls are nicely decorated with framed prints, pictures and a banjo clock.

An arch leads to the dining room that is fully carpeted. A nine piece mahogany dining suite has a table with a pair of tripod legs, a credenza, a china cupboard and six shield back chairs. A corner cabinet holds Claudine's collection of Precious Moments porcelain along with their 50th anniversary mementos. The walls are papered with a pale green and white damask pattern paper. There are framed pictures of the walls. French doors open into a cozy sun room furnished with a wrought iron, glass top table and six chairs and a wrought iron love seat. There is a green carpet on the floor and three windows in the room have blinds and overlook the trees and shrubs.

A hall from the living room leads to a gray and white tiled bathroom with a vanity and a tub and shower. In the hall there is an antique library table with an antique banquet lamp. Lots of nice prints on the walls.

Three guestrooms are off the hall. One is carpeted in a pale lavender carpet. It is wall papered in a Victorian pattern wallpaper and matching window treatment. It is furnished with a six piece washed pine suite that includes a full-size bed, dream chest and night stands. There is an antique doll house on display.

Another guestroom is furnished with a black lacquer four piece bedroom suite. There is a full-size bed dresser, chest, cedar chest and a white leather chair. Japanese prints are on the walls papered with a grass woven wallpaper. The room is carpeted and had drapes over shades.

The third guestroom is a two-room suite. The sitting room has an upholstered love seat, ladies desk, chair and television. French doors lead to the bedroom that has a French Provincial queen-size bed, dresser, and chair. A striped wallpaper is on the walls and curtains and drapes are at the windows. Both rooms have a light gold carpet.

Claudine serves a full breakfast consisting of juice, fruit, sausage and eggs, potatoes and sausage gravy, coffee cake and coffee, tea or milk. If you are not a big eater, a Continental plus breakfast includes orange juice, a fruit cup, homemade coffee cake and coffee tea or milk.

Upon arrival the DuRall's offer homemade cranberry, banana or pumpkin bread and coffee.

THE GABLES B & B: 404 Darst Road, Ferguson, 63135. (314) 521-2080. A two room suite and two guestrooms. Four miles from Lambert St. Louis International Airport. No smoking or pets. No children. John and Claudine DuRall, innkeepers.

DIRECTIONS: From I-270, exit 28 on the Washington/Elizabeth exit. Go south on Elizabeth approximately 2 miles to Darst, turn right and go 1 block to Darst and Clay. Driveway is on Clay. From I-70, exit on 240 at New Florissant Road. Go approximately 2 miles and turn right on Darst.

GEANDAUGH HOUSE, A CHRISTIAN BED & BREAKFAST
St. Louis

It has been said the Geandaugh House was, at one time, an inn for travelers during the opening of the West. Known as the "Prairie House," the small story and a-half home supposedly dates back to the 1790s. The Federal style brick addition was added in the early 1800s. Falling into ruins and scheduled to be demolished, the house was rescued in 1985 by Gea and Wayne Popp. Restored and with a new lease on life, it once more welcomes travelers.

To the right of the entry hall, in the 1800's addition, a parlor is furnished with a French provincial sofa and two upholstered chairs, a mission style rocking chair, coffee and end tables and a very unusual secretary desk that displays a collection of pottery barbershop buildings. There is an antique hanging lamp and an antique wall clock. White curtains set off the blue walls.

The dining room has a fireplace, an antique marble top sideboard, a large oak table and chairs and a great court cupboard. Note the original floors and the huge oak cabinet that was used in a pharmacy shop.

Gea serves a full country breakfast starting off with juice and fruit followed by eggs, sausage, gravy and pancakes. Or, if a lighter meal is more to your liking, a continental breakfast of juice, fruit and cereal is available. With either choice there is always homemade breads, biscuits, muffins and coffeecake along with jams, jellies, coffee, tea or milk.

Next to the dining room is the Grandmother's room furnished with an antique full-size iron bed, a birch dresser, and antique trunk and a mahogany wardrobe. Antique pieces include an oil lamp and a mantel clock. The room is decorated with dusty rose walls, handmade quilts and "mother pictures." A private bath has a curtained claw foot tub with shower.

From the front hallway in the older part of the house, you climb the original staircase to three guestrooms. Plump embroidered pillows and Irish lace curtains welcome you to Lady Elizabeth's Room in the front of the house. Named for the Countess of Cerai, on the Isle of Gurnsey, who was the first owner of the land where the early portion of the house was built, it has light green walls trimmed in saffron yellow. The three piece turn of the century oak furniture features a pineapple motif, on the 6-foot bedstead, a wash stand with towel bar and a matching dresser with mirror. An armchair, an antique metal floor lamp, and an initialed cedar chest complete the picture. The water closet, partitioned with wooden folding doors, and the sink and screened claw foot tub are in the room.

The Amor Room is named for the family that owned the property for over seventy years. The father, a merchant from France had three daughters who grew up in this house. Spacious and airy, the room is furnished with a 1930's bedroom set which includes a queen-size bed, dresser and chest of drawers. There is also a cedar chest and an upholstered chair with a floor lamp. The room has a private bath similar to the Lady Elizabeth Room.

The Preacher's Room reflects on Wayne Popp's life as a pastor. Browse through the many religious books, with a little Ellery Queen thrown in. It is furnished with maple twin beds, a chest, a pair of rush seated, ladder back chairs, an antique trunk and a bookcase. A private bath with claw foot tub and shower is just outside the door.

Wayne is adding a huge indoor patio in the back of the house. He has a brick floor laid and has put in the large skylights and windows. It should be ready to enjoy later this year. He is also installing a commercial kitchen in this area.

GEANDAUGH HOUSE B & B: 3835-37 S. Broadway, St. Louis, 63118. (314) 771-5447. Open all year. Four guestrooms with private baths. No pets. No smoking in house. Children welcome. Gea and Wayne Popp, hosts.

DIRECTIONS: Call for reservations and directions.

LAFAYETTE HOUSE BED & BREAKFAST
St. Louis

Lafayette Park, the city's first park, was established in 1836 on land that was once the city commons. The area became quite fashionable in the 1850s, and wealthy citizens were building their huge mansions on the street facing the park. This particular house was built by James B. Eads, builder of the Eads bridge, for his daughter, Margaret, as a wedding present. It is a 14 room brick, Queen Anne Victorian mansion built with the finest materials available. Walnut woodwork, 14 foot ceilings, large rooms with fireplaces and a beautifully carved walnut staircase are just a few of the amenities.

Lafayette House is owned and operated by Annalise Millet. It is St. Louis' oldest and largest bed and breakfast, established in 1986.

In the entrance hall, the carved walnut staircase, mantel and woodwork are all original. A huge living room has a fireplace, plenty of comfortable seating, books and magazines galore.

The pastry chef, Annalise, will treat you to a full breakfast with juice, fresh fruit, homemade breads, puff pastry, muffins and blueberry gingerbread. There are always jams and jellies, coffee, tea or milk. Various entrees are served which may include crab stuffed quiche, Belgian waffles with warm blueberry compote, fresh peach stuffed french toast, bacon and egg strada, blintzes, and omelets. It's all served in the large well furnished dining room at the mahogany Duncan Phyfe table capable of seating twelve guests.

There are four bedrooms on the second floor and a large lounge area with a television and a refrigerator for soft drinks.

The Lafayette Room is the most popular guestroom. It is a large airy room fully carpeted and still retaining the original speaking tube and old style brass fixtures. It has among the furnishings a large four poster bed. There is a private bath with tub and shower.

The Angel Room is bright and cheerful room with a beautiful view of sunsets. It has a four poster bed. The Morning Room with a queen-size bed, patchwork quilt, and marble mantel make this room a great place to wake up and start your day.

The Eads Room is furnished with a wrought iron bed with a Battenberg lace canopy, an Empire style dresser and a sofa. One wall is exposed brick. These three guestrooms share a large bathroom with tub and shower.

On the third floor is a four room suite with private bath that accommodates six to eight persons. It has a large bedroom, a sleeping and a reading alcove, a large living room with television, and a kitchen with refrigerator, sink and an apartment-size stove.

The Victorian Room is as romantic as it's name implies. Originally the library, this room has been transformed into a cozy getaway. A queen-size bed piled high with pillows beacons you to relax after your day, but before you close your eyes be sure to slip into the oversized jacuzzi.

LAFAYETTE HOUSE B & B: 2156 Lafayette Ave., St. Louis, 63104. (314) 772-4429, (800) 641-8965. Website: http://www.bbonline.com/mo/Lafayette. A four guestroom and a four room suite with both private and shared baths in an 1876 historically significant Queen Anne mansion overlooking Lafayette Park and the historic district. Full breakfast served. Children welcome. No pets. Minutes away from downtown St. Louis, antique shops, dining and popular attractions. Anna Millet, innkeeper.

DIRECTIONS: From the north, take I-70 east through downtown to I-44 west. Exit at Jefferson. Go right one block to Lafayette and right on Lafayette on block to house. From the west, take I-44 to Jefferson. Left one block to Lafayette, then right one block. From west on 40/61 go east to Jefferson. Right about 1 mile to Lafayette. Left one block to house.

JAMIE L. MºILROY© 93

LEHMANN HOUSE BED & BREAKFAST
St. Louis

B y the mid-1860s, Lafayette Square had become the most prestigious residential area in St. Louis. In 1866, Benton Place, named for Thomas Hart Benton, (now the oldest private street in the city,) was established. Number 10 Benton Place was originally built for Edward Rowse, a wealthy financier. However, it is remembered as the residence of the second owners, Frederick and Nora Lehmann, who resided at #10 Benton Place for thirty-one years.

After Mr. Lehmann's death, it passed through many hands and was in a sad state of disrepair when Marie and Michael Davies rescued it in 1992. Hoping to return it to its original splendor, the Davies have put in many hours on the still ongoing restoration of the 20 room Romanesque Revival mansion they now call home. Careful restoration of the oak, maple and cherry woodwork is ongoing and successful uncovering of the original Anaglypta wallpaper in the dining room is complete.

The extra large foyer has a huge brick fireplace. There are a pair of Victorian arm chairs and a table. In an alcove is a 1920's carved sideboard.

The parlor, to the right of the entry, has an onyx fireplace with a cherry mantle. There is a five piece Victorian parlor set, an English chest, an Empire secretary, drop-leaf work table and a three tier table. An oriental area carpet is on the floor. A turret off the parlor has a baby grand piano, two plant stands and an oriental carpet.

Anyone would enjoy breakfast in this dining room. The English oak paneled walls, beamed ceiling, huge fireplace and the built-in buffet look as they did one hundred years ago. A seven piece, highly carved dining set is right at home here, along with the crystal chandelier. Three windows overlook the side yard, which is graced with many trees and shrubs.

Across the hall from the dining room is the paneled library with a great wood-burning fireplace. The walls are lined with glass enclosed bookcases. In the middle of the room is a Victorian game table and two Victorian chairs.

Moving through the foyer with its Tiffany-style glass windows and up the grand staircase to the second floor, you will find three guestrooms off the wide hall. The Sun Room at the front of the house has a queen-size bed that sports a Laura Ashley spread, a marble top lamp table, a unique walnut dresser, a rocking chair and occasional tables. The fireplace mantel is solid cherry.

The President's Room with its wood-burning fireplace and golden maple flooring is furnished with a king-size brass headboard bed, a Chippendale style mahogany chest, a love seat, Boston rocker and an antique table used as a night stand. There is a private bath.

The Maid's Room, furnished much as it would have been when two maids occupied it, has a full-size iron bed, barley twist dresser, oak chest, two night tables with reading lamps and an upholstered arm chair. A gray wall-to-wall carpet is on the floor, lace curtains and drapes at the windows.

The World's Fair Room is so named to honor Frederick Lehmann's efforts in helping to bring the 1904 World's Fair to St. Louis. This sunny inviting room with its Victorian floral wallpaper overlooks the expansive yard and garden adjoining the house. It is furnished with a queen size brass bed, a wicker side chair, an upholstered arm chair that folds out into a twin bed, an oak chest of drawers, an oak armoire and a Victorian Eastlake dresser. Lace curtains are at the windows, and a plum color wall-to-wall carpet is on the floor. There is also a fireplace (for show only). The bath is shared.

On the third floor is the Map Room, which has a gas fireplace. The room is furnished with a four-poster mahogany tester bed with canopy, a Queen Anne style high boy, vanity, an Empire chest and a pair of wicker chairs with table. There is a private bath.

The Davies plan to open a two-room suite with a private bath in late spring or summer of 2000.

Guests can savor a varied breakfast of fresh fruit, home baked breads and enticing egg dishes with breakfast meats. Cereal, toast and jam are available and there is piping hot coffee and tea, fruit juice and milk.

LEHMANN HOUSE B & B: #10 Benton Place, St. Louis, 63104. (314) 231-6724. A 20 room 19th century mansion. Four guestrooms. Open all year. No pets. No smoking. Children welcome. Marie and Michael Davies, innkeepers.

DIRECTIONS: Exit onto Jefferson from either Hwy. 40/64 or I-44. Turn right off 40 or left from I-44 and go to Park Avenue. Go left from 40, or right from 44. Take Park to Benton on your left.

NAPOLEON'S RETREAT
St. Louis

Designated St. Louis' first historic district, Lafayette Square boasts the largest collection of Victorian-era architecture in the nation. In 1997, the neighborhood was chosen by Better Homes & Gardens and Architecture Magazines as one of the "ten prettiest painted places" in the country. A "walk & gawk" tour through Lafayette Park, the oldest city park west of the Mississippi, or along a narrow side street is always a must.

Napoleon I was consul of the French republic in 1803 when the Louisiana Territory was sold to the United States. In 1815, he "retreated" from the battle of Waterloo (hence the name of the inn).

Entering the house through huge, ornate doors, you are in a small hallway with oriental area rugs, a small antique table and house plants. A walnut staircase leads to the upstairs guestrooms.

To the right of the hall, a parlor, with pale yellow walls, yellow drapes, and a brass chandelier is furnished with a camel back sofa upholstered in burgundy stripe, a pair of barrel back chairs upholstered in blue and a French Provincial arm chair, an English tea table and Federal style end tables.

Pass through large pocket doors and you are in the formal dining room furnished with an antique oak Belgian sideboard, a small hunt board with a silver tea service and a French country pine dining table and chairs. An antique banjo clock hangs on the wall along with an antique gold-leaf mirror.

Four guestrooms and a carriage house suite, all with private baths, cable TV, private telephones, robes and fine soaps and shampoos are available, each furnished with period antiques and reproduction pieces.

The second floor Burgundy Room has burgundy walls, stenciled fleur-de-lys and white woodwork. The large windows have mini blinds with ecru waterfall-style drapes, and the floor has beautiful lattice-design carpeting. There is a 1920's tapestry on one wall. The room has a queen-size half tester bed, an antique marble-top bow chest, ornate Napoleonic-style mirror, wing back chair and writing desk.

The second floor Lafayette Room is furnished with a queen-size spindle headboard, a pair of glass top night tables with glass lamps, two wing chairs with coffee table, an antique Empire dresser and walnut writing desk. Victorian green walls, wall-to-wall carpeting and white curtains with gold swags compliment the five large windows.

On the third floor, the Napoleon Suite, nearly forty feet long, has a three-piece matching antique bedroom set, queen-size bed and writing desk. The sitting area offers a cozy setting with sofa, two chairs, coffee table and wet bar with refrigerator. The room has dark teal-green wall-to-wall carpeting and sponge-painted teal and soft green walls.

Off the New Orleans style courtyard, the Carriage House suite offers an intimate sitting room with dining area, kitchen and bath on the first floor. The second floor has a loft bedroom which looks down onto the living room area. A balcony off the bedroom overlooks the garden. The furniture, including a queen-size bed, are wrought iron. A large antique walnut desk is in the bedroom area. Large prints of French advertisements from the early 1900s accent the 18 foot ceilings. The bath has a shower/tub combination.

The Garden Room, also off the garden courtyard, offers complete privacy and relaxation. French Moroccan green with striped curtains offers a tranquil setting. A handpainted mural over the queen-size bed adds a unique background to this very romantic room. The furniture includes a wing chair, writing desk and armoire. The large bath has an oversized spa tub and shower.

A full breakfast is provided in the dining room or during the spring and summer, the courtyard. House blend coffee, juice, muffins and breads and seasonal fruit is served each morning, along with a main entrée such as Belgian waffles, French toast, quiche or omelets. Lemon scones are a specialty of the inn. Reservations a must!

NAPOLEON'S RETREAT B & B: 1815 Lafayette Avenue, Historic Lafayette Square, St. Louis, 63104. (800) 700-9980 or (314) 772-6979. A circa 1880 Second French Empire Victorian townhouse with four guestrooms and a carriage house suite, all with private baths. Open all year. Children over ten welcome. No pets or smoking inside. Jeff Archuleta and Michael Lance, proprietors.

DIRECTIONS: From Hwy. 40/I-64 eastbound, exit at Jefferson. Go south to Lafayette (4th traffic light). Turn left. Inn is one black past the park. From the airport, take I-170 south to 40/I-64. From Illinois, take I-55 south to I-44 west to Jefferson Ave. Turn right and then right on Lafayette. From the south, take I-55 north to the Lafayette St. exit, then left on Lafayette two blocks.

SEVEN GABLES INN
St. Louis /Clayton

Inspired by Nathaniel Hawthorne's novel, *The House of the Seven Gables*, a St. Louis architect designed this structure in the early 1900s as two separate apartment buildings with offices and shops on the ground floor. The two buildings had an open walkway between them. For almost 80 years, the buildings have stood here in the heart of Clayton, St. Louis County's administrative center.

In 1986, after a complete renovation, the buildings have been transformed into the Sterling Hotels and Resorts that offers every modern amenity with hospitality reminiscent of a traditional European style country inn. The inn has been designated a National Historic Landmark. It is also a member of the Paris based Relais & Chateaux, a select group of the world's finest small hotels and restaurants.

Entering the building, you will find there is no formal lobby. A wide hallway, that was the outside walkway, which joined the two buildings, acts as such. The hallway is furnished with several antique pieces. Nice vintage prints and paintings are on the walls. At the end of the hallway is a pleasant sitting area with chairs and a writing desk. Large bay windows look out over a garden courtyard which is enclosed by a high lattice work fence on all sides. One of the focal points of the inn, the courtyard has a brick floor, European style street lights, black wrought iron furniture, and beautiful flowers and shrubs including an old mulberry tree.

The guestrooms on the second and third floors are reached by climbing a winding staircase and walking through thickly carpeted halls with antique pictures, engravings, and brass lighting on the walls.

Guestrooms overlooking the courtyard are called Garden Court rooms, while other tucked away under the eaves and gables are called Gable rooms. These come in a variety of shapes and sizes with alcoves, nooks and crannies.

The Old World atmosphere is prevalent throughout the inn offering the quiet elegance of another place and time. Each of the 32 graciously appointed guestrooms are different, but all are furnished in authentic European country style. They are decorated with imported Louis XVI style furnishings and art. Televisions are hidden away in period armoires. All have state of the art phone systems. Private baths are stocked with exclusive imported toiletries.

The guestrooms all have either king or queen-size beds. Some are antique French sleigh beds, others are antique brass or reproductions. Each room has writing desks, upholstered wing back chairs and ottoman, dressers or chests and other antique pieces. Rooms are fully carpeted, have plush comforters, and display antique prints and pictures on the walls. There are also two apartments available.

Dining is one of the highlights of Seven Gables. There are two restaurants on the first floor off the lobby. Gourmet dining is in the tradition of the grand hotels of Europe. The dining room is a formal, yet intimate French restaurant with a nationally renowned reputation for its excellent food and eminent wine cellar. Jackie's is an informal, turn of the century French Bistro serving light and full meals at breakfast, lunch and dinner. From May through October, the landscaped Garden Court is open for lunch among the flowers and dinner under the stars. A full room service menu is also available.

Breakfast is not included in the room rate. However, Seven Gables does offer a special weekend package which includes breakfast among other amenities.

SEVEN GABLES INN: 26 N. Meramec Ave., Clayton, 63105. (314) 863-8400. A 32 room European style hotel featuring two fine gourmet restaurants. Breakfast, lunch and dinner are served to the public. Open year round. No pets. Children welcome. Dennis Fennedy, manager.

DIRECTIONS: The inn is located on Meramec between Maryland and Forsythe. From I-70 or I-270 up north, exit on Hwy. 170 south and go to Ladue Road. East on Ladue to Meramec. Right to inn. From I-270 south of I-70 exit at Hwy. 40/61 east. Exit at Brentwood. Go north to Forsythe, Turn right to Meremac. From downtown take 40/61 to Hanley. North on Hanley to Forsythe. West to Meramec. Right to inn.

Section Five

MISSOURI'S WINE VALLEY

Augusta

Ashley's Rose B & B
Augusta Wine Country Inn
Clay House B & B
Lindenhof B & B
Old Town Augusta Inn
Quarry House B & B

Beaufort

Wild Wind Farm

Hermann

Angels in the Attic
Aunt Flora's
Birk's Gast Haus
Captain Wohlt
Drei Madelhaus
Esther's Ausblik
Hermann Hill
　Vineyard & Inn

Kolbe Guest House
Little Log Cabin
Market Street B & B
Meyer's Hilltop Farm
Nestle Inn B & B
Patty Kerr Gasthaus
Pelze Nichol Haus
Reiff House B & B
Strassner Suites

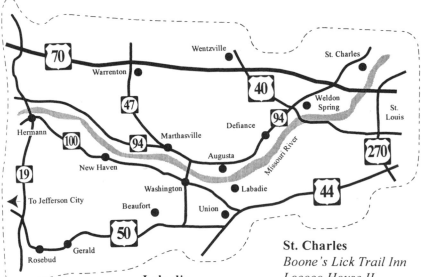

St. Charles

Boone's Lick Trail Inn
Lococo House II
The Geery's B & B
Mueller's B & B
Old Elm Tree Inn

Labadie

Hunter's Hollow B & B
Staats B & B

Defiance

Das Gast Nadler Haus
Parson's House B & B

Femme Osage

Femme Osage House

Gerald

Bluebird B & B

Marthasville

Concord Hill B & B
Gramma's House B & B
Little House B & B
Windhomme Hill B & B

New Haven

Senate Grove B & B

Washington

Du Bourg B & B
La Dolce Vita B & B
Schwegmann House
Washington House B & B
Weirick Hoelscher Estates

If you enjoy quaint river towns, spectacular scenery, great restaurants and antique shops, Missouri wines, history and tranquility, by all means make reservations at a bed and breakfast and plan to spend a couple of days exploring the Missouri Wine Valley Region. For a free Missouri River Wine Country Directory/Calendar of events, call (636) 239-2715.

The region is bounded by I-70 on the north, I-44/Highway 50 on the south, Highway 19 on the west, and I-270 on the east. Two highways dissect the area: 94 from St. Charles and 100 from St. Louis.

This is my favorite area of Missouri, and Highway 94 is my favorite highway. It stretches 140 miles from the Mississippi River to Jefferson City using the Missouri River as a guide. It is a winding, twisting, hilly road. One moment you are high up in the hills thick with hickory, oak, and cedar forests with unbelievable views of the rolling countryside. The next finds you in a peaceful valley, just a stone's throw from the Missouri River.

The road is a window to the pastoral Rhine Valley that early German settlers found so much like their Fatherland. Along the road are small towns, quiet and peaceful, each having its own red brick or white frame church and adjoining cemetery. Augusta, Defiance, Dutzow, Case and Marthasville. Century-old farmhouses, freshly painted with green shutters stand next to huge old barns.

And, it's the country in which Daniel Boone and his family settled in the late 1700s: The Femme Osage Valley. In fact, just off Highway 94 on Route F, standing on a wooded hillside, is Missouri's most historical spot, the Daniel Boone Home. Begun in 1803 and completed in 1810, the house would be home to Daniel until his death in 1820. It has been restored and furnished with many of the belongings of the great frontiersman. There is the room and the bed in which he died, the parlor, and the kitchen as well as other rooms. Tours daily. Call for tour prices and times.

Adjacent to the Boone House grounds is a village. This collection of historical structures has been moved to the Boone House site and are included on the tour. The village currently consists of five structures, including the circa 1838 Earle Peters Chapel, which is available for weddings, a wealthy merchant's house, a one-room schoolhouse, and a cabinet maker's shop. Additional structures will be added, including the historic Sappington Dressel House from St. Louis, which is currently being reassembled on the site.

Many well stocked antique shops can be found along Highway 94, and Missouri wines abound in the wineries along this route.

Back on Highway 94, just east of Augusta, is Bob and Judy Slifer's *Montelle Winery* at Osage Ridge. Situated on a bluff 400 feet above the Missouri River, it commands a spectacular view of the river, the town of Augusta and the surrounding frames and vineyards. Guests may tour the winery and nearby vineyards, sample the wines, walk among the shade trees along the ridge, and sit at outside tables to enjoy the scenery. Fine cheese, locally made sausage and freshly baked bread is available for those wishing to picnic. (636) 228-4464.

Ashley Rose B & B, Augusta Wine Country Inn, Clay House B & B, Lindenhof B & B, Old Town Augusta Inn, and Quarry House B & B are in Augusta.

The historic town of Dutzow, founded in 1832 by Baron Von Bock, was the first German settlement in the Missouri River Valley. Here you can tour the modern facilities of James and Mark Blumenberg's Blumenhof Vineyards, named after the family's ancestral farm in Germany. Their German heritage can be seen in the winery's friendly, relaxing ambiance. A wide range of wines is produced from grapes grown at Blumenhof's vineyards. Located on the Katy Trail on scenic Highway 94, you can sample the wines and picnic on the deck and grounds in a Teutonic setting. (636) 433-2245.

Another place you might want to stop at especially if you're looking for nice antiques is the *Femme Osage Antiques* of Dutzow. Janet Hines, the owner, specializes in Missouri antiques in walnut and cherry. Everything I saw here was in pristine condition and included a walnut step back cupboard with fruit pulls, a very nice pair of mahogany corner cupboards, two S-rolltop desks, an oak chifferobe, a marble top Victorian parlor table, an early rope bed, a dry sink, several work tables, a walnut wash stand, an oak ball and claw china cabinet, a great walnut Victorian dresser with glove boxes and unusual beading, a walnut dresser with a wishbone mirror, a pine chest, a Jenny Lind bed and a Victorian wardrobe. Located on Hwy. 94 in Dutzow. (636) 433-5860.

At the junction of Highway 94 and Highway 47, turn right to the Boone Monument Road. About a mile down this road, a large boulder marks the site of the original graves of Daniel and Rebecca Boone.

Back on Highway 47, go through the little town of Marthasville to Route O. Then go two miles to the *Luxenhaus Farm* sign. Old log buildings from the early 1800s have been moved to Bob and Lois Hostkoetter's property and completely restored. On the third weekend in October, *Luxenhaus Farm* holds its Deutsch Country Days Festival featuring outstanding costumed craftsmen from throughout the Midwest who demonstrate the German skills of the 1800s. Bowl carving, doll making, sausage making, spinning, weaving, and woodcarving are some of the forty demonstrations. All kinds of German foods are served. (636) 433-5669 or 239-7777.

Gramma's House B & B is at Marthasville. Concord Hill B & B and Windhomme Hill B & B are a few miles west of Hwy. 47 just off Hwy. 94.

Before you come to Marthasville, Highway 94 makes a turn to the west and continues its way along the Missouri river. There are little towns like Treloar, Holstein, and McKittrick that you shouldn't miss seeing. From the intersection of Highway 19, Highway 94 heads west to Jefferson City.

A good starting point for Highway 100 is just at the junction of Manchester and Woods Mill Roads (Highway 141). Travel west on Manchester. Once you pass through the suburbs of Ballwin and Ellisville, Highway 100 will take you through some beautiful countryside and popular river towns.

Past the little town of Pond on Highway 100 you will come to Gray Summit. Here is the Shaw Arboretum with a 10 mile trail for those wishing to hike through an area which preserves a typical example of Ozark landscape. From Gray Summit take Route MM to Ralston Purina's research farm. Feeding experiments are conducted on all types of farm animals and domestic pets in an effort to continually improve Purina's pet chows.

Follow Highway MM into Labadie, a small hamlet, which at one time was a busy farm town. Platted in 1855, the town is named for Sylvester Labaddie, Jr. and Sr. who were given this property as a Spanish Land Grant in 1800. The residents of the town dropped one "d" in Labaddie's surname. By the turn of the century, Labadie was a thriving railroad town. The Colorado Railroad and the Missouri Pacific crossed at Labadie as that was the first cut in the limestone bluffs west of St. Louis. The old Bethel Church built in 1868 is on the National Register of Historic Places and should not be overlooked. Today, Labadie is a quaint, quiet little town that looks much like it did during the mid-1800s. Many of the buildings date back to the 1850s and have now been restored to hold shops and restaurants. Hunters Hollow B & B and Staats Waterford Estates B & B are in Labadie.

On Front Street, in the old general store, St. Louisans Richard Hoey, John Bartley and Chef Chris Hancock have opened the *Hawthorne Inn,* a family restaurant serving lunch and dinner. The luncheon menu features appetizers, soups and salads, specialty pizzas, pastas, ten different types of sandwiches, a kids menu and desserts. Entrees include Sicilian strip, garden chicken, and cod. Each is served with a house salad and roasted potato. Dinner entrees are Hawthorne filet, tenderloin Labadie, Hawthorne strip, garden chicken, chicken marsala and filet of cod. Desserts include apple pie and cheesecake. (573) 451-6910.

As you leave town, turn right on Route T to head back to Highway 100. Turn right again and head for Washington. Go west to New Haven. Just before you get there turn south (left) on Robller Vineyard Road and proceed to the first gravel road. Turn right and go 1/8 mile to the winery at 275 Robller

Vineyard Road. The *Robller Winery* offers a complete line of wines from dry to sweet. They specialize in producing wines with a focus on French hybrid varieties. Take advantage of the picturesque countryside, relax in the tasting room and sample the wines, bring the kids and the picnic basket and enjoy. (573) 237-3986.

Back at Highway 100 continue west to New Haven. Four miles west of New Haven, make a right on Route B and go 5.5 miles to Berger and the *Bias Vineyards* of Jim Bias. Golf carts take you on a tour of the vineyards. Spend a while in the wine gardens to enjoy the view and taste the different varieties of their wine. (573) 834-5475.

Back on Hwy. 100, continue west to New Haven. About a half mile past New Haven, turn left on Route E then right on Route VV. This will take you to Senate Grove B & B.

To travel the southern boundary of the region, take I-44 west from St. Louis for twenty miles to *Six Flags over Mid-America.* It is one of the most popular fun parks in the country, offering over 100 rides, shows and attractions.

Nearby, the town of Eureka, founded in the 1800s, is a must for antique hunters.

The Firehouse Gallery and Antiques, located at 131 S. Central and owned by Mary and Bob Zier, is housed in Eureka's original fire station. The shop combines art and antiques. They had a double door walnut wardrobe, circa 1880, an Eastlake sofa, a step-back oak cupboard, a yarn winder, a small mahogany breakfront, a pair of marble top lamp tables, an unusual mahogany desk, a maple corner cupboard, a spinning wheel, a cradle type butter churn, and an oak wall telephone. They also have prints by nationally known artists such as Gary Lucy, Terry Redlin and Jesse Barnes. There is a collection of theorems, bird plates, transfer stoneware and World's Fair memorabilia. (314) 938-3303.

Continuing along I-44 from Eureka, take the Union exit at Highway 50. The best restaurant between St. Louis and Jefferson City along Highway 50 is *Brock's Chicken Inn* located at 340 Highway 50 West in Union. Brothers, Paul and Andy Karakasis, purchased the business from the original owner. They continue to serve the best chicken in the area, along with farm raised catfish, ribs, pizza and delicious barbecue. They have added a variety of Greek entrees. Open 7 days a week for breakfast, lunch and dinner. Menu service or buffet. (573) 538-8604.

From Highway 50 in Beaufort, take Highway 185 south for two miles to the old Noser Mill. Built in the early 1850s, this pioneer stone flour mill is the only water mill standing in Franklin County. The original log dam was replaced by the present one in 1910. Just down the road from the mill is the wonderful old stone house which once belonged to the owner of the mill. Bob and Anita Beckmann purchased the building and are restoring it to its original state. They hope to open their bed & breakfast in the next year or two. Be sure to watch for it. I promise you it will be something very special. One of the stone buildings on the premises is now the *Beckmann's Noser Mill Antiques,* located at 5106 Noser Mill Road. (573) 484-4170. Anita has a circa 1870 Lincoln desk, an 1860 oak yarn winder, an early pine bucket bench, a hanging wall cupboard, a pine spice rack, a circa 1840 walnut wardrobe, a cherry jelly cupboard, a walnut tavern table, a beautiful circa 1830 walnut corner cupboard with the original mustard yellow and robin blue and green paint. There was also a cherry meal bin with the original red paint, a circa 1840 harvest table, and an 1870s pine kitchen cupboard with bins and drawers. She also had baskets, quilts, loom rugs, woodenware, yellow ware, crocks, jugs, wooden bowls, pictures and lots of country primitives.

The last town along the southern boundary of this region is Rosebud. There are about half a dozen nice antique shops here. I stopped in at four of them. *Heady's Rock Island Hotel Antiques* is full of interesting things. She had a wooden oak ice-box, a really rare iron Wells Fargo gold shipment box, an oak store counter desk, a caned Lincoln rocker, a walnut blanket chest, a walnut step back cupboard, a large red tin bin, marked "Flour - Bread and Cake," a pierced tin 12 panel door pie safe, and an original hanging oil lamp. She has copper luster, graniteware, cut glass, and molds. There was a Red Wing 30 gallon crock, a creamer, sugar and spooner in ruby red flashed glass and some RR items including a lantern with purple glass lamps. (573) 764-2224.

Next door is the *Gift Room Shop.* Pete Weatherford, the owner, pointed out a glass door kitchen cupboard, several opossum belly cabinets, wash stands, an old metal ice box, a spool cabinet, a round oak table, a nice oak dresser, a barber's chair, a large brass oil lamp (converted), a library table, a metal Daisy churn, a walnut pie safe, four kitchen cupboards and three high back beds. There was an oak wash stand with four drawers and a door. There were also lots of framed prints and pictures, graniteware, linens, crocks, very nice hand painted plates and bowls, plenty of primitives, and kitchen tools. (573) 764-4330.

The last shop I visited was *Kountry Klassics,* where I found a combination of antiques, collectibles and well done craft items. Bev Klousner, the owner, invited me to browse. She had a very nice oak bonnet top dresser, a large wicker baby carriage, a library table, kitchen cupboard, an oak wash stand, a kitchen granite top work table, a Lincoln rocker with a cane seat, a two door oak armoire and a sideboard. Crafts included dried florals, quilts, lace, metal sign reproductions, framed pictures and prints and dolls. There is a year-round Christmas shop will all kinds of pieces. (573) 764- 4144.

From Rosebud, take Highway T south five miles, then turn left on Blue House Road for one mile to the *Log Cabin Pottery.* Viva and Charles Detert restored this 150 year-old lob cabin, where she wheel throws or hand builds beautiful pieces of pottery. Vibrant blue, green and rose as well as natural tones are used to create unusual and charming tea and coffee pots, pitchers, bowls, plates, mugs and even the popular spatterware. These make ideal gifts for any occasion and it well worth the short drive. (573) 764-2049.

The northern border of Missouri's wine country begins just west of St. Charles on I-70. You can also take Hwy. 40/61 west to I-70. Just before the junction of I-70 and 40/61 is a very special shop called *Wagon Masters Antiques*. I spent about two hours talking to Kim about their operation here. It is a large antique shop and I enjoyed looking at the 40 or more antique horse drawn sleighs, doctor's buggy, pony and horse carts, a U.S. mail buggy, a two seater sleigh, farm wagon, a 1930s ice wagon and a rare spindle seat circa 1878 buggy. In the antique portion, there were copper kettles, crocks, spinning wheels, yarn winders, a cranberry picker, wooden rakes and pitchforks, a wooden candle dryer, a huge immigrant chest, a jelly cupboard, a goat wagon, a wall coffee grinder, graniteware, saddles, wooden wagon wheels, buggy seats, decoys and tools of all sorts. (636) 625-2727.

Traveling west on I-70 takes you to Wright City, where one of my favorite restaurants is located. Since 1924, people have come from all over to enjoy the all you can eat chicken dinners at Big Boy's. This family style restaurant serves good country food and plenty of it. Besides chicken, they also have all you can eat ham or fish, served with mounds of side dishes. The soups, breads and desserts are homemade. Whenever I take I-70, I make it a point to stop here for breakfast, lunch or dinner. (314) 745-2200.

AUGUSTA

Augusta is a typical old German-American town, barely touched by the twentieth century. It was founded in 1836 by Leonard Harold, a settler who followed Daniel Boone to St. Charles County. He laid out the town on government land he purchased in 1821. The site was chosen for its excellent Missouri River landing. Incorporated in 1855, the town then known as Mount Pleasant, was predominantly German. These settlers had been attracted to the area by glowing descriptions of the land written by Gottfried Duden. Augusta became a prosperous agricultural area, growing mainly grain, livestock and grapes. The town was a trading center supporting craftsmen, merchants, wineries and hotels. In the 1870s, flooding caused the Missouri River to cut a new channel leaving the town without its boat landing, but with several hundred acres of fertile bottom land which still provides much of the town's income.

Before Prohibition, when Missouri ranked as the second largest wine producing state in the nation, there were no fewer than thirteen wineries located in the small, narrow Augusta valley. Of the five medals awarded to wineries at the St. Louis World's Fair in 1904, four went to the wineries of Augusta. With the onset of prohibition, Augusta became a sleepy hamlet until 1968 when the Mt. Pleasant Winery, which had been in operation from 1881 until 1920, was reopened. Here you will find the flavor of the Old World in the cellars and historical buildings. Tours are given regularly and you can view the complete operation of the winery.

Visit the tasting room, then relax on the terrace and enjoy a peaceful afternoon. To whet your appetite, the *Augusta Grocery* on the grounds have a selection of cheeses, sausage, juice, crackers and bread. Located at 5634 High Street. (636) 482-4419.

As other towns have gone by the wayside, Augusta, with its 300 residents, is now a thriving small town. Most of the tourist interest, which was spurred by the revival of the vineyards, has blossomed with the start of the many home based businesses you find there today. Shops feature everything from antiques to wood carvings.

The *Augusta Winery* is located at High and Jackson Streets. (636) 228-4301. The winery, built of stone and wood, features a pleasant airy tasting room with friendly salespeople to assist in your selection of wines. There is a beautiful outdoor wine terrace where you can enjoy a chilled bottle of wine ranging from dinner wines to sweet dessert wines, all handmade from local grapes. This is a great place for a picnic lunch, as locally produced cheese and sausage is also available.

Vic Brown's *Augusta Wood* specializes in solid wood furniture of walnut, cherry and pine. Here you can find paneled blanket chests, hall trees, benches, coffee tables, chairs and shelves. There are upholstered camel back love seats, chairs and hidden recliners. Beautiful Heritage display cabinets, ornate iron beds, a pine connestoga cupboard, and tables. There are unusual lamps, metal statuary, bird houses, music boxes, carved birds, tapestry throws and quality made toys. Numbered and signed art prints from nationally known artists such as Thomas Kincaid, Jesse Barnes and Terry Redlin are available. Located at Walnut and Ferry Streets. (636) 228-4406.

Located at 5595 Walnut, Kitty Covell's *Augusta Emporium* is housed in the historic Fritz Tiemann building, built in the 1860s. Almost everything about the building is original. Kitty had a 1920s nine piece dining room suite, an antique organ, a kitchen cupboard, a marble top dresser with candle stands, a nice chest of drawers, drop leaf table, a Victorian parlor chair and a dated 1866 lift-top plantation desk. She also had vintage clothing, books, toys, oil lamps, lots of costume jewelry, old fishing lures, painted bowls and plates, glassware, wooden kitchen utensils, coffee grinders, quilts, bottles, tins and old silhouette geese decoys. (636) 228-4024.

When you get hungry, there are several restaurants for you to try. The *White House Restaurant* is located in a great historic building at 5567 Walnut Street. Built in 1885, it was completely renovated by the owner, Alan and Kathryn Fraizer. Open for lunch and dinner, the Fraizers have created a varied menu that includes pasta, seafood, chicken, beef dishes and steaks. They also serve salads, soups, desserts and sandwiches. Don't pass up the famous White House hamburgers. A child's menu is available. (636) 482-4048 for reservations and information.

Paul and Maggie Moeser's *Ashleys Rose Restaurant* on the first floor of Ashleys Rose B & B at 5501 Locust, serves luncheon and dinner. A fresh fruit plate, Missouri cheese and sausage plate, homemade soups and salad and a variety of sandwiches are offered at luncheon. The dinner menu includes wiener schnitzel and homemade potato pancakes, slow roasted prime rib, steak Diane, calf liver with bacon and onions, a variety of delicious chicken entrees, sole Oscar, stuffed flounder, catfish and fried shrimp. Dinners include salad or homemade soup, vegetable and muffins. For dessert choose from Black Forest Cake, German chocolate cheesecake, peach cobbler or coconut cream pie. (314) 482-4108.

ASHLEYS ROSE INN
Augusta

Listed on the National Register of Historical Places, the Staudinger/ Grumke House was built in the early 1850s by German born August Staudinger, a watchmaker. In 1865, Staudinger left Augusta and sold the building. Later when a saloon keeper named Grumke owned the building, it became known as the "Sharp Corner." Some say that bootleg liquor was made here during prohibition. The bricks that make up the eleven inch thick walls in the two story home were handmade in Augusta.

These old buildings always seem to be waiting for someone to breathe a little life back into them. And, so it was with this historical home, when Larry and Diana Sadler purchased the building and began their long task of renovation. Now the house has been completely restored back to the original design with center halls and rooms on each side. Most of the woodwork, windows and doors are original.

Paul and Maggie Moeser now have their Ashleys Rose B & B on the second floor. As you enter the house, on the first floor, you are in a hallway with an entrance on the left that leads to the Moeser's restaurant. Diana Sadler's Locust Street Antiques is across the hall on the right. An enclosed staircase to the second floor guestrooms still has the original wooden walls. At the top of the stairs, a hall has a braided rug runner. Maggie has as antique marble top dresser here. Antique prints are on the walls.

The two guestrooms on the floor have 10 foot ceilings, the original floors and woodwork. Three six over six paned windows give the rooms lots of light, making them bright and airy. Both are decorated with antique prints. One room is furnished with a full-size antique four poster bed with quilts, and eight foot two door armoire, an antique dresser with glove boxes and candle stands, a caned Lincoln rocker and a Victorian love seat. A maple table and an antique table, both with lamps, are used as night stands. The floors have throw rugs on them. One wall is papered in a crewel design. A tin and wood chandelier hangs from the ceiling. A private bath has paneling on three walls and exposed brick on the other. It has a double head shower

Across the hall, the second guestroom is fully carpeted. It is furnished with a full-size antique four poster bed with antique coverlets on it, an upholstered sofa, an antique wardrobe, a drop leaf table with an antique mirror above it, an upholstered wing chair, a pair of night tables with lamps and an early 1900s rocking chair with upholstered back and seat. Lace curtains are at the windows. A private bath has a double head shower.

Maggie serves breakfast in the restaurant before it opens to the public. Juice, fresh fruit in season, bacon or sausage with American fried potatoes are served with a ham and cheese omelet. She also offers french toast with bacon. Always there is jam, jellies, toast, coffee, tea or milk. The restaurant is open for lunch and dinner to the general public.

As Augusta is right in the middle of the wine country, with two wineries in town, you are close to all of the wineries between here and Hermann as well as the antique shops and fine restaurants. In fact, there is so much to see and do, you could easily stay for a week or more. For a weekend stay, there is a complimentary bottle of Missouri wine.

ASHLEYS ROSE B & B: 5501 Locust, Augusta, 63332. (636) 482-4108. Open all year. No children. No pets. Smoking on balcony and in the smoking section of the restaurant. Paul and Maggie Moeser, innkeepers.

DIRECTIONS: From Highway 40/61 or I-64, go to Highway 94. Exit and go west to Augusta. (follow signs) Located on the corner of Locust and Lower Streets. From Washington, take Highway 47 across the Missouri River to Highway 94. Go west and Exit at Augusta.

JAMIE L. MCILROY © 99

AUGUSTA WINE COUNTRY INN
Augusta

Situated on a hilltop overlooking the picturesque town of Augusta, this house was the former Meyer House, built in 1887. It has been elegantly restored by the owner, Alan and Kathryn Frazier. Most of the floors are original as is the woodwork, doors and windows. A huge balcony with six large pillars has a porch swing. The property has been landscaped with trees, shrubs and flowers, along with an herb garden.

A small entry hall is carpeted in a floral design. A winding staircase takes you to the three guestrooms and common room on the second floor.

To the right of the entry, is a first floor common room. I watched Kathryn as she very professionally decorated the room for Christmas. The black background carpet has a colorful floral design. The walls are white on three sides. On the last wall below a chair rail, a local artist painted a flower garden behind a picket fence. Above the rail, she painted a large scene of rolling hills which also portrayed the Frazier's four properties. It is furnished with an antique round table and four Chippendale style chairs, a player piano, a federal style inlaid hunt board, and a large server with a designer lamp on it. Sheer curtains drape the bay windows and a chandelier hangs over the table. The room is decorated with pictures and dried and silk floral arrangements.

From the common room you walk into the dining room. A large, brick fireplace on a raised hearth goes from floor to ceiling. The floor is carpeted wall to wall with an ecru sculptured carpet. A long oak table and six oak chairs are placed before a large window. There is a striped upholstered sofa and a pair of upholstered wing chairs. There is also an unusual blue and white painted cottage table with a brass lamp. A hutch holds a classic gold rim dinner service and crystal. One wall is papered green and two walls are papered in a red and green casual pattern Four huge windows, and with bookshelves on either side of it is next to the fireplace. Two overlook the porch across the front and the lawn.

The inn features three guestrooms with private baths. You can enjoy total privacy as the guestrooms and common reading area are located on the second floor with access to the balcony.

At the top of the staircase, the Mary Frazier Suite is to the left. The original floors have area carpets on them. The woodwork is painted green. The wall covering is a black, mauve and green stripe on three walls and a small mauve print paper on the other. A matching border is at the ceiling. It is furnished with a queen-size Wrought Iron bed with a canopy of rose vines and wrapped lace, a desk and chair, an early 1900's vanity, an art deco-era wardrobe and an upholstered camelback sofa in green. Pale green accordion shades and swags are at the window. The marble bath has a walk-in shower.

A common room has a large area carpet, an upholstered sofa, an open arm chair, a glider rocker, a round coffee table, a bamboo table for games, and oak server, refrigerator, and a rattan and wrought iron bakers rack holds the coffee maker, condiments and cups. A lavender marble pattern wall paper is on the walls. A pair of French doors lead to the balcony. There are two round rattan topped tables with wrought iron bases, two chairs and a sofa.

Off the common room, the Power's Suite has wall-to-wall burgundy carpet. Lace curtains are over mini blinds. It is furnished with a queen-size reproduction of an antique bed, and antique marble top Eastlake dresser with glove boxes, a cheval mirror, a 1920's vanity and a pair of white upholstered Queen Anne style arm chairs. A "Gone With the Wind" lamp is on the dresser. Trudy Marshal, a local artist, painted grape vines around each window and the doors. A nice large bath has a tub and shower.

The Turnbull Room has a large black and white area carpet. Four large windows have black and white swags over blinds. There is a fireplace. It is furnished with an ornate wrought iron, queen-size cream color bed, an antique English mirrored dresser, a pair of tan Queen Anne style wing chairs and a unique table and lamp. Black and white stripe paper on the walls and a wide border of classic Greek design is at the ceiling. The bath has a tub and shower.

At 7:00 a.m., coffee and tea, a roll or coffee cake is served upstairs in the common room. Then at 9:00 a.m. there is always a fruit compote with a sauce, a very special stuffed French toast with apple or strawberries in season. Or, eggs Benedict, or Strata served with sausage or bacon.

AUGUSTA WINE COUNTRY INN: 5619 Fifth Street, Augusta, 663332. (636) 482-4307. Fax: (636) 228-4016. Open all year. A three guestrooms inn with private baths. Not suited for children. No pets. Smoking on porch or balcony. Alan and Kathryn Frazier, innkeepers.

DIRECTIONS: Take Jackson Street off of Hwy. 94 to Augusta. Stay on Jackson Street south and turn right on Fifth St. Inn is on the right hand side.

H.S. CLAY HOUSE BED & BREAKFAST
Augusta

D r. H.S. Clay, an 1873 graduate of the Missouri Medical College in St. Louis, built this house in 1885 for his second wife, Marie/ they raised their family of four sons and five daughters here. Dr. Clay passed away soon after the birth of their ninth child, leaving Marie to raise their family. Marie lived in the house until 1948, when she moved to Poplar Bluff to live with her son. The current owners, Alan and Leigh Buehre, purchased the home in 1991 and began the final phase of its restoration.

Entering from a spacious front porch, you are in a hallway that has a black and white tile floor. Old St. Louis prints are on the walls and a collection of cut glass decanters are on display.

The common rooms of the Clay House reflect the Victorian's wonderful penchant for clutter. The Red Room is to the left of the hall. This is a most interesting room. In a window nook there is an antique game table and two Hitchcock chairs. A jigsaw puzzle is always waiting for completion. A collection of books, magazines, decoys and baskets are on an old bench in front of the window. An end table had an old well pump made into a lamp. A green plaid camel back sofa is facing a fireplace, while a red brocade sofa is at a right angle to it and also faces the fireplace. On the walls is a collection of antique fishing gear, framed casting flies and lures, Civil War rifles, powder horns and framed hand colored lithographers proof prints of whaling ships.

Right from the hall, the parlor has a fireplace with a collection of twenty-six candle sticks. There is an upholstered love seat, a brocade armchair, an antique wardrobe, an antique tavern table with four Hitchcock chairs. A collection of baskets are on three of the walls. An oriental rug is on the floor and lace curtains at the windows.

Original Battenboard is on two walls of the dining room and a braided rug is on the floor. Two brass chandeliers hang over a long oak table with six Hitchcock chairs. Antique China cabinets hold Leigh's dishes and glasses. Model sailboats, steins and all sorts of collectibles can be found here.

French doors lead into the kitchen filled with vintage gadgets on display. The kitchen doors open onto a large deck with several seating arrangements and umbrella tables. A great place for coffee. Flowers are everywhere. A large oval swimming pool is two steps down to another deck where there is seating arrangement here also.

On the second floor, three guestrooms are uniquely furnished with collections of antiques, fine art, down comforters and gracious finishing touches. In the front of the house overlooking the garden, Marie's Room is furnished with a queen-size four poster pencil bed with hand made linens, a bedside table and lamp pair of white wicker chairs, a wicker table and reading lamp, a built in bookcase, and a low chest with an antique dressing mirror. The walls are papered in a pink and blue print, a oriental rug is on the floor. The windows which are on two sides of the room have shutters.

Courtney's Room is furnished with wrought iron, four poster, canopy queen-size bed with a white douvet and hand-made quilt, a pair of wicker chairs, a wash stand with a mirror, end tables and lamps. A oriental rug is on the hardwood floor and muslin curtains at the windows. A floral patterned paper is on one wall, the other three have a border chair rail. There are two built-in book cases.

Three sides of Robert's Room also have windows. The original floors have oriental rugs and shutters are on the windows. It has a queen-size four poster canopy bed with white bed linens, a pair of upholstered chairs, a lamp table and lamp, plant stand and a quilt rack. Decorations including died floral arrangements are very nicely done.

The Tree Top Suite is on the third floor. In the sitting area, there is a pair of leather wing back chairs, a small floorlamp for reading and a sofa table. There is a collection of antique duck decoys. In the small library there is a Mission rocker, bookshelves and library lamp. In the bedroom there is a small rocking chair at the foot of the bed, a pair of leather wing back chairs, a slant front desk, a Mission style oak bookcase, a sofa table. In the turret area there is a drum table and a pair of floral wing back chairs. A fireplace is always ready to add warmth and coziness. The private bath had a claw foot tub, separate glassed in shower and private balcony.

Upon arrival, home baked cookies, fruit and teas are served. Later on, appetizers, cheese and crackers and wine are served at "happy hour." And, a turn down service includes ports, and I.B. Nuts chocolates.

A full gourmet breakfast is served from 9 to 10 a.m. A choice of two juices, freshly ground coffee, and sixteen types of teas. Then start with sauteed bananas with brown sugar, pecans and a brandy glaze. Entrees would be custard French toast with candied, pepper bacon and sage sausage. Or, Eggs Benedict with country fried potatoes, an omelet or quiche with a breakfast meat. Always fresh fruit, home baked breads or muffins.

H.S. CLAY HOUSE B & B: P.O. Box 184. Corner of Public and Walnut Streets, Augusta, 63332. (636) 482-4004 or (888) 309-7334. E-mail: hsclayhouse@msn.com. Website: www.augusta-missouri.com. Open year round. A three room, two suite country Victorian house in town with private or shared baths. Not suited for children or pets. Smoking on porch and decks. Bicycles available for the Katy Trail. Lots of amenities. Alan and Leigh Buehre, innkeepers.

DIRECTIONS: Take I-70 or Highway 40 to Highway 94. West to Augusta. (see signs). Located on corner of Public and Walnut Streets. Call for information, reservations and directions.

LINDENHOF BED & BREAKFAST
Augusta

This Victorian farm house, built around 1850, was the home of the town blacksmith for many years. It is a well maintained home painted in favorite Victorian colors of cream and blue. The wrought iron fence in front is original.

Step back in time as you step onto the porch of this vintage Victorian home filled with elegant antiques and plump, cozy furnishings. Each guestroom is unique in decor and feature either queen-size (reproduction) or double-size (antique) beds as well as comfortable seating areas. Upon arrival guests are treated to refreshments. Friday night guests are treated to wine and cheese and Saturday arrivals are offered flavored coffees, liquors, or cocoa with pie or cookies. Feel free to take a plate of cookies to your room, or have wine and cheese in the garden by the pond. A cookie jar filled with Biscotti is always found on the tea cart and cold drinks are always available in the stocked guest refrigerator, including ice cold milk for those cookies.

Two guestrooms are on the first floor and feature in-room private baths. The Victorian Suite, located in the oldest part of the home, has a private porch and entrance. The focal point in this room is an Eastlake bed draped in lace from ceiling to floor. The walls are painted a deep cranberry and all the woodwork is white. There is an armoire filled with an assortment of antique treasures, a full-size sofa for reading and relaxing, a Victorian walnut chest of drawers, a walnut gateleg table, and a built-in bookcase. Guests who book this room are treated in the morning to a tray of coffee and the daily newspaper, which are left on their porch.

Clara's Cottage Room is located in the main portion of the home and has a large four-poster bed with decorative curtains and dried flowers serving as a backdrop behind the headboard. There is a huge walnut knockdown wardrobe that dates from about 1860. An antique vitrine displays a collection of music boxes and vintage photos and dates from about 1880. A marble top parlor table serves as a nightstand and a mahogany piecrust table sits beside the loveseat. This room also has a television available.

Alvina's Room, the Rose Room, and a large hall bath take up the entire second floor and is perfect for family or friends wanting their own private space. The Rose Room has a white iron bed with a drapery of white eyelet. There is also a white wicker daybed filled with pillows that is perfect for lounging and reading and can accommodate an additional person if needed. A beautiful hand-painted table adorned with roses is at the foot of the bed and two turn-of-the-century oak dressers complete the room.

Alvina's Room is quaint and cozy with a garden theme. A white iron bed is draped in pink and green curtains. There is a reading alcove with stained glass torchere and white wicker rocker. A collection of old quilts are displayed in a small cabinet. All rooms are equipped with individual heating/cooling units that assure climate-controlled comfort. Handmade quilts and hand-crocheted coverlets top all beds.

Head out into town to enjoy the local architecture, vintner's specialties, shopping or cycling. Enjoy dinner at any of the town's fine establishments and when your day is done, return to the inn and the plush robes we provide and head out to the jacuzzi spa for a relaxing up-to-your-neck soak.

In the morning, a bountiful breakfast will be served in the parlor on antique china. Our menu changes daily but may include baked German-apple pancakes, Belgian waffles with black cherry sauce, scrambled eggs with cheese and roasted red peppers, delicious omelets stuffed with spinach and mushrooms, hickory smoked bacon, savory browned potatoes, fresh fruit compotes and juice, tea, and coffee.

The Lindenhof owners, Debbie and Bill Schaefer, will be glad to make any arrangements that will make your stay perfect for you: fresh flower arrangements, customized picnic baskets, massage therapy, birthday cakes and balloons, private breakfast for two... just let them know ahead of time.

LINDENHOF B & B: P.O. Box 52, 5596 Walnut, Augusta, 63332. (636) 228-4617. Open year round. A four guestroom farm house in town with private or shared baths. Children welcome. No smoking. No pets. Debbie and Bill Schaefer, innkeepers.

DIRECTIONS: Take I-70 of Highway 40/61 to Highway 94. West to Augusta. (see signs). Located on the corner of Walnut and Jackson. Just five minutes from Washington on Highway 47 across the Missouri River to Highway 94. Then east to Augusta.

OLD TOWN AUGUSTA INN
Augusta

In the 1860's Rudolph Dammarca, who had immigrated to America, was listed in the town of Augusta as a tobacco manufacturer. During the Civil War, Rudolph served with the 3rd Missouri infantry. Later records show he built this house. The original house had a brick (made in Augusta) first floor and a frame second floor. Later a summer kitchen and house was built.

After Clyde and Holly Stratton purchased the property, they combined these two buildings adding, modernizing and renovating. The outcome is this great stone, brick and cedar home, surrounded by trees and gardens overlooking the Katy Trail and fields beyond.

Entering the house, you are in a large room where the early portion has the original walls of stone and brick, log beamed ceilings, wide plank floors and deep set windows with 6 over 6 window panes. Some of the panes are original also. There is no electricity in this portion of the room. A wrought iron chandelier with candles hangs over a long trestle table and eight chairs. There is also an early wood burning cook stove (looks only), a breakfront with Holly's stemware and dishes and a lower part of an opossum belly cupboard. Clyde has a curio cabinet, which houses a collection of quartz crystal. Breakfast is served in this room. In the renovated portion of the room, there is a piano, an upholstered rattan sofa and two matching chairs and an antique trunk. A floral carpet is on the floor of the older part. Holly has several large, line plants. This area is a common one for guests. P.S. There's electricity here!

The Fireside Suite, on the 1st floor has a brick fireplace which holds a woodburning stove. It is furnished with a full-size futon bed, a night table with reading lamp and a ladderback chair. Sliding doors open out. A patio and a deck furnished with wrought iron outdoor furniture. Nearby is an herb and vegetable garden. The room has wall-to-wall carpet and original artwork is on the walls. A sitting groom is fully carpeted. It has an upholstered sofa in a floral design, a small table and lamp, a 1920's radio cabinet, a round pedestal table and a rocking chair. A large picture window with draw blinds has a view of the distant fields and woods.

On the second floor, the Pecan Tree Suite has a queen-size four poster bed. A 1900's music cabinet and a small marble top wash stand are used as night tables. A carved art deco buffet with a marble top, a Swedish wood and upholstered rocker and ottoman are part of the furnishings. The w-w jade green carpet, floral drapes on three windows, ten foot ceilings, white walls with nice framed prints and several large line plants make this a comfortable room. A private bath has a sit down shower, What was once a summer kitchen and smokehouse has been made into a sitting room and small fully equipped kitchen. The floor is original as is the wainscote ceiling. There is also Japanese print wallpaper. Clyde built the brick woodburning fireplace. An upholstered sofa opens into a full-size bed. Holly uses organic items to decorate.

Also, on the second floor, the Balcony Suite is in the front of the house, overlooking the Katy Trail. A floral carpet covers the original plank floors. It is furnished with a queen-size, hand crafted short poster bed, wardrobe, a small table and chairs, a night stand with a reading lamp and a day bed. The walls are English Tutor style using the original hand hewn logs and plastered. It gives a great effect. A door opens out a large balcony with seating and a porch swing. There is a private bath with showers.

Breakfast is served family style and consists of an exotic blend of juices and also orange juice, fresh fruit in season and an entrée: an omelet with either fresh vegetables from the garden or ham or sausage and cheese. Or maybe waffles or pancakes prepared with fresh ground organic grain and served with meat and real maple syrup. Or times it could be eggs Benedict. Always fresh breads and muffins with jams and jellies, a variety of teas, hot chocolate and fresh ground organic coffee. You won't go away hungry.

On arrival Holly serves cheese and crackers and a refreshing drink. Iced tea or lemonade in summer, hot chocolate or hot apple juice with a cinnamon stick. This will hold you until you get to one of Augusta's good restaurants.

OLD TOWN AUGUSTA INN: 5549 Main St. Augusta, 63332. (636) 482-4654. Open all year. Two suites and one guestroom, all with private baths. (A fourth guestroom in the making.) Children welcome. No pets. Smoking on patio or porches. Holly and Clyde Stratton, innkeepers.

DIRECTIONS: Take Highway 40-61 to Rte. 94. Turn south and proceed to Augusta. The inn is located at the corner of Main and Public.

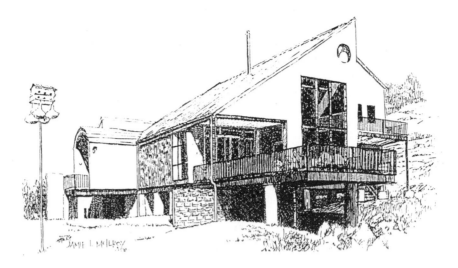

QUARRY HOUSE BED AND BREAKFAST INN
Augusta

I never would have believed that a quarry which had been mined for 100 years, then abandoned for 10 more, would ever be turned into a wonderful spot such as this.

Hank and Jean Macler who had been looking for a place to live was told about the area known as the Missouri Weinstrasse, a road from St. Charles to Jefferson City. A road of winding curves and hills and also some of the most beautiful country in the state. After several meetings with the quarry owners, the Maclers purchased the quarry and 250 acres of weeds, brush and several quarry ponds. Then to build their home.

Now five years old, Quarry House is a contemporary style of architecture. It is unlike any home I have ever been in. The first floor has an open floor plan with ceilings 20-25 feet high. A sitting area and a dining area has a green tile floor and a two story window. What a spot to view the quarry and lake. Positioned in front of these windows are three upholstered sofas and an upholstered chair that surround a large coffee table. The dining area has a really large round table with eight Chippendale style chairs. Three china cabinets hold glassware, collectibles and figurines. Pictures and plaques along with pieces from the straw market in Haiti decorate the wall.

A family room/library has a leather sofa and two chairs. There is a computer and a 35" television. Bookshelves have books and mementos of Hank and Jean's travels.

Sliding doors from the library lead onto a huge deck overlooking the quarry. There are two tables with chairs that offer a respite from either a long day, or just to take in the view.

A large lower level guestroom is fully carpeted. It is furnished with a washed pine dresser and a king-size bed which can be made into two twin beds. And, the colors! Greens, yellows, and pinks. The bath has a red tile shower, a red sink and chest walls. Posters and prints decorate them. Windows overlook a future garden.

A spiral staircase takes you to three guestrooms off of a balcony that looks down on the area below. The walls to the second floor are in colors of lavender, green and coral. At the top are mobiles of tropical fish.

Guestrooms feature a private bath and compact refrigerator. Both waterbeds and conventional mattress beds are available. Bathrobes are furnished and each room is stocked with books, games and toys to entertain the child in each of us.

Down the balcony hall, the second guestroom has a queen-size black bed, end tables, and a dresser.

Framed prints and posters decorate the one lavender and three white walls. This room overlooks the odd-looking stone walls of the quarry. The bath has red and gold wall paper a lavender sink and colorful towels.

The last guestroom is fully carpeted and had three white walls and one green one. It is furnished with a queen-size bed, a blond Danish modern dresser, a chest and a pair of bedside tables. The bath has a purple sink and colorful towels.

At the end of the carpeted balcony, a porch invites you to relax and watch a sunset or a sunrise.

A bountiful breakfast is served at your leisure in the morning. Breakfast in bed is available upon request. Fresh squeezed orange juice, fresh fruit plate in season, homemade muffins, and yogurt, eggs, bacon, or sausage Jean's specialty dish apple crisp. Coffee, milk or tea.

There is a lot to see and do at Quarry House. Relax in front of the big screen television, shoot a game of pool, fish in the eight acre lake, watch for wildlife and birds, or hike the nature trails leading to the Missouri River of just savor the solitude of country life from one of the two balconies. You'll enjoy Quarry House.

QUARRY HOUSE B & B: 4598 S. Highway 94, Augusta, 63332. (636) 228-4070 or 1 (888) 470-0929 for reservations. Fax (636) 482-4103. Open all year. Smoking outdoors only. They do accept children conditionally. Pets o.k. They have dogs and cats in residence. Bike or hike the Katy Trail using the Maclers private access road. Hank and Jean Macler, innkeepers.

DIRECTIONS: Quarry House is seven miles east of Augusta on Highway 94. Watch for their blue mailbox on the left side of the road. The driveway is on the right.

WILD WIND FARM
Beaufort

I stood on the deck of Wild Wind Country Inn, looked out across the 10-acre lake, then up into the forested hills that almost surround the property.

Bo McGinnis, the owner, had taken an old farmhouse sitting on 178 acres and completely renovated it. Then he added a wood and stone addition. A large deck with a hot tub and swimming spa overlooks the landscaped lawns. All of the old farm buildings remain, adding to the charm of Wild Wind. A large maple tree with a swing shades the deck.

Melissa has designed and built a beautiful garden, complete with a running brook. All kinds of shrubs and flowers bloom here from spring until autumn.

Guests have the use of the living room, dining area and den on the first floor. The den has a large fireplace and is furnished with a leather love seat and a recliner rocker, a bookcase with a variety of reading material, and a beautifully crafted cherry wood game table with tapestry covered chairs. A large bearskin rug in on the floor. There is also a television and sound system.

In the new addition, the living room is furnished with an upholstered sofa and a pair of arm chairs. An unusual deer horn chandelier hangs from the ceiling. Watching the fish in the fish tank is certain to soothe any jangled nerves.

The dining room, just off the living room, is rather unusual. The room is round with a cathedral ceiling. Breakfast is usually served here, but in warmer months the deck is used.

There are three guestrooms. One is just off the side entrance. It is a large airy room that is beautifully decorated. It is furnished with all new furniture including a queen-size mahogany four poster bed, matching highboy, night tables and lamps, and an upholstered chair. It has nice wallpaper and carpeting. The old beaded ceiling remains.

An enclosed staircase in the side entry hall leads to the second floor guestrooms. At the top of the stairs, a sitting room is furnished with a sofa that opens into a bed, a small electric organ, television, VCR, and a game table with chairs. Off this sitting area are two bedrooms, both newly decorated and carpeted. One contains a heavy oak, four poster bed, an antique dresser, night table, wash stand, and a rocking chair.

The other room has oak twin beds, a dresser, chest, and an antique trunk. The views from both rooms overlook the fields, woods and some of the outbuildings.

The bath, with tub and shower, can be entered from either bedroom. This upstairs area is meant to accommodate a family of six or two couples travelling together. The entire second floor, under the eaves, has sloped ceilings making it very cozy.

Talk about a country breakfast. Melissa goes all out to provide for guests. Most of the food served is fresh from the farm. There is Bacon, ham or sausage with eggs, biscuits and gravy, American fried potatoes, fruits, juices, breads and pastries, several varieties of gourmet coffee, and tea or milk.

There is lots to do while visiting here including fishing in the lake (boat furnished), hiking, picnicking, bird watching and, of course, the hot tub or swimming spa. It's a beautiful place with very nice people.

WILD WIND FARM: 5852 Highway 185, Beaufort, 63103. (573) 484-3110. Open from May 1 to December 1. A three guestroom home on 178 acres. A perfect spot to watch Mother Nature. Close to the wineries and antique shops in Washington and Augusta. No pets. Children welcome. Smoking on decks., Bo and Melissa McGinnis, innkeepers.

DIRECTIONS: From I-44, take Hwy. 50 west at the Union exit and proceed to Beaufort. Then take Hwy. 185 to the right for 2.5 miles. Just after you pass a Christmas tree farm, turn right at a log cabin to Wild Wind.

DAS GAST NADLER HAUS BED & BREAKFAST
Defiance

When you look at Dave and Jacquie Nadler's home you would never believe that it was once a small one and a half story farm house, built in 1904. Dave's grandfather lived in the house until the 1950s. It has been completely renovated and enlarged. One of the nicest additions is the extra large front porch filled with wicker furniture.

The entry, off this porch, is furnished with a spinet piano, a pair of wing chairs and a tier table. The entry hall, sitting area and dining area are separated by furnishings rather than walls. The sitting area has a fireplace and is furnished with a pair of love seats upholstered in white.

The dining area has a large hexagon oak table with eight high back chairs, a grandfather clock and a library table. A ceiling panel light over the table provides ample illumination. It makes a good spot to do jigsaw puzzles. The Nadler's have a good supply.

Off the entry, a 32' by 14' sunroom has windows around two sides. It has a large stone fireplace, an eight person hot tub and a juke box. There is white wicker seating and a wrought iron glass top table with four matching chairs. The room is fully carpeted.

The four first floor guestrooms share two baths, one with tub and the other with a shower. To one side of a large central area are two guestrooms and a bathroom. One guestroom is carpeted and has blinds at the windows. The walls have white paneling to the chair rail and cove molding at the ceiling. The room is furnished with a queen-size bed with a paisley spread, a cane back rocking chair and a round lamp table with reading lamp.

The second guestroom has carpeting in a floral design on a black background. The queen-size bed has a floral bedspread. There is a pair of wing chairs, a small night table, and a round lamp table with reading lamp. These rooms can be shared by a family or two couples traveling together.

On the other side of the central area are two more guestrooms. The third guestroom has a hooked rug on the floor and is furnished with a 1930s queen-size short poster bed, a pair of pink wing chairs and a round lamp table with reading lamp.

The fourth guestroom has a queen-size bed, a maple dressing table, a lamp table and lamp. The second bath is shared by these two room. All guestrooms are attractively appointed and have clock radios.

A spiral staircase from the central area leads to a carpeted tower room that has seating and a card table, plus a good view of the town. There is also an exercise room here. It has comfortable furniture and a television. Be sure to make use of this room.

A large covered pavilion is furnished with outdoor furniture including a table with benches, a chaise lounge, a refrigerator and grill for guest use. If you have children with you, be sure to check out the animals and if you come in the fall be sure to ask about the moonlight hayrides!

A full breakfast is served in the dining area. It consists of fresh squeezed orange juice, a fresh fruit plate in season, an egg casserole, potatoes with link sausages, homemade breads and muffins, caramel coffeecake, coffee, tea, jams and jellies all served family style.

DAS GAST NADLER HAUS B & B: 125 Defiance Road, Defiance, 63341. (636) 987-2200. Open all year. Children welcome. No pets. No smoking in guestrooms. Four guestrooms with two shared baths. Close to the Katy Trail, wineries and the historic Daniel Boone Home. Dave and Jacquie Nadler, innkeepers.

DIRECTIONS: From I-70 or I-64 (40/61 to Highway 94. South on 94 to Defiance. Turn right at S curve on Defiance Road. 1/2 block to Das Gast Nadler Haus.

PARSONS HOUSE BED & BREAKFAST
Defiance

In 1842, Thomas and Phoebe Parsons left Virginia and settled on this hill overlooking the Missouri River valley. That same year they started building their Federal style home.

The Parsons House, originally heated by five fireplaces, now has the modern comforts of central air conditioning and heat although three fireplace are still working. The house retains the original doors and floors, porches, high ceilings and antique light fixtures. Furnishing include antiques, family heirlooms and pieces collected by owners, Al and Carol Keyes, during their travels.

The house sits on eight acres and the award-winning gardens are delightful for relaxing in the hammock, the old fashioned swing or the bubbly hot tub.

A large entry hall has the original woodwork, doors, windows and floors. There is a long sideboard and a desk on oriental carpets.

To the right of the entry the "gathering room" is for guests to enjoy. It is stocked with books, games of other times and musical instruments. It is furnished with a circa 1650 German "box-table," a camel back sofa, a French provincial chair, an ornate marble top wash stand, coffee table, two arm chairs, an antique rocker, a French provincial hutch and a piano. Large bookcases are on each side of the fireplace, and a curio cabinet holds Carol's china doll collection. An antique lamp hangs over a table and chairs where breakfast is served.

Afternoon tea is served on the thirty foot porch at the rear of the house with windows across two sides. It is furnished with wrought iron table and chairs, a television and wicker chairs. You can see the old log beams. The first and second floor porches provide a view of the Katy Trail bikers and walkers.

The Garden View Room captures the country atmosphere as you look down into the herb and flower gardens and out to the fields beyond. The brick fireplace is closed but the original mantel is still here. The floors are painted, the woodwork is white with yellow walls and a wallpaper border print. White curtains are at the deep set windows. Area rugs spruce up the floors. The room is furnished with a queen-size Jenny Lind bed, a circa 1856 French armoire, a wash stand painted green, a pair of upholstered chairs and a bedside table. It is decorated with quilts, pictures and a stained glass chandelier. There is a private bath.

The Van Dyke Room features one of the home's working fireplaces. From this room you look out across town to the Missouri River valley. It is furnished with a 1920s Jenny Lind full-size bed, chest and vanity, a pair of upholstered chairs and a rocker. A large rag rug in on the floor, blue curtains at the windows and there is white woodwork. Pictures and quilts are part of the decor. There is a private bath.

Phoebe's Suite is a large room with views to both the gardens and the valley. It is papered with a flower print in blues and pinks on an off-white ground. Furniture consists of a queen-size Eastlake bed, an Eastlake chest, a hand carved table flanked by wing chairs. Crisp white curtains, quilts and Godey prints complete the decor. The bath is private and has a strawberry pink claw foot tub.

Breakfast is served in the gathering room or on the porch. Carol serves a full breakfast which might consist of cherry juice, hot fruit soup in winter and a chilled melon soup in summer, cinnamon rolls, apricot/walnut bread, sherried eggs and spiced bacon. She varies her morning meal with a variety of homemade breads and egg combinations. There is always coffee, tea, cocoa or milk.

PARSONS HOUSE B & B: 211 Lee Street, P.O. Box 38 Defiance, 63341. (636) 798-2222 or (800) 355-6878. Open all year. Three guestrooms with private baths. Children 8 and older. No pets. Smoking on porches. Al and Carol Keyes, innkeepers.

DIRECTIONS: From St. Louis, take Hwy. 40/61 (I-64). Cross the Missouri River and turn south on Hwy. 94. Go nine miles to Defiance, turn right on 3rd Street, go one block up the hill to Lee Street.

FEMME OSAGE HAUS BED & BREAKFAST
Femme Osage

Nestled in the beautiful and historic Femme Osage Valley, the Femme Osage Haus is a typical farmhouse built more than 100 years ago. Most of the house stands now, as it was built, with very little being changed over the years. The previous owner, a 95-year-old German widow of the town blacksmith, lived here for 75 years, from 1915 until 1990. In fact, a wagon wheel, now in the yard and purchased at an auction, was from his blacksmith shop.

The present owners, Jim and Becky McCollum, added the gold fish pond and back garden area with a screened arbor, swimming pool and hot tub.

Guests arrive through the sunroom with its green and white ivy furniture and a view of the garden. This is a year-round porch used as a breakfast room with a wood-burning stove, pine paneled walls, summer decor and lots of live plants. A wonderful place to relax and enjoy yourselves.

The guest quarters are on the second floor. A common room for guests is very interesting. You can still see the hand-hewn uprights along two walls, old barn wood, 20 inches wide on one wall, and a small red print wallpaper on the other. There is a sink with a coffee maker, a small refrigerator and a microwave oven. Coffee, tea and popcorn are provided. The floors are original. The ceiling comes to a peak with several beams. It is furnished with a daybed that opens to a king-size bed, an old steamer trunk for an end table, an oak bookcase with books and games, an antique rocker, a 1920s wind-up Victrola, a chifferobe and a round table with four rush seated chairs. An oriental carpet is on the floor and the walls have antique prints and plates.

The Morning Glory Room has an antique, carved high back, full-size bed, an antique marble top dresser with candle stands, a bookcase with reading material, an antique potty chair, a lyre back oval table and lamp, a cedar chest and a small Victorian love seat. Becky gave the walls and ceiling a different look by painting them blue with a feather duster. The floors have wall-to-wall gray carpet, the woodwork is white and white lace curtains are at the windows. There is a private bath with a shower.

The Violet Room is furnished with a queen-size brass and white metal bed with a hand made quilt, a wooden garden bench, a white bird cage on a stand, an antique table with a "Gone With the Wind" lamp, and a shaving mirror. A chair rail of a violet pattern paper border is painted lavender below and a lavender design above. White and green floral drapes over white blinds are at the windows. The woodwork is painted white. A door leads to a balcony overlooking the town.

Downstairs, the country kitchen has a round table and high back oak chairs, a hoosier cabinet and a red antique rocker. One wall has wide, old barn wood painted red, two walls have gray paneling with a chair rail, and one wall is the original wooden wall. On the tops of the cabinets and on the walls, Becky has all kinds of collectibles and antiques.

Becky serves a full country breakfast that includes juice and coffee in your room an hour before breakfast. She serves juice, fresh fruit in season, a hot potato and pepper dish and French toast with cherry sauce. Bacon and sausage, homemade poppy seed muffins, homemade jellies, jams and apple butter are served with all entrees.

Upon arrival, Becky offers apple cider in the winter and iced tea in the summer along with chocolate chip cookies or lemon bars.

Jim and Becky have four acres of the original farm with the old red barn, corn crib and chicken house. A patio has outdoor furniture. There is a garden, trees, lilac bushes and flowering quince. And, a great view. It's the perfect getaway. Go out, sit under the stars in the hot tub, relax in the porch swing, or take a stroll through this historic town of Femme Osage. The church, schoolhouse and cemetery all date back to 1830.

FEMME OSAGE HAUS B & B: 4383 Cappeln-Osage, Femme Osage, 63332. (636) 482-4005. Open all year. Not suited for children. No pets. Smoking on balcony, deck or in sunroom. MC/Visa and Discovery cards. A two room B & B with private baths. A variety of activities available in the nearby towns of Augusta, Dutzow, Washington, or Hermann. Jim and Becky McCollum, innkeepers.

DIRECTIONS: From Hwy. 94 and the town of Augusta, take 94 south approximately 0.5 mile and make a right turn (west) onto Hwy. T. Follow Hwy. T about 5 miles to the town of Femme Osage and make a right turn on Cappeln-Osage Road. The Femme Osage Haus is the first farmhouse on the left.

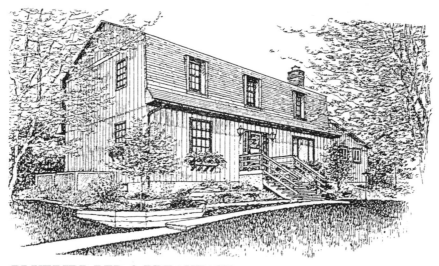

BLUEBIRD BED & BREAKFAST
Gerald

A winding lane lined with oak, pine and maple trees leads to Mary Jane and Don Boettcher's bed and breakfast home. It resembles a peaceful English country setting. There are so many varieties of trees and shrubs and hundreds of flowers. And so much privacy!

At the end of a living/dining combination is a large brick fireplace which holds a collection of Roseville pottery on the mantelpiece. This area is furnished with a sofa and a pair of wing chairs. The coffee table displays a collection of knives, locks and watches. An antique glass door cupboard holds a collection of silver plate. A picture window overlooks the wooded area. There is an oriental area rug laid over the wall-to-wall carpeting.

At the other end of the room is a French Provincial table with cane back chairs where breakfast is usually served. A sofa table holds a cut glass collection and breakfast dishes that have a different pattern on each place setting. The walls display fish prints, a fly rod and many nice decorations. An unusual mahogany roll-top desk has 37 drawers.

A family room has a sofa and love seat, a mahogany secretary, an upholstered recliner rocker, an antique trunk for a coffee table, an antique platform rocker and an old checkerboard table. There is a television and VCR. A door opens to a screened-in porch furnished with wicker and wrought iron.

Four guestrooms are on the second floor. In the Captain's Quarter's note the colorful nautical map, the steamer trunk, ship models, brass lanterns, and a pottery crock filled with rolled up maps. The room has twin beds, an antique upholstered rocker, a glass door secretary desk and a pair of captain's chairs. The floor has wall-to-wall carpeting with an oriental area rug over it. The door has an authentic port hole.

The Wild Bird Room is furnished with a queen-size four poster bed, a pair of night tables with lamps, an antique chest and a rocker and captain's chair. Small area rugs cover the floor. Above the chair rail is pheasant wallpaper print in teal. Below the rail is a paper with a small all-over print. The room has duck decoys and bird prints as decorations.

An extra large bath has a tub and shower. It also has a collection of bird houses and small decorator pieces. The walls are done in a plaid paper. This bath is shared by these rooms or contracted privately.

The Garden Room is a large room with an oriental carpet. It has a king-size French Provincial headboard, an antique chest, wardrobe, night tables and lamps, a small rocking chair and a lamp table with a reading lamp. One wall is papered in a print and the other walls are painted off white. A bird print border is at the ceiling. The bed comforter, drapes and table linens match.

The Star Gazer Room is named for astronaut Susan Helms, a daughter of close friends. Susan's "picture wall" contains memorabilia from her three launches. The room is furnished with a double low poster bed, a night table in matching maple, a small deacons bench and a quilt rack. The blue and white walls have a print of stars and there is a real telescope-for stargazing of course. The carpet is blue and white. Pictures of earth, as seen from space, are on the walls. A large bath with shower is shared by the two rooms or contracted privately.

Breakfast consists of fresh squeezed orange juice, in season, fresh grapefruit and orange sections with Grand Mariner, french toast, cheese pie, Canadian bacon, grilled tomatoes and steamed asparagus, sweet rolls, honey wheat bread and fresh ground coffee. With advance notice Mary Jane will prepare a gourmet dinner.

BLUEBIRD B & B: 5734 Mill Rock Road, Gerald, 63037. (573) 627-2515. Open all year. Children over 11 welcome. No pets. Smoke free indoors. Smoking on deck, except during high fire alert. A four guestroom home with two baths. Don and Mary Jane Boettcher, innkeepers.

DIRECTIONS: Take I-44 to Union Exit (Hwy. 50) Proceed west to Gerald. Turn left at first intersection in Gerald (Hwy. H) and proceed on H across the Bourbeuse River. Go 1.8 miles to Mill rock Road. Turn left and go .2 miles to first driveway on your right. Take driveway to the Bluebird.

HERMANN

Hermann, nestled among the peaceful hills along the Missouri River, looks like a little piece of Europe transported to Middle America. And no wonder, for it was founded by the *Deutsche Ansiedlumgs Gesellschaft zu Philadelphia*—the German settlement of Philadelphia—to be a colony where German Fatherland's language and customs would be preserved.

Scouts were sent to Illinois, Indiana, Missouri, and other places to select a site. They chose Missouri, perhaps because it was home to Friedrich Muench and Paul Follenius, leaders of the Settlement Society of Giessen, which had hoped to found a German state on this continent.

The society had given the proposed town the name of Hermann. They also drew plans for the town naming many of the streets in honor of both German and American heroes (Franklin, Gutenberg, Schiller, Mozart, Washington, Goethe and Jefferson). The main street, Market, was to be 10 feet wider than the Market Street of Philadelphia because the society felt that someday Hermann would be larger than Philadelphia.

Anxious to get the settlement underway, the society sent 17 members to Missouri in the winter of 1837-38. They came up the river on the last boat of the season, landing at the site on December 6, 1837. In the spring, 230 people made the trip to the new colony. By 1839, the population had grown to 450. When the society in Philadelphia disbanded, Hermann became incorporated and the colony was on its own.

One of the settlers first concerns was shelter. To meet this basic need, the people utilized both the natural resources and the German building style. The end result can be seen today in the orange-pink brick and stone buildings. The brick was made from the clay found around Hermann. The stone is limestone and sandstone, also prevalent in the area. In keeping with the local wine industry, many of the houses have wine cellars.

Soon the hills and valleys surrounding Hermann, like the Rhine Valley in Germany, were covered with vineyards and orchards to support a growing wine industry. By 1900 this village was exporting more wine than any town in the United States.

Though the perfect German colony never fully materialized, the dream is alive in today's historic Hermann. In fact, 108 buildings are listed on the

National Register of Historic Places. These historic buildings have been renovated and used to house antique shops, art galleries, restaurants, bed & breakfasts and other places of business.

There are again three wineries in Hermann. *Stone Hill Winery* was established in 1847 and the entire winery is now a National Historic District. The huge underground arched cellars are said to be the largest in the country. At one time, Stone Hill was the world's third largest winery with over a million gallons of wine produced yearly. Jim and Betty Held conduct tours of the premises, have a tasting room and patio, and some spectacular views of Hermann from the grounds. This place is a must see on anybody's list. (573) 486-2221.

Another must is the *Hermannhof Winery* on First Street. Jim and Mary Dierberg purchased the winery in the 1970s and spent three years restoring it. It, too, is a historic site and all of the ten stone and brick cellars and the smokehouse are open daily for tours. Visitors can picnic in the garden area, taste the many varieties of wines, and are able to purchase homemade sausages in the food shop. (573) 486-5959.

The *Adam Puchta Winery* is Missouri's oldest continuously owned family farm winery. In 1839, John Henry Puchta brought his family and his wine making skills from his native Bavaria to the Frene Valley near Hermann. Here he planted vineyards and built a house and arch wine cellar of native stone. The Puchta Winery was recognized for its quality wines until prohibition destroyed the industry. In 1988, Tim Puchta moved into the old family home, restored the vineyards and the original buildings. Now, you can tour the stone wine cellar, view the original stone wheeled grape crusher and wine press, taste the award winning wines and enjoy locally made cheeses and sausages in the tasting room or out under the trees. (573) 486-5596 or 486-2361.

Needless to say, Hermann has some exceptional antique shops where you are welcome to browse or buy.

Pete's Plunder at 202 E. First Street specializes in oak, pine and walnut furniture, along with jewelry and glassware. Pete Canady, the owner, has an impressive variety of furniture to choose from, including early Missouri pieces. When I was there I saw a walnut wishbone dresser, a three piece, carved walnut parlor suite, a walnut jelly cupboard, a cherry Empire dresser, a walnut two door wardrobe, a set of six Hitchcock chairs, a one drawer walnut table, an immigrant trunk, an English linen press, a six drawer chest on chest, a two drawer two door walnut wardrobe and a walnut day bed. Other pieces included a Stickley 60" round oak table, an Arts and Crafts oak buffet, a carved oak bookcase with glass doors, an oak Lincoln desk, a wicker oval table, a round table with four rush seated chairs and a Japanese decorated tea cart. There was also silver plate, brass items, sets of dishes, frames prints, a wall telephone, crocks, quilts and primitives. (573) 486-3900.

Countryside Antiques, owned by Carrie and Dodie Williams, has some early furniture in mint condition. Among the pieces I saw here were a walnut and butternut baker's cabinet, a nice pine jelly cupboard, a circa 1850 chest, an S-roll-top oak desk with raised panels, a walnut pie safe, a great pine harvest table, a walnut served, a very early bucket bench, a dry sink, a walnut pegged corner cupboard, a walnut tapered leg one drawer table, a circa 1800 Walnut jelly cupboard, a walnut two drawer table, a small table with four Windsor chairs, an early cupboard with five shelves and one drawer in the original paint, several nice wall shelves, a copper apple butter kettle and the top of an old pine cupboard that would make a great hanging wall cupboard. They also had baskets, wooden kitchen utensils, yellow-ware, toys, framed prints, quilts, nice crocks and primitives. Located at 110 E. First Street. (573) 486-2039 or 249-3467.

There is also the *Countryside Antique Gallery* located at 338 E. First Street. (573) 486-5307. It contains five or six rooms plus an old stone wine cellar filled with a lot of nice things including a shaker style yarn winder, a walnut flat wall cupboard, an early painted pie safe, a five leg table in Walnut, a marble top walnut wash stand, a Victorian love seat, a cherry Empire chest of drawers, a mission oak bookcase, a butcher block table, a walnut and pine pegged pie safe, a walnut four drawer cupboard, a walnut washstand, Victorian wash stand, a wooden coffee box and a hand-made walnut bookcase desk. There were lots of old tools, decoup, kitchen woodenware, quilts, apple peelers and all sorts of small items.

When you get tired of shopping and want to try some Hermann food, let me make a few suggestions. The *Wein Stube* at Hermannhof Winery is like stepping back into colonial times. It is furnished with old tavern tables and chairs, an antique corner cupboard holds steins, and a large fireplace with a collection of antlers on it. Wide board floors give the room a look of antiquity. You can have German style sandwiches such as bratwurst, summer sausage and German bologna. Soup is served in the winter and potato salad in the summer. 330 E. First Street, (573) 486-5959.

I like Ben Stella *Leija's Landing Restaurant.* You can enjoy fine dining in a warm country atmosphere, surrounded with primitive pieces of farm and early country life. The menu offers German dishes such as Roulades of beef, sauteed chicken livers (Bavarian style), grilled bratwurst and knackwurst sausage, sauerbraten and schnitzel. But there are also steaks, beef liver, prime rib and country fried steak. You can also order New England scrod, boiled red snapper, jumbo fried shrimp, Atlantic cod and halibut steak if you are in the mood for seafood. All dinners are served with homemade soup and salad bar and choice of potato. Don't forget a bottle of Hermann wine. Located at 4 Schiller Street. (573) 486-2030.

VINTAGE RESTAURANT AT STONE HILL WINERY
Hermann

I would have to say Vintage Restaurant is my favorite restaurant in Missouri. It has all the ingredients of a fine restaurant: charming ambience, delightful staff, and of course, unexcelled cuisine.

Jim and Betty Held, owners of Stone Hill Winery, have done a magnificent job of renovating this hundred-year-old stable at the winery into a dining establishment listed as one of the "best restaurants in America." So come in, hang your hat on a hitching post, take your seat in what was once a horse stall and enjoy a memorable dining experience.

Lunch entrees include fresh New England seafood, a wine country picnic (an assortment of cheese, fruit and a pate served with mustard and assorted breads), smoked German sausage and schnitzel, Jaegerschnitzel, and a fantastic hamburger.

The dinner menu offers filet of beef Oscar and breast of chicken poivon rouge with angel hair pasta. German entrees include wiener and pork schnitzel. Seafood is flown in from New England and the icy waters of the North Atlantic to assure only the freshest and finest New Brunswick salmon, New England scallops, and Maine crab. Entrees include your choice of potato du jour, baked potato or wild rice and freshly prepared vegetables.

All desserts are prepared fresh daily. The Black Forest Cake is great.

VINTAGE RESTAURANT: At Stone Hill Winery, Hermann. 65401. (573) 486-3479. Open all year. Call for reservations & hours.

ANGELS IN THE ATTIC BED & BREAKFAST
Hermann

Angels in the Attic, listed on the National Register of Historic Places, is a three-story brick Victorian mansion built by William Klinger in 1878. It was one of the earliest of the pretentious homes built by successful business men in Hermann. Klinger owned the steam-powered Hermann Star Mill. It is now home to Lynn and Frank Stephens.

When you enter the inn, you step back in time to the elegance and grace of a bygone era. The magnificent, carved cherry wood staircase is most unusual. There is also a hall seat, wicker chairs and an antique library table.

Off the hallway, the parlor still retains the original ceiling medallion, the original brass, gas chandelier, now electrified, and a beautiful stained glass window. There is a large floral design area carpet, and a highly carved mantel with a tile fireplace. It is furnished with an upholstered sofa and wing chair, an unusual antique Missouri-made bookcase secretary, an antique oval table with four antique chairs, a pie crust tri-pod table and six antique cane-bottom chairs. Lynn serves her guests breakfast in the parlor, with candlelight from the candles n the fireplace.

Lynn and Frank offer four rooms, all decorated with furnishings from another time, which have been collected over many years. Each of the rooms have private bath, designer bed linens on extremely comfortable beds and the room's own angel.

The Gardenside Room is everything one would want in a private retreat! A two-person whirlpool, breakfast in bed and a fireplace. It is furnished with a king-size wrought iron bed, a round bamboo table and two chairs, a rattan tea cart, wicker chest and reading lamps. It has wall-to-wall carpet, a gas burning fireplace, and in the back, a two-person jacuzzi with a hand-held shower head. This private room is located off of a large secluded brick New Orleans-style courtyard, landscaped with trees, shrubs and brick-edged flower gardens.

Two guestrooms and a sitting room are on the second floor. The Englishman's Room is furnished with a queen-size high back bed, an English dresser, tea cart, an upholstered, damask William and Mary style chair and night tables with reading lamps. A tile fireplace is surrounded by a heavily carved mantel piece, for show only. A floral carpet is on the floor and white sheer curtains are at the windows. The private bath is furnished with a whirlpool for two and a shower.

The Bridal Bouquet Room has a queen-size four poster canopy bed, an antique dresser with glove boxes and candle stands, an antique drop-leaf table with a reading lamp, an upholstered love seat and an antique sewing machine base. Nice circa 1920 framed prints are on the walls that have faux marble wallpaper. Puffy Roman shades are at the windows. There is a television. The private bath has a tub and shower.

The sitting room has a wicker love seat, table and chairs, a sewing machine base that holds a coffee pot and condiments, and an open arm chair. Framed prints are on the floral design wallpapered walls and an area rug is on the floor.

On the third floor, The Captain's Lady Room has a queen-size wrought iron bed, a pink stripe upholstered wing chair, a library table, and a television. There is a private bath with shower. A sitting area, under the eaves, has seating and a table. A coffee maker assures fresh morning coffee or tea. There are plenty of games and such to entertain you.

Breakfast is served from 9 to 10:30 a.m. If you like morning coffee, have a cup or two in your room before breakfast. A full breakfast consists of seasonal juice, a fruit plate, French toast with raspberry sauce or quiche with mushrooms. It could be eggs souffle or Frank's banana pecan waffles with maple syrup. The entrees include a breakfast meat and coffee cake.

ANGELS IN THE ATTIC B & B: 108 E. Second Street, Hermann, 65041. (573) 486-5037 or (888) ANGEL53. Open every day. All year except the last three weeks in January. A four guestroom with private bath. No children or pets. Smoking outdoors. MC/Visa, Discovery and American Express accepted. Http://www.bestinns.net/usa/mo. Frank and Lynn Stephens, innkeepers.

DIRECTIONS: From I-70, turn south onto Hwy. 19 (Exit 175). Go south 15 miles to Hermann. Hwy. 19 becomes Market Street. Go two blocks and turn onto Second Street. Or, from I-44, go west on Hwy. 100 (Washington Exit). Go 45 miles to Hermann. Hwy. 100 becomes First Street. Turn left at Schiller, go one block and turn right onto Second Street.

AUNT FLORA'S BED & BREAKFAST
Hermann

The known history of the building and lot known as Aunt Flora's B & B began when George Bayer purchased the land in 1837. After several changes of ownership, it was sold to George Schneider in 1854, who built this historic brick house with the traditional tin roof and dormer windows. Known as the Schneider-Brendel House, it had seven owners between 1854 and 1990, when the current owner, Irene Flora Habsieger purchased it intact with the antique furniture that is still here in the house.

Two guestrooms, located on the second floor, are reached by the original staircase. Old beaded tongue and groove walls are original as are the floors, dormer windows and the woodwork.

One guestroom is furnished with 1920s vintage twin beds and a matching dresser. There is also a cedar chest, a rush seated arm chair, night table with lamp, a platform rocker and a television. The room is very cozy located under the eaves with a beamed ceiling. The walls are chair rail high then slope toward the ceiling. Three walls are wallpapered in a blue floral and stripe print. The fourth wall is the original beaded woodwork. There are white curtains on the dormer windows. A hall bath has a tub and shower.

Another guestroom with beamed ceilings has a full-size bed covered with a handmade quilt, a chest, dresser, two rocking chairs, quilt rack, a mini-refrigerator, and a television. A night table has a "Gone with the Wind" lamp. The wall as are papered in a floral print and the two dormer windows are curtained. There are pictures, house plants and a nice floral arrangement. This room has a private bath attached.

Downstairs, in the dining room, a full breakfast is served. Irene prepares breakfast starting with steaming, fresh ground coffee served with a nicely arranged fruit plate, selected according to the season. In addition, a basket of freshly baked bread and a hot egg souffle dish right out of the oven makes this meal at Aunt Flora's something to remember.

The room is furnished with an antique oak table and chairs, a hutch, hand-made pie safe and a German shrank. A cobbler's bench is used for plants. An antique safe (Schnitzel banc) is one of several nice antique pieces. The room is papered in a green floral design.

In a quaint cottage garden setting with herbs, hollyhocks, other flowers and shrubs is Aunt Flora's Summer House. Tucked away on the back portion of the lot, this little building predates the Civil War, although no records have yet been found to verify it. However, in the walls, were found newspapers dated prior to the war along with a child's shoe from the same period which are on display.

This "gingerbread house" is complete with living room, kitchen, cozy attic bedroom and a bath with whirlpool tub and shower, and a large porch with table and adirondack chairs.

The sitting room has a fireplace and a queen-size sleeper sofa. The kitchen has refrigerator, microwave and an antique cupboard holding antique dishes. From the kitchen, the enclosed stairway with its original wide tongue and groove paneling, leads to the second floor loft and a quaint bedroom. It is furnished with a queen-size bed covered with a handmade quilt, an antique wash stand, a rush seated arm chair and an antique lamp table with reading lamp. Floral curtains with green swags are over the windows. A portion of the original wooden ceiling is still intact.

The original double brick outhouse still stands in the back yard as a reminder of the "Good Old Days."

AUNT FLORA'S B & B: 127 East 5th Street, Hermann, 65041. (573) 486-3591. Open all year. No children under 8. No pets. Smoking on porches only. A minimum two night stay during Maifest and Octoberfest weekends. Anniversary and wedding specials. Central location in the historic district of Hermann with easy access to museums, restaurants, wineries, antique and craft shops. Will pickup Amtrak travelers. Gift certificates available. Irene Flora Habsieger, innkeeper.

DIRECTIONS: Located in the Historic District of Hermann. Call for required reservations and directions.

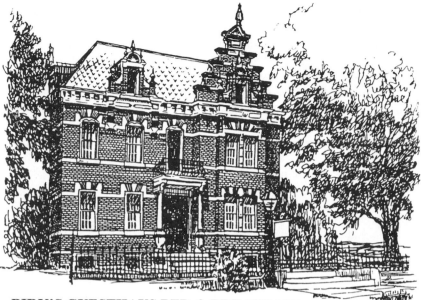

BIRK'S GUESTHAUS BED & BREAKFAST
Hermann

If murder mysteries are your thing, be sure to participate in Rick and Dianne Pankau's Birk's Mansion Mystery Weekend held in their three-story Victorian home.

Built in 1886 by George Stark, one of the owners of the Stone Hill Winery, at one time the third largest winery in the country, the mansion reminds me of something that Alfred Hitchcock would fall in love with.

The interior of the house has the marvelous look of baronial opulence, 10 foot doors with transoms, beautiful woodwork and fixtures.

On the first floor, a parlor has red wall-to-wall carpeting, which also is in the dining room. It is furnished with a Victorian square grand piano, a Victorian sofa and two Victorian armchairs. A large brass chandelier can't be missed. Lace curtains are at the windows.

The dining room still retains the original carved marble fireplace. Six unusual chairs with carved faces on the back are placed around a large dining table. A vintage china cabinet holds pink depression glass.

There are nine guestrooms, seven with private baths and two that share a bath. All of the rooms have a homey touch, but each are different, creating their own look.

Five of the guestrooms are on the second floor. At the top of the stairs, an area has an upholstered sofa, a coffee table and a slant front desk. There is also a television. Rooms are numbered rather than normal.

One has a king-size brass bed, an antique wardrobe, a wicker glass top table and three chairs, and a reproduction of an antique dresser.

Two is furnished with a king-size brass bed, an antique fainting couch, an English dresser and a bookcase.

Three has a fireplace with gas logs. There is a king-size brass bed, a burled wardrobe, a marble top dresser and a roll top desk.

Four is furnished with a full-size iron and brass bed, an antique dresser and a platform rocker.

Five has a full-size brass bed an antique chifferobe and an antique dresser. Rooms four and five share the bath.

On the third floor are the remaining four guestrooms. Six is furnished with a three-piece mahogany queen-size bed, a matching chest and dresser, a rocking chair and a bedside table.

Seven has an antique, carved queen-size high back bed, an oak low boy chest, bookcase and a washstand.

Eight is furnished with a queen-size wrought iron poster bed with a lace canopy, an antique dresser, a rocker and two matching bedside tables with lamps.

Nine (last but not least) has a full-size brass bed, an antique oak dresser, bookcase and a pair of nightstands. There is also a Jacuzzi in this room.

A full breakfast is served in the L shaped main dining/family room. Three tables have seating for up to twenty-four people. There are a piano, a television and a table for cards or games, and, there are plenty of games.

Breakfast starts off with juice, fresh fruit in season. Then the entrée is served and could be an egg casserole served with hash browns, sausage and cinnamon rolls. Or maybe a French toast casserole: a layer of French bread, cubed on the bottom of a casserole – then a layer of cream cheese followed by a layer of cubed French bread. It's soaked overnight in a rich egg mixture.

But the real attraction here is the mystery weekend, played on the first weekend of the month, excluding Octoberfest weekends. It is put on by the owners and their family who plays characters such as the butler, maid and even as guests. After arrivals Friday night, wine and cheese appetizers are served in the dining room. At 7:30 p.m. dinner is served. The scene of the mystery will start to unveil with the suspect's clues and other aspects of the soon-to-be-crime at this time. The next day is spent scurrying to investigate, interrogate, and attempt to solve the mystery, and unmask the villain. Guests have not only enjoyed the mystery but the new found friends who participated.

BIRK'S GUESTHAUS B & B: 700 Goethe St., Hermann, 65041. (573) 486-2911. Open all year except Easter. A nine room guesthouse mansion. No pets. Children welcome. Smoking outside. Rick and Dianne Pankau, innkeepers.

DIRECTIONS: From I-70, take Hwy. 19, 15 miles to Hermann. At 6th St., go west 3 blocks and turn south on Goethe 1 block.

CAPTAIN WOLHT INN
Hermann

The Captain Wolht Inn is located in the heart of Hermann's National Historic Register District. It consists of three properties that include two separate circa 1840, two story brick buildings that were built adjoining each other. The third building was Captain Wohlt's frame home, built in 1886 as his retirement home. It sets at the top of a hill just a few feet behind the other property. Charlotte Reed is the owner.

In the west building, the Peter's Suite has an entrance from the street. Entering the house, you are in a setting room, furnished with a barley twist day bed, an antique platform rocker, an upholstered Martha Washington arm chair, a small barley twist table, a coffee table and a television on a lady's desk. The bedroom has a queen-size four poster bed and two marble top stands with lamps are used as bedside tables. An antique immigrant's trunk is at the foot of the bed. The bath has stone walls on two sides and a kitchen has one stone wall and a fireplace, once used for cooking.

You enter the Poeschel Suite, on the second floor, above the Peter's Suite, from a deck on the upper level. It is furnished with an upholstered sofa, an upholstered arm chair, an old wash bench used for a coffee table, a wrought iron ice cream table with four chairs, television, floor lamp and an antique wooden rocking chair. The bedroom had an antique, queen-size bed, and an antique parlor table, an antique schoolteacher's desk and a child's rocker. The bath has a claw foot tub and shower. A door leads to a balcony.

On the first floor of the adjoining building, the Wicker Suite's entrance is from the street. A sitting area has a love seat, coffee table and two armchairs all in matching wicker. There is a wrought iron ice cream table and a floor lamp. The bedroom has a cannonball four poster maple bed, a pair of wicker night table and lamps a wicker desk and chairs. The bath has a shower.

Captain Wohlt's home has five guestrooms, each with a private bath with a tub and shower or a shower only.

The entry hall has the original staircase. The hall has blue headed paneling below a chair rail, with print patterned wallpaper above.

To the left of the entry, a large guestroom is furnished with a queen-size four poster bed, a dresser and a matching night table. A sitting area has an upholstered love seat and a floor lamp. It is carpeted in a gray carpet. The woodwork is blue and lace curtains are on the windows.

To the right of the entry, a large dining room is furnished with an antique oval table and six ladder back chairs. Two tables, one with four ice cream chairs accommodate the inn's guests at breakfast.

The second floor has two guestrooms. One has a full-size white poster bed, a wicker armchair, a pair of night tables, a Windsor chair and an antique table with a reading lamp. It has gray wall-to-wall carpet and lace curtains on the 4 over 4 panel windows.

The other guestroom is furnished with a king-size bed with a spindle headboard, a deacon's bench, a Victorian chair and a small one drawer work table. Lace curtains are at the window. A door leads to a private balcony.

On the third floor, under the eaves, are two guestrooms. The sloping ceilings unique nooks and dormer windows give these rooms an attractive, intimate atmosphere. Both are carpeted and have lace curtains at the windows. One is furnished with a full-size Jenny Lind bed covered with a patch quilt, an antique Peerless sewing machine with a marble top, a night table and lamp. The other room also has a full-size Jenny Lind bed with a hand-made quilt on it, an antique rocker, a pair of night tables with bureau lamps and a rush seated rocker and straight chair.

All of the guestrooms of Captain Wolht Inn have carpeting, dried flower arrangements and pictures. They are all decorated very nicely to give Charlotte's guest a warm and cheerful feeling.

Enjoy a full breakfast, beginning with freshly ground coffee. Have your first cup before breakfast on the brick patio, then to the dining room at Captain Wohlt's house. Breakfast consists of juice, fresh fruit in season, then French Toast or a baked egg, each with sausage, ham or bacon. Homemade tea bread, coffee, tea or milk.

CAPTAIN WOLHT INN B & B: 123 E. Third Street, Hermann, 65041. (573) 486-3357. Open all year. These historic buildings with three suites and five guestrooms. Families are welcome. Infant accommodations in the Poeschel Suite. Children under 12 stay free in their parent's suite. A smoke free inn. No pets. Missy is the resident dog and B.J. is the cat. Charlotte Reed, innkeeper.

DIRECTIONS: From St. Louis: I-70 west to Hwy. 19 south, then 15 miles to Hermann. Or I-44 to Hwy. 100-Washington exit, west to Hermann.

DREI MADELHAUS BED & BREAKFAST
Hermann

S itting in the heart of the National Historic District of Hermann, Drei Madelhaus B & B is a charming neo-classic brick home. Built on one of the first lots sold in the town, the building dates back to 1849. Mr. Kessler used it as his residence and a real estate office. Originally just one room on the first floor and one room upstairs, it was built as so many of the German houses of the early period, flush with the sidewalk. An addition of other first floor rooms was made in the mid-1890s. There is a small brick and wood cottage with a patio in back and a grape arbor on one side of the house. Flower gardens and shrubs decorate the yard.

The owners, Artur Hohl and Connie Czeschin, moved to Hermann from Seattle, Washington and purchased this bed and breakfast renaming it Drei Madelhaus (three girls house) after their three daughters. Connie's family is originally from the area and Artur, a native of Germany, is also a potter. Anyone with a love of fine crafts will be delighted to visit his showroom where you will find cookie jars, vases, dishes, bowls, cups and saucers and candle holders for sale. He is now producing garden fountains and hand carved and fired tiles in German heritage designs.

With the owners living away, this is a comfortable pleasant place to relax for a single party or a group.

In the keeping room or parlor, the original floors of yellow pine show the age of this house. There is a great Rumford fireplace. It is furnished with a sofa, and antique rocker, a Queen Anne coffee table, a lamp table and lamp and an antique chiffarobe which holds a television and VCR. A table and chairs are set in a bay window. The walls are papered in a cheery white and red flowered print.

A small fully equipped kitchen, papered in a burgundy print, is furnished with a refrigerator and stove and is available for guests to use. An old original door leads to the second floor guestroom. French doors open onto a patio with a wrought iron table and chairs; a nice place for breakfast in warm weather.

A downstairs guestroom is furnished with a 1920s style full-size bed and a matching dresser. There is also a table and lamp, a floor lamp, an antique straight back chair, and an antique coat rack. A hand woven wool rug is on the floor. The walls are papered in a pale green below a chair rail with a rose pattern above. White cottage curtains are at the windows. There is a heated mattress pad on the bed, as there are in each of the guestrooms. There is a private bath

The second floor guestroom, under the eaves, is furnished with a blue antique iron full-size bed topped with a handmade quilt. The rest of the room is in white wicker and includes a sofa, rocking chair, arm chair, coffee table, flower box and two bookcases that are used as end tables. The walls are papered in a beige marble pattern and dark blue curtains are at the windows. There is a private bath with a shower.

The private cottage at the back of the property is furnished with a full-size bed and a single bed covered with handmade quilts, a futon, a Boston rocker, and a small table and chairs. Both of the rooms in the cottage have handmade rugs on the floors, and green and white curtains at the windows. Shelving, to display samples of Artur's pottery, goes around all the walls of the two rooms. There is a private bath.

Connie and Artur serve a real German style breakfast. It consists of boiled potatoes that are sliced, fried onions, mushrooms and fried bratwurst. There is juice, and either fruit cup or 1/2 grapefruit, and apple cake. Artur rises each morning at five a.m. and bakes homemade bread. It is served fresh and hot accompanied by jams and jellies, coffee and tea.

DREI MADELHAUS B & B: 108 Schiller Street, Hermann, 65041. (573) 486-3552. A charming two guestroom house with private baths and additional small cottage for two-four with private bath, in the historical district. Open all year. Smoking on patio. Well-behaved children welcome. Close to the Katy Trail. Artur Hohl and his wife, Connie Czeschin, innkeepers.

DIRECTIONS: From Hwy. 100 east, go to Schiller Street and turn left. The cottage is in the first block. From Hwy. 19 take Second Street to Schiller and turn left 1/2 block. Reservations are a must.

ESTHER'S AUSBLIK BED & BREAKFAST
Hermann

Here is an immaculate brick bungalow built in 1939 and landscaped with many types of shrubs, flowers and tall trees, including a pecan tree. Many songbirds make their home on Esther's property and once in a while you may spot a red fox. Across the street is an old stone wall that overlooks the Missouri River. There is a great view of the boats coming and going.

Off the entry hall, the living room is furnished with a love seat, two marble-top fern stands with lamps, a piano (which you are welcome to play), an upholstered recliner, two chairs with cane sides and an entertainment center with a television set. The room is carpeted wall to wall and the fireplace always has a fire in the wintertime.

A carpeted sunroom, off the living room has eleven windows on three sides. Breakfast is usually served here, so there is a table, a pair of straight back chairs, two upholstered benches and a tea cart. Coffee is available.

The dining room is furnished with a French country dining table with six chairs, a small library table and an unusual corner cupboard. There is a marble-top Eastlake washstand and a marble-top buffet. The windows are shuttered. On occasion, breakfast is served here.

Esther puts a great breakfast on the table. She has several entrees and any of them will be more than enough to satisfy the hungriest appetite. The list includes Quiche Lorraine, bratwurst baked in wine, a fluffy omelet served with fried potatoes, sausage, onions and seasonings, or scrambled eggs with biscuits and mushroom gravy. There's always juice, a fruit dish of some type, homemade breads, jams and jellies and coffee, tea or milk.

Two guestrooms are on the first floor. The Riverview Room has a four piece matching bedroom set with queen-size bed, glass door armoire, dresser and night table. There is also a pair of Italian period chairs, a French upholstered arm chair. Lace curtains are at the windows and a small brass and crystal chandelier hangs from the window. Two walls are paneled while the other two are papered. A wall-to-wall salmon colored carpet is on the floor. There is a private bath.

The Country Classic Room on this floor is furnished with a white iron queen-size bed with an antique green and white quilt, an antique marble top circa 1850s dresser with candle stands, an antique walnut marble top wash stand with a back splash, a small night stand with a glass fairy lamp. It has a private bath with tub and shower. Notice the rare New England painted sleigh.

The Victorian Room, a second floor guestroom, has a pair of Jenny Lind twin beds pushed together, a lamp table with a reading lamp and a chair. There is a great circa 1830 marble-top dresser with a hand-carved mirror and a matching chest. Scatter rugs are on the floor and bedroom curtains at the windows.

The Under the Eaves Room, the second upstairs guestroom, has a queen-size antique reproduction oak bed, a matching dresser and a seven drawer chest. The quilt, pillow shams and balloon curtains are matched. There is a glass top and brass table and a chair.

Between the two guestrooms is a sitting area furnished with a sofa, a three drawer chest, a lamp and an ice cream table with four chairs. There is a refrigerator. A large private bath is shared by both rooms. However, if the occupants of these two guestrooms are not traveling together, Esther rents only one of the rooms.

In the rear yard there is a nice brick patio with a wrought iron glass top table, four cushioned chairs, two lawn chairs and a barbecue. A large tree shades the area in summer. The yard is landscaped with many shrubs and plants and a nice herb garden.

Another sunroom has a rattan sofa and chairs, a coffee table and lots of plants. It also has an eight person whirlpool tub. A door opens onto the patio.

ESTHER'S AUSBLIK B & B: 236 West Second Street, Hermann, 65041. (573) 486-2170. A four guestroom bungalow with three baths, facing the Missouri River. Open all year. Children during the week. No pets. Smoking only on the patio. Will pick up at Amtrak. Ideal for weddings and anniversaries. Esther Heberle, innkeeper.

DIRECTIONS: From Market Street (Hwy. 19/100) proceed to second street. Turn west on second.

HERMANN HILL VINEYARD & INN
Hermann

Situated on a bluff and surrounded by a vineyard, the backdrop for your stay here is an ever changing panorama of Hermann and the Missouri River Valley. Their Bavarian style house was built by Terry and Peggy Hammer for use as a bed and breakfast inn as well as for their own living quarters. Nothing has been spared to assured your comfort, privacy and freedom to set your own pace.

Each of Hermann Hill's spacious guestrooms feature large fireplaces with gas burning logs, high ceilings, French doors, solid oak woodwork, stained glass, private balconies and luxurious private baths with Jacuzzi style tubs for two, a TV/VCR, CD player, robes and a refrigerator.

Off the foyer, a large living room is furnished with a pair of sofas with tapestry upholstery, two Queen Anne arm chairs, coffee table, a marble top lamp table, an oak entertainment center with television and CD player and disks. The ceramic tile floor has an area carpet.

In a small alcove off the kitchen, a round oak table and chairs have a great view.

The dining room has a beamed ceiling and a beautiful stained glass back light in the ceiling. The room is furnished with a pedestal table with carved spindle back chairs and a pair of antique china cabinets with curved glass, holds silver, cruets, and cut glass. Three walls are painted green and the fourth wall is glass.

A staircase or an elevator takes you up to three guestrooms on the upper level. The Virginia Seedling Room is furnished with a king-size brass headboard, but they may be turned into twin beds if you prefer. There is a marble top antique washstand, bedside table, a mirrored armoire, an antique lamp table, and a pair of spindle back chairs. A large window offers a grand view.

The Cynthiana Room has a king-size sleigh bed, a secretary, bookcase, a marble top washstand, a Victorian table and two chairs. Two wall lamps are over the bed for reading.

The Norton Room is furnished with a king-size sleigh bed, an armoire, a marble top washstand, a rocking chair and an antique lamp table.

An exercise room on the lower level has a marble top antique sideboard with a microwave oven, a treadmill, exercise bike, Nordic-track and a weight bench for guests to use.

Back in the entry hall, take the stairs or elevator downstairs to two more guestrooms. The Vignoles Room has a king-size sleigh bed, and a pair of antique night tables with reading lamps. An antique oak wall phone and an antique mantle clock are part of the decor.

The Port Room is furnished with a king-size sleigh bed, two cane seated chairs, coffee table, a rocker and lamps. In all of the guestrooms Peggy and Terry have decorated the walls with the works of local artists.

Peggy serves a full breakfast with juice, always fruit and an egg dish, potatoes, English muffins, blueberry muffins, waffles or pancakes. There is cold cereal, coffee, tea or milk and jams and jellies. Ask Peggy about any special dietary needs.

Here you can sleep late, have breakfast in bed, walk to a nearby winery, explore a quiet old town, shop the many antique and craft shops, visit the many restaurants or simply relax and contemplate the view.

HERMANN HILL VINEYARD & INN: P.O. Box 555, Hermann, 65041. (573) 486-4455. Fax 573-486-5373. Open all year. No pets. No "smokers." A fine guest house inn with private bath and jacuzzi. MC/Visa, AE, and Discover cards accepted. Wheelchair accessible. Terry and Peggy Hammer, innkeepers.

DIRECTIONS: From Market Street (Hwy. 19) turn west onto Sixth Street, then left (south) on Washington and then right (west) on West Tenth. Hermann Hill Inn is at the top of the hill. Watch for signs.

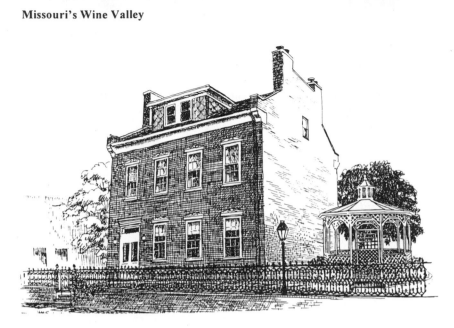

KOLBE GUEST HOUSE
Hermann

Facing the Missouri River, just a stones throw away, is yet another early Hermann building that has withstood the changes of time. The Eitzen House was built by Charles Eitzen, a councilman and shop keeper, in 1850. The front portion is the original 1850 structure with all the original woodwork, floors, and 12 foot ceilings. All built with fine German workmanship.

It's a great house and Mary Kolbe, the owner, is a great person. I'm sure you'll like her. The first floor contains Mary's parlor for her guests to use. It has several features: a marble fireplace, high ceilings, and deep set six over six pane windows. An oriental carpet is on the floor and the walls have original art work. Just part of the furnishings include a huge walnut armoire, an antique drop-front desk, a pine secretary bookcase, a burled antique parlor table and an antique hired-hand day bed. Gathered around the fireplace is an upholstered love seat, two wing chairs and a 16th Century six paneled oriental screen.

The breakfast area has a pedestal table with seating for ten people and an antique walnut step back cupboard that is very unusual.

At the top of the stairs, the South Wing Suite is two steps down from the landing. The sitting room is furnished with an antique desk, a pair of wing chairs upholstered in a crewel pattern, a chaise lounge and a Chinese document cabinet lacquered in black and gold with raised figures. There are three shuttered windows overlooking a gazebo and garden.

The guestroom has an Oriental carpet and walls papered in a teal green with a black stripe. The green matches the woodwork. There is a queen-size wrought iron bed, an upholstered wing chair, a lamp table and lamp and a cedar chest. The windows are also shuttered.

Back to the hall and up three steps will take you to the Eitzen Suite. An oriental carpet is on the floor in the sitting room. There are two windows with lace curtains. There is also a fireplace with an antique mantel clock on it. It is furnished with a 1920s sofa, an ornate coffee table, a pair of burgundy wing chairs, lamp table and lamp, an antique wardrobe and an iron day bed. The bedroom is furnished with an antique fainting couch, a four poster queen-size bed, a walnut butler's desk, a wig stand dresser with a collection of Mary's china and porcelain and an antique walnut table and chair. There are nice picture and floral arrangements. A private bath has a shower.

The Blue Room has an oriental carpet, an Eastlake full-size bed, night stand with lamp, a wing chair upholstered in a blue stripe, an antique library table and a parlor chair. Three of the walls are solid blue beneath a chair rail and a floral print above it. There is a private bath.

A full breakfast of breakfast meat, eggs, fried potatoes, fresh bakery goods, orange juice, fresh fruit, and coffee or tea is served in the first floor kitchen.

KOLBE GUEST HAUS: 214 Wharf Street, Hermann, 65041. (573) 486-3453. Three guestrooms with private bath in circa 1850 home. Open all year. Children welcome. No pets. No smoking. Mary Kolbe, host.

DIRECTIONS: Coming into Hermann on Hwy. 100, (First Street) from Washington, turn right on Gutenberg and go one block to Wharf Street. From Highway 19, (Market Street) turn east onto First Street (Hwy. 100) and go to Schiller. Turn left and go one block to Wharf Street.

A LITTLE LOG CABIN IN THE WOODS
Hermann

For a change, take the road less traveled and discover a world of natural beauty at this delightful bed and breakfast owned by Clyde and Ellen Waldo. You'll find them as charming as their cabin.

Nestled in the woods of the Clear Creek Valley, a modern log guest house is yours to enjoy. The cabin contains three bedrooms, living room, dining room, kitchen and porch. Outdoors a picnic area is available, including a Weber kettle and picnic table with benches.

Entering the cabin, you are in a large room that has cathedral ceilings and a large stone fireplace. What better place on a cold winter's night, than in a cozy cabin with a roaring fire in the fireplace? The room is furnished with a sofa and love seat, a coffee table, antique desk, television with satellite dish, and VCR with a collection of movies. The floors are random planks with two braided area rugs. The walls are of log on three sides. In this room, as in the others, there are many beautiful framed photographs of Ireland, Germany, Hermann and the USA by the award winning artist, Mary Silverwood-Potts.

Off the living room, a dining area has planked wood floors and two log walls, one of which is decorated with a handmade quilt. A wagon wheel light fixture hangs over an antique five legged table with chairs. There is also a small drop leaf table and a marble top washstand. Lace curtains are at the windows.

A fully equipped kitchen is available for guests.

Down the hall from the living room, three guestrooms are available. The Green Room is furnished with a king-size pine headboard bed with a handmade quilt, a pair of end tables, chest, a wicker coffee table and rocking chair and a floor lamp. Two of the walls are log. The other two are plastered. White cottage curtains are at the window. This room has a private bath and shower.

The Autumn Room has a king-size poster headboard, an upholstered arm chair, an antique oak dresser, an antique night stand and a lamp table. An earth-tone handmade quilt is on the bed and white cottage curtains are at the windows.

The Red, White and Blue Room has a high-back carved antique oak bed, two night tables, an antique round lamp table with a reading lamp, a pair of caned chairs, an antique two drawer dresser. A tan carpet is on the floor and cottage curtains are at the windows. All three guestrooms have a basket of complimentary toiletries. These two guestrooms share a bath.

Guests are treated to a delicious gourmet breakfast served in the cabin at the time you decide. The meal consists of juice, fruit compote and coffee or tea. The following entrees are available: Log Cabin breakfast of an egg casserole with Monterray Jack cheese, sauteed onions and mushrooms served with ham and apple walnut cinnamon biscuits, or baked french toast and sausage, a breakfast pizza of eggs, hash browns, cheddar and Parmesan cheese, egg omelet with hash browns and homemade muffins.

There are trails you can walk, on the privately owned 275 acres. A restored 1900 one room schoolhouse is available to tour, birds and wildlife to watch, fossils to find and plenty of relaxation. Nearby Hermann offers a golf course, wineries, antique and craft shops, fine restaurants, and historical sites.

Incidentally, as the owners live nearby, you have the cabin to yourself and total privacy.

A LITTLE LOG CABIN IN THE WOODS: RR 1, Box 471, New Florence, 63363. (573) 252-4301. Open all year. No smoking. No pets. Clyde and Ellen Waldo, innkeepers.

DIRECTIONS: From I-70 take exit 175 (New Florence/Hermann). Turn south on Hwy. 19. Go 1.8 miles to Strube Road. Turn right. Go 3.4 miles to Whiteside School Road. Turn right. Go 1 mile to bed & breakfast on left Owners live nearby.

MARKET STREET BED & BREAKFAST
Hermann

This turn of the century frame Victorian home was built in 1906 by Doctor Ernst Haeffner, and still has the original woodwork and light fixtures. How long he lived here, I couldn't say, but in 1935 it was turned into the Commercial Hotel and remained as such for forty seven years. It must have been a pretty good hotel!

The property has a large back and side yard with huge old trees, shrubs and flowers. Of course, there is a front porch, but you'll find the swing in the side yard rather than on this porch.

The entry hall has a fine oak staircase. Large pocket doors lead to the dining room. It is carpeted with an oriental rug. Lace curtains are at the windows and the walls are bordered in a floral print. The hall has an antique desk, antique clock and a table with a Gone-with-the-Wind lamp.

The parlor is furnished with a sofa and matching arm chairs, end tables with brass lamps, and a coffee table displaying old photographs. There is an antique Eastlake lady's chair, an antique rocking chair with upholstered seat and back, and a small table and lamp. An antique etagere holds porcelain pieces. The room is carpeted and lace curtains are at the large bay window.

The dining room has a blue oriental carpet over original pine floors. An oak mantelpiece is above the tile fireplace. There is a nice turn-of-the-century dining set. The seats and backs of the chairs are upholstered with a blue check fabric. A carved wall shelf hangs over the buffet. There's an antique trunk, a crank phonograph, an antique oak sideboard and a five drawer stand which holds a collection of cylinder phonograph recordings. A large copper wash boiler holding pine cones and a kerosene lamp collection help convey a feeling of long ago. Lace curtains are at the bay window.

At the top of the staircase, is a sitting area for guests. An area carpet is on the floor and there is a hanging lamp. There is an old Victrola, a pair of upholstered chairs, a large round table and bookshelf with lots of books. Nice paintings are displayed on the walls.

One of the guestrooms has a large bay window overlooking Market Street and is hung with muslin curtains. The room is carpeted and has a floral print wall paper. It is furnished with a queen-size iron bed with a white coverlet and a green dust ruffle. There is an oak washstand with a lamp, an upholstered rocker and a 1920s dresser. The room has a private bath with shower.

Another guestroom has floors that have been painted and waxed. The gray walls have a dark red and blue border at the ceiling and muslin curtains are at the windows. The room is decorated with old crocks and baskets. The furnishing consist of an antique full-size ornately carved Victorian bedstead with a handmade quilt, a walnut dresser, an upholstered arm chair and a small open armed settee. There is a private bath with shower.

The third guestroom has an antique walnut, queen-size bed, an easy chair with ottoman, a chest and mirror and a round lamp table with reading lamp. An area rug is on the floor and the walls are papered with a striped pattern and display nice antique prints. There is a private bath with shower.

Roberta and Van serve a hearty breakfast in the dining room. There is orange juice, fresh fruit in season, along with homemade coffeecake. She prepares hash browned potatoes with nestled eggs and peppercorn bacon. Delicious jams and jellies, coffee, tea or milk.

MARKET STREET B & B: 210 Market Street, Hermann, 65041. (573) 486-5597. Open all year. No children, pets or smoking. Visa/MC accepted. Within walking distance of most shops, historical sites, wineries and restaurants. Amtrak pick-up provided. Van and Roberta Garrison, innkeepers.

DIRECTIONS: Easy to find. Market Street (Hwy. 19) is the main north- south street in Hermann.

MEYER'S HILLTOP FARM BED & BREAKFAST
Hermann

Eldon and Maggie Meyer's Hilltop Farm is a perfect place for those who have never tried a bed and breakfast. The Meyers take great pride in seeing that their guests are comfortable. Within minutes of arrival you are on a first name basis and chatting over a cup of tea or coffee and cookies.

The house itself has an air of friendliness. The front porch has an old-time swing, attractive plants and a wonderful 15-mile view, which includes their weathered grey barn and outbuildings, pastures and woods.

The entry hall is carpeted and has an antique dresser with glove boxes and candle stands. An oriental runner carpets the hallway.

Off the entry, the parlor has beige wall-to-wall carpet. A brick fireplace has a wood burning stove insert. The room is furnished with a sofa and matching love seat, a piano, an upholstered recliner, coffee table, a knock-down wardrobe, a dry sink and a round table with reading lamp. Books, a stereo and CD player with many choices of CDs are for guests use. Tieback curtains are at the windows and nice prints are on the walls.

The carpeted dining room has paneling above the chair rail. There is a large oval table with six matching chairs, a hutch, and a corner cupboard. A brass chandelier hangs over the table. Lace curtains are a the windows, pictures on the walls and house plants about the room.

The second floor hall has an antique trunk, an old chalkboard, a child's rocker and a high chair filled with teddy bears. Blue and white curtains are at the windows.

The two guestrooms are decorated with antiques and country collectibles. They have private baths with showers, television with remote, clock radios and in-room controls for air-conditioning.

The Blue Room has a large oval braided rug on the original floor and the walls are painted a light blue. The room has a queen-size iron and brass bed with a drunkard patterned quilt, an antique lamp table and lamp, a pair of rush seated chairs, an antique oak dresser and a washstand with an antique pitcher and bowl set.

The Peach Room is furnished with a king-size iron bed covered with a floral comforter, an antique plant stand used as a night table, an antique washstand, a wing chair, a small rocker and antique marble top Eastlake dresser. An oval carpet is on the floor.

Adjoining the main house, but with its own entrance, a country two-room suite has a fully equipped kitchen including coffeemaker and microwave. Maggie keeps sodas, coffee, tea and popcorn on hand for guests. A green carpet covers the floor and the windows have blinds with swags. The room has a sofa that opens into a queen-size bed, an old wrought iron sewing machine that holds a television, an antique table with reading lamp, and a small table with two chairs. The room is decorated with many pictures, house plants and dried floral arrangements. The bedroom has a queen-size antique bed with a floral spread and matching pillow. There is an oak dresser that has a hat box, a night table, and lamp. The walls are a pale peach and the tie-back curtains match the bed linens. The private bath has a large jacuzzi for two. There is a private porch complete with swing. An ideal suite for honeymooners.

Awaken to the aroma of freshly baked pastries and coffee, then enjoy a leisurely breakfast of juice, fresh fruit, homemade jams and jellies. Maggie serves two main courses. Either a double cheese quiche with buttermilk, oatmeal pancakes. Or a breakfast casserole and German fried potatoes. Sausage, bacon or ham is served, with either a cinnamon or caramel bun. Maggie will also prepare stuffed french toast. You'll love this place.

MEYER'S HILLTOP FARM B & B: RR 3, Box 16, Hermann, 65041. (573) 486-5778. Open all year. No smoking inside. No pets or children. A 75-acre cattle farm with two guestrooms and a suite. Half a mile to the Katy Trail. Schwinn bikes available. Eldon and Maggie Meyer, innkeepers.

DIRECTIONS: On Hwy. 19, two miles north of Hermann. 13 miles south of I-70.

NESTLE INN GUEST HOUSE
Hermann

Nestle Inn is not an old house when you compare it to some of Hermann's circa 1840's and 1850's houses. I imagine it was built around the turn of the century during the peak of the Art's and Craft's style of architecture. It is a very warm and friendly home. It also has one of the best views of the Missouri River and surrounding countryside that you'll see. All you have to do is walk a slight hill which is part of Nestle Inn's backyard. The view from the bluffs is fantastic.

Entering the house from the front porch, you enter into a large living room that is fully carpeted. A large brick fireplace has a raised hearth. Some of the furnishings include a love seat upholstered in colors of cream, sage green and mauve. There are five upholstered wing chairs, four in sage green and one than matches the love seat. There is also an Eastlake parlor table, a slant-front bookcase desk and a television. The walls are painted white and there are lots of live plants.

The dining room, just off the living room has English style panelling on the walls painted white. A large bag window holds more live plants. Stained glass inserts are on the windows. It is furnished with a maple drop leaf table with Windsor chairs, a matching maple hutch that holds a collection of Japanese figures.

A first floor guestroom has blue wall-to-wall carpeting. The paneled walls, painted white, have Japanese framed prints on them. Lace curtains and swags are at the windows. It is furnished with a king-size bed with colorful floral bed linens is set in an alcove. There is an octagon table and two rattan chairs, a leather massage chair and a corner bookshelf with a television. There is also a gas log burning fireplace and a private whirlpool tub with dual shower heads.

A four room suite is on the second floor includes a sitting room and three bedrooms. At the top of the stairs, to the left, a room has a four person hot tub, a tile top table and three chairs, a rattan table with a coffee maker, a microwave and a television. A bath with a tub and shower is down the hall. A bedroom off the hall is carpeted in a blue print pattern. Sheer curtains and white drapes are on the windows. It is furnished with a queen-size maple spindle headboard, a bedside table and reading lamp, a dressing table with a lighted mirror and a pair of rattan chairs and a table with a lamp.

Across the hall another bedroom has a queen-size bed, a bedside table a Victorian table and two chairs and a chest with a brass lamp. Mesh curtains and burgundy drapes are on the windows.

A sunny sitting room makes up the four room suite. There is a gas log fireplace, an upholstered love seat, an antique day bed and a coffee table. This suite will accommodate from one to three couples, and it is rented that way, to either one, two or three couples together.

Donna serves a delicious home-made breakfast. Orange juice, fresh fruit in season, coffee, tea or milk. Donna makes a vegetable egg pie with seasoned spices, or cream and fruit filled French toast or German pancakes. All of the entrees are served with a breakfast meat.

Upon arrival, a welcome basket of crackers, cheese spread, chips, candy and fresh baked chocolate chip cookies.

The yard with that great view of the river is landscaped with trees, shrubs, and a flower and spice garden. There are seating arrangements with an umbrella table and chairs and a chaise lounge. A huge bonfire pit is sometimes used for bonfires.

NESTLE INN GUEST HOUSE: 215 West Second Street, Hermann, 65041. (573) 486-5895 or (573) 973-7090. Website: www.nestleinn.com. E-Mail: nestle@ktis.net A first floor guestroom with a whirlpool and a second floor four room suite with a fireplace and hot tub. No pets. Outside smoking. Children welcome. Donna Nestle, innkeeper.

DIRECTIONS: From Highway 100 or 19, go south on Market Street to Second St. Turn west on second street. Go to 215.

PATTY KERR GASTHAUS
Hermann

The earliest section of this house is hand hewn half-timbered construction. Built for J. B. Idemann in 1840, it is one of the oldest houses in Hermann. In 1859 when the street was graded to its present level, John Quandt acquired the property and added the east room, which is built of wood frame, and the entire first story, constructed of brick. The brick smokehouse was built around 1892. For many years, the house was occupied by Frederick Kraemer, a shoemaker, who had his shop on the first floor. The newest addition to the property is the quaint cottage on the east side of the house.

To enter the main portion of the house, stairs lead up to the second level. Through the French doors is the keeping room. One wall is the original exposed brick while the other three are papered in a plaid design. A large window with shelves, holds house plants and some of Todd and Nancy's favorite keepsakes. The room has a large oval table and four matching chairs, an antique china cupboard with oval glass door which holds small antiques. There is an antique Victorian table, a Victrola, and two straight back chairs. French doors open out onto a patio with a hot tub and a garden. And what a garden it is; hollyhocks, tulips, lilac, honeysuckle, roses and iris among the rock walls and garden paths. Sit at the table and enjoy a beautiful sight.

A living room with original beams, has a fireplace and is furnished with a sofa, an antique rocker, a handmade, built-in bookcase with a collection of oil lamps. Lace curtains are at the original six over six pane windows. A shelf above the fireplace has a collection of plates. One wall is of exposed brick and the others are painted beige with mulberry trim and woodwork.

On the first floor, the Iris Room has an electric fireplace. It is carpeted wall to wall and has throw rugs on top. The walls are green above a chair rail and red below. The room has an Amish four poster bed that has floral bed linens, night table and lamp. The original log beams remain, as do the handmade inside shutters. A small area has a refrigerator and a coffeemaker for guests to use. There is a private bath with shower only. This room has a private entrance from the street.

Just a few feet away from the main house is a two room cottage furnished with a full-size Amish four poster pencil bed with purple and green bed linens. The bed is high enough to require a step stool to get into it. There is a table and two chairs. The mulberry walls have green trim woodwork. A bay window holds plants, shells and other "treasures." A large milk can holds dried flowers. The sitting area has a white iron day bed. There is a private bath with a claw foot tub/shower.

A light continental breakfast is available and consists of juice, fruit and a pastry. Coffee, tea or milk. It is served in your room.

PATTY KERR GASTHAUS: 109 East Third Street, P.O. Box 434, Hermann, 65041. (573) 486-2510. Two guestrooms and two room cottage with private baths. No children or pets. No smoking. Two day minimum stay during festivals. Reservations a must. Nancy Satre, innkeeper.

DIRECTIONS: Call for reservations and directions.

PELZE NICHOL HAUS BED & BREAKFAST
Hermann

Here is a wonderful opportunity to step back into the mid-1800s and visit an intact German farmstead. The main house, tenant house, barn and smokehouse have all been built with handmade bricks from the kiln on the property. Listed on the Register of Historical Places as the Vallet-Danuser House, it was built by brickmaker, Adam Vallet, in the 1850s. The beauty of this house is that so much of the original work is still there: the floors, six over six window panes, the simple woodwork, mantels, and walnut staircase. Even the original shutters are stored in the basement.

Adam's son, Frederick, purchased his father's property in 1861. In 1925, after more than 80 years in the Vallet family , the land was sold to Walter Danuser. In 1980, Walter's son, Elmer, sold the property to the City of Hermann. But fortunately, the house with 7.8 acres was sold separately to a couple from Kansas City. At that time the house and outbuildings were virtually unchanged from the day they were built: no plumbing, one light bulb in each room, fireplaces for heat. The present owners, Jack and Chris Cady, are only the fourth family to own the house.

Upon entering, you are in an entry hall furnished with an antique Lincoln desk and a unique wooden lift-top school desk. To the left of the hall, the Keeping Room is sparsely furnished. A harvest table and ladder back chairs stand before a fireplace with its original mantle. Guests may breakfast here as a baby grand player plays soft Christmas music in the background. Primitive and antique Christmas decor compliment the simple elegance of the room. Or, guests may enjoy the ample library by sitting comfortably on the overstuffed plaid sofa facing the fireplace. Another bookcase is filled with beautiful old Blue Willow china. Throughout the room are many pieces of Americana, including a hanging lamp, an antique clock and a large apple butter kettle with pine cones. An oriental carpet is on the floor and the walls are painted tan, with woodwork painted sage green.

In the dining room are long harvest tables with old benches and ladder back chairs. An antique cupboard holds Frankome china, while a four door cupboard holds a collection of antique toys, Santas and Easter rabbits. A corner hutch displays old copper utensils, spatterware, and red ware. A primitive cupboard has another collection of toys and things.

The second floor hall has some of the Cady's wonderful Christmas collections. The two guestrooms are decorated in comfortable primitive furnishings. Each has its own bath. One guestroom is furnished with a queen-size four poster pencil bed covered with blue and red plaid bed linens. The tan painted walls are offset with woodwork painted tavern red. Muslim curtains are at the windows. In a sitting room there are two wing back chairs, a loveseat and a wrought iron floor lamp.

Across the hall, a second guestroom has a queen-size four poster tester bed with an antique quilt on the tester. Artisan crafted bent willow furnishings include arm chairs with colorful cushions at a round table, a table and a chaise lounge. There is an old bench for a side table and a wrought iron floor lamp. The woodwork is pale blue and muslin curtains are at the windows.

Chris and Jack serves a gourmet breakfast with second helpings. It might begin with custard French toast, homemade apple butter or jams, stewed apples in spiced wine followed by local brat with oven fried potatoes and eggs benedict. Or there is stuffed pork chops with sage dressing, American fries, applesauce and English muffins. Or maybe cheddar cheese pie.

In order to meet the need for an intimate fine dining establishment in Hermann, Chris and Jack opened their Harvest Room and Keeping Room to private dinners by reservation only. If a group of four or more couples (up to a maximum of 18 persons) requests, the Cadys will present a lovely 6 course dinner, prepared and served by them in a leisurely, relaxing atmosphere. The "prix fixe" menu for the meal will be planned with the diners' suggestions. Dinner wine is provided by the diners. If your group is interested in a dining experience other than the evening meal, the Cadys will be more than happy to work out another plan for you. They entertain club groups for luncheons, as well as groups of friends for showers, birthday, and other special celebrations. Outside the confines of their lovely home, the Cadys will see either to arranging a catered party, or can also cater it themselves.

Although neither Chris nor Jack is formally trained in the culinary arts, both have years of experience and strong genetic influences related to the kitchen. They have recently completed a year of teaching classes for the Dierberg's Market chain in St. Louis, with a culminating appearance on the television show Everybody Cooks. They again begin a round of wonderful recipes for the Dierberg's classes in the fall of 1999 through the year 2000. Plans are underway for a unique, classic cookbook with that special Cady touch.

In the 40 by 18 foot vaulted stone and brick wine cellar that forms the foundation for the historic Pelze Nichol Haus, Chris has created a wonderful gift shop filled with unique seasonal gifts from fine craftsmen. She also showcases her own artistic creations: miniature fur and clay Pelze Nichol Santas; German Easter rabbits; hand crafted miniature witches, as well as life-size garden witches.

In order to round out their schedule, both Chris and Jack are proud to be featured in the annual spring and fall Hermann Garden Club tours. Chris features her own art work during the annual Artists of Hermann Studio Tours. Jack, dressed in furs and capes and original costume, portrays Pelze Nichol himself at various functions at the Stone Hill Winery and at the Deutschheim State Historic Site. The couple is proud of their German heritage and works to preserve it in themselves and in Hermann.

PELZE NICHOL HAUS B & B: P. O. Box 147, Route 2, Hermann, 65041. (573) 486-3886. Two guestrooms with private baths in historic brick farmhouse. Open all year. No children, pets or smoking. Chris and Jack Cady, innkeepers.

DIRECTIONS: Located 1.3 miles east of the Missouri River bridge on the north side of Hwy. 100. Call for reservations and directions.

REIFF HOUSE BED & BREAKFAST
Hermann

Built in 1871, the Reiff House was originally used as a home with a small butcher shop located in the adjoining building, which is now a courtyard. In 1896, the building was purchased by John Reiff and his wife. If you were a traveler to the bustling river port of Hermann in the late 1800s, you might have stayed at the J. Reiff Hotel and Tavern; enjoyed the fine Hermann beers and wines and the friendly hospitality dispersed by Amelia and John Reiff.

The building retains its original details, Flemish bond brickwork, wrought iron balcony, twelve foot ceilings, four-panel doors and heart of pine floors. It sits in the heart of Hermann's Historical District.

Today, Sue Scheiter, owner and innkeeper, dispenses the friendly hospitality of the Reiff House and invites guests to share this historic home. Upon arrival, guests are offered a complimentary bottle of local wine.

To the left of the entry hall, a very cozy parlor is furnished with a blue and white upholstered sofa and matching love seat, an upholstered Martha Washington chair, a Boston rocker, and a rocker recliner. A carpenter's antique tool box is now a lamp table. A large entertainment center holds a TV/VCR, a stereo and shelves with a collection of porcelain oil lamps and other small collectibles. A table and chairs for two by the fireplace is a perfect spot to sit and talk.

A 125-year-old stairway with a walnut railing leads to the second floor. Each of the rooms has its own refrigerator, coffeemaker, cable TV, VCR, and telephone. A large outdoor hot tub is available and Sue encourages guests to reserve time for a European facial or a relaxing massage.

The J. Reiff Room is decorated with florals, antiques and reproductions. It is furnished with a king-size cherry canopy bed trimmed in lace at the top, a wicker loveseat and chair, a bachelors chest, a pair of end tables and an entertainment center with a television. It is wallpapered with a burgundy, cream and brown floral stripe pattern. The woodwork is painted in a jade green color. An oriental carpet is on the floor. Green inside shutters are on two windows and an exclusive balcony overlooks Market Street. The private bath is just outside the door and has a shower.

The Ivy Room is decorated in white, navy and rose. There is a king-size iron bed with hand quilted coverlets, a circa 1890s dresser, an ice cream table and chair, an upholstered wing chair, a blue and white checked upholstered love seat, a floor lamp and a brass and glass top table and an antique hanging lamp. There are plenty of plants and dried floral arrangements. There is also a fireplace. Lace curtains are at the windows along with inside shutters for evening privacy. The private bath features a two-person hot tub with shower.

The Melon Room is furnished with a queen-size antique iron bed with a hand crocheted spread. There is an open arm chair, a gentleman's dresser, a night table with a lamp and a wrought iron table. Green inside shutters are at the windows. The walls are painted in a colonial mustard color and are partially paneled with old beaded boards. Photographs and old prints portray the special charm and history of the inn. There is a private bath with shower.

In the mornings you are greeted with wonderful German pastries, country breads and spreads, fresh fruit, juice, delicious coffee and a full country breakfast served in the gracious antebellum dining room.

The dining room is furnished in cherrywood 18th century reproduction furniture, including a pedestal table, a china cupboard, a lowboy server and footed silver chest. The plate rail holds part of Sue's Blue Willow china collection, which accents the blue Persian rug under the dining table. In one corner is a grandfather clock handmade by Sue's father. Wooden shutters over Battenburg lace curtains open to afford a view of Market Street. This congenial setting can accommodate six to eight people for a sunny breakfast and transforms to an elegant candlelit room for the Inn's gourmet dinners. Intimate dinner for two is offered in the parlor by the fireplace.

Described by one guest as "The most elegant dining in Hermann," gourmet dinners are available to the public by advance reservation. The menu for the evening is determined by the first reservation. Entree choices include grilled quail with herbed wine sauce, bay scallops with wine celery sauce in pastry shell, roast stuffed pork tenderloin and twelve ounce Kansas City strip steak. Two seatings are offered nightly, at 6 and 7:30 p.m. The five-course dinner with coffee and three wine pairings is quite reasonably priced. It is Sue's pleasure to provide a delicious, memorable dining experience for visitors to Hermann.

During mild weekends and all festivals, the Courtyard Biergarten is filled with live music, food and drink. You can join in the festivities or watch from the comfort of your room.

REIFF HOUSE B & B: 306 Market Street, Hermann, 65041. (800) 482-2994 for reservations. A three guestroom historic house with private baths located in the center of Hermann's historic district. Open all year. No smoking. No pets. Visa, Mastercard and Discover. Sue Scheiter, innkeeper.

DIRECTIONS: Located on the main thoroughfare in Hermann - Market Street (Hwy. 19). Reservations are a must and should be made very early for any special festival day.

STRASSNER SUITES
Hermann

This three story building that houses Strassner Suites was built by one of Hermann's first settlers in 1881. It was first used as a dry goods store, and later as a harness and saddlery business. To be over a hundred years old, the building is in tip-top condition.

Today the building houses the family owned and operated Strassner Furniture Store and Upholstery Shop. The second floor has been completely renovated and decorated as a charming bed and breakfast with a private entrance separate from that of the furniture store.

This remodeling project, which took place in 1992, was a family project. The owners and their five daughters and son-in-laws, all dug in and contributed in painting and wallpapering. A couple of doors and walls had to be moved and private bathrooms added, and the transformation was one that awed them all. I'd like to tell you that I think this is one of the brightest, most cheerful and cleanest places I have been to. Everything is absolutely spotless and very tastefully decorated.

Upon entering the B & B, the first feature you see is the beautiful Victorian staircase that invites you into a common area, where there is a wing-back chair and side table with a lamp. Look around and you will find beautifully papered walls in hues of peach and cream, with accents of green. All the furnishings are new and the rooms are fully carpeted. Adjoining this area is the guest kitchen, to which you have full privileges throughout your stay. The kitchen is equipped with a microwave and refrigerator. It is here where a full breakfast is served.

Breakfast may consist of an egg dish with bacon, sausage, or ham either baked in or on the side; French toast or homemade waffles; fresh turnovers, or cinnamon rolls; fruit; juice and coffee. One thing is for sure—you won't leave hungry!

From the common area you will enter one of the two private suites. Each is a two-room suite consisting of a living room and bedroom, and of course, a private bathroom. The window, wall, and bed coverings in these rooms coordinate with the entry, in shades of peach and green.

The living room in each suite is furnished with a nice easy chair for your relaxation during your visit, as well as a sofa that folds out into a queen-size bed, which would accommodate another person or two if you so desire. There is cable TV with HBO in the living room, as well as a small dinette set.

The adjoining bedroom in the suite is furnished with a brass and iron bed and a matching dresser and night stand. Beautiful pictures adorn the walls in every room (of course, all are on sale through the Furniture Store!). The private bath off each bedroom has a shower.

The two suites are the B & B's only accommodations, which makes it the perfect choice for two couples traveling together. Located in the heart of Hermann's Historic District, gift and antique shops, restaurants, and one of the local wineries are within walking distance.

The owners of this B & B are very hospitable and strive to make this a very comfortable and clean home-away-from-home. They do not live on the premises, allowing you to have complete privacy; but they are there during the day and available if you need assistance with anything. It is their desire to make your trip to Hermann and to the Strassner Suites one worth remembering.

STRASSNER SUITES B & B: 132 East Fourth Street, Hermann, 65041.

NO LONGER IN OPERATION.
CLOSED OCTOBER 1999.

HUNTER'S HOLLOW BED & BREAKFAST
Labadie

The white frame building that houses both Hunter's Hollow Bed and Breakfast and Restaurant was built in 1908. At various times it housed a store, post office, and an apartment. It was completely renovated by Don Wolfsberger, a St. Louis Businessman and civic leader, for the restaurant, Hunter's Hollow. The bed and breakfast came shortly thereafter.

The decor of the restaurant is of a British hunting lodge with a rich, deep green wallpaper and beige, green and maroon plaid curtains. Large and small mounted game species decorate the walls. Adjacent to the dining area is the casual Decoy Lounge that gets its name from Don's antique decoy collection.

In the summer there is an open air patio with umbrella tables, a picturesque gazebo, and huge clay pots of flowers. Hunter's Hollow is a perfect getaway. You can a enjoy a day in the small town visiting the various antique shops, touring nearby Washington, and then having your dinner in the restaurant or served to you in the B & B apartment above. Top it off with a little time in the Decoy Lounge.

A private staircase, leading to the six room suite on the second floor, is decorated in pastel shades of blue wallpaper, blue print carpeting, and blue woodwork. Antique prints on the walls give a hint of what to expect. A small hall at the top of the stairs has an antique table holding a huge dried flower arrangement, an antique bench, and a tapestry wall hanging.

A dining room has a sofa, a leather arm chair, a pair of wing chairs, and an antique upholstered Lincoln rocker. An armoire holds a television. The unusual carpet is maroon with vases and flowers woven in the pattern. Curtains and a draped valence cover the windows. There are beautiful antique prints on the walls and various flower arrangements. A perfect room to enjoy the complimentary bottle of chilled Missouri wine.

The dining room has a highly carved Jacobean dining suite with barley twist legs. Another flower arrangement and a pair of carved candlesticks serve as a table centerpiece. The huntboard displays a collection of pewter and antique tiles. The room is wallpapered in a blue and pink floral pattern. An oriental carpet is on the floor.

A front guestroom has a four-poster bed with a blue comforter, an end table with old brass lamps, a dresser, and an upholstered chair with ottoman. The walls, papered in deep maroon, have antique prints on them.

A back guestroom has blue and tan striped wallpaper and a blue woven rag rug. It is furnished with twin antique sleigh beds with blue print comforters, a table with a metal hunt scene lamp and a small chest.

The kitchen has a stove, refrigerator, table and chairs. Blue print wallpaper and blue woodwork set off a collection of antique duck prints.

The private bath, with a blue and red pattern wallpaper, has a tub with shower. Brass lights and antique prints are on the wall.

Just down the road from Hunter's Hollow, at the top of Hunter's Hill are two private guest houses. The first is called the Fox and Hounds. It is said that nearly a hundred years ago, the town blacksmith raised five children in this handsome home. Decorated in the manner of a private hunting lodge, this romantic two story cabin boasts hand painted walls an antique four-poster bed, his and hers wardrobes and a full bath, upstairs. Downstairs, guests can enjoy the elegance of the formal dining room, relax in the comfort of the plush living room, or watch the birds from the brick patio and Victorian sitting porch in front of the house.

The sixty year-old cabin called the Compleat Angler, with its full width sitting porch has been transformed into a fisherman's paradise. Sir Isaac Walton's 19th century fly-fishing "bible," The Compleat Angler, inspired the whimsical theme carried out in the country style furniture and accessories. On display are the proprietor's prized collection of hand tied flies and antique English rods. Fish figures adorn the wallpaper, drapes, pillow, lamps, and even the light switches. Guests will delight in the inventiveness of the decor and also in the generously proportioned rooms, which include a fully equipped eat-in kitchen, a walk-in closet in the master bedroom and an oversized shower with seat.

The Fox and Hounds will sleep two adults while the Compleat Angler will sleep up to four overnight guests in comfort. Rooms are air conditioned and smoke free. Both feature television, refrigerators, microwave or toaster ovens.

Guests will enjoy waking up to a sumptuous continental breakfast with fresh fruit in season, orange juice and fresh brewed coffee.

As a guest of Hunter's Hollow Inn, you'll see beauty and wonder everywhere. Birdwatchers can enjoy the more than fifty species of birds that make the Inn their home. A few miles' scenic drive will transport bargain hunters to Gilberg's Perennial Farm and nearby antique shops and flea markets. Sample the wines of Augusta, Dutzow and Hermann; hike the trails at the Missouri Botanical Garden Arboretum in Gray summit; visit the historic Daniel Boone home in Defiance or the animals at Purina Farm. Or, spend a peaceful evening stargazing from a comfortable rocking chair. Hunter Hollow Inn belongs to the Missouri Weinstrasse with five wineries in the area.

HUNTER'S HOLLOW B & B: Washington and Front Streets, Labadie, 63055. (636) 742-2279 or (636) 458-3326 (St. Louis). A six room apartment with two bedrooms over Hunter's Hollow Restaurant, plus two guest cottages just a few blocks away. Children welcome. Henry P. Ruggeri, manager.

DIRECTIONS: From I-44, take the Gray Summit exit, then follow Hwy. 100 east abut one mile. Go left on Hwy. MM for about four miles. Then right on Hwy. T to the intersection of Washington and Front Streets in Labadie. From Manchester Road (Hwy. 100), in Ellisville, go to Hwy. T and turn right. Follow T through St. Albans and about seven miles further to Labadie. From Hwy. 94, take the Dutzow exit onto Hwy. 47 south and proceed seven miles to Hwy. 100. Turn left and go to Hwy. T. Turn left and Labadie is about eight miles further east on Hwy. T.

HUNTER'S HOLLOW RESTAURANT
Labadie

Located in the quaint town of Labadie, you'll find a truly great restaurant with the ambience of an English hunting lodge.

Chef Brian O'Brien, graduate of the Culinary Institute of America and formerly of Old Warson Country Club, uses only the finest products of the region—game, fish, beef, and fowl—with fresh fruits and vegetables from the valley.

Open for lunch and dinner, Hunter's Hollow serves great appetizers, homemade soups and salads. For lunch there are sandwiches and specialty dishes. Entrees include Portabello sandwiches, New England style crabcakes, Hazelnut Chicken and hickory smoked baby back ribs.

The evening menu features rack of lamb, stuffed quail, Long Island duck, hunter style pheasant, and fresh seafood, selected daily.

Vegetarian dishes are available upon request.

Be sure to save room for dessert: ice cream profiteroles and house made cheesecake.

HUNTER'S HOLLOW RESTAURANT: Washington and Front streets, Labadie, 63055. (636) 742-2279 or (636) 458-3326 (St. Louis). One of the finest restaurants in the State. Henry P. Ruggeri, manager.

STAATS WATERFORD ESTATE BED & BREAKFAST
Labadie

In 1849, one J. Perkins left his home in Virginia with his wife and 10 children. They came with a wagon train that included 11 other families and settled in Missouri, in the Labadie area. In 1850, Perkins had brick layers from the town of Washington, build this Federal style house. Today, 10 of the original homes are still standing, including the Perkins home. In 1976, a two-story Greek Revival home was added.

Now, enter Lucille and Charles Staats. For years, Charles has been a collector of memorabilia from the Civil War era. His mother had told him stories of his grandfather, a German immigrant, who fought in the Civil War with the 12th Missouri Infantry Company C, a German speaking unit, which served with General Franz Siegel.

In 1991, a friend of the Staats, told them of this house in Labadie that was for sale. The place had been completely restored and decorated. Within three hours after looking at it, they signed a contract and moved in, bringing their treasure trove of the Civil War with them. Wagons and buggies are displayed in the barn. Medical, photographic and other artifacts are displayed throughout the house.

When they decided to open a B & B, the 1850s wing offered a perfect setting. So when you check in at Staats Waterford Estate, you will find yourself being welcomed into a day in 1861, at the home of a Civil War surgeon.

You enter the B & B area from a glassed-in summer porch in the 1850s portion of the house. A Victorian wicker baby buggy is most interesting. A door leads to the foyer that has a circa 1858 pump organ and two saddles.

Off the foyer, the parlor of 1860, has green wall-to-wall carpet. A chair rail has flocked wallpaper in a pale green design over it. Green drapes are over white curtains. Alcoves on either side of a marble fireplace hold bottles and other small items from the Civil War period. It is furnished with a burgundy upholstered sofa, loveseat and wing chair. A Victorian parlor table and two Victorian chairs are in the center of the room, under a crystal chandelier. A seven foot display cabinet holds original surgical implements and a complete set of dental implements. A uniform is also on display.

The dining room has red wall-to-wall carpet. The walls have a chair rail with a red pattern flocked wallpaper above it. Red drapes are over white curtains. There is a marble fireplace. It is furnished with an antique cherry wood pedestal table with a carved swan base, and Victorian chairs. A table holds a circa 1840 music box. A mannikin wears a vintage 1860 ball gown from the summer home of the Benoist Family at Oakland House in Affton, a St. Louis suburb.

On the second floor, The Empress Theodore Room is fully carpeted with grey carpeting. Grey drapes are over white curtains, and an antique three globe brass chandelier hangs from the ceiling. There are twin cannonball poster beds with pink bed linens. The testers are draped with pink lace. There is a pair of French Provincial wing chairs on either side of a table with a reading lamp, and a Victorian rocker. A ball gown from the era of the Mexican War and a Victorian frock is on display. There is a private bath.

The Federal Room has wall-to-wall green carpeting. A patterned pale green flocked wallpaper is over a chair rail. It is furnished with a queen-size, four poster bed with a broken pediment head and footboard with green and white bed linens. There is a chaise lounge, a pair of club chairs, a table with a lamp and a bookcase with small artifacts displayed. A small dressing room has a vanity. There are some interesting framed items. A private bath has a shower and tub.

These two rooms share the Mathew Brady sitting room. It has a floral upholstered love seat and two huge circa 1860 cameras. Many framed photographs are Civil War reproductions. Off this room is a glassed in smoking porch with a four piece wicker set.

One half hour prior to breakfast, Charles serves fresh ground coffee and juice to your room. Breakfast is served in the dining room by Charles, wearing a full dress Civil War surgeon's uniform. There is a fresh fruit compote, cinnamon butternut pancakes, scrambled eggs and maple flavored bacon. Breakfast is varied. It is served on fine china, with crystal and silverware on linen tablecloths and napkins.

STAATS WATERFORD ESTATE B & B: 4550 Boles Road, Labadie, 63055. (636) 451-5560. Open all year. Two guestrooms with private baths in a circa 1850 home. No pets. Outdoor smoking. Not suitable for children.

DIRECTIONS: From I-44 west, exit at the Washington Exit 251 (Hwy. 100). Go north and turn right on Hwy. T. Then turn left on Boles/Dunn Springs Road. Then stay to the right on Boles Road and follow it to the Inn, on your right.

CONCORD HILL BED & BREAKFAST
Marthasville

Tucked away in the tiny agricultural community of Concord Hill (population 40), well away from the main roads, Concord Hill B & B is a circa 1886 farmhouse originally including fifty acres of surrounding ground. Partitioning of the homestead to children and relatives, over the years, resulted in reduction in the estate to about twenty-five acres. The house was being used as two unit apartment house for several years before being acquired, along with one and one half acres of ground, in the 1980s and being completely restored into a bed and breakfast. Jim and Vicki Cunningham acquired it from Nick and Karen Cipponeri in 1993.

The house has completely new heating and central air-conditioning, new plumbing, including modern bathroom fixtures, and new windows. A new wraparound porch was added at that time. Guests get a great view of the distant hills and fields. On the property is the original smokehouse, circa 1886, a chicken coop from the 1950s and a newly constructed carriage house. The chicken coop is active with laying hens and colorful roosters for the interest of the guests.

There are two bedrooms available in the main house, each with an adjoining bath. Each bath has a full tub and shower and is accessible directly from the bedroom. A door to the central hallway makes the baths available to all guests when groups book the entire house.

A day room adjoins the rear bedroom and allows access to a loft where two queen-size oriental futons can accommodate groups along with the bedroom(s) below.

The front, Sunrise Room, is furnished in turn of the century furniture including a full-size bed, upright chest of drawers and a mirrored dresser. This room has a view of the morning sunrise and is enjoyed by guests who are early risers.

The rear, Sunset Room, is furnished in more recent furnishings including a queen-size low four poster bed, a dresser from Jim's grandfather's family and a cedar chest from his mother. This room has a grand view of the open countryside to the west, including colorful sunsets.

Above the newly constructed Carriage House, is a romantic getaway room with wrought iron full bed and an antique 6-foot clawfoot tub in the center of the bedroom. Lavatory and watercloset are discretely tucked behind a partition out of view. This room is perfect for honeymoon couples or those wishing a more secluded and private atmosphere.

A full breakfast specializing in dishes that utilize the herbs and produce from the garden is served. They also specialize in preparing interesting dishes that will nutritionally equip guests for a vigorous day of bicycling on the nearby Katy cycling trail, located only 1.25 miles down the hill. The trail runs east 35 miles to St. Charles and west 150 miles to Sedalia, and offers spectacular views of the Missouri River and the high bluffs and other interesting geologic features. Wildlife is always available for viewing and photographing.

Concord Hill is located in the heart of Missouri's wine country and within a half hour drive of eleven award winning wineries. Antique shopping nearby in several area. Guests will find excellent casual and formal dining at restaurants in nearby Washington, Labadie and Hermann. After returning, relax and enjoy a bottle of local wine and the hot tub located outside on the deck. Stars are always clearly visible in the dark country sky and owls and coyotes can be heard on a warm summer evening.

CONCORD HILL B & B: 473 Concord Hill Road, Marthasville, 63357. (636) 932-4228. Open all year. No smoking inside. Children welcome. No pets. Cash and personal checks accepted. Two large guestrooms and a loft that can comfortably sleep five adults. Jim and Vicki Cunningham, innkeepers.

DIRECTIONS: Take Hwy. 94 west from Marthasville three miles to the Village of Peers. Turn right on Concord Hill Road, 1.4 miles to Concord Hill B & B.

GRAMMA'S HOUSE
Marthasville

"Over the river and through the woods to grandmother's house we go..." Do you remember that song? Well, a visit to Gramma's House bed and breakfast is just like a visit into the past. That's precisely what Jim and Judy Jones want to do...bring back memories to those of us fortunate enough to remember a setting such as this one. As you drive up the lane to the house, you get a feeling of peaceful solitude. No hustle or bustle here.

The house, which was once part of a 176-acre farm, is believed to have been built in 1839 by Judge Hieronymos Ulffers. A two story addition was built in the 1890s. The judge and his wife lived and farmed here for about fifty years. In 1986, Jim and Judy bought the house and 7 acres for use as a bed and breakfast.

The home is a large two story white frame farm house, so typical of those built during the 1800s. A nice porch, complete with old wooden porch swing, is on the side of house where you enter.

In the large, bright dining room, the pine floor is covered with an oriental rug. A corner cupboard, a Queen Anne dining table and chairs, and a 1920s radio are among the furnishings. Large windows with white curtains overlook the surrounding countryside.

Upstairs, in the original part of the house, is a large airy room with painted floors and walls. Granny's Room has an antique wash stand, a 1930s full-size bed with a handmade quilt, an upholstered chair, antique rocker and a two door mirrored armoire. The mauve colored walls have vintage children's clothes displayed on them. There are white lace curtains and area throw rugs. There is a private bath with shower.

Also upstairs is the Grand Canyon Suite, with a queen-size bed, separate large sitting room and private bath with a large shower. This very spacious suite is decorated in western décor.

Gramma's House also features two cottages away from the main house. The Old Smokehouse Cottage is perfect for someone wanting a cozy atmosphere. Rustic charm in a sitting room with fireplace, a sleeping loft and a private bath with claw foot tub. The Playhouse Cottage also has a fireplace and a private bath. It is decorated in a Victorian style.

Judy serves breakfast in the dining room. A typical menu consists of juice, fresh fruit in season, an omelet with cheese, ham and hash browned potatoes, homemade breads, muffins or biscuits, jellies and jams, coffee, tea or milk. Another entree might be homemade cinnamon french toast, with sausage, bacon or ham.

The Katy Trail, which runs right through Marthasville, is a great place to hike and bike. Bike rentals are available in town.

One of the nice things about staying here is Jim and Judy's real interest in making you feel at home. It is very informal and you can feel free to come and go as you choose.

GRAMMA'S HOUSE B & B: 1105 Hwy. D, Marthasville, 63357. (636) 433-2675. A two guestroom house with two guest cottages with private baths. Open all year. Full breakfast included in room rate. Mastercard and Visa. Website: www.grammashouse.com. Jim and Judy Jones, hosts.

DIRECTIONS: Located one hour west of St. Louis. Take I-70 to Warrenton. South on Hwy. 47 for 15 miles to Marthasville. Take Hwy. D through town about 1 mile to Gramma's House on the left. From I-44, take Washington exit (Hwy. 100) to Washington. Go north on Hwy. 47 about 5 miles to Boone Monument Rd. Follow paved road 1 mile, cross bridge, go left for abut 100 yards to Gramma's House.

LITTLE HOUSE BED & BREAKFAST
Marthasville

Located alongside the scenic and new nationally known Katy Trail, the Little House is a cozy turn of the century two-bedroom cottage that has been refurbished into a quaint and charming bed and breakfast. With the owners, Jerry and Rita Hoelscher, living nearby, you have the privacy of the whole house. It includes a living room, kitchen/dining area, two guestrooms and a bath.

You enter into the living room from the front porch. It has white paneled walls, wall-to-wall carpeting, and green swags over mini blinds. The walls are decorated with framed photographs of views of the local area. The room is furnished with an upholstered green plaid sofa that opens into a queen-size bed, to accommodate a family or a larger group using the trail. There is an upholstered rocker recliner, a reproduction of an old time ice box that is used as a stand for the color cable television. A blanket chest is used as a coffee table and for storage for bed linens. There is a maple rocking chair, a sofa table, a quilt rack, matching end tables and an arts and crafts birdhouse made into a reading lamp.

The kitchen is a nice old-fashioned one. It is paneled chair rail high and wallpapered above. There is a ceiling fan as there is in each of the rooms. It is completely furnished with a stove and refrigerator. There are cooking utensils, dishes and silverware. So, if you are inclined to cook, have at it. There is also a phone.

A hall from the kitchen leads to the two guestrooms and bath. One of the rooms is furnished with a full-size bed, and a small library table. The walls are white with a stenciled chair rail. One wall has the original beaded board. Throw rugs are on the floor and blue and white curtains at the windows.

The other guestroom has wall-to-wall carpeting, the walls are white and the woodwork is green. Green and red floral swags are over miniblinds. More framed black and white photographs are on the wall. Rita is quite a good photographer. She has an eye for good subject matter. One that really caught my attention was of a lone tree shrouded in an early morning fog. The room is furnished with a Mission style queen-size bed with a green plaid comforter and pillow. There is a lamp table and lamp beside the bed. There is a quilt rack holding towels. Dried floral arrangements are on the walls and on a table.

Upon arrival, Rita offers cheese and crackers. Wine for birthdays or anniversaries. Rita furnishes homemade coffeecake and fresh fruit in season.

Bike rentals are available just up the street, and Rita has a shed, which can be locked for those on the trail. You are close to most of the wineries, shops and restaurants in Dutzow, Augusta and Washington—which also hold many annual events.

THE LITTLE HOUSE B & B: 403 Depot Street, Marthasville, 63357. (636) 456-8230. 1 (800) 483-2587. Open all year. No pets. Smoking on porch. Children welcome and under age 7 stay free. A two guestroom cottage with bath. Jerry and Rita Hoelscher, hosts.

JANE L. McILROY ©96

WINDHOMME HILL BED & BREAKFAST
Marthasville

Located high on a hill overlooking the Missouri bottomlands and the Katy Trail, Nick Cipponeri's Windhomme Hill was once an Indian campground. In 1915, Edwin Hoeft built this nice frame home and farmed the surrounding acres.

Dining plays a large part of your stay here. Nick is a talented and creative chef with ten years experience owning and operating a successful restaurant. His love of gardening, a passion for cooking and a desire to provide warm hospitality to a few people at a time, led him to Windhomme Hill, where over the years, dining and cooking are a unique part of your stay. Guests are free to help harvest fresh produce and herbs from the garden, and learn from the chef as dinner is prepared. Then, share an exquisite meal with the host and other guests. This is part of a package Nick offers at an additional charge.

A long front porch has a porch swing and a terrific view for miles around. Some of the largest trees I've seen offer summer shade and an outdoor hot tub offers soothing relaxation.

The large wallpapered foyer has an area carpet and a teak elephant four feet high. There is an antique drop leaf table, two antique chairs and a Remington bronze statue. A staircase leads to the second floor guestroom.

The parlor is furnished with a sofa, a leather wing chair, a wing chair with matching ottoman, bookshelves, a glass top coffee table and two matching end tables, and an antique burled walnut, slant front secretary. The oak woodwork is original as it is throughout the house. The room is wallpapered.

The dining room has a large bay window with lots of plants and a plant stand. There is an antique jelly cupboard, a 1920s buffet, a long table with eight chairs and an antique arm chair. The walls are papered and nice framed prints are hung throughout, oriental carpet is on the floor and a brass chandelier hangs from the ceiling. Baskets of all types fill one corner of the room.

There are four guestrooms. The Blue Room, with a porch overlooking the valley and patio, is furnished with a full-size bed with matching bed linens, an antique dresser, a Chinese etagere with a collection of porcelain, a plant stand with a dried floral arrangement and a bench at the foot of the bed. An oriental area rug is on the floor, white lace curtains and a large bifold screen. Blue striped wallpaper is below a chair rail, solid blue above.

The Green Room has an unusual bed. It's a queen-size that fits snugly into an alcove and is about four feet from the floor. Underneath the bed are drawers. There is also a built-in corner cupboard with books and a television, a 1920s sofa, a Victorian floor lamp with a beaded fringe shade and a Chinese chest. It also has area carpets and cloth shades with colorful swags. The walls are papered in a green print pattern. A private bath with shower is in the room.

The Room-with-a-View furnished with a full-size poster bed with a handmade quilt. A huge armoire, with built-in customized drawers, holds a television. There is an antique washstand, a pair of wing chairs and an antique table sits in a bay window. The walls are papered and pale floral print, area carpets are on the floor.

The Bed View room has a built-in bed in front of the windows. At the foot of the bed facing the windows are built-in shelves and drawers that hold a television and collectibles. There is an arm chair, blanket chest, an oak stand with glass shelves and a wicker hamper. It's papered in a blue floral print. A private bath with shower is just outside the door.

Nick serves a garden fresh, full country breakfast, which varies from day to day. Always juice, fresh fruit in season, home baked breads, homemade jellies, jams, fresh ground coffee, tea or milk. Main courses could be farm fresh eggs (gather your own), sausage or ham, biscuits, and gravy. Maybe stuffed French toast, omelets or quiche.

WINDHOMME HILL B & B: 301 Schomberg Road, Marthasville, 63357. (636) 932-4234. Closed January. For reservations and pre-arranged dinners call 1 (800) 633-0582. Well mannered children welcome. No pets. Smoking on Porch. Nick Cipponeri, innkeeper.

DIRECTIONS: Call for directions and reservations.

JAMIE L MᶜILROY ©

SENATE GROVE INN
New Haven

The builder of this house was F.W. Pehle who was born in Prussia in 1839. Coming to America, he settled in the New Haven area and became a naturalized citizen in 1860. He was one of the founders of the Republican Party in Franklin County. He fought for the Union Army in the Civil War. In 1881, Pehle became Franklin county's first State Senator. This brick house that the Senator built in 1884, used only local materials. The brick was made on the Pehle farm, and the stone that was used for the foundation and window sills came from a quarry in the vicinity.

The inn offers spacious grounds for the guests to walk the trails. Bring your fishing pole and fish one of the three ponds. Bring your horse, you are welcome to ride the property. They also have two riding arenas.

To the left of the entry, a parlor is furnished with an upright piano, an upholstered sofa and armchair, a library table and a leather recliner. A corner bookcase has plenty of reading material. There is a television, and a VCR with movies. The original floors (now very shiny) have area carpets. White sheer curtains are at the windows and there are live plants.

The shiny floors of the dining room also have area carpeting. It is furnished with a queen Anne style dining set that includes a table with six chairs and a buffet. While curtains at the windows have green swags.

A large country kitchen overlooks one of the ponds and the farm outbuildings. It has beaded board paneling up to the chair rail and painted white above. It has a table and six matching Windsor chairs, a hutch and an antique oak washstand. There is a microwave oven and a toaster oven.

A first floor guestroom is furnished with a queen-size wrought iron and wood bed and a matching chest, dresser and vanity. There is a twig and wood rocker, a Martha Washington armchair, and a night table with a reading lamp. Three windows with white curtains have a view of the farm. There is a private bath with a tub and shower.

From the entry in the front of the house, a staircase leads to the three second floor guestrooms. One has a queen-size brass bed with blue and red bed linens, two night stands with lamps, a 1930's dresser, a Boston rocker, a brass coat rack and a wardrobe. White café curtains with swags are at the windows, the floor has throw rugs. A live ficus tree is in the room. A bath with a tub and shower is in the hall.

A second guestroom is furnished with an early 1900's full-size bed and a matching chest, a wardrobe and a night table with a reading lamp. A white bedspread and a handmade quilt are on the bed, white café curtains and swags at the windows and area carpets on the floors. There is a private bath with tub and shower.

The hall has a door that leads to a porch that runs the width of the house. The guestroom is furnished with a queen-size short four poster bed, a pair of night tables and lamps, a very early wooden armchair with a padded seat and back, a wardrobe, a quilt rack and an antique trunk at the foot of the bed. A green and white handmade quilt is on the bed and white curtains are at the three windows.

On the weekend, breakfast consists of juice, fresh fruit in summer, a frozen fruit cup in winter. Scrambled eggs with either sausage or bacon, home baked bread or muffins, bagels or English muffins. Jellies, jams, coffee, tea or milk. On weekdays, a continental breakfast of fruit bread, cereals, bacon and eggs, coffee or tea is served.

SENATE GROVE INN: 4554 Kohl City Road, New Haven, 63068. (573) 237-2724. Open all year. No smoking in house. No pets (horses, yes). A Great place to wake up and the birds singing. Tom Straatmann and Mary Weseman, innkeepers.

DIRECTIONS: From I-44 take the Washington exit, Hwy. 100. Go west to New Haven. About a quarter mile past New Haven, turn left on Hwy. E Turn right on Hwy. VV. Turn left when you see the Senate Grove Inn sign. From I-70, take the New Florence exit, Hwy. 19 to Hermann. Turn left on Hwy. 100 (just over the bridge). Turn right on Hwy. VV and look for Senate Grove sign.

ST. CHARLES

St.Charles, settled before the Revolutionary War, was the first permanent white settlement on the Missouri River. Each of the people who have lived here has imprinted something of its culture on the area. During early days, St. Charles was the funnel through which French trappers, Spanish explorers, American pioneers, and German immigrants flowed out towards the western fur trade, the rich soil of the plains, and California gold.

The first settler, Louis Blanchette, nicknamed the hunter, was a French-Canadian who came here in 1769 with his Pawnee wife, Angelique. He built a cabin near the mouth of the creek, now named after him. Soon other French-Canadians arrived, and gradually their scattered cabins grew into a village. The village took its name from the bluffs which the Creoles had called Les Petites Cotes (the little hills). In 1781, there were just a half a dozen houses and in the succeeding ten years this number increased to no more than twice that amount.

Under Spanish encouragement, many American settlers came to the territory. Among them were the Boones — Daniel and his wife, Rebecca and their sons, Nathan and Daniel Morgan, and various relatives, who arrived in St. Charles during the late 1790s.

In 1803, the vast unexplored West, roughly designated as Louisiana, became American territory. The following year, the Lewis and Clark Expedition, commissioned by President Jefferson, stopped at St. Charles. They were to chart the course of the Missouri River and the Columbia River westward to the Pacific. At this time, in spite of the daily arrival of Anglo-Americans, the French culture was still predominate.

Two years later the expedition returned with charts and fabulous tales, and the race for the empire began. St. Charles, at that time the last outpost of civilization, began to bloom. ·

On October 13, 1809, St. Charles was formally organized as a village. Three years later, under the provisions of the new territorial government, the old District of St. Charles was reorganized as one of Missouri's five counties. St. Charles remained the seat of Government.

During the War of 1812, the Indians were aroused against the French and American settlers, and St. Charles and the surrounding territory required the protection of a series of forts. Though several outposts were attacked, St. Charles was not molested.

After the war, restless Eastern farmers began to pour into the Missouri River valley. The dust of the town's streets never settled. Many of the milling throng were to become famous. There was General John Augustus Sutter, in whose California millrace the nugget was discovered that precipitated the great California gold rush. There was also Mother Rose Philippine Duschesne, who was later to receive religious honors.

In 1820 Missouri was admitted into the Union, and St. Charles, already the territorial capital, was designated as the temporary State Capital by the first legislature, which met in St. Louis. The general assembly convened on the second floor of three adjoining brick buildings, which the town provided, rent free.

On March 10, 1849, St. Charles was incorporated as a city. In this same year, the dust of its streets was once more stirred by a wave of restless, westward moving people. The California gold rush was on. But the frontier, too, had moved beyond the town. Independence, St. Joseph, Liberty and Westport had become the outer limits of civilization and St. Charles had reached its greatest period of expansion.

Today, after over two hundred years of history, St. Charles has moved once again into the mainstream of activity.

The first State Capitol building is still there and has been restored and furnished as it might have looked in 1821. The main streets of old St. Charles are still brick paved and the original 18th and 19th century buildings have been lovingly restored. These buildings now house over eighty shops and restaurants in the largest historical district in the State.

Visitors shouldn't miss seeing *The Lewis & Clark Center* at 701 South Riverside Drive. Here, you will find displays depicting the Lewis and Clark expedition. You can see the animals they saw, the unknown plants they discovered, and artifacts from the many Indian cultures they encountered as they explored the western portion of the United States. (636) 947-3199.

Along with the antique shopping, there are also some great gift and craft shops. For instance, *First Capitol Trading Post* at 207 S. Main Street has one of the largest displays of collectibles you will ever see. There are hundreds of M.I. Hummel figurines from Germany, more than 500 Lladro porcelain figurines from Spain, more than 500 current and retired Precious Moments figurines, and literally thousands of items from other great art houses in Europe and the United States like Waterford and Swarovski crystals, Fenton Art Glass, The Franklin Mint, Disney, Lenox and more. The displays go on and on and you can find everything from a $5 Beanie Baby to sculptures that sell for thousands of dollars. You won't believe this place even when you see it! (800) 582-4895 or (636) 946-2883.

Miss Aimee B's is located in the historic Martin-Becker House at 837 First Capitol Drive. First of all, you can have breakfast here. Omelettes, breakfast potato and sausage pie and sweets such as cinnamon raisin bread pudding. I tried the bread pudding. It was one of the best I've ever had. Lunch includes baked chicken salad, Florentine crepe pie and delicious sandwiches. Then shop the marketplace on the second floor for antiques, home and garden accessories, children's books, dolls, candy bouquets, jewelry and accessories, night wear and Boyd's Bears. (636) 946-4202.

On the lower level of the Newbill-McElhiney House, step back in an atmosphere reminiscent of the 18th century at Donna Hafner's *Haviland Platter Cafe.* There is a huge fireplace, a very early antique corner cupboard and an old brick floor. It's as cozy a place as you'll ever see. Hundreds of pieces of Haviland china are on display. Donna features French dining, specializing in homemade soups, sandwiches, and desserts served fresh daily. Be sure and try her peach cobbler and ice cream. Upstairs on the first floor is a great museum. Several of the rooms are furnished as they would have been in the mid-1800s. And, a lot more Haviland. Located at 625 Main Street. (636) 946-7155.

Another place I like is the *St. Charles Vintage House Restaurant.* The one hundred thirty year old building is so picturesque, you will think you are in a Bavarian wine garden. Gus and Rita Holzwarth serve great Bavarian and American cuisine. Sauerbraten with potato pancakes, wiener schnitzel and bratwurst are some of the favorites, as is the beef roulade. You will find it hard to resist the fresh apple strudel and Black Forest cake. Located just one block from the Station Casino Riverboat at 1219 S. Main Street. (636) 946-7155.

Cafe Beignet at 515 S. Main Street was erected in 1811 and was home of the famous Eckert's Tavern. The tavern complex included a blacksmith's shop, wagon repair yard, and a livery stable. Mr. Eckert, a former buffalo hunter, served such popular menu items as smoked buffalo tongue and buffalo steaks. In 1821, Thomas Hart Benton made his famous speech from the porch demanding that a free public school be established in St. Charles. The home now serves as *Cafe Beignet,* a cozy little restaurant with a comfortable atmosphere. *Cafe Beignet* features Cajun/American food and traditional style breakfast. Exclusive private parties. Patio dining. Open 7:30 a.m. to 3 p.m. Tuesday through Thursday; 7:30 a.m. to 9 p.m. Friday. 7:30 a.m. to 4 p.m. Saturday and Sunday. (636) 946-3000.

MOTHER-IN-LAW HOUSE RESTAURANT
St. Charles

One hundred and thirty years ago, Francis X. Kremer married young French girl. She became so homesick for her mother, that Francis sent for her and brought his mother-in-law to St. Charles. He built the first duplex in town in 1866. He and wife and family lived on one side and his mother-in-law lived on the other.

Today, if Francis were to visit this duplex, she would find a charming Victorian restaurant. The walls are papered in Victorian patterns, there are hanging lamps and on the walls an impressive collection of still life prints from one hundred years ago. Francis does not come back, but some say the ghost of his mother-in-law haunts the house.

While you await her appearance, try the homemade soups and the daily luncheon special. Or there are salads, several variations of hamburgers, chicken and roast beef.

The dinner menu offers prime rib, New York strip steak, filet mignon, chicken dishes, and fresh seafood that includes sole Oscar, stuffed founder, and lemon pepper sole. All dinners are served with rice or potato and a salad bar.

The owner, Donna Hafer, also offers a homemade coconut cream pie and a cherry cream pie for dessert.

MOTHER-IN-LAW RESTAURANT: 500 S. Main Street, St. Charles, 63301. (636) 946-9444. Open all year. Reservations are advised, especially on weekends. Lunch served Monday - Saturday 11 a.m. - 2 p.m. Dinner served Tuesday - Saturday 5:30 p.m. - 9:30 p.m.

JAMIE L. MC ILROY © 96

BOONE'S LICK TRAIL INN
St. Charles

In the early days of St. Charles, the site that now houses Boone's Lick Trail Inn sat on a strategic location, for it was here one could enter the Boonslick Road originally blazed to serve Boone brothers at their salt manufacturing works. This road became the settler's route to Arrow Rock, at which point the road joined with the Santa Fe Trail.

The inn, built in the 1840s, is a typical Federal style building built of handmade brick, quarried limestone and hewn timbers. Today, it is in the heart of the National Historical District, a delightful ten block area with cobblestone streets, gas lamps and over 100 shops, boutiques and restaurants. Paul and V'Anne Mydler purchased the house in 1981 and have done extensive restoration work on it.

Entering the inn from the front door, you are in a small hallway. (Note the stencil artistry.) To the left is a parlor furnished in antiques that V'Anne has collected. There is a table and chairs used for guests at breakfast, a leather camel-back sofa, two wing chairs and an antique chest that doubles as a coffee table. Note the huge antique bolting counter, which was once used to store fabric in an old-time general store. It now acts as V'Anne's buffet table at breakfast time. Area rugs, antique prints, pictures and plants all tend to make this a most inviting room.

A primitive cupboard and a large dining table with six chairs are in the dining room. The cupboard holds some of Paul's decoy collection. Freehand herb stencils bring spring to this sunny room. Breakfast is served here and in the parlor. V'Anne offers a full breakfast of juice, fresh fruit in season, fresh home baked pastries and V'Anne's specialty lemon biscuits. A main entree could be either an egg casserole, french toast or German pancakes. All are served with English muffins or toast, homemade jams and jellies, and of course, your choice of coffee, tea, milk or cocoa. A special warm fruit is served in winter.

All five guestrooms at the Inn have private baths. The rooms are quaintly furnished with cozy comforters, lace curtains and ceiling fans. The furnishings are not pure Victorian, pure 18th Century, early American, primitive or art nouveau, just pieces of all the above are the decorating styles of the inn.

The two guestrooms on the first floor garden level each have their own entrance. One has a queen-size bed. A handmade duck patterned quilt hangs over the bed on a rack. A large drum table with lamp and a bookshelf with plenty of books complete the room. Cream and gray Berber carpeting softens the contemporary feel to this room that appeals to business travelers. The other room has a four poster queen-size bed, an antique sausage leg table and a carpenter's work bench, which was used to teach carpentry to children in school.

On the gallery porch above, two more guestrooms have private entrances. One room has a country farmhouse look with queen bed and a pair of nightstands and a simple ribbon stencil border at the ceiling. The other room has a queen antique iron bed and antique white wicker furniture. Note the hand-stenciled ivy border at the ceiling.

In the third floor attic loft room, you'll find a small balcony with a view of the Missouri River. It is the largest room furnished with a queen-size bed, antique dresser, and a table for two overlooking the Historical District. Breakfast on a silver tray is an option. There are future plans for a master bedroom and bath on the second floor. The bedroom overlooks the historic brick street, the Western House, Blanchette Creek and Boone's Lick Road.

A unique feature of the inn for the outdoor enthusiast, is seasonal duck hunting on the Mississippi flyway with Paul Mydler. You rise early in the morning, go to Paul's duck club and have a go at your skills. Hot coffee and a breakfast snack is provided for hunters.

BOONE'S LICK TRAIL INN: 1000 S. Main Street, St. Charles, 63301. (636) 947-7000. Fax: (636) 946-2637. (8 a.m. to 5 p.m.) Open all year. No pets. No smoking. Children welcome. Website: www.booneslick.com. E-mail: Innkeeper@booneslick.com. V'Anne Mydler, proprietress.

DIRECTIONS: From I-70 exit at Fifth Street, north to Boonslick Road, then right approximately five blocks to inn.

THE GEERY'S BED AND BREAKFAST
St. Charles

This circa 1890's home was built by a Mr. And Mrs. Alexander, and is presently owned by Chevalier and Dame, Peter and Marilyn Geery, who have given it Victorian elegance with a Scottish flair.

When you step through the door of this nicely decorated home, you will find it pleasantly furnished with antiques and reproductions that create a cozy atmosphere and warm inviting hospitality. The entry hall with a paneled oak staircase and walls covered with a burgundy sculptured wallpaper. It has a large grandfather cock and a mirrored hall seat.

French doors lead to the ladies parlor that has an English scenic print wallpaper. There are some very nice framed prints of English scenes. Hardwood floors have an area carpet. It is furnished with a 1930's upholstered wood trimmed sofa, a marble top coffee table, an upholstered Federal style sofa also with wood trim, a pair of antique Eastlake chairs, a Victorian parlor chair, and antique tripod drop leaf table, a piano and a Victorian parlor table.

Pocket doors lead to the gent's parlor that has a corner brick fireplace and a bay window. An area carpet is on the floor. It is furnished with a blue and red plaid upholstered sofa that face a pair of upholstered wing back chairs. A large brass and glass display case is full of Peter's collection of toy miniature soldiers. (This is a must see) The walls are decorated with framed hunting prints.

French doors from the front hall and a door from the gent's parlor lead to a dining room with beamed ceilings. An oval table with a matching breakfront, buffet and a server are part of the furnishings. A crystal chandelier hangs over the table. Several wall shelves hold porcelain pieces. White walls have stenciling on the ceiling. Gold and off white drapes are at the windows.

Each of the three guestrooms have been given their own personality. The staircase takes you to the second floor where you will find a small room that serves as a sitting room for guests. Theirs is an antique day bed, a bookcase, a pedestal table, television, a butler's tray table with a lamp and two curio cabinets holding a doll collection. Shutters and curtains are at the windows. The walls have a yellow, blue, green and red floral print paper.

At the top of the stairs, Roselea's Room is named for Dame Marilyn's mother. Polished to a lustrous glow, a king-size brass bed is the focal point. There is an English burled armoire and a matching vanity with an Eastlake chair. A wicker chaise, an upholstered open arm, wing chair and a round table are part of the furnishings. A mint two-toned green wallpaper covers the walls. The floor has an oriental carpet.

The Alexander Room, named for the original owners of the house, is furnished with a full-size iron bed, an antique circa 1860 marble top, splash-back washstand and an antique armoire, both from Scotland. There is a pair of Windsor chairs, a bedside table and lamp, a gentleman's valet and a small marble top table and lamp. Green floral area rugs are on the floor, and gold swags over blue drapes on the windows. The wall have a gold and blue paper.

Named for Sir Peter's clan, the Lindsay Room has a circa 1860 four poster tester bed, and antique Scottish three mirrored dresser, two pedestal tables with lamps at the bedside, an upholstered open arm chair, and an upholstered chair that has a carved back and sides. It came from Peter's relatives in Scotland. A corner tile woodburning fireplace is just the thing on cold mornings and nights. A door opens onto a balcony with a rattan glass top table and two rattan chairs. Breakfast here if you wish.

A three course Scottish breakfast is served consisting of hot or cold cereal, juice, homemade bread and bagels, jams and jellies and homemade marmalade. Then there are eggs, bacon or sausage, mushrooms and tomatoes fried and coffee, tea or milk.

THE GEERY'S B & B: 720 N. Fifth St., St. Charles, 63301. (636) 916-5344. Fax (636) 916-4702. E-mail: peeryktj1@aol.com. Open all year. Smoking on porches. No pets. Within a very short drive to the Historical District with its shopping and restaurants. A three guestroom home. Peter and Marilyn Geery, innkeepers.

DIRECTIONS: Take I-70 to Fifth Street exit North. 1 1/2 miles to 720 N. Fifth St. From Hwy. 270 to Hwy. 370 West, take third St. exit, right to Tecumseh (1 1/2 block) to Fourth St. right on Morgan to left on Fifth St. 1 1/2 blocks to 7620 N. Fifth.

LOCOCO HOUSE II
St. Charles

Leo and Rhona purchased this house in 1991 and since 1994 it has been a B & B. It is their second one; their first being at Jefferson Barracks. Now you can get a massage, use the hot tub and even be able to have a good old-fashioned pajama party (for the women). I'm sure the subjects you talked about then have changed, but the fun and friendship have not. Lococo House will host your party, including snacks for evening, cozy, comfortable guestrooms, a private sitting area and a delicious home cooked breakfast. You bring the "jamies." Rhona will do the rest.

Entering the house, you are in a rather large foyer, with an oriental carpet, two vintage wedding dresses on display, and an antique writing desk. There are lace curtains. A spindled and paneled staircase leads to the second floor guestrooms.

The living room is furnished with a plaid sofa and a matching love seat, a pair of red wing chairs, an antique lamp table and lamp, coffee and end tables and a music stand. A walnut mantle surrounds a tile fireplace. There are lots of books, magazines and plants. A pocket door leads into the dining room.

The dining room has a round table and four captains chairs, a 1930s table and six chairs, a buffet and a hutch with a collection of blue and white china in the Royal Homes of England pattern. Lace curtains are at the windows, a brass chandelier hangs from the ceiling. There is also a player piano, a love seat and a wardrobe holding a television.

On the first floor, off the front hall, the Pink Room is furnished with a 1930s waterfall style full-size bed and a matching dresser, two chairs and a pair of end tables with small hurricane lamps. There are hooked area rugs and lace curtains.

On the second floor, the Brown Room has two full-size beds, a wardrobe, an antique trunk, a rocking chair and a matching straight back chair with upholstered seat, a night table, floor lamp and a television.

The Blue Room, with a fireplace, has a 1920s four poster full-size bed with a matching chest and vanity, a rocker with upholstered seat and back, cedar chest and a day bed for a third person. A braided rug is on the floor.

The Green Room is furnished with a full-size bed, a circa 1879 rocking chair, which belonged to Rhona's grandmother, a night table, floor lamp and a television.

The guestrooms share two large baths that have claw foot tubs and showers.

Outside, a covered gazebo has a hot tub and grill. A wrought iron table and chairs are on a porch overlooking large trees, shrubs and flowers.

On arriving, Rhona offers warm apple pie and coffee.

The Lococo's serve a full breakfast with fresh squeezed orange juice, fresh fruits in season, Lococo House french toast with bacon and sausage and browned potatoes. Coffee, tea or milk.

LOCOCO HOUSE II B & B: 1309 North Fifth Street, St. Charles, 63301. (636) 946-0619. Fax (314) 940-7134. Open all year. Children welcome. No pets. Smoking allowed. Five guestrooms with two shared baths. Outdoor spa, murder mysteries, health weekends and special occasion packages. Rhona and Leo Lococo, innkeepers.

DIRECTIONS: Take I-70 to Fifth Street exit in St. Charles. Go north for two miles. Lococo House is on the west side of the Street.

MUELLER HOUSE BED & BREAKFAST
St. Charles

This turn of the century home was built around 1908 and has been restored to its original splendor. With pocket doors, transoms and original lighting fixtures in some of the rooms, it is like stepping back in time. It is owned by Ray and Ruth Mueller, who still put time in making their home just so. Ruth is a twin sister to a very dear friend of mine, who also has a B & B. I know Ray and Ruth Mueller make every effort to combine comfort with beauty.

The house has a nice large front porch, surrounded by trees and shrubs. A fairly good-sized entry hall has a nice hooked area rug on the floor, lace curtains on the windows, and a striped wallpaper design on the walls. It has an antique round table, a slant front desk, an antique baby buggy and a corner cupboard that holds a collection of porcelain.

To the right of the entry hall, the parlor has a marble fireplace with an oak mantelpiece. The 11-foot ceiling gives a sense of spaciousness. It is furnished with a pair of floral tapestry upholstered high back lone seats, an organ (you can play) a cabinet holds a television and a VCR. There is an end table with a reading lamp, a Queen Anne style coffee table and a doll collection in a curio cabinet. Lace swags are over blinds on the windows, a hooked rug on the floor and the walls are decorated with dried floral arrangements and pictures.

The dining room has a circa 1910 matched dining set that includes a table, six chairs, a court cupboard and a buffet. There is an upholstered wing chair and a china cabinet with more dolls. There is a large bay window with lace curtains and swags and a built-in cupboard.

On the second floor, Sadie's Room is fully carpeted. Floral drapes are over blinds at the window. It is furnished with a queen-size sleigh bed with a tapestry bed spread a matching, ornately covered chest and mirror. There is a Queen Anne table and an upholstered love seat, a color television.

Miss Agnes' Room was named for one of the early owners of this house. It is furnished with a rise covered four poster bed, an antique armoires, a library table, a bedside table with a reading lamp, a wicker love seat and ottoman and a quilt rack. There is also a color television.

Both Sadie's Room and Miss Agnes' Room share a bath that has been updated for your convenience. It has a Jacuzzi whirlpool tub or shower at your disposal, but the original built-in cabinets were retained.

On the third floor, this suite is just the right place for seclusion and privacy. It has a queen-size, New Orleans style, iron bed and a solid cherry dresser and mirror. It has a cozy sitting area by the palladium windows in one dormer and a reading area with a chaise lounge, a floor lamp and a thick cushion in another dormer. There is a private bath and cable television.

Breakfast is served in the dining room on the antique carved oak table with a lace tablecloth, cloth napkins, crystal and fine china. Their bountiful breakfast includes old-fashion French Toast, eggs, bacon, and homemade biscuits, sausage gravy and a hot fruit plate. Coffee, tea or milk. Nothing wrong with that.

On arrival, Ruth offers an iced drink in the summer lemonade or iced tea. And a hot drink in winter, hot apple cider or hot chocolate. You will find candy on your pillow at night.

MUELLER HOUSE B & B: 710 N. Fifth St., St. Charles, 63301. (636) 947-1228. Open all year. No pets. Smoking on porch. Not suited for children. Three guestrooms. Two shared, one private. Jacuzzi in the shared bath. Close to Historic District, French Town and Casino. Ray and Ruth Mueller, innkeepers.

DIRECTIONS: Take I-70 to the Fifth Street exit and go North 1.4 miles to 710 N. Fifth Street.

OLD ELM TREE INN
St. Charles

The inn was named by it's owner, Martha Kooyumjian, for the magnificent 160 year elm tree that is in the back yard. It is supposedly the largest elm tree in St. Charles. I don't doubt that at all.

The house was built in 1904, by Robert Belding, a prominent resident of the city, editor of the St. Charles Banner newspaper. Over the years, the house has had many owners, and when Martha purchased it she had it completely restores to its' original Queen Anne Victorian charm. Martha has also decorated the house with fine 19th century antiques. It has also been newly papered and painted throughout, professionally landscaped and a gazebo built. The wrap around verandah adds to its southern mid west style charm.

The entry hall is furnished with a grandfather's clock and an antique hat rack with a mirror. It is lit by a brass chandelier. The walls have a green and white striped paper below a chair rail with a green print paper above.

To the left of the hall, the parlor has a unique corner bay window. There is also a large gas fireplace that has a Victorian brass clock and matching candelabras. An Oriental area carpet is on the floor. It is furnished with an upholstered Victorian sofa, a pair of upholstered Victorian arm chairs, a marble top coffee table, an antique organ, an antique corner table with an antique brass and marble lamp and a small round lamp table. The room is papered with a white on white patterned print wall covering.

The dining room has a hooked area rug on the original floor. A plate rail is on the wall. A rose stripe wallpaper is below a chair rail and a floral print is above. A crystal chandelier hangs over a double tripod dining table with six high back chairs. There is also a buffet, a barley twist, marble top lamp table and a vintage radio cabinet. Sheer curtains are on the windows, and elegant framed pictures are on the walls. A corner door leads to the veranda.

To the right of the hallway, a small parlor has a huge mirrored, antique armoire, a rose upholstered wing chair, a marble top plant stand and a large round lamp table. An area carpet is on the floor. It is wallpapered in a small print burgundy pattern paper.

A library is furnished with an antique slant-front bookcase desk, an antique marble top lamp table and a brass floor lamp, a small oak game table sets in the middle of the room with four antique barley twist chairs. There is a large bookcase. Sheer curtains are at the windows, an area carpet is on the floor. The walls are papered with a burgundy print above a chair rail and a burgundy paisley floral below.

On the second floor, under the eaves, are three guestrooms, with cable television, telephones and private baths. These are all very cozy and intimate rooms, and sure to please the most.

The Rose Suite is furnished with an antique, queen-size bed, topped with a comforter and piled high with pillows. Brass wall lamps are over the bed. A built-in bookcase holds a porcelain tea set. There is also a small wall table, an upholstered armchair, and a black lacquered desk and chair. White shutters are on the windows and a gilt-framed mirror is on the wall.

The Bridal Suite is at the front of the house and is furnished with an ornate, brass antique queen-size bed with a sculptured spread. A small-carved chest is at the foot of the bed, a plant stand holds a vase of silk flowers. There is a ball and claw bench and a night stand and lamp. A sitting room has wall-to-wall carpeting. It is furnished with a white upholstered love seat, an upholstered chair, a small end table and lamp, a 1920's wardrobe and an upholstered arm chair in a green print

The World's Fair Suite has an antique Eastlake queen-size bed, an antique marble top chest and wash stand and an octagonal table. A sitting area has an upholstered Victorian sofa, an upholstered are chair and a tripod table.

Martha serves breakfast in the dining room. The table is set with fine china, crystal and flowers. Breakfast consists of Eggs Benedict served with smoked maple sausage, pumpkin bread with homemade apricot marmalade, oranges soaked overnight in champagne, fresh fruit in season and coffee, tea or milk. This is just one of a variety of menus.

OLD ELM TREE INN: 1717 Elm Street. St. Charles, 63301. (636) 947-4843. Website: www.oldelmtreeinn.com. Open all year. Smoking on the veranda. No pets. Three guestroom suites with private baths. Close to Missouri's first capitol, Main Street shops and restaurants, Historic French Town, and the St. Charles River front casino. Martha Kooyumjian, innkeeper.

DIRECTIONS: From Fifth St. go to First Capitol Drive, then left to Kingshighway and right to Elm. Go left on Elm. Parking in rear private spot.

WASHINGTON

Washington, with a distinct Old World flavor, is a tranquil community on the Missouri River. The town was platted by William W. Owens in 1828. Its first German settlers came in 1833 purely by chance. Twelve families from Hanover, Germany arrived in St. Louis. Finding no boat leaving for the Illinois country, their original destination, they decided to go up the Missouri in search of a home. They landed at what is now Washington. Then, it was little more than a tavern and ferry crossing. As a result of a good river landing site, Washington was foreseen as a most promising river port. After Owens' death in 1834, his wife, Lucinda, and son-in-law, John F. Mense, continued with the town project. The town of Washington was officially founded on May 29, 1839.

Washington is an old town for this part of the country, and the early brick homes attest to the confidence the pioneers had for their future. Henry Tibbe invented the corn cob pipe here and his gracious home is still a showplace. John B. Busch started a brewery here in 1855. His splendid second empire mansion still stands as the V.F.W. Post. One hundred year-old churches with their Gothic spires, Greek Revival cottages, and Victorian townhouses are common throughout the old residential sections.

Just a few years ago, Front Street was lined with warehouses, commercial buildings, and homes in disrepair. But now, the waterfront buildings are restored and refurbished to cater to leisure time activities: wineries, antique and craft shops, restaurants, and art galleries.

There are several places here you don't want to miss. *Gary Lucy,* an internationally known artist, has his studio at 231 W. Main Street. His original paintings are on display on the second floor along with displays of beautiful handmade models of steamboats (not for sale). His limited edition prints are on the main floor. The Lucy's have expanded and now occupy the building next door as well. It houses not only the works of other artists, but pottery, lamps, decoys, picture frames and a number of other selections of fine art including dinner services, music boxes, furniture, plates, crystal and tile bottom trays. (636) 239-6337.

Washington's *Historical Society Museum* displays artifacts from the early town. It traces Washington's evolution from a ferry boat landing into the commercial and cultural center of a German-American settlement in the lower Missouri Valley. 113 E. Fourth Street. (636) 239-0280.

For all the antiquers, there are several places in and around Washington that you won't want to miss Four miles south on Highway 47, then one half mile west on Clearview Road, you will find J.K. and Joyce Reynold's *Willow Creek Antiques.* In a 150 year old log barn consisting of 5,000 square feet and a new 1,000 square foot addition. You will find treasures ranging from A to Z. As Joyce showed the new additions, I saw a two door mirrored wardrobe, a heavy carved library table, a great circa 1840 birch secretary, a walnut stepback cupboard, a Rosewood chest with mirror, a side by side secretary, a circa 1830 pine chest, a Lincoln desk, a Missouri oak library table, and an oak stepback cupboard. In the barn I saw a lift top spinet desk, an English marble top wash stand, an old metal bath tub, an immigrant's chest, an oval wicker table, a spinning wheel, a bakers' rack and a maple baker's cabinet. There were all kinds of crocks, oil lamps, old tools, tins, baskets, linens and primitives. Glassware included carnival, depression, cut and pressed. This is a great place to explore for "yesterday." (636) 583-5247.

A place of great interest is Crosby Brown's *Fort Charrette Trading Post and Museum*, which is housed in a log cabin that once stood across the Missouri River from the circa 1762 French village of La Charette, just west of Washington. It was moved to save it from destruction. The village was the last western settlement on the Missouri River in 1804, according to Lewis and Clark, who stayed here on their western trip. The fort is dramatically restored and furnished as a late 1700s local fortified French-Indian fur trading post. Antiques dating from the 18th and 19th centuries, collected for more than 50 years are on display. Located at 4515 Old Highway 100 East. (636) 239-4202. By appointment only.

Attic Treasures is located in the Washington House B & B at 100 W. Front Street. A blend of the old and new can be found in a street level shop. Antiques included are an ornate parlor table, kitchen cupboard, china cupboard, oak bookcases, vintage lace, prints and pictures, painted plates and bowls and bird cages. Newer or reproduction pieces include tea sets and lemonade sets, bird houses, cups and saucers. Sue Black, owner, also carries the Heartland line of candles. (636) 742-4360.

When you're ready to take a break, don't pass up the *Basket Case Deli & Creamery Hill Cafe*. During the day both places (with a common lobby), serve twenty varieties of specialty sandwiches, each a work of art. They are well-known for their daily fresh seafood selections. At night, the *Creamery Hill Cafe* puts on a different face. White tablecloths, fresh flowers ... the works. Menu offerings include rib loin steaks, filet mignon, Norwegian salmon, shrimp scampi, chicken marsala and several great pastas. Entrees come with your choice of salad or homemade soup of the day. Wonderful cheesecakes and homemade pies. 323 A West 5th Street. (636) 239-7172.

Built in 1850 as a hotel and restaurant, *Mense's Landing* has a casual family atmosphere. Some of the best soups I've tasted I had here. Gary Mense features a variety of homemade pizzas, salad bar and sandwiches. You can dine inside with authentic 1800s ambience and charm or outside on the dining patio. Located at 300 W. Front Street. (636) 239-4359.

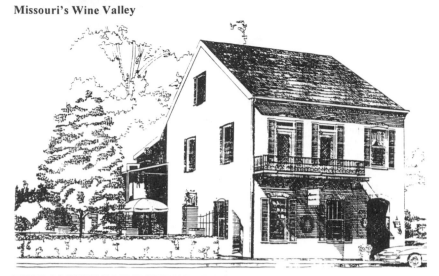

THE AMERICAN BOUNTY RESTAURANT
Washington

Here is a restaurant I know you are going to like. Around 1850, Bernard Weiss built a home and tobacco store here on Front Street. As with many German buildings, it has withstood the ravages of time, weather and sometimes, neglect. Now one hundred and fifty years later, in the same building, Chef Brian and his wife Trina Manhardt have opened the American Bounty Restaurant, a quaint country inn. Completely renovated, this charming restaurant is one of the finest in the area. The restaurant has been written up in Midwest Living and Southern Living Magazines.

Enjoy a casual lunch inside by a fireplace or on the shaded brick patio facing the river. Choose from soup, salad and sandwiches. Entrees include chicken breast encrusted in sage and potatoes with a vegetable medley, grilled Parmesan polenta, or grilled fresh salmon fillet brushed with herbed honey and dijon glaze, with fresh vegetables, sour cream and scallion rice blini.

Evening menu offerings include grilled strip steak, packed in Front Street rub and topped with medallions of crawfish butter, served with fresh seasoned vegetables and Parmesan polenta, or maybe grilled boneless cuts of pheasant with rum cured black currants and chive butter, served with seasoned fresh vegetables and Parmesan polenta

Don't miss the green apple cobbler with maple batter and sauce anglaise.

THE AMERICAN BOUNTY RESTAURANT: 430 Front Street, Washington, 63090. (636) 390-2150. Fax 390-4013. Reservations are advised for dinner. Chef Brian and Trina Manhardt, proprietors.

ELIJAH MCLEAN'S RESTAURANT
Washington

Overlooking the Missouri River, the Elijah McLean home was one of the first residential structures in Washington and one of the finest. It was built by Dr. Elijah McLean who came to Franklin County in 1824 to practice medicine and in 1829 he was elected to the State Legislature.

In the early 1960s, the home's main parlor was remodeled and extended to its present sixty feet. The second floor was removed and made the arched twenty-four foot high ceilings. The chandeliers are said to have been brought to this country from a museum in England. This room is now called the 'Grand Dining Room." Until 1980, it was a private home. It is now an exceptionally fine restaurant, owned by Taylor and Kiki Strecker and Jorge and Marilyn Maldonado.

The luncheon menu features pasta, several chicken dishes and fajitas. Most meals are served with either a cup of soup or a salad.

The dinner menu selections are served with a cup of soup or house salad, fresh vegetables and choice of potato. The roast prime rib of beef is the house specialty. There is also filet mignon, sirloin steak, tournados of beef bordelaise and fried shrimp. German specialties include calves liver, wienerschnitzel and jaegerschnitzel.

Don't forget to make a selection from the fabulous dessert tray.

ELIJAH MCLEAN'S RESTAURANT: 600 W. Front Street, Washington, 63090. (636) 239-Wine or Dine. Please call for hours and reservations.

DE BOURGE HOUSE BED & BREAKFAST
Washington

This brick, story and a half home was built around the turn of the century during the high point in America's Arts and Crafts period. It was originally a two family home that was built by shoe washers from the old shoe factory located one block from this location. It has been fully restored to reflect the arts and craft style of architecture. The first thing I noticed about the house was the absolute cleanliness and the way the floors glistened.

Entering the house from the front porch, the living room has area carpets on the floors, the walls are painted a medium shade of yellow. Lace curtains are at the window. The room is furnished with a green upholstered love seat with Queen Anne style end tables with lamps at either end. A great antique armoire, a coffee table brass floor lamp and a pair of upholstered open armchairs.

An archway leads into the dining room. There is an oriental carpet on the floor, lace curtains are on the windows. It is furnished with an antique oval walnut table and four green and gold striped upholstered chairs. There is a 1930's carved walnut buffet with candle sticks, a brass lamp and porcelain pieces. A large round mirror is set in a gilded likeness f the sun rays is over the buffet. AS corner display cabinet has a glass collection. There are three antique spindle back chairs and a tea cast.

A small porch off the kitchen has a wrought iron table and two chairs. It would be an ideal place to have a first cup of coffee. A privacy fence is around the back yard. A huge old elm tree shades a patio that has an umbrella table and chairs. There are shrubs and flowers.

Three guestrooms are on the second floor. At the top of the stairs there is a hall table with a coffee maker. At the front of the house one of the guestrooms is furnished with a queen-size bed with hand made quilts and lots of pillows. There are two round bedside tables with lamps and a green wicker rocker. A long wall shelf holds dried flower arrangements, and a few nice pieces of brick-a-brack. The walls are a pale yellow. The windows have lace curtains with green and lavender striped drapes. An oriental carpet is on the floor.

Off the hall a second guestroom is furnished with a brass and white metal day bed which opens up into a king-size bed. There is also a small cane seat rocking chair, an oak chest on chest and a night table with a reading lamp. The walls are painted a pale green, that shiny floor has an oriental area carpet and the windows have lace curtains with floral drapes.

Also off the hall, a third guestroom has a king-size four poster rice bed with a floral spread, a wicker rocking chair, a wooden chest on wrought iron legs is at the foot of the bed, a pair of bedside tables with lamps, an antique dressing table and a ladder back chair. The walls are pale yellow, lace curtains with floral drapes are at the floor. Gail De Bourge just had a private bath with a clawfoot tub installed in this room.

At the end of the hall a shared bath has a tub and a shower. It is decorated very nicely.

Gail serves a full meal in the dining room. It includes juice, a fruit dish, homemade bread and muffins, coffee, tea or milk. As Gail varies her breakfasts, it could be an egg, sausage and cheese casserole, or a breakfast pizza, how about French Toast with syrup and powdered sugar, served with sausage, ham or bacon.

I like the town of Washington and go there quite often. I like the shop and especially the restaurants. Gail has two bikes and its only a few miles to the Katy Trail She also has Amtrak pickup and delivery with advance notice, and with advance notice she can arrange for special dietary needs.

DE BOURGE HOUSE B & B: 119 Johnson Street, Washington, 63090. (636) 390-4898. Open all year. A three guestroom home with private and shared baths. We cater to adults but do accept children conditionally. Smoking outdoors. No pets. Gail De Bourge, innkeeper.

DIRECTIONS: Call for reservations and directions.

LA DOLCE VITA BED & BREAKFAST,
VINEYARD & WINERY

Washington

Perched atop a hill with a million dollar view, Wayne and Marcy Halbert's La Dolce Vita B & B, Vineyard and Winery is either a romantic escape, a peaceful getaway or the perfect place for a business traveler. The contemporary ranch home was built in 1995 and has a two-acre vineyard 20 feet from a rear patio.

The lower level of the house includes guest quarters two guest bedrooms with private baths, a keeping room and a covered patio area.

The Cynthiana Room, named after the grapes grown here, is furnished with an antique, white ornate iron bed, with a Dresden Plate quilt, an antique dresser with a cut glass lamp, an upholstered wing-back chair and a night stand and lamp. The walls are pale green, has nice pictures and the floor is fully carpeted. There is a private bath with shower,

The Vintage Room is furnished with a queen-size wicker bed that also has a hand-made quilt, a bedside table, a 1920's dresser, an upholstered wingback chair and a wicker table. It is fully carpeted and has a colorful area rug on top of it. Old time framed prints are on the pale yellow walls, It has a private bath with shower. Both guestrooms have views of the vineyard.

The keeping room, which is fully carpeted, is furnished with upholstered floral sofa, an upholstered wing chair, an antique Morris recliner, a bookcase with books and magazines, a wrought iron glass top coffee table and end table, a desk and chair and a small bar. There are live plants and pictures on the wall including a poster with scenes from the movie, La Dolce Vita. It's a great place for early morning coffee. Glass doors open onto the patio. The covered patio has a glass top table and four cushioned chairs and a chaise lounge. There are live plants and the vineyard 20 feet away. This is a deal place to spend time just relaxing.

On the first floor, a portion of a large open area has an antique harvest table with a church pew and four chairs, a vintage Victrola, and an antique cupboard containing all kinds of "things." Breakfast is served here.

Glass doors open onto a cozy screened-in porch, furnished with a white wicker set which includes a sofa, a pair of arm chairs, a coffee table and a lamp table. There is also a four-piece wrought iron set, which includes a table and four chairs. Lots of live plants and that million-dollar view of the countryside. If you wish and the weather is no object, breakfast can be served here.

A full breakfast is served from 8-9 a.m., and consists of several varied entrees. There is always orange juice, fresh fruit in season, coffee, tea or milk. The entrees could be either French toast, eggs Benedict, Belgium Waffles, all served with ham or sausage. I almost forgot the cinnamon rolls. At check-in, beverages include, wine and a cheese smash is offered.

The vineyards and winery produce up to 400 cases per year of premium Cynthiana wine. Their grapes are hand picked, sorted, crushed and fermented for 6-8 days. The must is gently pressed and the wine transferred to stainless steel tanks for secondary fermentation. Then over winter, the wine is cold stabilized. By April, the wine is put into American oak barrels to age for at least 9 months. After bottling, the wine is rested until it's sold. The winery is not open to the public for tasting.

LA DOLCE VITA B & B: 72 Forest Hills Drive, Washington, 63090. (636) 239-0399. Fax (636) 239-7279. Website: Ladolcevitawinery.com Open all year. A two guestroom with private baths and keeping area. Smoking on patio. Not suited for children. Am Exp/MC/Visa honored. Wayne and Marcy Halbert innkeepers.

DIRECTIONS: From Washington, take Hwy. 47 east to Country Club road. Turn left to Forest Hills Drive. La Dolce Vita is second house on right.

SCHWEGMANN HOUSE BED & BREAKFAST
Washington

Completed in 1861, this well preserved three story, red brick Georgian mansion is a prime example of the architecture and craftsmanship that typifies contruction in Missouri by the early German immigrants along the Missouri River. This stately home was once the residence of John F. Schwegmann, a native of Hanover, Germany who ran a flour mill nearby on the riverfront. The parlors, warmed by the glow from the fireplace, graceful staircase, high ceilings and tall windows create an old fashioned country elegance. It is listed on the National Register of Historic Places.

The owners, Cathy and Bill Nagel offer nine 1860 era guestrooms with private 1996 baths. Each is charmingly decorated with antique furnishings and handmade quilts. There are two parlors in the house. One, the Garden Parlor is used for serving breakfast. The other, the River Parlor is used for guest comfort, where each evening you are offered homemade goodies along with tea and coffee. It is furnished with an antique love seat, upholstered chairs, an antique secretary and an oriental carpet. The fireplace is the focal point. There are parlor games, music, and books relating to the area, for your pleasure. Faux painting decor by a local artist is exhibited throughout the home.

The first floor guestrooms include the Wide Missouri Room with its rose tones complemented by floor to ceiling draperies with lace panels framing a glorious river view. The antiques will remind you of a European boudoir. It has a queen-size bed.

Just a few steps away is the Garden Room,. This delightful room is brightly decorated with antiques. A tree of life quilt and floral bouquets are part of the decor. It has a queen-size bed.

On the second floor, John and Mary's Room, with two double beds offers a glimpse of the family and Washington's past. Handmade quilts, antiques and a comfortable rocker make you feel at home.

At the top of the stairs, the Orient Express Room is a sunny corner room with queen-size bed that overlooks the garden and offers a view of the river. The theme is set by an antique oriental table and two oriental prints.

The Riverview Room, with two double beds, offers a panoramic view of the wide Missouri. Antique satin quilt hangings with their pale colors of peach and green compliment the dark antique furnishings. Eyelet curtains, and everlasting bouquets add the final touches.

The Jolly Boatman's Room has three prints of artist, John Caleb Bingham's Boatmen on the Missouri River. A handmade quilt, and antique oak furniture create a setting for the original false fireplace mantel. Queen-size bed and comfortable upholstered reading chairs.

The Miller's Suite has its access from a sitting porch on the second floor nestled in the boughs of a giant pecan tree. This private suite with a queen-size bed boasts a massage tub for two, a chilled bottle of Missouri Wine and breakfast delivered to the door.

Nestled in the eaves of the third floor, the large rustic Garret Room has views of the river to the west and north. Wide plank floors and treasure's from Granny's attic will bring back childhood fantasies. There is a queen-size bed, and a matching marble top dresser and washstand.

The Anniversary Room is another special room for romantic evenings. A queen-size bed, an old trunk with an antique wedding dress, and an antique rocker by the window overlooking the garden and river await your stay.

At breakfast in the Garden Parlor on the patio you are served freshly ground coffee, assorted teas, fresh fruit, and Schwegmann house specialities. A sample breakfast might include German apple pancakes, grilled ham, cranberry oatmeal scones and zucchini bread. Another breakfast would be a three cheese egg strata, grilled smoked turkey, apple strudel, and mini muffins.

SCHWEGMANN HOUSE B & B: 438 W. Front Street, Washington, 63090. (636) 239-5025. Reservations (800) 949-2262. A Historic inn with nine guestrooms with private baths. Open all year. No pets. Children welcome Sunday through Thursday. No smoking. Inspected and approved by Mobil Travel Guide and BBIM. Website: www.schwegmannhouse.com. Cathy and Bill Nagel, innkeepers.

DIRECTIONS: On the riverfront in Washington.

WASHINGTON HOUSE
Washington

Washington House was originally built around 1837 to serve travelers and trappers along the Missouri River in what was soon to become the town of Washington over the last 160 years. The house has undergone numerous changes, both in architecture and use. After first serving as an inn, it has at various times, been a general store, riverboat captain's home, boarding house, fish market, speakeasy, restaurant and an apartment. Now, however, it has been authentically restored and once again is welcoming guests to its early 19th century charm by Terry and Sue Black.

As a bed and breakfast, Washington House offers the feel of a time long past, combined with contemporary comforts. The rooms offer views of the Missouri River and have independently controlled heating and air conditioning.

The entrance to Washington House, like so many early German houses, is right at the sidewalk. The entrance hall is furnished with a circa 1830 Empire desk and a windsor chair.

There are two guestrooms on the second floor. The first room is furnished with a four poster, queen-size canopy bed that has a handmade coverlet. There is a pair of upholstered wing back chairs, a chest and a television. A buffalo rug is on the bare original floors. Burgundy colored drapes are at the windows. The white walls are stenciled at the ceiling. There is a fireplace in the room for show only. The private bath has a claw foot tub.

The second guestroom also has a queen-size four poster canopy bed with an antique quilt on it. There is an antique wardrobe, a chest, a drop leaf table, two spindle back chairs, a rocking chair and a television. The original floors have throw rugs on them. Green and white checkered swags are at the windows, and the walls are painted green below a chair rail and off white above it. It also has a private bath.

In the second floor hall, there is an antique marble top dresser with a wishbone mirror, and a coffee maker for that first cup of coffee. There is also a small refrigerator. The walls are painted in a colorful crewel pattern.

Breakfast is not served at the Washington House, but a full breakfast (included in the room rate) is served at Cowan's Restaurant, a Washington favorite, just a few blocks away.

Designated a National Historic District, Washington Landing was first settled by "Old Americans" from Kentucky, Tennessee and the Carolinas during the 1840s and 50s. So, take some time and enjoy a relaxing evening or weekend in early Missouri. There are antique and gift shops, art galleries, fine restaurants and nearby wineries. Cross the river and hike or bike the Katy Trail. Or, leave your car at home, and relax and ride Amtrak to Washington and Washington House.

WASHINGTON HOUSE: 100 W. Front Street, Washington, 63090. (636) 239-2417 or (636) 742-4360. Open all year. A two guestroom inn overlooking the Missouri River. In the heart of the historic district. Children welcome. No pets. Due to the historic nature of the building, no smoking. Terry and Sue Black, innkeepers.

DIRECTIONS: From St. Louis, take I-44 west to Hwy. 100 (the Washington Exit). Go west 10.6 miles to the sixth stoplight at Hwy. A. Turn right on A (Jefferson St.) to Front Street on the river. Turn left, one block to Lafayette, etc. From I-70, take Hwy. 47 south across the Missouri River bridge to Third Street. Turn right on Lafayette.

WEIRICK ESTATE BED & BREAKFAST
Washington

The land on which Weirick Estate B & B is built was originally deeded to a John Caldwell in 1833. In 1838 it was part of a tract purchased by Elijah McLean. The southern portion, the back of the house now, was built in 1879. Upton Weirick, an official with H. Tibbe & Son Manufacturing Company, which made corn cob pipes, bought the property and built the rest of the house in 1895. In 1923, the house passed to Frank Hoelscher and for seventy years and three generations, it remained in the Hoelscher family, until it was sold to Gary and Cindy Grosse.

The house features the original 12 foot ceilings, picture moldings, woodwork, transoms, marble fireplace and the wooden staircase. The ten room Victorian home is in tip-top shape, and has been elegantly decorated throughout with family heirlooms and antique furniture.

The hallway has a new black and white tile floor, which was common at that time. The hallway also serves as the entryway to the home. There is an antique mantelpiece and an iron stove holds tourist information. The morning breakfast menu is placed here the night before. There is white paneling below a chair rail in the hall and up the stairs. One wall in the hall is papered in a large rose pattern paper. Up the stairs, a foot wide border at the chair rail, are of hand-painted roses.

To the right of the entry hall, the large parlor is carpeted in gray wall to wall. A very unusual gray and white striped wallpaper has a two foot wide border about a foot beneath the ceiling. The room is furnished with a pair of Queen Anne camel back love seats, a small butler's tray table, a baby grand piano, a broken pediment breakfront, an eight leg octagonal table, a glass top server, a Victorian chair, an antique armoire and a Martha Washington arm chair. The marble fireplace holds some great pieces. In a large three bay window with lace curtains, there is a pedestal dining table with six Chippendale chairs. Breakfast is served here, but you can also use it for games and puzzles.

The guestrooms are on the second floor. The Honeymoon Room is large, with a bay window and a fireplace. Lace curtains are at the window. It is furnished with a queen-size four poster rice bed, an antique cherry chest and mirror, an antique armoire, a Queen Anne writing desk, a floral wing chair and a bentwood rocker. The walls have a blue floral and stripe paper and a blue carpet. A great view of the river.

The Grandparent's Room has three large windows with lace curtains. A green and white striped wallpaper is below a chair rail while a floral design print is above. It is furnished with two full-size iron beds and night tables with lamps. There is cable television. Two wicker chairs, a 1920s dresser and chest.

The Anniversary Room has a white antique, full-size iron bed, a cherry wood secretary, two white wicker chairs. An antique dental cabinet serves as a night stand.

At the top of the stairs, a sitting area has a green and white striped love seat, a sage-green wicker chair and two bookcases with lots of books.

Breakfast entrees include a breakfast lasagna with sausage, three cheeses, eggs and noodles, served with (foccia) Italian bread.; sherried eggs with cheddar cheese and sherry on an English muffin with peppered bacon; eggs benedict and hash browns;. Or, corned beef hash with a poached egg. All are served with juice, fresh fruit, homemade varieties of muffins and nut or pumpkin bread. Coffee, tea or milk.

Upon arrival, guests are offered free samples from the small craft brewery in the cellar.

WEIRICK ESTATE B & B: 716 West Main Street, Washington, 63090. (636) 239-4469. Open all year. No children under 12. No pets. No smoking inside. Visa/MC. Pick up and return to Amtrak Station. Gift certificates available. Gary and Cindy Grosse, innkeepers.

DIRECTIONS: Call for directions and reservations. Near downtown.

Section Six

LAKE OF THE OZARKS REGION

Bland
Caverly's Farm B & B

Bonnots Mill
Dauphine Hotel

California
Memory Lane B & B

Columbia
Gathering Place B & B
Missouri Manor B & B

Dixon
Rock Eddy Bluff B & B

Fulton
Loganberry Inn
Romancing the Past

Hartsburg
Globe Hotel B & B

Jefferson City
Huber's Ferry B & B
Jefferson Inn

Lake of the Ozarks
Cliff House B & B
Ginger Point B & B

Versailles
Hilty Inn B & B

Warrensburg
Brawley Creek B & B
Camel Crossing B & B
Cedar Croft Inn

Waynesville
Home Place B & B

Westphalia
Werner House B & B

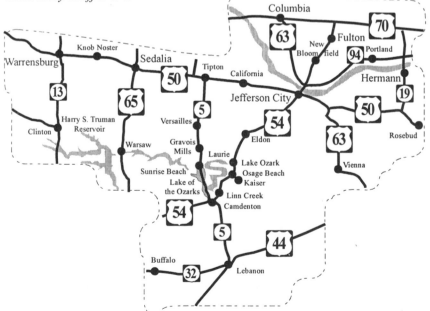

The Lake of the Ozarks is the heart of a scenic historic vacation land that attracts more than four million travelers every year. The Lake of the Ozarks Region is an area of superlatives. Here, visitors can find Missouri's largest lake, state park, fair, and university.

Since the opening of the Bagnell Dam in 1931, the lake has become one of America's finest vacation areas. Its 650 billion gallons of water are perfect for just about any kind of water fun imaginable. And its 1,375 miles of shoreline, twisting and turning through forested Ozarks terrain, create hidden coves and natural areas for hikers, photographers, and nature lovers.

The Lake of the Ozarks, which gives the region its name, and its neighbor, Truman Lake, with almost 1,000 miles of shoreline, offer a chance to fish, boat, ski, swim, or enjoy the multitude of near-the-water attractions that have developed in this popular vacation spot. Forested hills and dramatic bluffs at the water's edge compliment the water fun in Missouri's heartland.

Several districts make up the Lake of the Ozarks Region. Bagnell Dam, responsible for harnessing the mighty Osage River and starting point of this great lake, is located on Highway 54, 42 miles southwest of Jefferson City. Free tours through the dam are provided by Union Electric Company. The nationally famous Bagnell Dam Gun Show is held in June. An annual Bluegrass Festival is held in the winter months in the Horseshoe Bend area off State Road HH. Lake Ozark is a small community just two miles from the dam. Cliff House and Ginger Point are located at Lake Ozark.

The Osage Beach area is located six miles southwest of Bagnell Dam on Highway 54, where the Grand Glaize arm of the lake joins the picturesque main Osage channel. The Lake of the Ozarks State Park lies immediately adjacent to this area. Besides spring, summer, and fall activities, winter sports are also available with snow skiing (man made). Visit the Lake of the Ozarks State Park. Missouri's largest with 16,872 acres near Osage Beach. There are swimming beaches, boat launching areas, picnic areas and horseback riding trails. The park offers tours through Ozark Caverns.

Camdenton area is called the Hub City of the lake. It is located on Highway 54 at the intersection of Highway 5, about 18 miles southwest of Bagnell Dam. The area is composed of the Niangua arm and the Osage arm of the lake. Breathtaking scenic views are abundant in this area, especially around the Ha Ha Tonka castle ruins. The area events include the Annual Dogwood Festival in April and the nationally famous Camdenton J-Bar-H Rodeo in July.

Naturally, the State Capitol at Jefferson City should not be overlooked. The Jefferson Inn and Huber's Ferry B & B are located here.

North of Jefferson City, in Columbia, education is the dominant theme. The sprawling University of Missouri, founded in 1841, was the first state university west of the Mississippi River. Stephens College and Columbia College are also here. Columbia is mid-Missouri's largest city with all the shopping and dining that implies. Missouri Manor B & B and The Gathering Place B & B are located in Columbia.

Westminster College, just to the east in Fulton, was the site of Winston Churchill's Iron Curtain speech in 1946. It preserves his memory today with a Memorial in the centuries old Church of the Aldermanbury, which was shipped in pieces from London to the campus of Westminster College and reassembled there. Loganberry Inn and Romancing the Past B & B are located in Fulton.

In mid-August, Missouri's State Fair is held in Sedalia. At California, you can learn about Missouri hams, while you tour the Burger Smokehouse. Memory Lane B & B is located in California. Parts of the old Butterfield Overland Trail, an early stage coach road, can be seen at Warsaw, along with a museum with items dating from the early 1800s.

In Warrensburg, the old Johnson County Courthouse is one of the oldest courthouses in the state. It was built 17 years after Missouri was admitted to the Union. Camel Crossing B & B, Cedarcroft Farm B & B, and Brawley Creek B & B are located at or near Warrensburg.

Among the caves in the area are Indian Burial Cave at Osage Beach, Jacob's Cave at Versailles, and Bridal Cave at Camdenton. Hilty Inn is located at Versailles.

Antique lovers, don't fail to stop at Jesse Carroll's antique shop on Highway 63 in Vienna. This is one of the better shops in the whole area. When I was here, Jesse had a circa 1860 walnut corner cupboard, a pegged jelly cupboard, an 1890 glass door kitchen cupboard, a high back, circa 1880 bed, an Eastlake walnut dresser with a marble insert and a Queen-Anne game table with a carved checkerboard top. There were crocks, quilts, a line of tools, glassware, Indian artifacts, oil lamps, granite ware, children's toys and miniature wooden models including a 1/6th scale threshing machine and a water wagon. This is a good place. (573) 422-3298.

Another unusual shop is John Viessman's Americana Antiques, located 1/2 mile north of Highway 63 and Junction 42 in Vienna. (573) 422-3505. He deals mainly in books and has about 50,000 of them. Categories include natural history, children's, military, cookbooks and early editions. John showed me a circa 1865 double wardrobe in walnut. It was six feet wide and nine feet tall. There was also a step back kitchen cupboard. There were many old tins, kitchen items, tools, art pottery, glass, primitives and toys. He is restoring his grandfather's log cabin to house the primitives.

Jerry and Sandy Shelton's Maries Hollow Herb Farm and Antiques is another place you should visit. They specialize in wonderful garden related antiques and garden furniture. There was, however, a double cupboard put together with square nails and with the original red paint, a corner cupboard, a scrub-top harvest table, an Adirondack bench, iron beds and Victorian plant stands. There are also quilts, enamel ware, vintage clothing, old patriotic items and some great early painted country furniture. Call for directions. (573) 422-3906.

Going east from Jefferson City on Highway 50, turn south on Highway 63 and take a look at some of the handiwork of the early German settlers of this region. There are mellowed stone houses of Germanic design, some early brick homes and white frame houses with huge old barns that enhance the natural beauty of the countryside. Four miles south of Highway 50 on Highway 63 is the town of Westphalia, where the prim stone and frame building crowd the main street. In 1835, a small group of Westphalian families settled near here on the Big Maries River. In the spring of 1837, a log chapel was built. Father Helias d' Huddeghem conducted the first mass. In 1848, the log chapel was replaced with the present St. Joseph's Church. This little town if certainly worth a few hours of your time to explore. The Westphalia Inn Restaurant and the Werner House B & B are located in Westphalia.

A few miles south of Westphalia, make a left turn onto Route E and you are heading for the town of Rich Fountain. It is typical of the many small German communities that grew up off the main highway and are sprinkled throughout this area. The town has both early stone and frame buildings with an atmosphere of simplicity and order. The settlement received it name because of the many clear springs in the neighborhood. The 250 Bavarian families who settled in the vicinity in 1842 had come to the United States to escape oppressive government restrictions. In 1998, Rich Fountain will celebrate one hundred and sixty years in the parish. The White Stone Inn restaurant is located in Rich Fountain.

The tiny hamlet of Bonnots Mill sits amid the hills and bluffs on the south bank of the Osage River, twenty miles east of Jefferson City. Take Route A north from Loose Creek for about seven miles. The oldest town in Osage County, was French Village, which stood very near the present site of Bonnots Mill. French fur traders were more than likely the first settlers. The Osage Indians would come to the town to sell or trade their animal skins. A flood in 1844 destroyed French Village and afterward, the remaining Frenchmen founded the town of Dauphine, named after a province in France. In 1838, Felix Bonnot left France for America and some years later settled in Dauphine. In 1852, he established a flour and sawmill here. People began coming to Bonnot's Mill to have their corn and wheat ground. The name Dauphine was slowly forgotten and Bonnots Mill took its place. The little town became a busy railroad center and river port. At one time, in the early days, there was a post office, wagon maker, blacksmith, saloon and a hotel. Today, Bonnots Mill retains all the charm of yesteryear. The old churches still stand and the old hotel is now the Dauphine Hotel B & B. Try Krautman's Korner for a good place to eat.

CAVERLY FARM & ORCHARD BED & BREAKFAST
Bland

David and Nancy Caverly have moved from St. Louis, where for six years, they had their first Caverly Farm Bed and Breakfast. Now they have a 57-acre farm, with a renovated the circa 1850 farmhouse in rural Osage Country and have opened Caverly Farm & Orchard Bed & Breakfast.

The farm is a great place for families to come and spend some time enjoying a world without noise and crowds. Dogwood and redbud trees in spring; fields of newly bundled hay bales in summer; bittersweet, red maple, sumac, oak, walnut and cedar trees share their many colors in fall; and even the shades of white and gray after a snowfall are all appreciated. There is an abundance of wildlife often seen on the farm.

The farmhouse has all modern conveniences including an electric stair-chair to the second floor for guests who need assistance with stairs. The renovation has preserved much of the ambiance of the old farmhouse. There is a parlor, dining room, a spacious screened-in porch and three guestrooms with private baths.

The parlor is furnished with a piano, a television and VCR, a video library and a variety of books and magazines. A turn of the century parlor set includes a love seat, two side chairs, an armchair and a platform rocker. There is an oriental carpet on the floor. The original beaded ceiling and a huge hand hewn beam have been retained.

The dining room also has the original beaded ceiling. It is furnished with a cherry table and ladder back chairs, a maple tea cart, a walnut sideboard, a built-in marble top serving area and a tall butternut hutch.

Glass doors from the dining room lead onto a spacious screened-in porch overlooking fields and a lake. It is furnished with a wrought iron glass top table and four chairs, a round side table with chairs and comfortable lounge furniture. Steps lead down to a play yard for children. Let them try the old rope swing.

The three guestrooms, each with a private bath, are on the second floor. A new upper hallway has a beaded wainscoting. A guest telephone is here, along with tourist information and a library.

The Garden View Room is furnished with a queen-size headboard bed with night tables and reading lamps on either side, a single hide-a-bed and a walnut marble top dresser. A round walnut table with a reading lamp sets in the corner. The walls are white and the woodwork is painted a deep, French blue. The floor is covered with a blue wall-to-wall carpet. The room overlooks the front garden.

The Valley View Room has a walnut four poster full-size bed with a pale rose woven spread, a walnut chest and mirror, night tables and a small library table with a reading lamp. The floor has a Berber carpet. The walls are white with deep rose woodwork. The room overlooks the lake, hay fields and woods.

The Farm Room is an ideal child's room. It has a trundle bed covered with a handmade quilt. There is an antique washstand, an oak chest, and children's chairs. A wide wallpaper border with a colorful farm scene is chair rail high. The room has a view of the lake, woods and Guest House.

Nancy serves a full breakfast consisting of juice, fresh fruit in season, fresh farm eggs with cottage bacon and sausage, homemade breads, jams, local honey, coffee, tea or milk.

Guests may enjoy the wildlife often seen on the farm; take in a weekend country auction; or visit the wineries of St. James and Hermann. Antique shops are found in nearby small towns. Several very nice restaurants are located within a reasonable driving distance.

CAVERLY FARM & ORCHARD B & B: 100 Cedar Ridge Road, Bland, 65014. (573) 646-3732. Open all year. Children welcome. No pets. No smoking in house. Nancy and David Caverly, innkeepers.

DIRECTIONS: From St. Louis take I-44 to Union exit, Hwy. 50. Follow Hwy. 50 through Rosebud to Hwy. 28 and turn left. Take 28 through Bland to Hwy. NN (about 2 miles west of Bland). Turn right and go 2 miles to County Rd. 737 (Cedar Ridge Rd). Turn Left. 1/2 mile to farm.

DAUPHINE HOTEL
Bonnots Mill

I will not forget the first time I saw the town of Bonnots Mill. It looked like a fairy book village nestled in the mountains of Europe. I may be over enthusiastic in my description, but it is a very quaint place.

Listed on the National Register of Historic Places, the building that houses the Dauphine Began as a two-room dwelling built in the 1840's. By 1875, extensive additions had been made to the building and it was operating as a hotel. The name Dauphine comes from the original name of the town.

In 1890, a prominent citizen named Alex Verdot purchased the hotel. His wife Adelaide and four daughters were responsible for the day to day operations. Because the town was situated along an important river and railroad transportation routes, the Dauphine did a thriving business, offering "First Class Cuisine; Excellent Rooms; Best Accommodations for Travelers" (from the 1891 Missouri State Gazetteer). One of the four daughters eventually got married and moved away, but the other three continued to run the hotel even after their parents passed away. By the 1930's however, the depression, combined with the increasing popularity of the automobile, ended the town's role as a center of county commerce. The hotel closed and the building served as a private residence for the three "Verdot Girls" until the last one passed away in 1970. For the next ten years the hotel stood vacant. Then, during the 1980's, restoration began. The current owners recently completed the restoration and opened it as a Bed and Breakfast Inn in the spring of 1997.

The hotel offers seven guestrooms, all with central heating and air conditioning. Most of the rooms have private bathrooms, including one with an antique claw-foot tub. All of the rooms are furnished with the original iron beds, handmade quilts, and antique dressers and/or armoires. Other items such as washstands, rocking chairs, and antique lamps and prints bring a feeling of nostalgia.

Guests enter the hotel through a lobby that is decorated to resemble a train depot with arts & crafts furniture, an old steamer trunk, and lots of railroad memorabilia. It's a great place to relax and learn about the area, with numerous books, games and puzzles available. Guests can also gather in the parlor, furnished with an antique sofa, chairs and love seats gathered cozily around a wood stove. For the musically inclined, there is an old-time pump organ as well as a Victrola. Breakfast is served in the dining room and family-style kitchen, which are also furnished with antiques, including an oak sideboard, pie safe and Hoosier cabinet. Eggs are cooked to order, along with a large selection of traditional country breakfast fare.

Outside, there is a lovely two-story porch with a view of the Osage River, a side porch with a swing facing the bird feeders, and several well-tended gardens. And don't forget to check out the old outbuildings, including the chicken coop and original three-stall outhouse.

Your hosts, Scott and Sandra Holder, left city life in Washington D.C., to come to Bonnots Mill where Sandra's ancestors first settled when they immigrated to this country in the mid-1800's.

DAUPHINE HOTEL BED AND BREAKFAST INN: P.O. Box 36, Bonnots Mill, 65016. (573) 897-4144. Website: www.dauphinehotel.com. Open all year. Children over 10 welcome. No pets. Smoking on porch. Sandra and Scott Holder, innkeepers.

DIRECTIONS: From St. Louis take I-44 west to Union exit (Hwy. 50). Take 50 west to Loose Creek (55 miles). Turn right on Hwy. A and go 6 miles to Bonnots Mill. From Jefferson City take Hwy. 50 east to Loose Creek (20 miles) and take Hwy. A. It's a very scenic drive.

MEMORY LANE BED & BREAKFAST
California

This Queen Anne Victorian house was built in 1894 by A.W. Yarnell, a local merchant. It was the first house in California to have an inside bathtub. It still retains all of the original stained glass windows and beautiful cherry wood woodwork throughout. Joe and Maryellen LaPrise sold their farm several years ago and moved to California to open this bed and breakfast.

The guestrooms feature antique furnishings while the remainder of the house is decorated with a blend of antique and modern furniture.

Antique lovers will enjoy the nostalgia of talking on an authentic crank telephone or listening to a Thomas Edison crank phonograph.

Entering the house you are in a large hallway that has the original staircase with a cherry wood bannister. It has been newly wallpapered since I was here last. Among the furnishings are a writing desk, a wall phone, Victrola, and a Victorian mirror. Area rugs are on the original floor.

A parlor for guests use contains a Victorian pump organ, an antique Edison phonograph with horn, and two wing chairs, a contemporary sofa, a pair of end tables and a coffee table all in Queen Anne style. It is wallpapered with a Victorian print, has antique pictures on the walls, and the original brass chandelier.

The carpeted dining room is furnished with an oak Jacobean sideboard, an antique oak china cabinet that is highly carved, a Victrola, an oak secretary, and a large oak table and chairs. The room has a nice fireplace and a bay window.

Memory Lane serves a full country breakfast to guests: juice, fresh fruit bowl, ham, bacon or sausage with eggs or pancakes, hashed brown potatoes, homemade rolls, muffins or biscuits, jams jellies, coffee or tea.

Three guestrooms are on the second floor All of the rooms have antique prints and pictures. Brook's Room has a matching three piece antique bedroom set that consists of a high-back, full-size walnut bed, a walnut washstand, and a walnut marble top dresser. A Victorian table holds a Gone-with-the-Wind Lamp. The room is carpeted, has lace curtains, original brass lights and is papered in a Victorian design.

Irene's Room has antique twin four poster beds, an antique treadle sewing machine made in 1915, a small marble top washstand, and a walnut dresser. It is carpeted, wallpapered and has the original brass light fixture.

The Yarnell Room is furnished with a full-size antique, ornate high back bed, a marble top dresser with glove boxes and candle shelves, a wrought iron washstand with antique pitcher and bowl set and a day bed for a third person.

A large bathroom has a claw foot tub with a shower and the original porcelain sink. The three guestrooms share the bath.

Soda and lemonade are served in summer and hot chocolate in the winter. Coffee is always available and a light snack is served in the evening.

Weather permitting, it's very pleasant to sit in the swing on the front porch. Or, wander down the brick walk in the yard, to the sitting arbor entwined with Clematis vines for shade and beauty.

MEMORY LANE B & B: 102 South Oak Street (Hwy. 87), California, 65018. (573) 796-4233. A three guestroom B & B with shared bath. Open all year. Well behaved children over 10 welcome. No smoking in guestrooms. No pets. Close to Burger's Smokehouse and more than 50 antique shops are in a 35 mile radius. Senior citizen and 4 day stay rates. Pets in residence. Joe and Maryellen LaPrise, hosts.

DIRECTIONS: From Jefferson City take Hwy. 50 west to California. Turn right at Oak Street (Hwy. 87) and go four blocks to the house.

THE GATHERING PLACE BED & BREAKFAST
Columbia

Cora Gans Davenport purchased this property in 1905 to build her private residence. The house was completed in 1906. The builder signed the last piece of siding high on the northwest corner of the house. Cora owned the home until 1918. Since then, it has been home to several widows and to four fraternities. During the 1960s, 70s and 80s, the owner of the house divided it into eight apartments.

Shirley and Ross Duff purchased the property in 1994 and a complete renovation and restoration was undertaken. The character of the four column front porch has been retained as were the twin bay windows.

The first floor is open to guests for reading, visiting or doing business. The entry hall has an 1858 cherry table. Old post office boxes hold snacks and a refrigerator has soda and water. The stairway is black walnut.

The hallway arch leading into the parlor was designed after the Ecce-Homo arch in Jerusalem. The parlor's black walnut floor has an oriental carpet. There is a gas log fireplace. In a bay window, a tripod table and lamp have a leather wing back chair on either side of it. The room also contains an upholstered sofa and a loveseat. There is also an antique walnut Lincoln desk, a display coffee table, an antique chest, a plantation desk and two upholstered arm chairs.

The dining room is furnished with four antique walnut tables and an antique cherry harvest table with Chippendale style chairs. There is a punched tin, three door pie safe and a jelly cupboard. A plate rail holds pewter rimmed blue and white plates. A blue wall is below a chair rail with a red and blue striped floral pattern above it.

The Gathering Place offers four queen-size suites and one king-size room. All have desks, telephones with data ports and cable television. Antique pieces in walnut, cherry and tiger maple are prevalent. The rooms have individually controlled heating and air conditioning. The five suites are named after favorite M.U. courses.

The Missouri History 101 Suite is on the first floor. The room is threshold free and fully handicapped accessible. It also has a separate sitting room. It is furnished with a queen-size canopy four poster walnut bed, an antique night table and reading lamp, and a blanket chest. An oriental area carpet is on the floor. There is a butternut corner cupboard an upholstered floral sofa, an upholstered arm chair and ottoman, and a small chest. There is a bay window.

The Textiles 202 Room on the second floor, features a king-size carved poster bed with antique textiles and quilts. There is an armoire, two yellow and blue plain upholstered wing chairs, a blanket chest, bedside table and reading lamp and a yarn winder. The bath has a Jacuzzi and shower.

The Wildlife Conservation 203 Room is furnished with a queen-size, handmade walnut bed with an Ethan Allen comforter, upholstered wing back chairs, and a night stand. The walls are burgundy and an oriental area rug is on the floor. Fishing lures and outdoor relics decorate the room.

The Children's Literature 204 Room has a queen-size four poster, tiger maple bed, a pair of blue wing back upholstered recliners, two antique tiger maple chests, a pair of bedside tables and a table and chairs. There are "kiddie" books and pictures. The bed linens are from Williamsburg. The bath has a Jacuzzi and shower.

The Chemistry 305 is on the third floor and has a sitting room. It is furnished with a cherry four poster queen-size bed, night stands and lamps, and a wing back chair upholstered in a red scenic print. A dental cabinet has an antique chemistry book. The sitting room has a blue plaid upholstered sofa, a wing back chair and ottoman, and an antique chest. Original artwork is on the walls and an oriental carpet is on the floor. The bath has a Jacuzzi and shower.

Breakfast is served between 7 and 9 a.m. There is a daily menu. It starts with juice, a melon medley, then a swiss cheese quiche with sausage links and croissants. A lighter menu might be a melon medley, yogurt, English muffins and coffee or hot tea.

THE GATHERING PLACE B & B: 606 South College Place, Columbia, 62201. (573) 815-0606 or (800) 731-6888. Fax: (573) 817-1653. Open all year. No smoking inside. No pets. Four queen suites and one king room with private baths. Shirley and Ross Duff, innkeepers. Kristin and Jim Steelman and Deiter Duff, right hands.

DIRECTIONS: From I-70, take Hwy. 63 south to Stadium Boulevard. Turn right and go to College. Turn right to inn. You can take Stadium Exit and go south to College. Left on College.

MISSOURI MANOR BED & BREAKFAST
Columbia

Built in 1930 for prominent businessman, W.C. Conley, this home in the style of an English manor, was once part of the sprawling University of Missouri campus. It is one of the few surviving grand homes in the area. It is now the residence of Lyria and Ron Bartlett, innkeepers of the Missouri Manor B & B.

Across the length of the back of the house, Ron has designed and planted an English garden. A large patio with lots of wrought iron furniture is a perfect spot for refreshments and conversation. Shrubs, hundreds of flowers, brick walks and a gold fish pond should relax anyone.

The entry hall has an ornate cherry staircase and a tile floor. On each side of a library table is an upholstered arm chair.

Off the hallway, the living room has a large bay with seven windows, each with fifteen small panes of glass. A sofa sits in front of it facing a fireplace that has a huge floral arrangement over the mantelpiece. There are also several tables and overstuffed chairs. At the end of the room, French doors lead into a small comfortable area with tile floors and a tile fountain on one wall. French doors lead outside.

My favorite room is the library. It has a corner wood-burning fireplace and floor to ceiling bookcases on two sides. A large window overlooks the garden. The room is furnished with a sofa and chair, a large round table with reading lamp and a marble top chest. A green carpet is on the floor.

In the dining room is a long English oak table that was in the Missouri Governor's mansion in the early 1900s. Ten ladder back chairs surround the table and a chandelier hangs over it. A heavily carved frame holds a large mirror on one wall. The room has English paneled walls below the chair rail with papered walls above. French doors lead to the front yard.

A sideboard breakfast of freshly baked pastries and muffins, several fruits, juice, cereal, coffee and specialty teas is served in the dining room.

A broad sweeping staircase leads to the four guestrooms. The second floor hall has a Queen-Anne sideboard and a French arm chair in a red checked fabric. All of the carpeting, wallpapers and fabrics used throughout the manor are from the Laura Ashley collection.

The Conley Room honors the memory of the builder of this fine home. Furnished in bird's eye maple, the sunny room has a full-size brass antique bed, a maple dressing table, night stand and an armoire that holds a collection of china and pottery rabbits. Floral patterned curtains match the bed linens. Two eight over eight paned windows overlook the garden. A private bath has tub and shower.

The Bridal Suite features the Stewart sitting room, named for Norm Stewart, former basketball coach for the UMC Tigers. This room contains a sofa, a table and three chairs, an antique desk, and a wing chair. The bedroom is furnished with a queen-size bed, a wing chair, an antique drop leaf table, a wicker bench, and an antique arm chair. Adjoining the sitting room is a large dressing room with six over six windows. There is a chaise lounge. The fully tiled octagonal bath area is in the turret adjoining the suite.

The Walton Family Suite honors the co-founders of Wal-Mart, Sam and Bud Walton who grew up in Columbia and attended UMC. This suite has two bedrooms, each with a dressing room separated by a shared bath with tub and shower. One room has a queen-size bed, an antique spindle back love seat, a pair of upholstered chairs, a lamp table, and a lady's desk. The other room contains an antique queen-size bed, wicker arm chair, round night table, wicker lamp table, desk and chair and a wing chair.

Missouri Manor is one of the most beautiful homes I've seen and I'm sure you will like both the Manor and your hosts, Lyria and Ron.

MISSOURI MANOR: 1121 Ashland Road, Columbia, 65201. (573) 499-4437. Fax: (573) 449-2971. Open all year. Not suited for children. No pets. Smoking on the grounds. Lyria and Ron Bartlett, innkeepers.

DIRECTIONS: From I-70 exit on Hwy. 63 south. Go to Stadium Blvd. and turn right. Cross old Hwy. 63. First road turn right on Ashland Road.

ROCK EDDY BLUFF COUNTRY BED & BREAKFAST
Dixon area

Just below Tom and Kathy Corey's home, two hundred feet below to be exact, the Gasconade River, one of the State's most beautiful streams, curves in a broad sweep against wooded hills, quickens over a shoal, then relaxes into a deep pool strewn with huge boulders. This place has been know for scores of years as "rock eddy."

Not twenty minutes after I arrived at Tom and Kathy's they pointed out a huge bald eagle soaring in circles about thirty feet away. Tom said it was one of the first pairs of nesting eagles in the State. They stay here year round. What an introduction to Rock Eddy Bluff Bed & Breakfast!

Surrounded by trees, shrubs and flowers, this place is ideal for those wishing to enjoy peace, solitude and simple country living. As you enter the two story frame house you are in a living/dining room combination. The living room has fireplace with a Vermont casting wood burning insert. A perfect place to enjoy lemonade or iced tea in the summer and hot chocolate or hot spiced apple cider in the winter along with cheese and crackers upon your arrival. The dominant feature of this room and the spacious deck outside, is a panoramic view of the river valley and hills spreading away to the horizon.

The dining room holds several pieces of antique furniture; a country cupboard and a round oak table with bow back chairs. Both areas are decorated with small antiques and pictures. Most comfortable.

The second floor guestrooms share a sitting area that has a sofa, antique pine love seat, and bookshelves, and is decorated with antiques and toys. One guestroom has a queen-size brass and iron bed with an antique quilt on it. An antique immigrants trunk, an Amish rocker, marble top walnut washstand, a marble top wishbone dresser, antique table, a television and a VCR. A door opens onto a small deck with seating. The other guestroom is furnished with a queen-size brass bed, an ornate buffet, an Amish rocker, a television, and a VCR. Nice pictures, carpets and ceiling fans are in both rooms. The bathroom with shower is shared.

Just down a lane from the main house, Turkey Ridge Cottage is nestled in a grove of trees. Three bedrooms easily accommodate six persons. All of the rooms are paneled, have wall-to-wall carpeting and ceiling fans. The cabin contains a complete kitchen with all linens, cooking utensils and fixings for an ample breakfast. A comfortable deck overlooks the valley

"Line Camp" is an 1880s cabin for those who wish to put the hectic urban life far behind them. Secluded in the timber near the river, the one-room cabin contains an antique iron bed, step back cupboard, cooking stove, wood stove, dry sink, table, antique icebox, and porch swing. Kerosene lamps provide light. Water is pumped from the well and, of course, there is a path to the bath. A comfortable deck overlooks the valley.

The Corey's serve a breakfast you'll remember. Typical main dishes include omelets, eggs Benedict, Bunkhouse biscuits and gravy, Belgian waffles, or breakfast casserole. Ham, sausage, or bacon, fruit juice, and muffins assure you won't be come away hungry.

There many things to do here. A private river access provides fishing, swimming and canoeing. For hiking or nature walks there are one hundred fifty acres to enjoy. Clifty Creek nature area and natural bridge are close by. Over seventy-five bird species have been counted on the property. Within view is the bald eagle nest and a great heron rookery.

Pictures and more on the web at: www.rockeddy.com.

ROCK EDDY BLUFF B & B: HCR 62, Box 241, Dixon, 65459. (573) 759-6081. (800) 335-5921 for reservations. E-mail: corey@rockeddy.com. Two guestrooms with shared bath, secluded cottage, and rustic cabin. Open all year. Smoking on deck or cottage/cabin. Children and pets welcome in cottage/cabin. MC/Visa/Discover accepted. Tom and Kathy Corey, innkeepers.

DIRECTIONS: Take Hwy. 63 south from Columbia 2 miles past Vienna to Hwy. 28. (about 65 miles) Go right for 11 miles to Rt. E. Turn left and go 7 miles to end of pavement. From Rolla take Hwy. 63 north about 23 miles to Hwy. 28. Left on 28 then as above.

LOGANBERRY INN
Fulton

T he Loganberry Inn, certainly one of the finest B & B's in Missouri, is in the heart of historic Fulton. This inviting turn of the century Victorian hosted Margaret Thatcher and Scotland Yard in 1996, and Polish President and Nobel Peace Prize winner Lech Walesa in1998. It is just ½ block from the Winston Churchill Memorial and Westminster College, site of the "Iron Curtain" speech. The Churchill Memorial is housed in an elegant Christopher Wren Church that was built in 1677 in London, England, and brought over to Westminster Campus as a fitting tribute and memorial to Churchill in 1969.

Carl and Cathy McGeorge purchased this elegant and comfortable 2 story painted lady with marble fireplaces, high ceilings, old-fashioned molding, and stained glass windows. A 300 year old black walnut tree frames the ½ acre garden with its shaded quiet of a Victorian gazebo, herb garden, grape vine covered trellis, flower beds and a cathedral of trees. The front porch is very inviting with Adirondack chairs and rocking chairs.

The Loganberry Inn has the hospitality and surroundings you want in a B & B. Carl and Cathy have provided private baths, TV, VCR, and phones, fluffy robes, baskets filled with amenities, very cozy beds with thick down comforters, and a quiet, private atmosphere. The surroundings are elegant and gracious, yet comfortable and uncluttered. The hosts are warm, amiable, and fun, and they love to indulge you. The Loganberry provides special pampering, such as Cathy's Special Recipe Chocolate Chip Cookies and milk at bedtime, or your own steaming pot of tea on a silver tray brought up to your room.

A full breakfast is included. One of Cathy's variations of homemade breakfasts is Strawberry Souffle, fresh, locally produced sausage, lemon & blueberry muffins, and fresh fruit with a homemade fruit sauce, juice and coffee or tea.

The large, double parlor is accented with a marble fireplace, walnut and cherry antique chairs and side tables. Upholstered sofas and loveseats provide for luxurious lounging. The dining room is one of the most elegantly put together rooms I have ever seen. The walls are papered in a Victorian print, and the lace and fabric window treatment perfectly frames sunlight streaming in the bay window at breakfast. The highly carved Queen Anne Hunt Board compliments an antique Oak table with spiral carved legs and French country chairs.

A hallway at the top of the stairs contains a small sitting area and a buffet where you can linger over early morning coffee. Four guestrooms are off the hall. The Margaret Thatcher room is elegantly furnished with a white iron and brass Queen-size bed, antique writing desk, antique armoire, serpentine dresser and rocker. The Westminster room, a crisp and chipper blue and white, has two antique brass double beds, antique armoire, and wicker chairs. The President's room is dramatically furnished with a king-size bed make from two antique French Ribboned walnut beds. Two comfortable window seats filled with pillows provide a beautiful view of the lawn, and are great to curl up in with a good book. The Kings Row room has a cozy canopy sleigh bed, antique wardrobe, desk and a unique and creative wallpaper treatment.

LOGANBERRY INN: 310 West 7th Street, Fulton, 65251. (573) 642-9229. Four guestrooms with private baths. Open all year. Children over 8 welcome. Smoking on porch. Carl and Cathy McGeorge, innkeepers.

DIRECTIONS: Take mile marker 148 exit off I-70 at Kingdom City. Head 7 miles south and take 2nd Fulton exit, Hwy. F. Left at stoplight on Westminster. Right at stop sign on Seventh Street. Inn is ½ block on right.

ROMANCING THE PAST BED AND BREAKFAST
Fulton

This large, white, three story Queen Anne home, built in 1868, will charm you from the moment you see it. It sets back from the street quite a bit and the large old trees and landscaping make it picture perfect.

The owners, Jim and Renee Yeager, have put a lot of love in this home. And it shows in many ways. You enter the house from a large wrap-around-front porch that has wonderful gingerbread on it. The entry hall has beautiful, ornate original woodwork, as does the rest of the house. A winding staircase is also original. A ladies and a gentlemen's Victorian chairs, a block front bonnet top and bookcase desk are part of the furnishings.

The parlor has a nice bay window with lace curtains and swags. Area rugs are on the original floors. Framed paints and pictures are on the walls papered in a colorful floral pattern. It is furnished with a Victorian sofa, an antique armoire, a Victorian parlor table and a drop front desk. An upholstered camel back sofa faces a unique fireplace and is a perfect spot to enjoy refreshments on a cold winter night.

The dining room also has a bay window and a fireplace with a mantle decorated with china and floral arrangements. It is furnished with a long oak dining table with carved tri-pod legs, oak chairs, and an oak buffet and china cupboard that holds Renee's dishes. There is an upholstered love seat and an antique piano, which you might like to play. There is a brass chandelier over the table and prints and pictures on the walls. Both the parlor and the dining room are filled with antiques.

There are three distinctly different Victorian guestrooms with black marble fireplaces. All are spacious with private baths, ceiling fans and A/C.

On the first floor, off the hall, Miss Jamies Study is decorated with a rich green, gold and burgundy Victorian wallpaper. Oriental throw rugs are on the floor. Bookcases on either side of the fireplace line an entire wall. The room has a carved antique high-back bed with burgundy bed spread and pillow shams, a Martha Washington arm chair, a desk, a settee, floor lamps on each side of the bed and a Murphy bed that opens for two persons. A new private bath has an ultra spa tub and a shower for two.

At the top of the stairs, a large hall is furnished with a drop leaf table, a pair of Victorian chairs, an antique wishbone dresser and a cabinet holding games, checker and chess sets.

The Renaissance Suite, on the second floor, is a romantic guestroom, adjoining sitting room and a large bath. The renaissance furnishings include an ornately carved antique high-back bed, a chest with carved fruit pulls, a wardrobe, an antique fainting couch, a wishbone dresser, end table and lamp and an antique mirror. The room has taupe color wall-to-wall carpeting. There is a wrought iron ice cream table and chairs. The black and white tile bath has a shower for two.

Also on the second floor, the Victorian Rose Room is bright and airy. It has an antique spool bed with crisp, white linens, a floral print upholstered love seat, a rocker, table and desk all in wicker, a table and a pair of ice cream chairs. There is gray wall-to-wall carpet, white lace curtains. The bath has a tub and shower and the original tile walls.

A screened in country porch has a wicker sofa, a coffee table and a table and chairs. Off the porch, a brick patio has a wrought iron table and chairs and a hot tub.

The large yard has huge trees, shrubs and flower gardens. Under one large tree is a hammock.

Renee serves a bountiful breakfast and can be enjoyed by candlelight in the formal dining room. One of her offerings is a strawberry and orange croissant filled baked French toast and a glazed ham slice, scones or muffins and hot bread or rolls. Juice, coffee, tea or milk. Or, hashbrown potatoes, eggs and ham baked in a casserole and served with homemade citrus syrup over in-season fruits. Hot breads or rolls.

Romancing the Past is within walking distance of nearby antique and gift shops, museums and the Churchill Memorial with its 17th century church of St. Mary the Virgin Aldermanbury. Westminster College and William Woods University offer Community Theater and displays of local art. I personally wouldn't leave this wonderful house.

ROMANCING THE PAST B & B: 830 Court St., Fulton, 65251. (573) 592-1996. Website: www.romancingthepast.com Open all year. Children over 10 welcome. No Smoking. No Pets. A three guestroom Queen Anne Home. Mastercard, Visa. Gift Certificates available. Jim and Renee Yeager, innkeepers.

DIRECTIONS: Call for directions.

GLOBE HOTEL
Hartsburg

In 1893, Herman Gungol, a tinsmith in Hartsburg, built this building and operated it as the Hotel Globe. In 1929, Herman and Amanda Osterlob bought and operated the building as the Hartsburg Hotel until 1950. They then rented rooms there. As the railroad trade slacked off, there was no reason to keep it open and from 1970 to the mid 1980's was an antique shop.

When Jeanette Crawford and her husband purchased the building in 1985, there was no heat as the rooms at one time used wood stoves in each room. The electric, Jeanette told me "...was a joke."

A complete restoration effort has been on going since 1993. It's a typical 1890's structure with gingerbread on the porch. It is a blue painted frame building, trimmed in white.

A double door entry leads to a parlor off the hall. The room has several area rugs and is furnished with an antique day bed, an upholstered chair, a desk and an open arm rocking chair.

The dining room has a colorful floral design carpet. It is furnished with a six piece 1930's style dining set that includes a dining table and four chairs, a server, an antique drop leaf table and a two piece buffet with a very nice carved, antique top. There is a large bay window.

At this time, there are five rooms available. At the top of the stairs, a hall runs the width of the building. A tall antique cupboard displays a collection of oil lamps on it. Bed linens and bathroom linens are stored inside. Also, in the hall are a half bath and a full bath. There is a washer and dryer available.

The rooms are numbered, keeping the original numbers. Room two has twin Jenny Lind beds with a hand-made quilt, and a small table and lamp. Blinds are at the windows.

Room five is furnished with a short poster full-size bed with an antique quilt on it, a 1920's wardrobe, and antique straight back chair and a small wash stand with a lamp. Blinds are on the two windows overlooking the street. The original floors are polished and have throw rugs on them.

Room six is furnished with an antique single-size metal bed with an antique quilt and an antique table and lamp. Area rugs are on the floors. A door adjoins room five. Nice for two parties biking together.

Room seven has an antique high back, full-size bed, which matches a marble top dresser. A chest, an open arm chair with a cane back and an upholstered seat. There is also an antique walnut wardrobe. An oriental style carpet is on the floor. Blinds are at three windows.

For breakfast, Jeanette serves homemade muffins, cinnamon rolls, bagels, yogurt, orange and cranberry juice, jams and jellies and coffee tea or milk.

The hotel sits on the Katy Trail, just 10.4 miles from Jefferson City on the trail, and 18 miles to Columbia. It is about 114 miles to St. Charles, the start of the trail and about 73 miles to its terminus at Sedalia.

GLOBE HOTEL: 60 S. Second Street, PO Box 89, Hartsburg, 65039. (573) 657-4529. Open all year. A restored 1893 Hotel. Children OK, no pets. Smoking outside. Storage for bicycles. Jeanette Crawford, innkeeper.

DIRECTIONS: From Kansas City or St. Louis take I-70 to Highway 63 exit south. Go approximately 18 miles to Route A. Turn right and go 5 miles to Hartsburg. Hotel is on the main street. From north or south take Highway 63 to Route A. Turn west on Route A to Hartsburg.

JEFFERSON CITY

The Missouri State Capital and the seat of Cole County, "Jeff City" as it is commonly called, sits on the steep bluffs of the Missouri River. It is named for Thomas Jefferson.

When Missouri's first general assembly convened in St. Louis in 1820, a five man commission was appointed to select a site for the State Capital on the Missouri River. On December 31, 1821, the City of Jefferson, a rudimentary settlement on the Missouri River was selected.

For a long time the city of Jefferson consisted merely of a dram shop, a foundry and a mission in the general neighborhood of Lohman's Landing—now the foot of Jefferson Street. The site was platted in 1822, and in May of the following year a contract was awarded to build a "good brick building, 60 feet long, 40 feet wide, two stories high, with fireplaces well finished," which was to serve as the capitol and governor's mansion. Erected on the site of the present executive mansion, it cost approximately $18,500.

The town was incorporated in 1825, and in 1826, when the general assembly moved there from St. Charles, the community had 31 families, a general store, a gristmill, a distillery, some tanneries and a hotel. The capital's slow growth during the early years prompted other towns to be considered as the new seat of government. The future of Jefferson City as the capital became doubtful and settlers hesitated to build in town. The matter was finally resolved.

In 1837 the capitol burned. The original State seal and almost all of the State records were lost. A new state house, costing $175,000 was built on the site of the present capitol. It was completed five years later. The city itself, meanwhile, acquired a more permanent aspect. Stage coach service was available and steamboats docked regularly at Lohman's Landing. Flour and gristmills were built and the tanneries and distilleries expanded. The development of the town was further accelerated by an influx of German immigrants.

Jefferson City was incorporated as a city in 1839. For nearly a decade, progress of the city was steady. Then, a tragedy occurred in 1849, when a steamboat stopped at the city and discharged cholera stricken passengers. More than sixty of them died, and for the next two years the plague stalked the countryside.

The trans-state line of the Pacific Railroad was completed between St. Louis and Jefferson City in 1855. However, when the train was crossing the Gasconade River, a trestle collapsed and the train was plunged into the river, killing 28 passengers. Because of this disaster, train service between the capital and St. Louis was not started until 1856.

The commercial promise of the railroad was soon obscured by the clouds of the approaching Civil War.

At the start of the Civil War, Jefferson City became a center of controversy over whether to remain or secede. The assembly could not come to a decision and decided to refer the matter to a convention. The convention voted to remain in the Union. However, Governor Jackson refused to recognize Federal authority and did not heed President Lincoln's call for troops. Federal troops took possession of the city, camping on Capitol Hill. The nearest approach to a battle came in 1864, when General Sterling Price came within four miles of the city. There was an exchange of artillery fire and Confederate cannon balls fell within the present city limits.

For ten years after the war,. Jefferson City made a slow recovery. It was not until the constitution of 1875 that a general peace of mind was restored. In 1881, Sedalia made an unsuccessful effort to wrest the capital from Jefferson City. An era of expansion began in the 1880s and brought substantial benefits.

Since the turn of the century, Jefferson City has developed from a small town into one of the State's leading cities. The present Capitol building was completed in 1917, after the old state house burned in 1911. Industrial changes have had little influence on the city, for politics is its principal business.

HUBER'S FERRY BED & BREAKFAST
Jefferson City

Huber's Ferry B & B is a magnificent example of Missouri-German architecture. It holds a majestic position high atop the bluffs overlooking both the Osage and the Maries Rivers. The house, circa 1881, is built of brick and is three stories tall. And, along with a huge red bard of the same period, have been placed on the National Register of Historic Places. William Huber, a descendant of early German settlers, a prominent farmer and a ferry owner, and his wife, Mary, were the original owners of the property.

David and Barbara Plummer purchased the property in 1982 and began restoring it that same year. The front porch was reconstructed from old photographs. A new shake roof was put on. It was tuckpointed, painted and a second floor galeria going across the entire house was restored. All of the floors, woodwork, doors and staircase are original.

Entering the house, a wide hall extends from the front to the back. Four large rooms make up the first floor. From the front hall, a door to the left leads to the dining room. With an oriental carpet. The mulberry walls have antique pictures and photographs of the 1800s. Lace curtained windows offer a view of the Osage River. A fireplace has an insert stove. The mantelpiece is heavily carved. A crystal chandelier hangs over a round oak table with eight matching buffet and a serving table.

To the right of the entry, a parlor is furnished with an upholstered Victorian sofa and a marble top parlor table with a unique antique lamp. An antique Eastlake mirror is over the table. An antique corner chair that once belonged to Barbara's grandmother, and a small Victorian love seat and matching chair are unique. A pie crust, tripod table with two circa 1890 chairs, sets in the center of the room under an antique handing oil lamp (not electrified). Two high-back spindle rockers are family heirlooms. A corner etagere holds small pieces of porcelain and china. The original floors have an oriental carpet. Lace curtains are at the windows. The white walls are decorated with gilt framed pictures of William and Mary Huber and of Barbara's great grandparents. For chilly mornings, and evenings, there's a wood burning "courting stove."

A door from the parlor leads to the library, furnished with an upholstered plaid sofa, a leather wing back chair, an antique spindle back rocker, a coffee table, a bookcase an antique parlor table, a bookcase, an antique open arm chair and a corner cupboard with a collection of transferware.

The second floor hallway, featuring Huber family and ferry photos, connects to four spacious guestrooms, each with a private bath.

The Maries Room has pale green walls, tan woodwork and lace covered windows, with a view of the old red barn and the Maries River. It is furnished with a queen-size iron bed and an antique single iron bed. There are two bedside tables with lamps, an upholstered wood trimmed wing chair and a coat rack.

The Osage Room has pale tan walls, lace curtains and a blue carpet. Some of the furnishings include a huge carved antique oak wardrobe, a queen-size bed, a small chest and an upholstered wing chair.

The Garden Room has pale yellow walls, yellow woodwork, lace cafe curtains and is fully carpeted. It is furnished with an antique wrought iron full-size bed with a floral spread and pillow shams. A wicker table and lamp, bedside table, an antique wicker rocker and a Singer and Childs treadle sewing machine. A dried floral arrangement is on a round table.

The William and Mary Room has a floral carpet, lace curtains and pale lavender walls. It has an antique queen-size Eastlake bed, an upholstered swivel rocker and an antique wash stand, a corner etagere and a large round table with a lamp.

Breakfast is served in the dining room using Barbara's family Haviland china, crystal and silver. Juice, seasonal fruit compote or melon salad, several variations of egg dishes, homemade bread and muffins and coffeecake. Or, maybe German pancakes with syrup served with country ham or thick sliced bacon. Jellies, jams, coffee, tea or milk.

HUBER'S FERRY B & B: HCR 33, Box 157, Jefferson City, 65101. (573) 455-2979. No smoking inside. No pets. Ask about children. Website: www.bbonline.com/mo/hubersferry/. David and Barbara Plummer, innkeepers.

DIRECTIONS: Located at the junction of Hwys 50 and 63, 12 miles east of Jefferson City. Coming from the west, turn right (south) onto Hwy. 63 south. Turn on Country Road 501. On your right almost as soon as you turn on 63. Go up the hill. You'll see the big red barn.

JEFFERSON INN BED & BREAKFAST
Jefferson City

Y ou won't find an inn more relaxing and comfortable than Jefferson Inn. The building is one of the great arts and crafts bungalows so popular at the turn of the century. Note the wonderful workmanship. The living room is furnished with a beautiful floral stripe sofa and comfortable. Overstuffed, traditional chairs to sit and relax with a drink or a good book in front of the huge brick fireplace adorned with soft sconce lighting over the mantel. A tall burgundy and pink floral arrangement sits on a period table in the front double window with lace curtains. A 1920's floor model Victrola, still operational, is in the corner. There is also a drop front secretary desk and bookcase. Sofa tables, magazine racks, fireplace shield board, sit on highly polished hardwood floors. An antique Keen Kutter glass case displays Limoge China from France, as well as other whimsical collectibles. Living and dining room walls have been redone and covered with rag paint in a cream and windrift beige color for a warm, romantic effect. French doors with stained glass on both sides of the fireplace lead to the Southern Magnolia Room with hot tub. Magnolia and Pomgranate garlands hang above the Levelor blinds around the glass enclosed room. Cream and sand colored wicker chair and bench, lush green plants, and flowers adorn the red tile floor. Soft lighting and a picture-perfect view of the State Capital dome complete this enchanting room—especially lovely at night.

The formal dining room is furnished with a reproduction of a Federal style cherrywood table that can seat up to ten people along with a matching lighted china cabinet full of beautiful glassware and china. A charming antique hotel coffee urn along with coffee grinders and a wooden pendulum clock compliment the room. Victorian wreaths and a French garden scene adorn the walls.

To the right of the entry hall, the Missouri Primrose guestroom is furnished with a 1920s full-size bed and a carved vanity. A television is on a Queen Anne style table. The walls are hunter green with a floral border at the ceiling. White woodwork, lace curtains, beige carpeting, plants, and pictures make this a most pleasing room. A private bath with stained glass, tub and shower is just outside the door.

The Wild Sweet William Suite, just down the hall, is furnished with a queen-size reproduction Victorian bed, a mahogany desk, night tables and a floor lamp. The walls have a green stripe paper. It has its own sitting room with a sofa, chairs and a television. There is a private bath with shower.

On the second floor, the Easter Blazing Star Room has a queen-size four poster, bed and a matching dresser. There is also a cedar chest, a small desk, night stand and a small table with a lamp. A wine carpet is on the floor, lace curtains at the windows and the walls are papered in a floral design. It has a private bath with shower. As with all of the second floor rooms, it is under the eaves, making it very cozy.

The Blue Star Room has a four poster, queen-size bed and a matching dresser. The room has wall-to-wall gray carpet, a blue and white striped wallpaper on the walls and lace curtains at the windows. There is a private bath with shower.

A sitting room has a small alcove with a drop leaf table and four painted chairs, two curio cabinets, a sofa, end table and lamp, two Victorian chairs, and a desk. A door leads to a small balcony.

The Dogwood Suite is furnished with a queen-size four poster bed, a matching wardrobe, an upholstered open arm chair, floor lamp, lamp table and a television. A green carpet is on the floor and green stripe wallpaper is on the walls. A private bath with shower.

Innkeeper, Geri Sims, will start your day off with a full country or gourmet breakfast with a variety of delicious dishes such as blueberry pancakes with bacon or link sausages, biscuits and gravy, quiche, crepes with fresh fruit, ham and cheese croissant breakfast sandwiches with melon compote, to name just a few. For those who prefer a lighter fare, a complete Continental breakfast of fresh fruits, muffins, Danish, bagels with cream cheese, jams, juice, coffee, tea, and milk is also available.

JEFFERSON INN B & B: 801 West High Street, Jefferson City, 65101. (573) 635-7196 or (800) 530-5009 for reservations. Open all year. Children over six welcome. No pets. MC/Visa, American Express and Discover accepted. Located new State Capitol building and the interchange of Hwy. 54, 63 and 50. Charles VanLoo, owner. Geri Sims, innkeeper.

DIRECTIONS: Call for reservations and directions.

CLIFF HOUSE INN
Osage Beach

I think Cliff House Inn could be a perfect place to experience the Lake of the Ozarks and everything it has to offer. Cliff House is a huge white frame, rambling place, built high on a bluff, some feet over the water level of the lake. It is quite a sight to sit on one of the decks and watch the action on the water. The wooded hills are alive with color in fall, and you can't get a better view of them than you can from here. There are a series of stairs and landings going down to the water. About forty feet of them. Great going down, but, you do have to come back up (the same way).

From the front of the house on the first floor, a shared entrance opens to a staircase leading to the top level of the home, and to the Morning Room and the Country Picnic Room. At the top of the stairs there is a common room that both guestrooms use. The stairs and common room are fully carpeted. A large brass 12 arm chandelier hangs from the vaulted ceiling. The walls and woodwork are white. An upholstered loveseat is in burgundy and shades of blue. There is a burgundy chair, a burgundy ottoman, an iron and wood glass top coffee table, an octagon table and reading lamp, a rattan arm chair and an iron plant stand holding live ivy. Green drapes are on French doors leading to a covered balcony with seating for four. You won't believe the panoramic view of the lake.

To the left as you come up the stairs, the Country Picnic Room has yellow walls decorated with fish pictures. Cafe curtains are over mini blinds at the window. The woodwork is painted white. A picnic basket on the floor holds towels and washclothes. You'll find two unusual things here. One is a column of four stacked bird houses, joined together and with a green and white shade, it makes a floor lamp. The other is a series of four large bird houses, each facing a different direction, joined together and a 2.5 foot square glass on top makes a table. The room is furnished with a king-size twig headboard. A vintage 1900 dining set is really put to good use. The buffet holds a television, the table and two chairs for games or coffee and a china cabinet for artificial plants. They are all painted white. There is a Berber carpet on the floor. Bath has a Jacuzzi and stained glass.

The common room is between the Country Picnic Room and the Morning Room.

The Morning Room has a Berber carpet on the floors. The sage green white woodwork walls have framed bird prints. It is furnished with a queen-size rattan head board, a chest, dresser, 2 mirrors, an antique steamer trunk, a wrought iron and rattan end table and two chairs, a night stand with a lamp, and a wicker table with a pair of artificial plants. There is a wonderful view of the lake from the windows. A built-in aquarium is in the room. A fireplace is visible from the bed or the luxurious shell-shaped Jacuzzi for two.

The Garden House is a favorite choice for honeymoons, anniversaries, or a romantic getaway weekend. You enter through a private court yard with an outdoor hot tub, and a view of the sunset from your private deck overlooking the lake. The woodwork and the walls are painted white. Miniblinds are on the 10 windows that surround the rooms on three sides. It is carpeted with Berber carpet. The high sloping ceilings give an air of spaciousness. There is a fireplace for those chilly fall nights. The deck has a wrought iron table and chairs. A large tree under the deck has grown up through it. I would imagine a hole was cut for it. The room is furnished with a queen-size pencil poster bed and canopy, a high boy with a bonnet tap, night tables and lamps, a 1920s coffee table. A small parlor has a small round table and two upholstered chairs, an antique drop front desk and an old dome trunk. There are live and artificial plants. A large bath has a walk-in shower with dual heads.

The L-shaped Rock Terrace Suite is the largest in the house and its decor is strictly western. It includes a private entrance, a living area, bedroom, sun room and an attached bath with a Jacuzzi tub. Enjoy the sunsets and cool evening breezes in front of the outdoor chimney on the deck. The suite is fully carpeted. Two French doors lead to the deck and a view of the lake. The living area is furnished with a Mexican cupboard with a pair of longhorns mounted over it. An upholstered sofa opens into a full-size bed. There is also a low chest for a coffee table, a floor lamp and live plants. The bedroom is furnished with a washed pine queen-size headboard bed with western motif linens, a matching dresser and mirror, a cedar night stand and lamp and a television. Just off the bedroom, a large room shares space with a dining area and a small sitting area overlooking the lake. The sitting area has an upholstered sofa and love seat in tones of bright tan and grey that face each other over a mission type coffee table. There is a washed pine wardrobe and a glass top table and lamp. A dining area has a Southwestern-style wooden table and four chairs. The deck has a four piece wood patio set and two upholstered seated chairs. Stairs go down to the main floor, where you can take another flight of stairs down to the lake. However, those stairs start about forty feet above the water line.

Anne serves a full breakfast that is delivered to your room. It consists of juice, fresh fruit would be either cantaloupe, honeydew melon, strawberries, or grapes. In winter, it would be a warm fruit compote. There is an egg dish with ham, bacon, or sausage and hash browns. Other entrees could be overnight French toast, sausage stuffed peaches with syrup, or powdered sugar, omelets, Belgium waffles, muffins, jam or jelly and coffee, tea or milk.

CLIFF HOUSE INN: RR 1, Box 885, Osage Beach, 65065. (573) 348-9726. Open all year. Four suites with private bath and Jacuzzis. A wonderful lake view. Children 12 and over. No pets. No smoking. MC. Visa. Check. Anne Baker, innkeeper.

DIRECTIONS: Turn onto State Road KK off Hwy. 54. Go left at "Y" (KK35). Stay left to Bay Point Condominiums sign. Turn left at KK 35P 0.5 mile to KK35PF. Turn left to gravel drive. Continue approximately 200 feet, and you're at Cliff House Inn.

GINGER POINT BED & BREAKFAST
Osage

G inger Point B & B is located right on the waters edge of the main channel of the Lake of the Ozarks. A totally private suite, it will accommodate up to eight people in the same party. It consists of the entire lower level of Eugenia and Leo Christeson's waterfront home.

Guests have their own private driveway and private 60' patio, (partially covered) surrounded by trees, shrubs and flowers, and their own private entrance. A walk leads down to a boat dock where you can fish, swim, boat or just sun yourself on the top deck of the of the dock and watch the lake activity. I on the patio, there is a swing, wrought iron furniture and a BBQ for guests use.

The guest suite is all open, but is divided into three distinct areas. A small kitchen is furnished with a refrigerator, microwave oven, coffee maker, toaster and sink. A private entrance leads to stairs that go up to the parking area and driveway. A glass and wood top table and six rattan chairs set before a large window that overlooks the patio and lake. Rust and wine color drapes can be pulled for further privacy. This same area has an upholstered floral print sofa and a matching rocker. The sofa opens into a full-size bed. There are tables and reading lamps and a television.

Another area is furnished with twin beds, four leather and rattan combination arm chairs, a glass top coffee table and a sofa table holding a small collection of Mexican pottery. Another large window with drapes looks out across the lake, there is a private bath with a walk in shower.

Another bedroom area at the back of the suite is more private. It contains a full-size bed and two sofas that opens into beds. This area also has a private bath with shower and tub.

The complete suite has chair rail high, rough cedar paneling. The walls above are white. The suite is decorated with Mexican items that Eugenia brings back from her yearly visit there, and with nicely framed pictures.

Eugenia leaves a Continental breakfast for her guests. There is orange and tomato juices, sweet rolls, English muffins, cold cereals, jams and jellies, coffee, tea and milk.

This place would be ideal for either a couple or a large party. Everything you would want is here. Just bring your boat and fishing gear and you're ready for an enjoyable weekend. It is open April through the end of October.

GINGER POINT B & B: Osage Beach, (573) 365-6839. A private suite with two baths. Smoking on patio and dock. No pets. Children welcome. Les and Eugenia Christeson, owners.

DIRECTIONS: Call Eugenia for reservations and directions.

HILTY INN
Versailles

D oris Hilty's circa 1877 Victorian home is located one half block from the town. There are several antique shops and the Royal Theatre, where local performers stage monthly plays.

To the left of the entry hall, a parlor is furnished with a camel back sofa, a pair of Queen Anne wing chairs, a floor lamp and a Queen Anne style lamp table and lamp. Lace curtains are at the windows and an oriental carpet is on the floor. A rose colored floral print, on a black background was imported from France.

Across the hall, a dining room has a mantelpiece. There is an oval, oak table with six oak chairs, an oak curio cabinet, several floor lamps, a pair of drop leaf tables, a wrought iron ice cream table and four chairs and in the bay window is one of the drop leaf tables and two antique chairs.

Hilty Inn offers four guestrooms each with private baths. Notice the burled newel post as you go upstairs to the guestrooms.

Thornleigh's Room is furnished with a queen-size bed, an antique dresser, a lamp table and lamp for reading, a plant stand and a love seat. It is a large airy room with the original "heart of pine" floors. An original closet has built-in drawers at the bottom. The room is wallpapered in a small floral design with stripes. Lace curtains are at the windows. The bed linens are white eyelet cotton.

The June Room is furnished with an antique Eastlake, queen-size bed, an antique wardrobe, a lamp table, a cane seated rocker, and an upholstered open arm chair. A sink has been installed in a small oak chest. There is a half bath with shower. Throw rugs are on the original pine floors. There are lace curtains in the bay window and the walls are papered in a striped floral pattern.

A door leads from The June Room down two steps, to a common area that has a pair of wing chairs and a sofa which opens into a bed, an antique wardrobe, floor lamp and a lamp table with a lamp. An oriental carpet is on the floor, lace curtains at the windows and walls are papered in a crewel design paper. You might want to have a early morning cup of coffee here and watch the news on television.

Alice's Room is furnished with a queen-size bed that uses a mantel as a headboard. A wicker table with a lamp for reading is by the bed. An oak rocking chair and an upholstered chair with ottoman has a wicker lamp table and lamp between them. There is a private bath with a tub and a shower. A door opens onto a screened-in porch with a swing and a wicker sofa.

The Hilty Room has a white iron, antique full-size bed, an antique dresser, floor lamp and an upholstered chair. There are black and white area carpets, white lace curtains and Battenburg lace for the shower curtains and bed linens. The white walls have a black and white ceiling border with a scene of holstein cows.

Doris serves a "more than enough to eat" breakfast. There is juice, fresh fruit in season, homemade muffins, jams and jellies and gourmet coffee and tea. Her main course could be a casserole with eggs, onions, zucchini and cheese, stuffed french toast, or scrambled eggs with American fried potatoes with onions and peppers. All are served with either sausage, ham or bacon.

A courtyard of old brick has a nice fountain and outdoor furniture. A great place for breakfast. Doris also has wedding receptions, anniversary and other special occasions here.

There are refreshments on arrival and candy in the rooms.

Hilty Inn is a nice place and Doris Hilty makes a perfect hostess. She wants to make sure your stay here is a pleasant one. I like her and I think you will, too.

HILTY INN B & B: 206 East Jasper, Versailles, 65084. (573) 378-2020. Open all year. 45 minutes to Lake of the Ozarks shopping and fine dining. A four guestroom home with private baths. Children over seven welcome. No pets. Smoking on porches. http://bbim.org/hilty/index.html. Doris Hilty, innkeeper.

DIRECTIONS: From the east or west, take Hwy. 50 to Tipton. Go south on Hwy. 5 to Hwy. 52. South on 52 to Versailles.

BRAWLEY CREEK BED & BREAKFAST
Warrensburg

John and Regina Hess' Brawley Creek B & B was designed to provide a secluded retreat for those seeking the serenity of the countryside. Appreciation for the natural world is built into the design of the home and the decor expands that theme. The Hesses have drawn the out-of-doors in, with accents of wood throughout, large windows, fabrics with leaf and floral patterns and rustic textures. The combined effect creates the ambiance of a simple time.

The house is situated in a forest only 50 feet from Brawley Creek, which runs through the property, and can be enjoyed from an expansive wraparound porch. Trails are being developed in the twenty acres of woods and fields for leisurely walks. An abundance of birds and wildflowers vary with the seasons, and turkey, deer, and raccoons are frequently seen, as well as an occasional fox or coyote.

Regina is a former health care professional and takes great pleasure in preparing healthy and delicious food and in creating a warm and welcoming atmosphere. John is a professional naturalist with interests in photography and woodworking. Both enjoy sharing their enthusiasm for the natural world with their guests.

Guests are encouraged to use the various sitting areas in the living room, dining room, upstairs foyer, and porches. They enjoy walking in the woods with their guests or just sitting and having a nice conversation.

The living room is carpeted wall to wall with Berber carpeting. Three huge windows have floor to ceiling bookcases on either side of them. It is furnished with a pair of arm chairs upholstered in a burnt orange color. An oak drop leaf table has a hanging lamp over it. There is also a floral upholstered love seat, another drop leaf table, and a hanging lamp and a rattan chair. A small inset has a pair of upholstered wing back chairs with ball and claw feet and a table and lamp. The room also has beamed ceilings and a wood burning stove.

The dining room has tongue and grooved walnut floors. There is an oak trestle table with nice Windsor chairs, an antique caned chair, a 1920s buffet, a wrought iron table, a floor lamp and two cushioned wicker chairs. The dining room walls as well as the living room is a gallery for local artists as well as John's photography. A door opens onto the porch furnished with Amish-made Adirondack chairs. A nice view of the woods and Brawley Creek.

The Den Guestroom on the first floor has wall-to-wall Berber carpet. One wall is of rough oak and the other three are grey. There is a queen-size bed, a built in desk, seating, a bedside table, a lounge and end tables. A picture window overlooks the woods and creek.

On the second floor, the Porch Room is fully carpeted. Lap siding is on one wall with the other three painted grey. It is furnished with a queen-size bed, two end tables with wrought iron lamps, a wicker chair and a lamp table and lamp. The private bath has a walk-in shower.

The Attic Room has a sitting area with a futon, book shelves, a desk and chair. The sleeping area has a queen-size bed, an upholstered barrel chair, a small dresser and mirror and two bedside tables with lamps. One wall is whitewashed with old house siding, the other three are off white. It is fully carpeted. There is a full bath with a tub and shower.

In all the guestrooms, Regina has crocheted Afghans. There are also handmade quilts covering the beds.

Breakfast can be served in the dining room, breakfast nook, or on the porch when weather permits. Homemade specialties include Belgian waffles with spiced apples and warm maple syrup, apple French toast with homemade apple syrup, stuffed apricot French toast with apricot syrup, Amish baked oatmeal with strawberries and nuts, Swiss cheese and mushroom quiche, spinach and sausage quiche, hot fruit and sausage, muffins and breads served with local Amish jams, and sweets such as cinnamon swirl orange bread, sticky orange biscuits, sour cream coffee cake and apple cider kringle. Seconds are highly encouraged. The coffees are made from special blends of coffee beans ground fresh, and are available prior to breakfast, as well as hot herbal tea and juices. Special dietary needs can be accommodated if informed at the time of reservation.

BRAWLEY CREEK B & B: 631 SW 51 Road, Warrensburg, 64093. (660) 429-6483. E-mail: brawleyc@iland.net. A wonderful place to get in touch with nature. Three guestrooms with private baths. No pets. Not suited for children. No smoking on premises. John and Regina Hess, innkeepers.

DIRECTIONS: From the intersection of US 50 and Hwy. 13 in Warrensburg, take Hwy. 13 south for seven miles to County Road 600. Turn right (west) on County Road 600 and proceed about 1.25 miles to County Road 51. Turn left (south) on 51 and proceed 0.25 mile to the wooded drive just before the bridge (631 SW 51st Rd.).

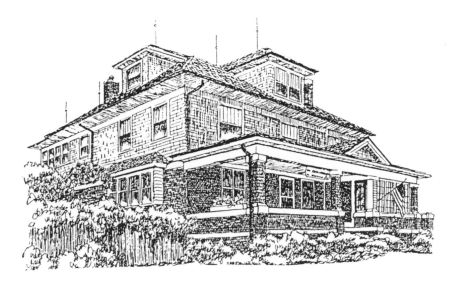

CAMEL CROSSING BED & BREAKFAST
Warrensburg

Ed and Joyce Barnes spent almost eight years, from 1978 to 1986, in Saudi Arabia, where Ed worked for a major oil company. During this time they purchased this large turn of the century house for their use when they would return home. Upon their return, they completely refurbished the house decorating it throughout with pieces of furniture and brick-a-brack they had been buying while overseas. To say the least, the house has a strong Middle East touch with oriental carpets, Chinese screens and many mementos of their time in the Middle East. Joyce began to collect camel paraphernalia such as camel bags, saddles, pictures, vases and figurines. Hence the name, Camel Crossing for the bed and breakfast.

You enter the house and are in an entry hall with large pillars leading into the 40 foot living room filled with unusual pieces: a chamfer chest from Taiwan, an oriental medicine chest, and several oriental carpets. A huge fireplace (great on chilly days and nights) is the focal point of the room. It has plenty of easy chairs, a sofa and a pair of monk's chairs. A small sunroom toward the front of the house doubles as a breakfast nook where, if you wish, your breakfast will be served.

A large dining room is also off the front hall. It has a colorful carpet from India, lamps from Damascus, and a lot of brass accessories. Breakfasts are served here. A large deck has been added to the back of the house, shaded by a large white mulberry tree. You may breakfast here, weather permitting.

A great staircase leads to the three bedrooms on the second floor. The bedrooms lead off a large hallway, which holds more of their collections.

The Rose Room has Victorian decor. There is an antique marble top dresser, a queen-size bed with a hand crocheted bedspread, a teak screen from India, and rugs from Turkey and Afghanistan, among other antiques. All the rooms are wallpapered and decorated with pictures and miscellaneous objects of interest.

The Butterfly Room has Chinese decor with a Chinese noodle cart, queen-size brass bed, oriental night stands, a chest and bachelor's chest. All are finished in black lacquer with Chinese designs. There is a camel saddle foot stool in this room, a Flokati carpet from Greece, and rugs from China. The room has a fireplace and a ceiling fan. The room gets its name from framed and mounted butterflies on the walls. A shared bath with shower and tub is just across the hall.

The third bedroom on the second floor is called the Celestial Room due to the cherubs and seraphs used in the decor. A queen Somma waterbed guarantees a serene night's sleep. For those who like the sound of the surf or rain on the roof—a sleep machine provides instant transition. The private bath has a shower stocked with a choice of bathing amenities.

Somer's Room is up a second flight of stairs. This private hideaway is done in country blue and ivories. Somer is now married but her room still has dolls and stuffed animals to pique the interest of young and the young at heart. "Adorable" or "Will you adopt me?" are frequent responses to this room. A small private bath (tub only) completes this sweet "suite." A family of five can be very cozy here but not crowded. Cable television serves the rooms. A second floor lounge is also available.

Breakfast varies according to the guests wishes as Joyce will prepare what you want, when she can. But you are assured of getting homemade pancakes, waffles, or french toast. The usual bacon and eggs are always available. When I visited with Joyce and Ed, they invited me to have lunch with them. They served two dishes I had never tasted, spanakopita and tonnota. Don't ask me what it was, but they were both delicious. And that just goes to show you that you are never too old to try something new.

Camel Crossing is a house where you can really feel at home and Ed and Joyce go out of their way to please. They succeed!

CAMEL CROSSING B & B: 210 E. Gay Street, Warrensburg, 64093. (660)429-2973. Fax: (660) 429-2722. A four bedroom B & B. Open all year. Air-conditioned. A full breakfast with room rate. No smoking in house. Well behaved children accepted. No pets. Just one hour from Country Club Plaza in Kansas City. Close to Sedalia for Missouri State Fair. Six blocks to Central Missouri State University. Member of BBIM. Ed And Joyce Barnes, innkeepers.

DIRECTIONS: From Hwy. 50 or I-70, take Hwy. 13 south to Warrensburg to the traffic light at the Circle K convenience store. Turn right on Gay and go 1/2 block. House is on driver's side.

CEDARCROFT FARM & COTTAGE ON THE KNOLL B & B
Warrensburg

Placed on the National Register of Historic Places, this secluded farmstead is in the middle of 80 acres of woods, creeks and meadows. It was built in 1867 by John A. Adams, a pioneer soil conservationist and a Union army veteran from the Civil War. His father had settled here in 1834.

Bill and Sandra Wayne (Sandra is the great granddaughter of John Adams) have renovated and restored the farmhouse to look much like it did in 1890. They have furnished the home with antiques and primitives. Cedarcroft offers two distinctly different accommodations, the 1867 Farmhouse and the new Cottage on the Knoll. The 1867 Farmhouse is ideal for antique–lovers and families while the Cottage is designed to provide all the romantic amenities in a secluded setting.

The guestrooms in the original part of the house consist of the original country kitchen, a parlor and a gathering room, all on the first floor. Bill and Sandra live in a new addition at the rear of the house, so the guests have complete run of the original house.

The parlor has a circa 1860 sofa, a mission oak library table, an oak upright piano, an antique Victrola, and a walnut secretary. Old family photographs are in antique frames.

The gathering room has a three piece mission oak living room set and an antique love seat. There is a satellite TV and VCR.

Tucked under the eaves on the second floor are two private guest quarters, rented to only one party. It consists of a two bedroom suite with the private bath on the first floor. Each room can accommodate up to four people and are named after Sandra's aunts.

Grace's room contains a pair of antique iron beds with antique quilts on them, an antique chiffonier, an old treadle sewing machine, antique trunk and a desk and chair.

Cora's Room is furnished with an antique full-size bed and an antique full-size walnut bed. Both have nice quilts and coverlets on them. The bottom of an antique Hoosier cabinet doubles as a night table. The old beaded board ceilings are original to the house.

The original kitchen still has the old wooden walls, now painted. It has been converted to a kitchen/dining room and has a round oak table and chairs, oak Hoosier cabinet, oak server, and an antique potato bin. Breakfast is served here. A "more than you can eat" country breakfast includes a main dish, surrounded by seasonal fruits or juice, Amish made spreads, hot coffee or tea and little side dish surprises. Specialties include real country biscuits and gravy, honeymoon waffles or a special country casserole. A typical evening snack, served at your convenience includes fruit, nut bread, cookies, fudge, ice cream and iced tea.

Cottage: The Cottage on the Knoll is located 150 yards from the main house, It contains a wood-burning fireplace, two-person thermal massage tub, pine king-size canopy bed, and two person shower. It has vertical pine walls and plank floors, a floral loveseat and a 25" satellite TV with VCR. The breakfast nook features his and hers coffeemakers and a small refrigerator. Guests receive a rose, a journal book to record their romantic memories, a disposable camera and a bottle of sparkling cider. The front porch features a glider swing to overlook the meadow and creek. Breakfast is served in the room.

CEDARCROFT FARM and COTTAGE ON THE KNOLL B & B: 431 SE "Y" Highway, Warrensburg, 64093. (660) 747-5728 or (800) 368-4944 for reservations. E-mail: infohh@cedarcroft.com Website: http:// www.cedarcroft.com. A two bedroom farmhouse or secluded cottage offering plenty of privacy. Open all year. Full breakfast and evening snack included in rate. Children in the 1867 Farmhouse only. Smoking outside only. MC/ Visa/Discover/American Express accepted. A close proximity to Western Missouri's attractions, including Windsor's Amish area and the State Fairgrounds in Sedalia. About an hour from Kansas City. Member BBIM and PAII. Bill and Sandra Wayne, innkeepers.

DIRECTIONS: From Warrensburg take Hwy. 13 about 5 miles south to Route Y. East on Y exactly 4.0 miles. Farmstead is on the north side of road. A long lane leads to the house. Look for large sign by gate.

THE HOME PLACE BED & BREAKFAST
Waynesville

The Home Place sits high on a hill overlooking the Rubidium Valley and surrounding countryside. It is indeed an impressive view. The house was built of native sandstone, by a William Hensley in 1940, on land that is the Civil Ware site of Fort Waynesville, a Union army garrison. This is a very quaint house, full of surprises. The large yard is enclosed with a white picket fence. Huge old trees shade the lawn.

As you enter the house, you are in a parlor, aptly named "Old Glory" because of the variety of military memorabilia from the Civil War and World Wars I and II., that belonged to Jean and Herb's families whose members fought in these wars.

There is a large braided rug on the polished floors. Facing a stone fireplace is a camel back sofa with an immigrant chest used as a coffee table. An antique organ, a gateleg table, a double schoolhouse desk, old blackboard and a rare free standing National cash register are just a small portion of the furnishings. At the end of the room is a good place to relax and listen to the old radio, the Victor Victrola or watch cable television. There are tapes of old radio shows and lots of movies. The area is furnished with a sofa and chairs, a dry sink and a lamp table and lamp.

On the lower level you can play checkers or other board games in a game room that is furnished with an ice cream table and chairs, an antique stove, and an unusual wagon train cupboard with original kitchen utensils. This room connects to the "Red Rooster General Store: dining room. It is furnished with a long table and chairs. Breakfast is served here. There are all kinds of antics to see: a floor model coffee grinder, butter molds, an old pump and wooden flour bin.

You can breakfast or enjoy an evening dessert and beverage in the Willow Tea Shop, a glassed-in sun porch with tongue and groove knotty pine walls and ceiling. Two 24 small paned windows are on one side of the room, while three picture windows are on another side. The room is furnished in white wicker: chaise lounge, and a pair of arm chairs, glass top table and four chairs. There is also a piano, an antique sideboard, and a child's goat cart from Germany.

Jean serves several versions of breakfast and you will certainly get enough to eat. Heart shaped waffles with fried apples and sausage, fresh fruit in season with strawberry sauce, homemade cherry almond coffeecake and your choice of oven fresh ground coffees. Jean also prepares individual omelet casseroles with ham, bacon, eggs, onions, green peppers and cheese along with hash browns or American fries and biscuits, a fresh fruit plate and apple kuchen.

The inn features four guestrooms. The Victorian Bride's Master suite has a six piece French bedroom set with a full-size bed, an armoire, marble to dresser and mirror and a marble top washstand, all heavily carved. There is a walnut Eastlake chair and a glass top table. A wedding dress that belonged to Jean's grandmother is on display.

The Wine and Roses Room has a Victorian bed, antique fainting couch, antique dresser with glove boxes and a small commode. Both of these rooms are on the second floor and have a private bath.

On the lower lever, the Missouri Gentlemen's room features a stone fireplace. It is furnished with an antique, full-size tall back bed, an oak dresser, oak dressing stand and an armoire.

The Childhood Memories room has an ornate curly iron and brass full-size bed, a walnut dresser and a night table with reading lamp. It is decorated with toys and vintage clothing. The room connects to the Missouri Gentlemen's room for a family suite.

HOME PLACE B & B: 302 S. Benton, Waynesville, 65583. (573) 774-6637. Open all year. Two guestrooms and two room suite with private baths. No pets. Children welcome. Smoking outside only. Hunting & fishing guides available. Jean and Herb Hiatt, innkeepers.

DIRECTIONS: From I-44 take Waynesville exit (Business loop 44). Proceed to town square. Turn left on Benton and go 1 block.

WESTPHALIA INN RESTAURANT
Westphalia

There are not too many restaurants in the State serving true, old fashioned skillet fried chicken. Not only do the owners, Tom and Melody Buersmeyer, serve it here, but other than hickory smoked, sugar cured ham, it is the only entree they offer.

The old brick building, erected in 1930, has had extensive improvements made on it. The original lobby is now an antique laden waiting area, where one can relax in comfortable chairs and rockers. The second floor has also been renovated and now houses the Top Story Lounge and a deck, where you can sit and visit before or after your meal.

But, back to the food. I have eaten here on several occasions and tried both the chicken and the sugar-cured ham. It was served family style along with real mashed potatoes and real gravy, green beans cabbage slaw, homemade bread, butter, strawberry preserves and coffee, tea or milk. The dessert is cheesecake or ice cream.

WESTPHALIA INN: Located on Main Street, Westphalia, 65085. (573) 455-9991. Reservations are recommended and are highly desirable. 5 p.m. to 8:30 p.m. Sunday 12 noon to 8 p.m. Closed Monday through Thursday.

DIRECTIONS: Take Hwy. 63 south three miles from the junction of Hwy. 50 and 63. Turn left onto County Rd. 600 (Main Street) and go approximately 3/4 mile. The inn is on your right.

WHITE STONE INN RESTAURANT
Rich Fountain

Built in 1892, this stone building was once the mercantile store in Rich Fountain, selling harnesses, clothing and most anything else that was needed for the farm or home. Then it closed in the mid-1950s and stood vacant for thirty years, until it was purchased and restored by the Zika family. All of the original shelves, floors, doors and windows are intact. The place is absolutely immaculate. As of August 1998 the Inn is owned and operated by Regina and Tracy Turley, both native Missourians.

The Inn offers a twelve ounce Kansas City Strip steak prepared to your satisfaction. A tender, boneless breast of Chicken Parmesan. Grandma Strayers cornmeal breaded, pan-fried catfish. A wonderful bowl of Fettuccine with a rich, creamy Alfredo sauce, and deep-fried Butterfly Shrimp. Thursday nights are reserved for the all-you-can-eat pan-fried chicken special. And the rest of the week is always a surprise. All of the entrees include homemade French Country bread, a fresh garden salad with crisp mixed greens and a medley of garden fresh vegetables, and your choice of two side dishes.

The Inn also offers an array of homemade desserts and an exquisite wine list. Beer and mixed drinks are also available.

WHITE STONE INN RESTAURANT: Highway E, downtown Rich Fountain, 65035. (573) 744-5827. Open for dinner Thursday from 5 - 8 p.m., Friday and Saturday 5 - 9 p.m., Sunday 11 a.m. - 6 p.m. Reservations are requested for parties of eight or more. Regina Turley, proprietor

Please visit the Inn on the Internet. White Stone Inn is featured in the "Outskirts" at www.getintostlouis.com/whitestoneinn.html.

WERNER HOUSE BED & BREAKFAST
Westphalia

arl Werner and his wife, Katharina, immigrated to the U.S. in the early 1850's. They had 10 children. Carl purchased land in Westphalia in 1878, and when his son August married, he sold him a lot. This house was built by August and his wife in 1885. At the death of August in 1914, the house passed to Alois Werner, August's son and his wife Rose. They had two daughters who ultimately sold the property to Sergio and Linda Fernandez, the current owners. It had been in the Werner family for over 110 years.

The house is a good example of "Missouri German" Architecture. All of the original walls, doors, windows and trim still stand as they were when built. The original porches are on two sides of the house. It is an excellent example of an urban farmstead, with the original summer kitchen, root cellar, and smokehouse still intact.

Entering form the front porch, an entry hall has a piano you might want to play. A walnut staircase leads to the second floor guestrooms.

A parlor is furnished with an L shaped upholstered sofa with one end being a recliner. There is also a 100-year-old roll top desk, a Queen Anne sofa table, an upholstered recliner rocker, an antique lawyer's bookcase, end tables and reading lamps and a wrought iron plant stand. There is an entertainment center with a television and VCR with 1,200 movies. White lace curtains have green swags, the woodwork is white and the neutral walls have pictures and an arrowhead collection.

The dining room has a bright floral design wallpaper under a chair rail and a yellow and white stripe paper above. Sheer curtains are at the windows. It is furnished with an antique table, two antique spindle-back chairs, a 100-year-old, hand-made church pew and a Mission style oak buffet. There are nice wall decorations including an antique wall clock. A door leads to a porch with adirondack chairs.

The very spacious guestrooms on the second floor were named for Sergio and Linda's children. Sonya's room is bright and airy. Green, white and pink wallpaper is below a chair rail and a mulberry color paper is above. A floral pattern border is at the ceiling. Throw rugs are on the floors and green and white café curtains and swags are on the windows. It is furnished with a full-size spindle head and foot, white iron bed with a floral comforter, a beside table with lamps, an antique Morris recliner, antique floor lamp and an antique dresser with glove boxes. There is an unusual hand-made beaded board closet.

Sergio's Room has a white queen-size bed, a white chest and a white dresser. There is a small rocker, a yellow metal floor lamp and two army bunk beds have been put to use as a queen-size bed. The windows have muslin curtains.

An area in between the two bedrooms is called just that, the in-between room, furnished with a bookcase and books, a game table and two chairs and a 1920's radio. A porch leads to a balcony. A large bath has a shower. If they have more than one occupancy at a time, the bath is shared.

Guests are served a full breakfast in the dining room between 7 and 9. There is orange juice, a fresh fruit salad, eggs, ham, rope sausage and hot bread, biscuits or pancakes. Always jams and jellies, coffee, tea or milk.

Upon arrival, Sergio and Linda offer ice tea or lemonade in the summer and hot chocolate or hot cider in the winter.

THE WERNER HOUSE B & B: 202 W. Main Street, Westphalia, 65085. For reservations call (573) 455-2885. Open all year. A two guestroom with shared bath in an original 100-year-old farmstead. No pets. Smoking on porches. Children welcome. Sergio and Linda Fernandez, innkeepers.

DIRECTIONS: From Jefferson City, take Highway 50 to Highway 63. Turn south for 4 miles to Westphalia.

Section Seven

KANSAS CITY AREA

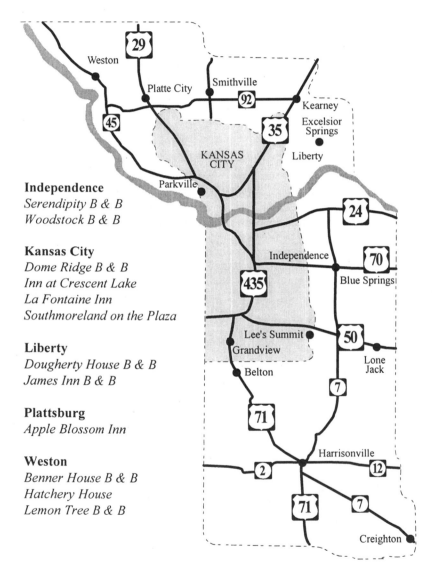

Independence
Serendipity B & B
Woodstock B & B

Kansas City
Dome Ridge B & B
Inn at Crescent Lake
La Fontaine Inn
Southmoreland on the Plaza

Liberty
Dougherty House B & B
James Inn B & B

Plattsburg
Apple Blossom Inn

Weston
Benner House B & B
Hatchery House
Lemon Tree B & B

KANSAS CITY

Big city fun, historic towns, and open countryside — all this and more is part of the Kansas City area's appeal. For a town that was only a tiny river landing when Missouri became a state in 1821, Kansas City has come a long way.

Kansas City has its start in two rip roaring frontier settlements: the Missouri River town of Kansas and the hell-bent-for-leather town of Westport, several miles south on the Santa Fe Trail. Francois Chouteau, an employee of the American Fur Company, established a post in the Kaw River bottom in the spring of 1823. It soon became known as the town of Kansas. It served as a depot from which other posts of the company were supplied and their furs collected. Traders, trappers, voyageurs, and laborers, with their families (about 15 or 20 families), came with Chouteau. In 1830, a flood destroyed Chouteau's warehouse, so he moved his little post a few miles east to the foot of the present Grand Avenue, where a ferry had been established by Peter Roy in 1828.

In 1819, the steamboat Independence proved the Missouri River could be navigated. The Indians in the area were removed in 1825. Now Missouri began filling up with settlers. In 1826, Jackson County was organized with the county seat 10 miles east of Chouteau's settlement at Independence. This soon became the principal outfitting point for the wagons with their freight heading to Santa Fe and Northern Mexico, and for immigrants going to Oregon in the early 1840s. The trail to Santa Fe lay west from the town of Independence. It crossed the Big Blue River some four miles south of the Missouri River.

In 1832, John Calvin McCoy, recognized an outcropping of rock just west of this crossing as a perfect landing levee for boats. He built a store here to cater to the needs of those returning from the Southwest and to catch some of the overflow business from Independence. The next year, he platted the town of Westport. Merchants from Westport received their goods by steamboat at the ferry landing four miles to the north, where Chouteau had set up his new post. The little town soon competed with Independence as the eastern terminus of the Santa Fe Trail.

In the meantime, the settlement at Chouteau's post, now called Westport Landing by both Independence and Westport, had grown into a thriving community. The Platte Purchase in northern Missouri opened the area for settlement in 1836. The meant more immigrants and trade. When fur traders, Ceran St. Vrain and William Bent, began hauling their freight from the upper Arkansas River directly to the landing in 1845, a precedent was established, which was followed by others. Westport Landing had a prosperous trade of its own. In 1838, when Gabriel Prudhomme, who owned the land, passed away, the Kansas Town Company purchased his farm of about 270 acres, platted it into lots, and named it Kansas. The site of the original town was the area now bounded by the Missouri River, Broadway, Forest Avenue and Main Street at Missouri Avenue.

Today, Kansas City is an appealing bland of history, parks, fountains, big city sophistication and Midwestern friendliness. Surrounded by surprisingly scenic countryside, Kansas City is the heart of a compact, diverse vacationing.

No longer civilization's last outpost, Kansas City has shed its frontier town image to become a thoroughly modern, cosmopolitan city. Tree-lined boulevards lead to fine shopping areas, restaurants, and night life. Ambitious developments such as the Country Club Plaza, 14 square blocks of Moorish architecture reminiscent of Spain, and American's first shopping center; the look of tomorrow at the 100-acre Crown Center with its entertainment, stores, restaurants, and hotel; and the dining and night life, combined with the unique shops in the courtyards and alleyways of historic Westport all complement each other. From downtown (don't miss City Center Square), to the suburbs, you'll marvel at Kansas City's varied shopping, cuisine and fun.

Fountains and parks add to the city's beauty. A rose garden now graces the site of the Civil War Battle of Westport at Loose Park. Scope Park, the second largest park in the United States, is one of the city's major attractions. You can spend a day at the zoo, enjoy nature trails, picnic sites, two 18 hole golf courses, or watch the summer productions at the outdoor Starlight Theatre. Or visit the 4,434 acre Fleming Park in Jackson County, which includes 1000 acre Lake Jacomo and the preserved historic buildings of Missouri Town 1855. Buildings from even earlier in the 19th century are preserved at Heritage Village in Hodge Park.

For more reminders of the past, see the World War I exhibits at the Liberty Memorial and ride to the top of its 216 foot tower. Museums, often in parklike settings, are also a part of the city's appeal. The renowned Nelson Art Gallery is the most famous, but others such as the Kansas City Museum of History and Science or the Museum of Regional History are also very worthwhile. Admire the huge Union Station of the pre-Civil War, Warnell House.

Entertainment in Kansas City takes many forms. Jazz can still be heard in the city that made it famous, but there's more. The Kansas City Philharmonic, Lyric Opera, and the Conservatory of Music are all popular, as are the Missouri Repertory Theatre and Kansas City Ballet. Dinner theatres, Tiffany's Attic and Waldorf Astoria, are well known.

See all this and you've just started. Shop for fresh produce and bargains at the outdoor City Market. Take a Missouri River cruise, or you can relive the frontier days at Trail Town, home of Benjamin Stables and the Kansas City Rodeo.

If pro sports are what you expect in a big league city, then you will feel right at home here, too. Royals baseball and the Chiefs football teams play at the twin stadium Truman Sports Complex. For those who would rather participate than watch, the city has room (facilities) for tennis, bicycling, running and other sports.

At the edge of the city, World of Fun, continues to draw kids of all ages with its rides and shows based on different sections of the world. La Fontaine Inn, Doanleigh Inn, and Southmoreland on the Plaza are all in Kansas City proper. Dome Ridge B & B is in North Kansas City.

Remember, There's more to the area than just the city. Nearby towns provide the extra things to see and do.

Just east is Independence, where pioneers once traveled along the Santa Fe, California, and Oregon Trails It became their last taste of civilization before they headed west. In Independence, a large city in its own right, the Harry S. Truman Library and Museum, is a major attraction. It has exhibits on the presidency in general and Mr. Truman's career in particular, plus his grave site. Other historic sites in the city include Mr. Truman's restored office and courtroom, and an 1859 jail that once held Frank James.

Independence also was an important stop during the Mormon migrations in the 1800s. It now is the site of a Mormon Visitors Center that features paintings, films, and other exhibits. In the auditorium, world headquarters of the Reorganized Church of Jesus Christ of Latter Day Saints, you'll see a museum and display gallery. Serendipity B & B and Woodstock Inn are located in Independence.

Farther east is Fort Osage. In the early 1800s William Clark built the fort, America's first outpost in the Louisiana Territory. The fort, overlooking the Missouri River, has been reconstructed for visitors.

North from Independence is Liberty, where Jesse James robbed his first bank. Today, you can visit the restored Jesse James Bank Museum. Also in Liberty, you'll find another reminder of the Mormon migration through the area: the Liberty Jail, where Mormon prophet Joseph Smith was confined in 1838-39. James Inn, Dougherty House B & B and Mercantile Manor B & B are located at Liberty.

At Kearney, a little further north, is the birthplace and grave site of Missouri's most famous outlaw, Jesse James. The house is just the way it was when he lived there.

Just north of Excelsior Springs on Highway 69 is *Watkin's Woolen Mill,* America's only 19th century (1850) textile factory with the original machinery.

For more history, head west to the Missouri River, then north to Weston, a former river port with more than 100 buildings pre-dating the Civil War. It is the oldest town in the Platte Purchase and has an entire district listed on the National Register of Historic Places. You can tour the family-run McCormick Distillery, American's smallest and oldest distillery, and visit the largest tobacco market west of the Mississippi. In Weston you will find the Benner House B & B, Hatchery House, LLC, and Lemon Tree B & B.

Parkville is a neat, historic river town just north of Kansas City on Highway 9. It is full of antique shops, where you can spend an entire day just looking. A good restaurant too.

South of Kansas City, you'll find open country, parks and lakes and historic towns such as Harrisonville and Belton. The Reed Wildlife Area, near Lee's Summit, highlights the scenic beauty which stretches to the city's doorstep. The world headquarters for the Unity School of Christianity is nearby. It's south at Unity Village with some 1,400 acres of woodland, gardens and fountains.

With all it has to offer, the Kansas City Area is impossible to summarize in one neat phrase. Surrounded by community lakes, wildlife areas, green hills, Kansas City's blend of history, urban excitement, and outdoor beauty, guarantee that his area has something for every taste. There's more waiting for you here than you might expect.

INDEPENDENCE

Indians first located and explored the rivers, streams and springs in this area. Daniel Morgan Boone, son of Daniel Boone, visited the site which was to become Independence. He lived in the area from 1800 to 1812 and trapped beaver on the Little and Big Blue rivers.

Lewis and Clark on their 1804-06 expedition chose the site for Fort Osage, which was established two years later. A treaty with the Osage Indians opened the area to homesteading on January 1, 1826. Jackson County was organized shortly thereafter. Settlers soon came from Kentucky, Virginia, Tennessee and the Carolinas.

Immigration to Oregon in the 1830s made Independence boom and when gold was discovered in California, many outfitted here.

The Latter Day Saints arrived in 1831. Trouble followed. They were expelled, and lost most of their land, including the acreage Joseph Smith, Jr. had purchased and dedicated as a site for a "Temple of the Lord."

Independence did not escape the Missouri-Kansas border troubles of the 1850s, which began and ended in guerilla bands raiding back and forth across the state line. As it was throughout Missouri, residents included both Confederate and Union sympathizers, who endured four long years of martial law. Two battles were fought in the Jackson Square area. The courthouse was used as a hospital and the old jail as the Federal Post.

Two railroads were built after the Civil War: the Missouri Pacific in 1865 and the Chicago & Alton in 1879. Independence was a typical wild west town.

By the turn of the century, Independence had become the county seat, with a reputation as an agricultural and livestock center. John A. Truman, moved his family to the county seat. First, they lived on South Chrysler and then they moved to a larger home on Waldo Avenue.

Harry S. Truman, Jackson County Judge, United States Senator, Vice President and 33rd President of our country was destined to take his place in history as one of the truly great Americans. He was gutsy and compassionate, straight-forward and profound, a master of the rough and tumble game of politics. An integral part of Independence, "Give 'em Hell" Harry's roots sank deeply into his adopted hometown. His boyhood homes, the summer White House, his first courtroom, a memorial statue, the Truman Library and Museum and his final resting place are all here.

SERENDIPITY BED AND BREAKFAST
Independence

Joseph W. Mercer was born in 1845. He served in the Confederate Army during the Civil War and was wounded three times and lost his arm in a battle at Pine Ridge, Arkansas. After the war he attended St. Louis Commercial College in St. Louis. Returning to Independence, he taught school. He was elected to the office of treasurer of the state in 1874, mayor of Independence in 1892 and ten years later he was an eastern Jackson County judge.

Joseph Mercer built this three-story fourteen-room brick house in 1887. It was constructed of pressed brick, and finished in mahogany, ash and pine. Doug and Susan Walter purchased the home in 1994, and are only the third owners. When Susan says "step back in time," she means it.

The parlor is overflowing with many different and unusual things. There is a circa 1881 square grand piano, an Eastlake secretary with glass doors, a Victorian love seat and marble top Victorian tables. From century old books that sport antique bookmarks in the bookcases, antique clocks, hand crafted framed Victorian florals to the ornately carved, mahogany mantle with a Victorian over-mantle, this whole house is filled with genuine articles of daily life that a 1900s era family might have used and enjoyed.

The dining room, too, is filled with the luxuries that a middle class family could obtain from the latest Sears or Wards catalogue of the 1890s. Flowered Bavarian china, Moss Rose dishes, majolica glassware and silver plated serving pieces fill the china cabinets and cover the circa 1880 marble top sideboard. Antique still life prints in antique frames fill the dining room walls. Breakfast is served on a antique walnut table. Period carpets are on the floor and lace curtains are at the windows. A chandelier with blue and amber crystals glows in the center of the room. Life-like German bisque dolls in their own chairs share this setting. Another doll looks down from her antique high chair. This is a treat for every little girl, and big ones too!

A full breakfast is served in the main dining room using antique china. You are served juice, fruit, breakfast quiche, muffins plus coffee, or tea. Breakfast also may be served on the porch, overlooking the garden, weather permitting.

Guest accommodations include two suites on the first floor of the carriage house. The Santa Fe Suite contains a queen-size bed and the Frontier Trails Apartment Suite contains a king-size and a twin bed. Both suites have full kitchens, dining areas and sitting areas. The Spirit of Independence Apartment Suite on the second floor of the carriage house has two bedrooms, with a king and a queen-size bed and is also more suitable for children. Breakfast is served in the main house.

In the main house, on the second floor, the Harry Truman, two room suite, furnished with a circa 1880 four-piece Victorian bedroom set, a carved, high back bed, wardrobe, dresser and a marble top washstand, all in walnut.

On the third floor, the Bess Truman two room suite with a full-size and a king-size bed. It also has a kitchenette, a dining area and a small sitting area. This "grandma's attic" is ideal for children as is contains many children's books, a child-size table and chairs and toys of grandma's era displayed in cabinets. Both of the suites have private baths with tub and shower. They can each sleep four people. All guestrooms have books, magazines, color TVs, radio and alarm clocks.

Interesting sights await outside in the garden. The brick edged flower beds are ablaze with color from spring into autumn. The side porch shelters the house plants in summer and provides a quiet place for watching the world go by. Many benches and chairs around the yard are ample enough to accommodate a house full of guests.

The owners, Susan and Doug Walter, have created this atmosphere for their own pleasure and enjoyment. Now you can share their home overnight.

SERENDIPITY B & B: 116 South Pleasant Street, Independence, 64050-3638. (816) 833-4719. (800) 203-4299. http://www.bbhost.com/serendipitybb. Open all year. Two guestrooms and two 2 room suite with Victorian decor. No smoking please. Well behaved children welcome. Inquire about extended stay discounts. Phone or write for descriptive brochure. Near Historic Independent Square and most tourist sites. Doug and Susan Walter, innkeepers.

DIRECTIONS: Call for reservations and directions.

WOODSTOCK INN
Independence

Nestled within Independence's famous historical district, the Woodstock Inn is just a short stroll away from everything you came to Independence to see! I have stayed here on several occasions during my state-wide travels and have always enjoyed myself and the owners, Todd and Patricia Justice, who had purchased the Woodstock in 1996 from the previous owners. They have made a few changes.

The building that houses Woodstock Inn was built in 1900 as a private home. From 1929 until the 1980s it was used as a workshop for imported collector dolls. It stood vacant for several years before Charles Woodstock purchased it. After renovating and adding a parking area, he opened it as Woodstock Inn.

The front door opens into a large room that has a small lobby on the left. It is carpeted and is furnished with an upholstered sofa, an upholstered chaise lounge, upholstered chairs and a pair of upholstered open arm chairs and a coffee table. There is also a TV and live plants. Thomas Kincaid prints are on the walls.

To the right as you enter, the dining room has a long oak table and spindle-back Windsor chairs. A refrigerator is for guests' use.

After a restful night's sleep, wake to a piping hot cup of coffee and take a seat at the table. Tempt your palate with the house specialty, gourmet Belgian waffles topped off with powdered sugar and smothered with specialty syrups or fresh fruit sauce, or sample their other breakfast entrees. It changes daily, but favorites include apple crepes, Swedish pancakes, ham and cheese stuffed French toast and garden-fresh frittatas. Always coffee, tea or milk.

There are eleven guestrooms, each has a private bath with shower. Three also have Jacuzzis. All of the rooms are carpeted, bright and cheery and extra clean. Each is tastefully and distinctively furnished. All have some type of upholstered chairs, be it a wing or tub chair. You can choose from Queen-size, double or twin beds. Antique quilts or comforters are on some of the beds.

Four guestrooms are on the first floor, down the hall from the lobby. Then up the stairs off a large landing there are seven more guestrooms. There is a sitting room on the second floor with a TV, an upholstered sofa, chairs and a coffee table.

At Woodstock, you will have the comfort and privacy of a small hotel, but you will find the hospitality of a bed & breakfast home. Woodstock Inn's category falls in between the two. Handicapped facilities available with ramps to front door. Private, lighted off street parking.

WOODSTOCK INN: 1212 West Lexington Avenue, Independence, 64050. (816) 833-2233. (800) 276-5202 for reservations. Website: www.independence-missouri.com. An eleven guestroom inn that includes two suites. All have private baths. Close to the Mormon Reorganized Church of Latter Day Saints Temple and also the Mormon Visitor's Center, Truman Home and Library and on the city bus route. Children welcome. No smoking. No pets. Ample off-street parking. Ten blocks to Historic Independence Square with plenty of antique shops. Visa/MC, American Express, Discovery. AAA approve and Mobil Guide and BBIM inspected and approved. Todd and Patricia Justice, innkeepers. Blanca Gonzalez, right hand.

DIRECTIONS: From I-70, exit north on Noland Road to 23rd Street. Left to Crysler Avenue. Right on Crysler, which becomes Lexington, to Woodstock Inn. Also I-435 to 23rd Street, east to Crysler. Proceed as above. Call for reservations and directions.

DOME RIDGE BED & BREAKFAST
Kansas City

Trees, trees, trees and more trees. In fact the whole 17 acres, that comprise Bill and Roberta Faust's property, are covered with trees. They do have a cleared area for parking, but that's it. No matter where you are on the property, you can reach out and touch a tree.

Bill should have been a master carpenter, as he built the entire house, decks, a lot of the furniture, cabinets and anything else that required tools. I envy anyone with these skills.

From the first floor, the geodesic dome rises 31 feet to the ceiling. It is built entirely of yellow pine. Wide decks surround the entire house, where you'll find many plants, outdoor furniture, song birds and some small animals. The last time I was here Bill had tomatoes growing in a garden on the deck. There is also a Jacuzzi with a whirlpool for guests' enjoyment.

Bill and Roberta's guests share the entire home. The living room has a wood burning stove on a raised hearth. Sofas and easy chairs are placed around the stove to get full benefit from it. I've not been here in winter, but my guess is, it's a cozy setting. Sliding doors and windows overlook the deck, with eight different exits to the outside.

A dining alcove off the living room has a 100 year old china cabinet holding crystal. Breakfast is usually served here; however, I would prefer mine in the most unusual kitchen I've seen. It is built entirely of tongue and groove pine including overhead and base cabinets, counters, ceiling and walls. And, it's not too much wood, either. The table looks out over the deck, and you guessed it, trees.

For breakfast there is generally juice, fresh fruit in season, with either Belgian waffles with fruit and whipped cream or California omelets with ham, bacon or sausage, and coffee or tea.

Stairs lead to a railed balcony on the second floor that is used as a library and sitting area. It has a sofa and a long book cabinet with all kinds of reading material.

Two guestrooms are on the first floor. One is furnished with a full-size bed, night stand, chest and rocking chair. It has a ceiling fan and television. A door opens onto the deck.

The other guestroom is furnished with a queen-size bed, chest an upholstered chair and a television. It, too, opens out onto the deck.

A guestroom on the third floor, at the top of the dome, is fully carpeted. It is furnished with a trundle bed, that opens into a full-size bed, an upholstered arm chair and a chest. It has a private bath with shower.

A lower level guestroom has a king-size bed with an ornate white iron and brass headboard, a television and radio. The private bath has a two person spa and a separate shower. There is also a private deck.

A family room on the lower level has a pool table, television, VCR and a CD player. The Fausts have over 500 movies, which may be viewed here or in guestrooms, and 200 CD discs. There is a half bath.

Just off the deck, near the kitchen, Bill built a 20 foot screened gazebo. It has two sets of wrought iron tables and chairs. Breakfast is great here.

For a great getaway, I don't think Dome Ridge can be improved on too much. If I'm wrong, write me!

DOME RIDGE B & B: 14360 N.W. Walker Road, Kansas City, 64164. (816) 532-4074. A four guestroom home north of Kansas City. Open all year. Spa on the deck. Totally private. No small children. No pets. No smoking. Bill and Roberta Faust, hosts.

DIRECTIONS. The best thing is to call Bill or Roberta and they will take your reservations and provide directions.

THE INN ON CRESCENT LAKE
Kansas City

Just north of Kansas City, the Inn on Crescent Lake is a prestigious, stately three story Georgian Colonial mansion with four huge white pillars. It has been combined with spacious, garden-like grounds and 22 acres of rolling terrain to provide the nostalgic seeker with a classic ambiance. The Inn is surrounded by two crescent-shaped ponds, historically known as Crescent Lake.

The owners and innkeepers, Bruce and Anne Libowitz, purchased the property in 1996, and after months of renovation and decorating, opened their inn.

The inn nestles well back from the road in huge pine and hardwood trees. The drive to the house crosses over the lake. A few steps take you between the tall pillars to the front entryway. Inside the foyer, a massive elegantly spindled staircase leads to the second floor guestrooms.

To the left of the entry, is a long living room with a huge brick fireplace flanked by two upholstered wing chairs and an overstuffed sofa. Adjoining the living room is a tiled floor solarium furnished with wicker table and chairs. It is a cross between a greenhouse and a sunroom and has views of trees, trails and the lake.

The Inns intimate light-filled dining room is fully carpeted. The windows have forest green drapes. White, crisp table linens are on all of the tables, each with four caned back chairs. The walls have a colorful floral wallpaper. Bruce and Anne Libowitz are both graduates of the French Culinary Institute in New York City and prepare the meals. A delectable breakfast can be enjoyed in the living room, dining room or solarium. Breakfast varies and could be chicken apple sausage, scrambled eggs with herbs, toasted English muffins and roasted rosemary potatoes. Or maybe blueberry pancakes with carmelized bananas and bacon.

Each of the Inns eight luxurious guestrooms and suites contain a collection of antiques and refined furnishings. Each room is decorated with its own charm and personality and features a large private bath, individual temperature control, cable television and toiletries.

Five guestrooms are on the second floor. The Fish Room with its fishing motif, features a king-size sleigh bed and a whirlpool tub and shower. It has a view of the pond.

The Striped Room is a romantic room with hand painted striped walls. This room has a king-size sleigh bed. An old fashion claw foot tub and shower will wash away stress. There is a view of the front lawn and pond.

The Peach Room is furnished with two twin beds or a king bed and features a whirlpool tub and a glass block shower enclosure in the bath. There is a pool and front lawn view.

The Train Room has a queen-size wrought iron bed, hardwood floors, and if you wish, a train that will chug around the perimeter of the room. The bath has claw foot tub and shower and a converted antique wash basin. There is a pool view.

The Art Deco Room is a cozy room that features a queen-size sleigh bed. The bath is tiled in black and white. The custom black shower or the red claw foot tub is the spot to relax. Your view is of the side yard and pond.

Two guestrooms are on the third floor. The ballroom is by far the largest of the Rooms. It contains a king-size bed, an alcove sitting area and a whirlpool for two. There is also a custom marble shower. Front yard and pond view.

The Tree House Suite boasts an arched ceiling and skylight. It has a king-size sleigh bed and a sitting room complete with an antique library table and club chairs. The bath has a claw foot tub and shower.

There is also a guestroom on the first floor, furnished in the same style as the others. The room and bath, however are designed to accommodate persons requiring wheelchair accessibility.

An in-ground pool as well as fishing, paddle boats, and walking lake trails can be enjoyed by guests. This is quite a place and I think you will be well satisfied. The Inn was even featured on Restore America with Bob Villa.

INN ON CRESCENT LAKE: 1261 St. Louis Ave., Excelsior Springs, 64024. (816) 630-6745. Fax (816) 630-9326. Website:www.crescentinn.com Open all year. An 8 room inn, in a beautiful Georgian Colonial mansion. Handicapped accessible. No pets. A smoke free inn. Not suited for children under 16. Visa/MC. Bruce and Anne Libowitz, innkeepers.

DIRECTIONS: From I-35 North, exit 20 (Excelsior Springs via Hwy. 69). Follow Hwy. 69 10 miles into town. In town, exit onto Hwy. 10. Turn right at Corum Rd.(the first traffic light on Hwy. 10). Follow Corum Rd to Hwy. H. Turn left on Hwy. H. The inn is located .4 miles down the road on the right.

LA FONTAINE INN
Kansas City

L isted on the Missouri Register of Historic Places, this beautiful, fully restored, all brick, circa 1910 Georgian Colonial Home, is one of Kansas City's newest places to stay near the Country Club Plaza. It is located in the neighborhood known as the cultural center of Kansas City. It is the home of Lionel Martin and Rick Winegar.

Upon entering the house, you are in a foyer that has white paneling chair rail high with a salmon color grass cloth wall covering above it. A great white staircase leads to the second floor guestrooms. A crystal chandelier hangs from the ceiling. There are side windows on both side windows on both sides of the front door, each with twenty-one small panes of beveled glass. There is a wonderful carved ceiling molding.

Spend the evening relaxing in the living room located off the central hall, in front of a large marble fireplace, enjoying complimentary wine and cheese. This room is furnished with an upholstered camel back sofa, a pair of French glass top tables a block front gentleman's chest, a pair of upholstered wing chairs, an Ebony baby grand piano, and entertainment center with a television, a sofa table and a wing back open arm chair. French doors open onto a covered porch. There are two rattan couches and a rattan chair.

The mahogany trimmed dining room is furnished with a mahogany triple pedestal table with twelve matching ball and claw foot Queen Anne style chairs. There is a marble top server and three large windows each have forty-light small panes of glass. The floor has an antique carpet. A crystal chandelier hangs over the table.

A sitting area at the top of the stairs has a breakfront, a leather wing chair a Queen Anne love seat and a Queen Anne side table and lamp.

Four elegantly appointed guestrooms, each with a full bath, are offered on the second floor. French doors lead from the hall to the Spring Room. Two walls of windows have white inside shutters. Two walls of windows have white inside shutters. Two walls are of exposed brick. It is furnished with a full-size bed, and open arm, upholstered high back chair, a pair of square tables with lamps. The bath has a jacuzzi and a shower.

The Winter Room was the original master bedroom. Decorated in yellow, green and burgundy, it boasts a carved four poster rice bed, a block front bedside table, and matching dresser, a pair of upholstered wing back chairs, a bonnot top high boy and a large antique mirror. There is a mahogany and marble trimmed wood burning fireplace. The original bath has a huge jacuzzi as well as a glass shower that can be turned into a steam room.

The Autumn Room, with a peach and green décor, is furnished with a curved four poster rice bed, a drop front desk and chair, a bonnot top high boy, a bookcase and sofa table with a lamp. Note the pair of beautiful finely woven leather arm chairs. A hooked area carpet is on the floor. The bath has an antique tub and a large glass shower that can be turned into a steam room.

The Summer Room, decorated in raspberry, white and green, adjoins a large private deck with a private hot tub. The room has a brass four poster bed, a mahogany bedside table, and upholstered open arm chair and an armoire. The bath has a corner shower.

You can gain entrance to the Elmore Truitt Carriage house by a carpeted staircase to the second floor and into the first room that is furnished with a pair of upholstered chairs, a refrigerator, sink and coffee maker. A second room has a queen-size sleigh bed, a night table and reading lamp, a television and a wicker chaise lounge. There is a small bar with a pair of bar stools. This two room suite is very cozy under the eaves. There is a bath with a claw foot tub and shower and also a jacuzzi. Outside, a great garden area has a fountain and outdoor furniture. There are two really huge trees.

Start your day on the porch with morning coffee or tea, followed by a full breakfast in the dining room. Martin prepares several entrée choices. A cheese, egg and ham souffle with hash browned potatoes, a cheese, egg and sausage strata with carmelized pears and yogurt, or chicken crepes with a cranberry and orange sauces. German pancakes are also served.

LA FONTAINE INN: 4320 Oak St., Kansas City, 64111. (816) 753-4434. Open all year. No pets. Outside smoking. No children. M/C, Visa, Discover and American Express.

DIRECTIONS: From I-70 in downtown Kansas City, take Main St. south to 44th street. Turn left and go four blocks to Oak St. and turn left.

SOUTHMORELAND on the Plaza
Kansas City

Since Colonial times, New England inns have set the standard for lodging hospitality. Cozy rooms trimmed in warm woods and bright brass, lit fireplaces, deep featherbeds, good sherry, and generous innkeepers have greeted the weary traveler. Now, this tradition of home-style comfort can be found at Southmoreland on the Plaza.

Century-old shade trees, native rock walls, sweeping lawns and formal gardens create a feeling of "country in the city." The Colonial Revival styling of this 1913 mansion inspired special touches reminiscent of New England bed and breakfasts such as open air decks, white wicker solarium, and elegant antiques. The common rooms of the inn, the all season veranda, spacious courtyard, and gardens are for guests' use.

Entering the front entry hall, a living room with a nautical theme is to the right. There is a Duncan Phyfe style sofa, rocking chairs, butler tray coffee table, and an antique roll top desk. An Austrian armoire holds a television, VCR, and 175-plus happy ending videos. The fireplace is the focal point of the room.

The dining room on the left of the entry is an authentic replica of an Early New England inn. A long antique harvest table is surrounded with eight ladder back chairs. Two smaller tables that match the large table were made at Pleasant Hill. Wing chairs are on either side of an antique dry sink that accents the room. A primitive hutch holds china in a Willow ware pattern. A large fireplace dominates the room.

A solarium, just off the dining room, contains beautiful white wicker arm chairs, tables, plant stands and lamps. The upholstery is navy and white. Old denim cloth was made into carpeting by the Jamesport Amish. This room looks cool even on the hottest days.

An all season veranda has recently been converted to a second all season dining room. Multi pane French doors and a handsome fireplace frame the enclosure. Tables for two provide a more romantic alternative to the harvest table's communal setting.

The courtyard has comfortable chairs, tables with umbrellas and an old-fashioned limestone barbecue. Nestled in the center of urban bustle is an island of serenity with a waterfall, pond and benches for quiet conversation.

An American gourmet breakfast is served in the New England style dining room or in the veranda dining room. It consists of a fruit course (frappes, mixed compotes, cold fruit soups), freshly baked batter breads and muffins and a hearty entree such as baked shirred eggs, omelet, eggs Benedict or stuffed French toast. On Saturday mornings, guests may have a BBQ breakfast.

The twelve guestrooms were named after notable citizens from Kansas City. The decor reflects the era and personality of the room's namesake. Each guestroom has a private bath and special features such as a private treetop deck, wood burning fireplace, or Jacuzzi.

The August Meyer room is a spacious, comfortable room with Civil War era furnishings in burled walnut and the option of twins or king-size beds. Located on the wheelchair accessible first floor, this room features a 2 person Jacuzzi.

The William Rockhill Nelson Room's traditional Colonial colors warm this spacious room furnished in Chippendale. Richly painted Irish hunt prints hang over the elegant, king-size bed with a hand-tied canopy. Plaid "Mr. and Mrs." chairs sit companionably by the wood burning fireplace.

The Kathryn Winstead Room is a sunny, cheerful room featuring a queen-size iron bed with bright brass cannonballs and is decorated in vintage Americana befitting the sponsor of Kansas City's favorite steakburger. After a long day, luxuriate in the unique 32" deep soaking tub or watch a croquet game from your private deck.

The Thomas Hart Benton Room's unique Mission era furniture, including a queen-size oak and copper four poster bed create historic context for select Benton works in a warm, comfortable guestroom. Private deck and full bath adjoin this room.

The Col. Robert T. Van Horn Room has a miniature porcelain Vermont Castings wood burning fireplace that compliments this authentic Cape Cod room. A cozy fire will warm you as you enjoy the queen-size bed with a splendid 6 foot carved oak headboard.

Kersey Coates' Pennsylvania Quaker roots were the inspiration for this room with its handmade Shaker furnishings and selection of artwork. A stately silver maple commands your view from the queen-size pencil post bed or the swing on the adjoining deck.

Leroy "Satchel" Paige Room is a tribute to Kansas City's baseball legend. He would have slept like a baby in the restored knotty pine sleeping porch outfitted with period pieces from the 1920s and 30s. This room, with a queen-size log bed boasts a Vermont Castings fireplace.

The Loose family's Massachusetts summer home "Searocks" is the inspiration for the Ella and Jacob Loose Room decorated in a navy and white nautical theme boasting an ornate, queen-size iron bed. A very private and spacious deck overlooks the courtyard.

The Clara and Russell Stover Room has many comforts including a two person Jacuzzi in the restored, original bath, a 13' x 15' private deck with wrought iron sunning chaises, and a queen-size brass bed. Pastel decorator themes are used here.

You might first notice the queen-size, four poster mahogany bed, flanked by brass lamps from the railroad club car, in the George Caleb Bingham Room, but the real treasures are on the walls — copies of Bingham portraits that have hung in this home since 1948. An adjoining oversized deck has a spectacular urban view.

Like Southmoreland's last three sets of owners, Mary Atkins was a teacher. Her bequest was the original endowment for Kansas City's art museum. The Mary Atkins Room honors this quiet soul, who would have enjoyed its coziness with copper accents (including a teapot collection), queen-size pencil post bed and the intimate little deck.

The William Gilliss Room, with the rich hunt colors, brass accents, and duck prints of the "gentlemen's library" decor, is inspired by Gilliss' bachelor status among K.C. founders. A queen-size pencil post bed and compact dormer deck are a part of this handsome guestroom.

SOUTHMORELAND on the Plaza: 116 East 46th Street, Kansas City, 64112. (816) 531-7979. FAX (816) 531-2407. As the only Mobil four star B & B in 20 states, Southmoreland is a twelve guestroom inn. One room handicapped accessible. Smoke free. No children under 13. No pets. 1.5 blocks to 300 shops and restaurants of the renowned Country Club Plaza. Mark Reichle and Nancy Miller Reichle, innkeepers.

DIRECTIONS: From I-70, take the Main Street exit south to 46th Street (one block north of Brush Creek and the J.C. Nichols fountain). Turn left. on 46th, go past Walnut to Southmoreland on the Plaza.

LIBERTY

On January 2, 1822, less than two years after the first permanent settlers entered the region, Clay County was organized and soon after, Liberty was platted. The new town boomed. Colonel Sheebael Allen's Landing, on the Missouri River a few miles to the south, was the main port for northwest Missouri during the period 1829-41, and Liberty was the outlet for much of the trade to the northwest Missouri area

As hemp, tobacco and the overland trade proved profitable, an aristocracy of ardently pro-slavery planters and merchants developed. The outbreak of the Civil War was received with mixed emotions. Some citizens advocated secession; some pleaded for maintenance of the Union.

On September 16, 1861, 700 State Guards ambushed a Union force of about 500 men near Blue Mills, some 4 miles southeast of Liberty. The Union loss was put at 17 dead and 80 wounded with the State Guards losing 5 men and 18 wounded.

During the mid-1900s many of Kansas City's citizens, trying to escape the urban city, moved to Liberty for its small town life. Today, the past and present coexist in the restored and maintained neighborhoods and downtown area of this historic city.

Liberty's special character can be seen in both the architecture and history of the downtown area, residential neighborhoods, museums, and educational institutions. Liberty has over thirty buildings listed on the National Register of Historic Places, as well as one of the oldest private colleges in Missouri, William Jewell College.

Liberty also has five Historic Districts which contain a wide variety of architectural styles including Queen Anne, Italianate, Dutch Colonial Revival, Greek Revival, and Craftsman bungalows. The Historic Districts: Dougherty, Jewell, Liberty Square, Lightburne, and Prospect Heights can be identified by the maroon and green oval signs.

The Clay County Visitors Bureau has information about upcoming special events and brochures from area attractions. The Visitors' Bureau would be happy to send you additional information about the Liberty area. They are located in the old Courthouse. (816) 792-7691.

DOUGHERTY HOUSE BED & BREAKFAST
Liberty

Major John Dougherty (1791-1860) purchased this property in 1837. Major Dougherty is remembered in history as working with the Missouri Fur Company, having close relationships with Chouteau, Picot, Lewis and Clark and General Doniphan. He was appointed Indian agent and served at Fort Leavenworth and Council Bluffs.

Major Dougherty's son, O'Fallon and his wife, Sarah, built this home in 1881 on land his father left him. The property stayed in the family until 1955.

In 1994, Bill and Sheri Ray purchased the home and began major restoration. Pine floors were refinished and once forgotten fireplaces now warm the rooms on cool evenings. The original red brick house was covered with stucco at the turn of the century. There are 17 rooms in all. Parlors and sitting rooms have comfortable corners for reading, a little television or making new friends. Gardens offer places to linger to enjoy the gazebo, fountains, hillside stream and an ornamental fish pond. You can enjoy your breakfast or evening desserts on the spacious wraparound porch.

The entry hall has oriental carpets. There is a German grandfather clock, an oak library table and a hall tree. An archway leads to the front parlor.

An oriental carpet covers the original floors. The setter and side chairs are hand carved. An Edison Victrola is in working order. There is a stack bookcase, and a circa 1850 mantel clock. The mirror was once in the Tom Pendergast mansion. French doors open into a sitting room.

The sitting room has a large bay window, 12 foot ceilings, as all of the first floor rooms have, and the original fireplace. It now burns gas instead of wood. A jukebox is a 1937 Wurlitzer, the second model made. It has been fully restored. There is a Mission library table, an antique oak sofa, two Mission rockers, an upholstered arm chair, a bookcase, and a plant stand. An antique Morris recliner, an armoire, and a round oak coffee table finish the room. French doors open to the dining room.

The dining room is furnished with an arts and crafts buffet, a slag glass leaded light fixture hangs above a golden oak five-legged table and six antique oak chairs. There is also an antique oak china cabinet, and an English sideboard. A Tree of Life pattern carpet is on the floor. There is also a bay window.

On the second floor, three guestrooms, each with its own private bath, blend antique furnishings, stained glass and accessories. There is individual control heating and central air conditioning. The guestrooms are named after a Dougherty family member.

The Sarah and O'Fallon Room is furnished with a queen-size poster bed, an oak washstand, an armoire, a pair of upholstered wing chairs, an antique chest, a stack bookcase and an oak side by side secretary bookcase. The bath has a Jacuzzi.

Hertie's Room, named for Sarah and O'Fallon's daughter Mary, has a queen-size metal bed, a pair of upholstered barrel back chairs. A hand-made pre-Civil War cedar chest and a barley twist leg tile back washstand. The fireplace is for show. The bath also has a Jacuzzi.

Katie's Room, named for another daughter, is furnished with an antique full-size brass bed, an English blanket chest, an armoire, an antique chest, a rocking chair, floor lamp, an English washstand, and a barrel back upholstered chair. The bath has a tub and shower.

Breakfast is served in the dining room and consists of juice, fresh seasonal fruit, homemade muffins, and bread. Sheri varies her menu so guests don't have the same breakfast on any other day. It could be zucchini friatatta served with Italian sausage and a potato casserole and sliced tomatoes, in season. Another menu might be any way eggs (your choice) with your choice of bacon or sausage, and homemade biscuits with sausage gravy. There is always jams, jellies, coffee, tea or milk.

DOUGHERTY HOUSE B & B: 302 North Water, Liberty, 64068. (816) 792-4888. Not suited for children. No pets. Smoking on porch. M/C and Visa accepted. Close to Jesse James Bank Museums and Liberty Jail Visitors Center. Ten minutes to Jesse James Home. Bill and Sheri Willoughley-Ray, innkeepers.

DIRECTIONS: From I-70 in Kansas City, exit north on I-35. Exit on exit #16, which is Hwy. 152. (It turns into Kansas Street.) Turn right on 152 and go approximately 3 miles to Liberty Square. Go left on Main Street to Franklin. Right on Franklin to Water. Left on Water Street to 302 N. Dougherty.

JAMES INN
Liberty

The James Inn is an unusual five room bed and breakfast located in a restored circa 1913 church, a few blocks away from the historical town square. Needless to say, a lot of renovation went on in the building. Owners David and Mary Anne Kimbrell designed the inn with romance in mind. They offer an intimate, relaxing atmosphere.

What was once the center aisle of the church is now a long hall that leads to a large open area where the alter used to be. To one side is a sitting area with a fireplace. There are upholstered chairs and a sofa, a rocking chair and various other pieces of furniture.

On the other side is the dining area. Seven antique tables with chairs assure privacy, but also invite socializing, if you desire. Notice the antique opossum belly cabinet. Before breakfast, enjoy an early morning cup of coffee in your room. Then linger over juice, fresh fruit in season, followed by either quiche or Belgium waffles. Coffee, tea or hot chocolate.

Each of the five guestrooms are decorated in soft colors and floral designs with warm antique furnishings. They all have cable television, radios and telephones. Illuminated by tall Gothic windows, four guestrooms are off the hallway on the main level. Each of the four has an unusual loft bath area that overlooks the bedroom. They are all decorated with nice framed prints and pictures along with house plants. Each of the four rooms has its own double Jacuzzi.

The four main level rooms all have queen-size four poster feather beds with cozy feather comforters, antique oak dressers, tables and rocking chairs.

To make your night even more romantic, the Honeymoon Suite has a fireplace at the bedside. The Deluxe Honeymoon Suite has two fireplaces, one at the bedside and one in the loft bathroom by the double jacuzzi tub.

The fifth room is on one level with a four poster featherbed, sofa, antique dresser and wardrobe. The large bathroom has a double jacuzzi tub, shower, and two pedestal sinks.

New in 1999 was the addition of two Spa Rooms, providing James Inn guests and the general public with massages, body wraps, facials, manicures, pedicures and aromatherapy. The Day Spa is the ultimate in relaxation and pampering. All of the guests can enjoy an outdoor Jacuzzi on a private deck and sauna in the spa area.

The Gift Shop, located by the front desk, offers aromatherapy products, lotions, soaps, and candles to enhance your special night.

You are invited to visit the James Inn website at www.thejamesinn.com for additional information on the many special packages available.

THE JAMES INN: 342 North Water Street, Liberty, 64068. (816) 781-3677. Fax: (816) 781-9132. Website: www.thejamesinn.com. Open all year. Winter rates from September 1 to May 15. Summer rates from May 15 to September 1. No children. No pets. Smoking in some rooms. Five guestrooms in an unusual setting and very nice. MC/Visa. David and Mary Anne Kimbrell, innkeepers.

DIRECTIONS: From I-35 north, take exit # 16 and turn east onto Hwy. 152 for 2 miles. Hwy. 152 turns into Kansas Street. On the square, turn left on Water Street and go three blocks north.

APPLE BLOSSOM INN
Plattsburg

This large two-story house with a wraparound front porch was built in 1910, and in the early years, many of the town's children took piano lessons in the parlor. In 1937, and for nearly a quarter of a century, it was the family home of the local pharmacist. It was then turned into apartments, had various owners and experienced a general decline. In 1992, Darrell and Charlotte Apple purchased the house, renovated and decorated it, then opened their Apple Blossom Inn.

Entering the house from the front porch, you are in an entry hall with an oak stairway, stained glass at the landing and French doors leading into the parlor.

A large hooked rug is on the original floors. There is a magnificent built-in floor to ceiling corner cupboard with leaded glass doors that holds a collection of china. There is an upholstered loveseat, an antique twist-leg parlor table with a reading lamp, an antique Eastlake parlor table, a pair of upholstered swivel rockers, a coffee table and an oak china cabinet. There is also a television. The woodwork is all original as is the ceiling molding. Old-time prints are on the walls that are covered with a floral print paper.

Sliding doors from the parlor lead to the dining room. A green tile corner fireplace has a mirrored oak mantlepiece. There is also a floor to ceiling built in cupboard. The room is furnished with an antique, round oak table with Queen Anne style legs and four chairs. There is an antique buffet and a china cabinet, and a grandfather clock along with a pair of upholstered club chairs. A raised burgundy floral wallpaper is above a chair rail. The bay windows have lace curtains.

At the staircase landing, a small sitting area has a cane loveseat, a chair and a magazine table with a reading lamp. You can have an early cup of coffee here.

At the top of the stairs, the Granny Smith guestroom is furnished with twin Jenny Lind beds with hand made quilts, a bedside table, a cane bottom rocking chair, a small dresser, and a quilt rack. A large hooked carpet is on the floor, lace curtains with a floral valance at the windows and the white woodwork is original. There is a private bath with walk in shower.

The Gala Room has a full-size bed, a pair of wicker night tables with lamps, a round wicker table with a reading lamp, an oak mission style chair and an oak drop front ladies desk. The walls are pink and white, The curtains and bedspread have pink and green flowers on a black background. The original bath has a tile floor. There is a tub and shower.

A small alcove down the hall has Charlotte's grandmother's small trunk and some heirlooms. What caught my eye was the train collection.

Breakfast is served in the dining room using antique china, crystal and silverware. Charlotte has several menus. Orange or apple juice, fresh fruit in season, muffins, scones or bread, jams and homemade apple butter. There is also coffee cake at the cook's whim. Entrees could either be apple pecan pancakes and apple blossom eggs wrapped in turkey bacon. Or, individual fresh herb souffle baked inside a ham shell. Then there's hash brown quiche with fresh herbs or ham and cheese quiche with hash brown crust. There are different apple blossom blends of fresh coffee. Weather permitting, breakfast can be served on the deck or patio.

An apple dessert of some kind along with a beverage is served in the evening.

CHARLOTTE'S APPLE BLOSSOM INN: Second and Broadway, Plattsburg, 64477. (816) 539-3243. Closed during January. Fax: (816) 539-3243. Website: www.bbonline.com/mo/appleblossom/. Three guestrooms with private baths. No pets. No smoking indoors but on patio or deck. Darrell and Charlotte Apple, innkeepers.

DIRECTIONS: From Kansas City or St. Joseph, take I-29 to Hwy. 116 (exit 30). Turn east and follow the signs to Plattsburg.

WESTON

In 1836 the Federal Government extinguished the titles to Indian Territories in Northwest Missouri, from which were carved six counties, called the Platte Purchase. Constant conflict between the white poachers and the Sac, Sioux, Fox and Missouri tribes had forced this act. It opened 2 million acres of Indian land for white settlers, mostly from the eastern and southern states who brought their customs with them.

Weston had its beginnings when Joseph Moore stated a claim in 1837, laid off a few streets and sold some lots. Soon immigrants from Austria, Germany and Switzerland were moving in and buying little home sites. Within a year the population had increased to 300. Shipping advantages on the Missouri River made the town a port for much of the growing overland traffic. Compact cottages began rising, tier upon tier, on the slopes surrounding the four block square that comprised the business district. By 1849, merchants of Weston had shipped 1,600 tons of hemp, and huge quantities of pork, lard, peltries, wheat and tobacco. As affluence came the early settlers, they built columned Federal style two-story houses fashioned like the homes they left in the south.

By 1853, Weston had a population of 5,000 and was the second largest port in Missouri. Hemp and tobacco were among the most profitable early crops. Steamboats jammed the river. The town became a main embarking center for the wagon trains moving west.

During the Civil War, loyalties were divided in Weston and Platte County. Border skirmishes between Missouri and Kansas were common and Quantrill's raiders were active in the area.

Disaster struck in the years between 1855 and 1880. Two fires destroyed large portions of the business district, and five floods, the last of which moved the river two miles away, left the port high and dry. The population dwindled to a fraction of its boom total. The Emancipation Act and the unwelcomed railroads spelled Weston's doom. Most of its citizens moved away. By 1890, only about 1,000 residents were left.

A few hardy souls remained loyal to Weston, and a slow recovery brought to town into the 1890's. At the turn of the century, a few large Victorian homes were built. Tobacco grew in importance in the 1890's and landscaping tobacco growers from the south came to capitalize on the excellent prices the crop was bringing. In 1928, five million pounds of tobacco were sold at Weston.

Today, the cultivation and sale of high-quality barley and tobacco products remain a force in Weston's economy. From the canvas covered tobacco bed in March to the chant of the auctioneer the following January, Weston's "brown gold" attracts countless visitors to the annual auctions in December and January.

Weston has nearly 200 pre-civil war homes and businesses in a 22 block area. In 1972, the Weston Historical District was entered in the National Register of Historic Places. Today, Weston is one of the oldest and most picturesque river towns in Missouri. Half hidden in a little valley between the Missouri River bluffs, the town offers visitors much to see.

Be sure to visit the New Deal Tobacco Warehouse, the McCormick Distilling Company, the oldest continually active distillery in the country, the Weston Historical Museum displays artifacts that was part of the religious, educational, cultural and business life in Platte County, largely from the Weston area, Pirtle's Weston Vineyards and Winery located in a church built in 1867. The winery produces a variety of wine which visitors can sample while walking through the vineyards near the building. Mission Creek Winery, the second in Weston, offers locally produced varieties. In addition to wine they offer a food and craft section in their building where you can also sample the wines.

As of now, there are three bed and breakfast inns in Weston and three restaurants.

AVALON CAFÉ
Weston

uilt in 1847, this antebellum house is one of the buildings that is
included in the National Register of Historic Districts. It was, at one
time, called "White Lace" for all of the lacy gingerbread which adorns
the long front porch. The café has been renovated, but keeping the integrity
of the building intact. The original living rooms have been turned into several
cozy dining rooms that seat 60 to 90 persons. The café is quaint by daylight,
but romantic by candle light.

Continental cuisine, prepared by chef/co-owners David Scott and Kelly
Cogan, offers a wide variety of dishes ranging from the Beef Tenderloin in
Missouri Bourbon Sauce to the American Lamb Chops in burgundy butter.
There is a nightly fresh seafood special as well as the western trio, which
offers a sampling of three menu items, each prepared with its own sauce.

Desserts include Double Chocolate Souffle Cake, fresh berry pies and
bread pudding in vanilla sauce, to name a few.

*AVALON CAFÉ: 608 Main Street, Weston, 64098. (816) 640-2835. Open all
year. Hours: Tues – Sat. Lunch: 11 a.m. to 3 p.m. Dinner begins at 6 p.m.
Sunday brunch: 11 a.m. to 4 p.m. Dinner from 5 to 8 p.m. David Scott and
Kelly Cogan, chefs/co-owners.*

THE VINEYARDS RESTAURANT
Weston

One of the things I like about what I do is the traveling. It's fun to drive around the state seeing different places and meeting new people. While I was in the town of Weston, Susan Keith and Steve Anderson of Apple Creek B & B invited me to have dinner with them. They wanted me to see the Vineyards Restaurant. If you ever get the chance to visit Weston, be sure and make a reservation to have dinner here. It is one of the better places in the state.

Sheryl Mock, the owner, has changed the menu somewhat, which now includes fresh grilled North Atlantic salmon with soy ginger shitake sauce, American lamb chops with French dijon sauce, a chicken breast wrapped in puff pastry stuffed with artichokes Romano, filet of beef with portabello mushrooms in Merlot sauce.

Everything is fresh cooked to order and accompanied with fresh vegetables. All of the breads, soups, and desserts are homemade. Try the warm brie with roasted garlic or fresh fruit.

The restaurant is small and very comfortable. Sheryl has added a lattice-covered patio with seating for 32 persons, and also had the front porch glass enclosed, with seating for 16 more. Tables have crisp, white tablecloths and napkins, fine china, crystal and silverware.

THE VINEYARDS RESTAURANT: 505 Spring Street, Weston, 64098. (816) 386-2835. Open all year. Reservations a must. Sheryl Mock, Chef/owner.

DIRECTIONS: From Kansas City, take I-29 north to Hwy. 92. Hwy. 92 west to Hwy. 45. North on Hwy. 45 to Weston.

BENNER HOUSE BED & BREAKFAST
Weston

Listed on the National Register of Historic Places, the Benner House is a fine example of steamboat Gothic architecture. It was built in 1898 by George Shawhan. He owned the distillery, which was the forerunner of today's McCormick Distillery.

John and Julia Pasley will see to it that your visit here will be a very special one. It is a perfect setting for a honeymoon, anniversary, or just a special time away. There are two large wraparound porches, one on each floor, where you can relax and enjoy this lovely old town. Maybe you'd like to tour the hills of Weston. If you like to walk, take a stroll along the historic streets and enjoy the many beautiful Antebellum homes, antique shops and gourmet restaurants.

The main parlor provides an especially inviting atmosphere for conversation and getting acquainted. It has a fireplace, for the colder months. The room is furnished with many nice antiques including an antique clock and a pump organ, which you are welcome to play. The room has a Victorian love seat and a pair of Victorian arm chairs. The original gaslight has been electrified, and the floors are the original clear pine.

You may curl up in a rocking chair with your favorite book in the sitting room, which has a collection of antique books.

The dining room has an antique oak dining table and chairs and an Eastlake marble top buffet. Small antique pieces include glassware of many kinds, old prints and pictures.

A full breakfast is served in the oldest of traditions in the Victorian dining room and is especially prepared for guests. Enjoy fresh fruit in season, juice, special homemade breads and muffins, egg dishes with ham or sausage and cinnamon rolls. John grinds and blends his own coffee.

Accommodations include four guestrooms all with private baths. The Victorian antique furnishings make each bedroom unique, warm and inviting. One has an antique double wedding ring pattern quilt on an iron full-size bed, an oak wardrobe, and an antique rocking chair. There are pink curtains, blue wallpaper, a ceiling fan and the room is carpeted.

Another guestroom has a three piece matching Eastlake bedroom set in walnut and a table and chairs. Plus a wicker settee for lounging or reading. Still another room is furnished with a circa 1880 Victorian ornate brass bed with a hand crocheted coverlet, an antique oak dresser, an oak plant stand, a pair of upholstered chairs, and an antique trunk filled with vintage clothes. The room is carpeted, has a ceiling fan and is decorated with old prints, house plants and small antiques.

The fourth guestroom has an antique bedroom set entirely of oak consisting of a full-size bed, armoire, and chest. Other pieces include a table and chair and an unusual Morris recliner. An antique "yo-yo" pattern quilt is on the bed. The room is carpeted, has a ceiling fan and is also decorated with house plants.

The four guestrooms share two large baths with tubs and showers and a half bath. Old kitchen cupboards hold linens, while an antique oak stand has bubble bath and bath salts. There is also a hot tub you are invited to use.

BENNER HOUSE B & B: 645 Main Street, Weston, 64098. (816) 640-2616. Open all year. A four guestroom home, all with private baths. For special occasions, arrangements can be made for wine, champagne, candy or flowers to be placed in your room. Children over 12 welcome. No smoking. No pets. Gift certificates available. Julia and John Pasley, innkeepers.

DIRECTIONS: Located 20 minutes north of Kansas City. Take exit 20 west off of I-29. Follow it to Weston. Call for reservations, information and directions.

THE HATCHERY HOUSE, LLC
Weston

In 1845, the mayor of Weston, Benjamin Wood, purchased land from the town and built this two-story, federal styled home, flanked on each side with brick fireplaces. Through the years, the house changed owners several times one of which, was David Holladay, Ben Holladay's brother.

In the 1930s, the home was converted into a boarding house. Quite often, due to the inexpensive rent, newlyweds and young couples occupied the apartments. As time passed, many of these young couples conceived and had their children while living here. Consequently, the townspeople coined the phrase "the hatchery" for the "hatching of babies."

The present owners, Bill and Anne Lane bought the inn and have added many of their own great antiques, to the home's collection. Both Bill and Anne pay close attention to detail and offer impeccable service as their guests enjoy the experience and tranquility of this wonderful house and Weston.

The parlor is fully carpeted and still has the original brick fireplace, now gas logs are used. There is a built in bookcase and the room is furnished with an upholstered sofa, an entertainment center with a television, coffee table, an upholstered wing back chair, and an antique trunk.

The Hatchery House has four guestrooms that have been named after someone who has had a significant part, past or present in this marvelous antebellum home. All the guestrooms have the original fireplaces, (now with gas logs) and private baths with tub and shower.

The Novle Wyatt Room is a spacious room furnished with an antique hi-back, queen-size oak bed with a church pew at the foot, a walnut armoire, reproduction icebox and an oak dresser. The original floors have an area rug, lace curtains at the windows and it's decorated with many quilts and linen doilies, a kerosene lamp and an antique pitcher and bowl.

The Holladay Room has a private balcony overlooking Weston's skyline and 100-year-old church spires. Enjoy the sunset from this peaceful space, which is furnished with a carved high back, queen-size antique bed, a matching dresser, an English tile back wash stand, a rocker, reading lamp and a drop front desk.

Clemmie's Suite is a romantic suite with two rooms inside an old-fashioned porch style entry. The sitting room contains an upholstered love seat, a marble-topped coffee table, an upholstered wing back chair and an antique pine wash stand. An antique dresser holds a sink. The floor has a large area carpet. An antique "Gone-with-the-Wind" lamp and a 1930's floor lamp are in the bedroom. The room is wallpapered in a burgundy and green floral.

The Payne's room is a spacious room furnished with a high-back carved bed, a mirrored wardrobe, an oak chest and mirror, a wrought iron day bed and an antique Victorian parlor chair. The walls have floral wallpaper border with pineapple stenciling around the windows and doorways.

The dining room is very different. A large open porch was enclosed and three double windows were installed on one side. The original slopping bead board ceiling is painted white, as are the original brick walls. A floral carpet is on the wide planked oak floor and lace swags are on the windows. It is furnished with five wrought iron ice cream parlor tables and chairs, and a 1922 gas cook stove. Breakfast is served in the dining room. Bill is the main cook and he varies the menu from day to day. On this particular day, they served orange juice, fruit compote, scrambled eggs, bacon, and French toast almondene. It was more than enough. You also had your choice of milk, tea or coffee (they have their own blend of coffee).

In the early evening, wine and cheese are served and at 9:00 a nightcap of decaf coffee and McCormick's Irish Cream.

I thought this was a truly great place plus the innkeepers made you feel right at home. I would recommend The Hatchery House to anyone.

HATCHERY HOUSE, LLC: 618 Short Street, Weston 64098. (816) 640-5700 or toll free reservations at (888) 640-4051. Open all year. Four guestrooms with private baths in the heart of historic Weston. Smoking outside. No pets. Children with prior arrangements. Bill and Anne Lane, innkeepers.

DIRECTIONS: From Kansas City take I-29 north to Tracy, exit 20. Turn west and go one mile through Tracy to Rte. 273. Turn north on 273 and go five miles to Hwy. 45/JJ junction. Take JJ into Weston. Turn left on Welt Street. Go two blocks to the corner of Welt and Short Street.

THE LEMON TREE BED & BREAKFAST
Weston

The house that is now called the Lemon Tree B & B was built in 1906 by Phil Doppler, a successful Weston dry goods merchant. Prior to building this house, the Doppler family resided in what is now referred to as the Lemon Tree Cottage, circa 1840. After moving into the Lemon Tree, Mr. Doppler sold the cottage, splitting up the two homes.

During the 1920s and 30s, the Lemon Tree changes hands several times and in the 1940s became the property of Mrs. Bess Beach. At that time, she had the house divided into four apartments. For thirty-five years it was known as Bess Beach's Boarding House.

In 1982, Jim and Pat White purchased the house and began renovation to return the home back to a single family dwelling. The present owners, Craig and Kim Rodgers, purchased the home in 1989 and have continued extensive renovations. It was named the Lemon Tree because it was yellow. Now, what was once Mr. Doppler's two homes are now the Lemon Tree B & B.

The three story Victorian home is open to guests, and the solarium, formal parlor, dining room and den can be enjoyed. Craig and Kim are dedicated to making your stay romantic, enjoyable and special. You will be welcomed with a bountiful hor d'oeuvres platter and a complimentary bottle of wine or other beverage. There is also a delectable evening dessert bar. When I was here, they had no less than 6 or 7 different pies, cakes and other good things.

The living room at the Lemon Tree is furnished with a pair of teal velvet sofas, two end tables that are McIntosh speakers with alabaster lamps, a huge marble top dresser from the mid 1800s and an antique Dutch wall clock.

The dining room has a large banquet table with Queen Anne chairs, two china cabinets, a pair of high back wing chairs and several display cases with collections of cut glass, crystal candle stick and beautiful Meissen porcelain.

The den has three upholstered love seats that form a U-shape around a large coffee table. One of the many interesting items here is a life-size rocking horse.

The glass solarium is one of my favorite places. Lace curtains are draped over the ceiling to floor windows. Wicker chairs, tables and a sofa are surrounded by large, potted live plants. You won't want to leave this room.

Three guestrooms, a common room and a glass solarium are contained in the antebellum cottage of the 1840s. The common room has two upholstered love seats facing each other over a large coffee table, an aquarium, piano, a pair of leather wing chairs and a corner cupboard circa 1760.

The solarium has glass on three sides, several large plants and is furnished with white wicker chairs, a sofa and tables. This is a wonderful spot to just sit.

French doors from the common room lead to one of the guestrooms. It is furnished with a queen-size high-back oak bed, a dresser, wardrobe and a cushioned wicker chair. Beautifully framed pictures are on the walls. There is a private bath with a tub and shower. A door leads to the deck and pool.

Another guestroom has a queen-size high-back oak bed and a matching armoire. An antique day bed (like grandma's) and a wicker chair are some of the furnishings.

The third guestroom is furnished with a queen-size carved bed, a marble top dresser and a huge mirror. There is a private bath. Each of these guestrooms have cable television with HBO and VCRs.

You will be awakened in the morning with fresh coffee and homemade cinnamon rolls or blueberry muffins, delivered to your room. Then a sumptuous breakfast is served in the keeping room, dining room, or weather permitting, pool-side, surrounded by an extensive collection of tropical parrots. Kim varies her menu. There is always several juices, fresh fruit in season, coffee, tea or milk. Entrees could be homemade fresh yogurt with cream and fresh fruit or bagels, cream cheese and smoked salmon and chives, maybe the fiesta breakfast of sausage and eggs baked in a pastry shell, with German fried potatoes and either pork chops or a Kansas City strip steak. Then there could be turkey crepes with fried potatoes and a baked or caramel apple. Last but not least omelets to order, served with pieogies.

LEMON TREE INN: 407 Washington Street, Weston, 64098. (816) 386-5367. Open all year. No pets. Smoking outdoors. Children over 10. Visa, MC and Discover. Craig and Kim Rodgers, innkeepers.

DIRECTIONS: Call for complete directions.

Section Eight

PONY EXPRESS REGION

Gallatin
The Ray Home B & B

Jamesport
Country Colonial B & B

St. Joseph
Harding House
Shakespeare Mansion

Trenton
Hyde Mansion

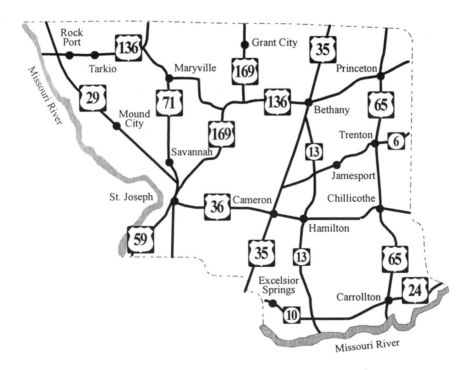

The Pony Express Region, encompassing all of northwestern Missouri, played a vital role in America's westward expansion. In the 19th century, the broad sweep of the Missouri River formed a natural boundary between the last outposts of civilization and the unexplored frontier. Lewis and Clark were among the first tourists, when they led their expedition up the Missouri River in 1894. The Pony Express Region's link with the frontier days is still evident with reminders of the Old West, including cowboys, Indians and outlaws.

Because of its strategic location, St. Joseph has served as a focal point for steamboat, stage and freight lines, and, of course, as the eastern starting point of the Pony Express.

The Pony Express Region is a land of surprising contrasts. The scenic beauty of windblown loess bluffs and fertile plains makes this a land to be seen and enjoyed. The rural character of this region makes it a natural for outdoor fun. The countryside, green and growing, is crossed by rivers and dotted with lakes.

Spread throughout the region, state parks, all with camping and water fun, provide activities for every taste. At Big Lake State Park, for example, you can boat, fish, or swim in a 625 acre Oxbow Lake. An easy drive from St. Joseph will also take you to Crowder State Park, near Trenton, with streams and trails, or to Missouri's smallest state park, 84 acre Lewis and Clark. You can also hike and picnic at nearby 422 acre Wallace State Park.

Fishing and other water fun is also available at several small lakes such as the Paho, Pony Express, Nodaway and Jo Shelby, or on the area's rivers including the Platte, Grand and Thompson. North Grand River is famous for its channel catfish.

While anglers are enjoying the waterways, hunters also find plenty to like in the area's plains and forests. Deer, rabbit and other upland game are abundant. Some of the best waterfowl hunting found anywhere is at Squaw Creek Federal Wildlife Area near Mound City. Each fall, ducks and geese gather here by the hundreds of thousands and in such great variety that the spot has been termed the Duck Mecca of the Midwest. Quail are popular as game birds in this part of the State and pheasants are moving into northern Missouri in ever larger numbers each year.

For all its beauty, northwest Missouri also has a fascinating history. This part of the State has more than its share of famous people, such as Martha Jane Canary (Calamity Jane), born in Princeton; Gen. Enoch Crowder, honored with a state park; soldier and statesman James Shields honored at Carrollton; J.C. Penney (catalog and retailing magnate), born at Hamilton (where you can see memorabilia of his life at a free museum); David Rice Atchison, 16 time president pro-tem of the U.S. Senate; and many others including Eugene Field and Dale Carnegie.

Take some time, too, to explore the Breckenridge-Gallatin area. Here Joseph Smith and his Mormon followers settled briefly in the early 1800s and identified the land of Adam-ondi-Ahman, believed by them to have been visited by Adam after his expulsion from the Garden of Eden. Another religious site in this area is Conception Abbey, a Catholic seminary at Conception Junction, noted for its beautiful frescoes and religious manuscripts dating back to the 9th century. Today, Amish farms dot the area, so you may find yourself sharing the highway with an occasional horse drawn black carriage.

Drive through the rolling hills that characterize the western edge of the region, through Mound City and Rock Port, and you'll find yet another surprise. At Tarkio stands an octagonal, three story building used in the late 1800s to house farm mules. Today, the Mule Barn Theatre offers professional summer stock productions as well as college theatre during the school year.

The Pony Express Region has enough history to fill a book. It has enough beautiful scenery to keep you breathless. It has a wealth of things to see and do for the whole family.

For the visitor, the open farm country means blue skies, unpolluted by industrial wastes and plenty of elbow room. The wide expanse of open country, broken only by rivers and forests, is ideal for outdoor fun.

THE RAY HOME BED & BREAKFAST
Gallatin

Listed on the National Register of Historic places, this seventeen room home features spacious guestrooms; two staircases; six fireplaces; stained, etched, curved and lead crystal windows. The home was built in 1896 by Anderson Ray and his wife Olive, prominent members of the First Baptist Church of Gallatin. The Rays were noted for their generous financial gifts to their church and to William Jewell College.

Bill and Jane Due purchased the house in 1988, and a seven year restoration followed. The house still contains all of the original appointments including woodwork, windows and floors. The publication, *America's Painted Ladies*, describes this home as "one of the loveliest ladies in the Midwest."

Entering the house off the wraparound porch, you are in a large foyer with a fireplace and a brass chandelier. There are two antique tables, chairs and a church pew. Take note of the beautifully carved oak staircase.

The parlor is fully carpeted and has an ornately carved mantle. Part of the furnishings include an antique organ, a Victorian sofa and chair, a pair of upholstered wing chairs, a Victorian lamp table and a grandfather clock. The room is wallpapered in a Victorian print.

The carpeted dining room has a tiled fireplace with carved oak mantle. The bay windows have cafe curtains and swags. There is a Chickering piano, an antique sideboard, a large dining table with eight chairs, a library table and two antique china cabinets holding cut glass and china. There is a great crystal chandelier. The room is papered in an ivy print.

A sitting room has a large bay window, a fireplace with a carved oak mantel, the original brass chandelier and is wall-to-wall carpeting. It is furnished with a pair of wing chairs, an upholstered cane back sofa, a French settee, television, a desk and an antique bookcase.

On the second floor, a guest sitting area has a small balcony. There is a Victrola, a table and two chairs, a pair of wing chairs, a television and VCR with plenty of movies. There is also a Victorian lamp table with a reading lamp, a carved 1920s radio and an antique parlor stove.

A front guestroom suite, carpeted wall-to-wall, is furnished with an antique Eastlake full-size bed with crocheted bedspread. There is also a Victorian settee, a pair of wing chairs, an ottoman, a Victorian table and reading lamp and a small English dressing table. The room is papered in a Victorian print. Lace curtains and swags are at the windows.

A middle guestroom off the wide hallway has a small balcony and a marble fireplace with a mahogany mantle. It is furnished with a four poster canopy bed with a lace canopy, a Victorian love seat, a bedside table with reading lamp, and a pair of Victorian arm chairs.

At the end of the hallway there is a small sitting area that has an old treadle sewing machine, a small 1930s cupboard, an antique rocker and an early model floor radio.

Just off the sitting area, a third guestroom has a bay window, an original brass chandelier and cafe curtains with swags at the windows. The room has an antique Eastlake full-size bed, a matching dresser, chest and mirror, a mirrored wardrobe and an antique table with reading lamp.

Dessert awaits guest arrival at Ray Home. Apple dumplings and lemon pie are among Jane's favorites. A full breakfast is served by candlelight. Juice, fresh fruit, stuffed french toast and fresh berry syrup, egg and sausage crepes with cheese sauce is a sample breakfast. Menu varies daily.

THE RAY HOME B & B: 212 W. Van Buren, Gallatin, 64640. (800) 301-STAY. Open all year. Children 12 and older welcome. Senior discounts. Smoking areas provided. Pets may be kenneled at local veterinarian with advance notice. Bill and Jane Due, innkeepers.

DIRECTIONS: From Kansas City take I-35 north to exit #61 (Hwy. 6). East on 6 to Gallatin. Call for reservations and directions.

JAMESPORT

To me, Jamesport, like a number of other quaint and unusual towns in Missouri, holds a lot of interest. I guess it's because I like to go back a hundred to two hundred years and try to feel what these early citizens felt as they settled and farmed the land. All too many of these small towns are slowly passing from the scene.

Jesse Harris and his family were the first white settlers in this area. The year was 1836. His neighbors, the Sac and Fox Indians, welcomed Jesse, so he built a log cabin near what is now Jamesport. Incidentally, his cabin is still standing in Jamesport City Park.

Jamesport was founded by James Gillian and Dr. James Allen. The town was incorporated in 1872 and began to flourish as a railroad town and center of commerce for the surrounding countryside.

In the 1950s, a group of Old Order Amish settled at Jamesport. Today, over 1,100 Amish residents live on about 150 farms in the area. Jamesport is only one of over 50 Amish settlements in the United States. Their religious beliefs go back to the days of the Anabaptist movement that began in Switzerland in the 16th century. Originally part of the Mennonite Swiss Brethren, they later separated from the Mennonites and came to America in the early 1700s.

The Amish lead a simple life. The plain people, as they are called, present a nineteenth century appearance as they travel the area in their horse drawn buggies, carts and farm wagons driven by family members doing daily chores or on their way to town. Their life is centered around hard work and their religious life. It is easy to spot their simple, neat, clean homes which have no window curtains. They use no electricity, own no automobiles, telephones, radios or televisions.

You can take a brief escape from today's hustle and bustle with a tour through the Amish farmlands. The Cedarwood's Amish Farmland Tours start at the Cedarwood restaurant in Jamesport and take a 30 mile tour, which takes about three hours.

In addition to the Amish tour, you may want to spend some time browsing in the interesting antique shops in Jamesport. And be sure to check out the many stores owned by the Amish, where you can purchase delicious homemade breads and pastries, spices, fabrics, hand loomed rugs and fresh vegetables.

COUNTRY COLONIAL BED & BREAKFAST
Jamesport

The original portion of the Country Colonial B & B was first sold in 1891, while it was a hotel. Over a hundred years later, Myrick and Janet den Hartog purchased the property and totally renovated the house to look as it might have when it was first built. The two story porch is a across the front of the earlier building. The addition was added at a much later time.

The entry hall is furnished with a lady's antique desk. There is an oriental area rug on the floor.

Off the hallway, a parlor is furnished with a baby grand piano and a 1920s style sofa and matching chair. A handmade armoire holds a television, games and puzzles and a VCR with lots of movies. There is a Victorian lamp table with a reading lamp, and a round coffee table. Lace curtains and drapes are at the windows and an art deco chandelier hangs from the ceiling.

The library has a built-in, wall to ceiling bookcase on either side of a patio door. They hold books of almost every description including a complete set of the works of Shakespeare. There is a walnut drop leaf table and chairs and an upholstered arm chair.

A large puzzle is always being worked on the table, so breakfast is served in the Kitchen. Here, a bay window overlooks the flower garden, bird feeders and a patio furnished with an umbrella table with chairs and a chaise lounge. The garden has a small fish pond and fountain.

The country kitchen, with brick floor, is furnished with an antique table and chairs and an antique cupboard. The room is decorated with Vintage kitchen collectibles.

The entry hall staircase leads to three guestrooms. The Veranda Room is furnished with a full-size Jenny Lind bed with lace canopy and a hand-made quilt. There is an upholstered arm chair, an antique dresser and mirror, a tripod lamp table at bedside and an old time steamer trunk displaying a collection of books, quilts and stuffed toys. A door opens onto a veranda that is furnished with wicker pieces and a willow porch swing. A private bath with tongue and groove walls, has a six foot copper bath tub. Godey's Ladies fashion prints are on the walls.

The Blue Room is just a bit smaller than the other two rooms, but is very cozy. A chair rail has blue print wallpaper above it and a stripe pattern below. An oriental carpet is on the floor and there is a cove ceiling. Blue drapes are over mini blinds at the window. The room is furnished with a full-size white iron antique bed, a rocking chair, an antique dresser with glove boxes and a pair of bedside tables. A private bath has a shower.

The Rose Room is furnished with a feather bed supported on a pre-Civil War rope bed. There is also an antique washstand, rocking chair and a wardrobe. A rose print paper is on the walls. There is a private bath with shower.

Breakfast served the morning I was here consisted of a fresh fruit mix, apple pancakes with apple syrup and bacon, a ham and grits casserole, a sausage and egg casserole, homemade Amish bread, monkey bread, Dutch letters (a puff pastry), and homemade coffeecake and coffee, tea and hot chocolate.

COUNTRY COLONIAL B & B: Downtown Jamesport, 64648. (660) 684-6711 or (800) 579-9248. Website: www.jamesport-mo.com/countrycolonial/. Chamber of Commerce Website: www.jamesport-mo.com. Open all year. A restored hundred-year old home offering three guestrooms with private baths right in the heart of Jamesport. 16 antique shops , 27 quaint craft specialty shops and 11 Amish shops. No children. No smoking. No pets. Myrick and Janet den Hartog, innkeepers.

DIRECTIONS: Call for reservations and directions.

ST. JOSEPH

St. Joseph, built on the bluffs that overlook the Missouri River and the grain and grazing lands of the western prairie, at one time bestrode the roaring trade lanes to California and Mexico. Today, it is Missouri's fourth largest city.

The site of St. Joseph was first visited by Joseph Robidoux, while on a trading expedition up the Missouri River in 1799. As an employee of the American Fur Company, in 1826, he was sent to establish an outpost at the mouth of Roy's branch in the Black Snake Hills. The next year Robidoux moved his post to the south bank of this stream. In 1834, Robidoux purchased the post from the American Fur Company for about $500.00.

In 1836, the Government, wishing to end the fighting between the pioneers and the Indians, made the Platte Purchase, which was approximately two million acres. Soon settlers began pouring in from other states.

In 1843, Robidoux had a town platted on the site of his settlement. He named it St. Joseph, after his patron saint. The town was declared the county seat in 1846. That year, the American, French, Creole, Irish, and German settlers had built 350 houses, two churches, a city hall, and a jail. The settlement of the Oregon Territory had swelled the immigrant tide, and St. Joseph, the last town in northwestern Missouri that had direct river communication with the East, was prospering. The staple commodities needed by the town were brought from St. Louis by way of the Missouri River. They were exchanged for furs and buffalo hides. Grizzled mountain men from the far West dressed in embroidered and fringed deerskin, walked about the streets.

The Pony Express became one of the most colorful and well-known chapters of St. Joseph history. On April 3, 1860, service was started with St. Joseph as the eastern terminus and Sacramento, California, the western.

It was from the Pike's Peak Stables that the young riders began their long 1,966 mile journey to the western terminus at Sacramento. Altogether, the Pony Express was in operation only 18 months before the telegraph made it obsolete. However, in that brief time the 400 young men and boys riding the Pony Express, provided a vital communications link across the continent and were credited with saving the West for the Union. in the crucial days of the Civil War.

For St. Joseph, the Civil War was merely the climax of a slowly gathering conflict. Predominantly Southern in its sympathies, the citizens here owned some 2,000 slaves. Guerilla bands used the town for a base and spread terror over most of the countryside. Almost 2,000 men went south from Buchanan County to join the Confederate forces.

Near the close of the war, the business boom, which had started in the North reach St. Joseph and continued into the era of railroad building. Freight companies were started and the livestock industry took a new lease on life. When the Civil War ended, Texas cattlemen started driving their cattle east to market Bypassing Sedalia, the cattlemen came to St. Joseph, bringing not only meat animals, but new stock. By the 1880s, St. Joseph was at the peak of postwar prosperity. In 1890, the city was said to have been the wealthiest city per capita in the nation.

Today, modern St. Joseph is a growing city with fine dining and shopping. Its theatre, music, parks and scenic boulevards have their own appeal for visitors. It's a city where travelers are as welcome now as during the pioneer days.

The Pony Express stables are open to the public as a museum, featuring exhibits that include fully equipped blacksmith and wheelwright shops of the mid-1800s.

Also in St. Joseph is the weathered home were Jesse James was shot and killed by Bob Ford. The home is a museum with exhibits on America's most famous outlaw, who was killed for the $10,000 reward in 1882.

More fragments of the past are preserved at the St. Joseph Museum housed in the 43 room Wyeth-Tootle mansion. Wide ranging exhibits in the century old building include artifacts from more than 300 Indian tribes and a huge display of mounted wildlife specimens.

The Patee House, once a fine hotel in the early days of St. Joseph, has been restored and today the four story building is known as the Patee House Museum. It draws visitors to see the reconstructed Pony Express office. The first Express headquarters was in the building. A wood burning locomotive, frontier businesses, and other Americana exhibits are here.

For a change of pace, wander through the Albrecht Art Museum, where American art is exhibited in a Georgian mansion with several acres of landscaped gardens. Or visit the unique Doll Museum with dolls from many countries and dolls dating back to 1800.

Don't pass up a visit to Kemper House, built in 1881. The antique laden home will give an insight into 19th century living. Along with furniture and everyday living needs from the past, there are many unusual antiques on display, about which little is known.

HARDING HOUSE BED & BREAKFAST
St. Joseph

Located in one of the oldest neighborhoods of St. Joseph, the Harding House was built on land that was part of a land grant signed by President Polk to William T. Harris in 1840. The wide variety of architecture in the area attests to the change in the building styles from 1840 to 1904. This house was built in 1904 for George and Minnie Johnson. He was the vice president of Wyeth Hardware Company, the largest hardware company in the world at that time. It was built in the American four square style, a new style with clean lines, using every square inch of space to advantage, and boasting bathrooms and closets not found in the more ornate Victorian homes. The interior is more reminiscent of the Victorian era. It has beautiful, old oak woodwork, an ornate carved staircase, and the original brass hardware. Fourteen gorgeous, beveled glass windows let hundreds of tiny rainbows dance throughout the house. Pocket doors leading to the living room and dining room have been restored by a local craftsman.

The living room has a working fireplace with a bookcase built-in. It is furnished with a four piece Victorian parlor set of sofa and chairs, a marble top table and an ornate mirror. There is an oriental carpet on the floor. Plenty of plants, china and porcelain make this a very interesting room.

The dining room has beautiful oak paneled walls with a plate rail. The walls are papered in a blue print above the rail. An oriental carpet is on the floor. The antique oak dining suite containing a china cabinet, small sideboard and round table and chairs are the main features. It also has an antique organ.

The hallway has an oak paneled sitting room with comfortable wing chairs, an antique desk and an old Victrola. Large oak pillars and a paneled stairway with a window seat leads to the guestrooms on the second floor.

A full breakfast is served in the dining room. It consists of country fresh eggs and cheese grits; or maybe french toast with ham, bacon, or sausage; or waffles or pancakes with whipped topping and strawberries. In the fall, Glen's famous fried apples and hot biscuits hit the spot. It's all served with juice, fresh fruit, and coffee or tea.

Upstairs are four guestrooms. One has an antique, walnut full-size bed with a high, carved headboard, an antique dresser with glove boxes, a small antique bedside table and an upholstered chair and ottoman. The bed has a crocheted spread. There are lace curtains with over drapes. Area rugs are on the floor.

An Eastlake queen-size bed, a marble top dresser, Eastlake upholstered chairs, and a table make up some of the furnishings in the second bedroom. A working fireplace is quite outstanding and great in the winter. It's a special room and ideal for newlyweds or anniversary couples. Sparkling cider is served on these occasions.

The third guestroom is furnished with an antique, iron queen-size bed, and an antique dresser. The room is decorated with lace curtains, blue swags, and blue walls. An oriental carpet is on the floor and an antique quilt hangs on one wall.

A unique, antique sleigh bed is in the fourth guestroom along with an empire chest, upholstered chair, old trunk and a rocking chair.

Two rooms share a bath, redone as it used to be with the old beaded walls and an antique pie safe for towels. It has a claw foot tub with shower. The other two rooms share a half bath and shower.

Harding House is centrally located and close to the Patee House Museum, Jesse James House, Pony Express stables, St. Joseph Museum, Alberechet Art Gallery, and the Doll Museum. Many antique shops are located in St. Joseph and the surrounding area.

HARDING HOUSE B & B: 219 North 20th Street, St. Joseph, 64501. (816) 232-7020. Open all year. A beautiful four guestroom home with two shared baths or two guestrooms with private baths. Children welcome. No pets. No smoking indoors. Glen and Mary Harding, hosts.

DIRECTIONS: From I-29, exit at Frederick Avenue in St. Joseph. Turn left to 22nd Street. Turn left to Faron Street. Then right to 20th Street. Left one block to 20th and Jules.

SHAKESPEARE CHATEAU BED & BREAKFAST
St. Joseph

This magnificent Queen Anne Victorian mansion was built in 1885 by Nathan Ogden, a wealthy banker. Designated a National Historic District, Hall Street was the site of some of the most pretentious and lavishly furnished homes during St. Joseph's golden age. Using only the finest material, these homes had quarry faced limestone to create ornate finials, decorated attic dormers, gables and parapets.

Once you step through the carved walnut doors and onto the hand-tiled floor of the foyer, you'll see some of the most beautiful, ornately carved woodwork and paneling of cherry, walnut and mahogany. A bronze bust of William Shakespeare was installed over the foyer mantlepiece. He still welcomes guests as he has over a century plus. There is a carved beamed ceiling, a floor to ceiling mantle around a tile fireplace, the original chandeliers and stained glass windows, of which there are 40 throughout the house give you a taste of what is to come.

To the left of the foyer, a parlor has a large bay window, a huge carved mantle around a tile fireplace, a brass chandelier, stained glass and burgundy carpeting. It is furnished with a pair of Queen Anne upholstered wing chairs, a carved antique drop leaf table, an upholstered sofa and a large round table with a floral arrangement.

Through a huge arch, the dining room has beamed ceilings, a carved oak fireplace mantle with a gilt mirror over it, an oriental carpet is over parquet floors, and floral wallpaper over a paneled chair rail. A pair of brass chandeliers hang over two dining tables with Queene Anne chairs. There is a reproduction of an Edison Victrola and an antique German court cupboard.

A drawing room has large bay windows with lace curtains, beautiful stained glass, an original tile fireplace has floor to ceiling carved mantle and an oriental carpet is on the floor and a brass chandelier hangs from the ceiling. It is furnished with an upholstered rosewood sofa, marble top tables and an ornately carved chair.

There are seven guestrooms. Each carries a theme from Shakespeare in its name. Four rooms are on the second floor and includes the Romeo and Juliet Suite with a marbleized fireplace and a whirlpool tub. A sitting area in a stained glass bay window has two parlor chairs and a table. The bedroom has a king-size antique half tester bed and an antique chest.

The Verona Room has a fireplace and a jacuzzi. It is furnished with a carved Victorian bed, a marble top wash stand and a carved Victorian dresser. The room is decorated in rich reds and gold tones. A bay window has stained glass.

The Midsummer's Night Dream has a king-size tester bed, a marble top antique dresser, an upholstered sofa and a marble top antique wash stand. A claw foot tub sits in the room across from your sitting area beneath stained glass windows.

The Crimson Rose Room is off the second floor rear landing. It is furnished with a heavily draped queen-size bed, a French writing desk, an upholstered camel back sofa and arm side chair and an iron table and lamp. The private bath has a 1918 iron tub and shower.

Three guestrooms are located on the third floor. The Juliet Suite has a king-size bed, a writing desk, an iron and wicker day bed which provides an extra bed if desired, a six legged table, a rocking chair and a wicker blanket chest. There is a private single-size whirlpool tub.

The Garden Suite features an open sitting area. It is furnished with an ornate king-size bed, an antique chest for a bedside table, a hiboy, a wicker love seat, two wicker chairs and a coffee table. The bath has a corner tub and a hand held shower.

The As You Like It Suite consists of two rooms. One has a king-size tall poster bed, an antique dresser, a wicker vanity and stool, a wrought iron table and a wicker chair. The sitting room has an upholstered sofa, wicker chair and a corner fireplace. The bath has a tub and shower.

A two-course breakfast consists of juice, a fruit compote in winter, fresh fruit and yogurt in summer. Stuffed French toast with ham or bacon or egg friatta. Hazelnut fresh ground coffee, tea or milk.

SHAKESPEARE CHATEAU: 809 Hall Street, St. Joseph, 64501. (888) 414-4944 and (816) 232-2667. Fax: (816) 232-0009. Website: www.shakespearechateau.com. Open all year. No pets. Smoking outside. Children 10 and over welcome. A wonderful Victorian mansion full of surprises. Craig and Kellie Ritchie, proprietors.

DIRECTIONS: Call for directions.

HYDE MANSION BED & BREAKFAST
Trenton

This handsome, colonial style mansion was the dream home of the 35th governor of Missouri, Arthur M. Hyde and his wife, Hortense. He was named to President Hoover's cabinet from 1929 to 1933. After a stay in Jefferson City and Washington, D.C., Arthur and Hortense returned to their home in Trenton. For years they toyed with the idea of building a new, more elegant residence. Unfortunately, Arthur did not live to see the house completed. He passed away in 1947. Mrs. Hyde decided to carry out the plans and lived in the house for several years. In 1975, she moved to St. Croix, Virgin Islands. She passed away at the age of 81.

In 1988, Robert and Carolyn Brown bought the house from the Hyde estate and completely restored the home.

You enter the house by way of a center hall with oak floors, Persian rugs, and an elegant stairway. Portraits of the Hydes are on the walls at the foot of the stairs.

The spacious parlor to the left is done in mauve and gray with white walls and lace curtains. A fireplace and grand piano are part of the room's features. It is furnished with a sofa and two club chairs. A pair of wing chairs are in front of the fireplace. In one corner is a love seat and coffee table, and two chairs and a lamp table are in another. Nicely framed pictures are on the walls. Here you can relax and visit with other guests.

The Browns prepare the breakfast each morning before departing for their real estate office downtown. Rosalie Snuffer, the housekeeper, comes on the scene and takes over with equal efficiency.

Carolyn likes to offer a variety on her breakfast menu. Eggs are cooked the way guests want them along with a choice of sausage, ham or bacon and hash brown potatoes. Then there are homemade blueberry muffins, biscuits or toast, fresh fruit and juice, coffee or tea.

Breakfast is served in the dining room. There are five tables with cotton floral table cloths. There are lots of house plants and nice pictures. For business persons, who need a little privacy, you may eat in a small breakfast room.

Guests have their choice of seven guestrooms, each having its own personality and decor. Carolyn painstakingly selected the wallpapers, paintings, curtains, pictures, bedspreads and carpeting to create a homey, but unmistakably refined atmosphere. Each room has its own private bath, cable television, telephone and desk area.

The six upstairs guestrooms are all cozy rooms under the eaves. Some have queen-size poster beds, some queen-size oak beds with matching chests and night stands. One also has a hide-a-bed in addition to the queen-size cherry bed. The dormer windows have small sitting areas.

All guests may use the comfortable upstairs den equipped with books, a television and game table. Or, you can relax on the screened-in back porch with its cheerful white wicker furniture. There is a rear entrance to the second floor, and guests are given a key so they can easily come and go. There is also a patio that is furnished with tables and chairs. It overlooks a garden and huge old trees.

HYDE MANSION B & B: 418 East 7th Street, Trenton, 64683. (816) 359-5631. A rambling seven guestroom home, where everything has been done to make your stay memorable. Open all year. Children over 12 welcome. No pets. No smoking in house. Carolyn and Robert Brown, hosts.

DIRECTIONS: From Kansas City, take I-35 north to Jamesport. Exit on #61 to Trenton. Turn right on 7th Street. From any north-south highway, take Hwy. 65 to Hwy. 6. Turn west into Trenton. Call for reservations.

Section Nine

LITTLE DIXIE REGION

Arrow Rock
Borgman's B & B

Boonville
Lady Goldenrod B & B

Fayette
Sweetbrier B & B

Lexington
Graystone B & B
Victorianne B & B

Marshall
Oliver Homestead

Mexico
La Paz B & B

New Franklin
Rivercene B & B

Pilot Grove
J.D.'s B & B

Rocheport
Katy O'Neil B & B
School House B & B
Yates House B & B

Sweet Springs
Inn at Patrick Place

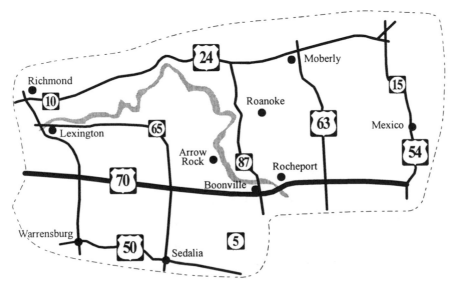

Shortly after the Louisiana Territory was purchased by the United States, the first of the early pioneers started to settle the region now known as "Little Dixie."

Most of these settlers came from the southern states of Virginia, North and South Carolina, Kentucky, and Tennessee. With them they brought their traditions and way of life, especially their love of fine horses, fox hunting and whiskey making.

I'm not sure where the boundary lines should be for the Little Dixie Region, and I don't know if anyone does. Someone told me it was more of a feeling than a physical boundary. So, for all practical purposes, here are the boundaries for this exciting region.

The southern border is I-70, west from the junction of Highway 54 at Kingdom City to the Boonville exit at 101. Then south on Highway 5 to Highway 50 (17 miles). West on Highway 50 to Highway 13 at Warrensburg (43 miles). (Warrensburg itself is in the Lake of the Ozarks Region.) The western boundary is from Highway 13 at Highway 50, north to Highway 10 at Richmond (45 miles). The northern boundary is east from Richmond on Highway 10 to Highway 24 at Carrollton (30 miles). East on Highway 24 to the junction of Highway 24 and Highway 15 at Paris (85 miles). The eastern boundary is from Highway 15 at Paris, south to Highway 54 at Mexico. Then, south on Highway 54 to I-70 at Kingdom City (42 miles).

The first place I would suggest you see is the town of Rocheport. Taking I-70, it is just eight miles west from Columbia, then exit at Route BB to the town. At one time, it was an important landing place and ferry crossing on the Boonslick Road. There is a nice little museum here and a circa 1845 Christian Church. During the Civil War, when Bloody Bill Anderson's guerillas made their headquarters here, Rocheport won the infamous title of the "Outlaw Capital."

The School House, Katy O'Neil and Yates House Bed & Breakfasts are located here. On your way be sure to stop off at *Les Bourgeois' Vineyard and Winery,* located on Highway BB atop the Missouri River bluffs. Here you can sample the table wines and try the cheese, sausage, fruit and breads, while you relax in the warm ambience of a small winery and enjoy a spectacular view of the valley below. (573) 698-3401.

South of Boonville, on Highway 135 in the heart of Little Dixie, is the small village of New Lebanon, with a total of three buildings and a population of 15. Two of the buildings are the 100-year-old school house and the 138 year-old New Lebanon Church. Both are listed on the National Register of Historic Places. The third building houses *Abe's Country Store,* owned by Jeannette Heaton. The store has the original counters, showcases, shelving, scales, cash register, and the remaining original merchandise that was on hand when the store closed. It's a real step back in time. Jeannette also has an antique shop here. The item that caught my eye first was a child's old farm wagon. There were lots of advertising tins and signs, crocks, quilts, and primitives. Note the Salesman's sample pot-bellied stove. (660) 366-4482.

By all means, plan to make a visit to several of the historic homes that are open to the public. *Pleasant Green Plantation House* dated back to 1820. The seventh generation of the builder, Anthony Walker, still owns the property. It is furnished with much of the furniture that once belonged to Anthony Walker. (660) 834-3945.

Then there's *Crestmead,* built around 1859. The farm was operated by slave labor until the end of the Civil War. Today the farm raises Shorthorn cattle descended from the herd established here in 1888. (660) 343-4140

Another place to visit is *Ravenswood,* an 1880 Victorian mansion. It was built by Captain Charles Leonard on 1,900 acres, established in 1824. Six generations of the Leonard family have lived here. (660) 427-5562. All of these homes are on the National Register of Historic Places.

The towns of central Missouri reflect fascinating history, a past shaped by men such as Kit Carson, Daniel Boone, Senators Thomas Hart Benton and Graham Vest, Dr. John Sapppington, and artist, George Caleb Bingham. A trip into the western part of the region is a step into frontier history. The old trails such as Santa Fe, Oregon and Great Salt Lake, passed through Missouri often following the course of major rivers where the going was easiest. Pioneers heading west using these trails on their way to the frontier liked what they saw and many went no further. Today, the little town of Arrow Rock remembers its days as an important stop on the Santa Fe Trail. By river and land, the great floor of western migration passed through. Now the town is a living relic of the past, with forty historic sites. Borgman's Bed & Breakfast is in Arrow Rock.

A short drive to Boonville with its preserved 19th century buildings is the site of Missouri's first Civil War Battle. It was fought here on June 17, 1861. Enjoy the drive along the river bluffs where Indian mounds are in evidence. Lady Goldenrod and Rivercene Bed & Breakfasts are located in Boonville.

A little further to the west, a major Civil War battle in Missouri was fought in Lexington. The Battle of the Hemp Bales is remembered today with a State Historic site centered around the red brick Anderson House. The town's beautiful old colonial courthouse, too, bears its scar. A cannon ball is still embedded in one column. The Graystone and Victorianne Bed & Breakfasts are located in Lexington.

Although it is not often that Missouri is mentioned in accounts of the Civil War, the fact is only two states has more Civil War battles than Missouri. Daniel Boone came to Missouri when "back east" got too crowded. He lived in the State for the rest of his life. Boonslick historic site is located, appropriately, near the town of Boonesboro, just north of Boonville. You'll also see history and traditions preserved at Moberly's Railroad Museum, the Chariton County Historical Museum in Salisbury, and the Audrain Country Historical Museum in the town of Mexico. La Paz Bed & Breakfast is in Mexico.

J.D.'s Bed & Breakfast is located in Pilot Grove. Another bed & breakfast in the Little Dixie Region is The Oliver House Bed & Breakfast in Marshall.

ARROW ROCK

A rrow Rock, once a bustling frontier town with a peak population of 1,000, is today a tranquil, unique village with an aura of the past found in few places in the United States. Its population today is approximately 130.

As was often the case, Arrow Rock developed into a frontier town because of its strategic location along a road to the West — The Missouri River. However, even before the white man appraised the value of the spot, the Indians had put Arrow Rock to good use. An Indian trail, crossing the entire state of Missouri, generally followed the course of the Missouri River. The channel of the river narrowed somewhat at Arrow Rock. Consequently, the Indian trail crossed the river there. Once across the river on the south side, the trail followed a break in the bluffs formed by a creek, to the high ground and then continued on West.

French explorers and trappers of the early 1700's were probably the first white men to see Arrow Rock. One of the earliest recorded comments about the place was made on June 9, 1804 by Lewis and Clark on their journey to explore the river to the West. Clark returned in 1808 on his way West to build Fort Osage. He observed on his trip back to St. Louis, that Arrow Rock was a "handsome spot for a town."

By 1817, there were enough settlers moving into and through the mid-Missouri area to justify a ferry at Arrow Rock. In November of that year, John Ferrill built a tavern at the ferry landing to accommodate the travelers. In 1820, the tavern and ferry were owned by David Todd, an uncle of Mary Todd Lincoln, the president's wife. Most of these settlers were from Kentucky or Virginia.

On September 1, 1821, William Becknell and his party of four left Franklin, Missouri on a trading expedition, which took them to Santa Fe. Franklin, Missouri was just across the river and downstream from Arrow Rock. This was the first of many expeditions to the country around Santa Fe, which all began at either Franklin or Arrow Rock, until Independence became established as an outfitting post.

The town of Arrow Rock was born on June 10, 1829, through the donation of a fifty acre tract of land. The town was platted by M.M. Marmaduke and was originally called New Philadelphia. The name was changed to Arrow Rock by an act of the Legislature in 1835.

Arrow Rock eventually became a business and social center for the area. From 1839 to 1840, Arrow Rock served as the temporary County Seat of Saline County. The year 1842 saw the Arrow Rock Lodge W55 F.F. & M. become the first Masonic Lodge in Saline County. "The Philamatheans," a local literary and debating club, was active in the 1850's. By 1860, the population had reached 1,000, river traffic to Arrow Rock was at its peak, weekly stage line service was established and a telegraph line was installed.

In its heyday, Arrow Rock counted among its citizens three governors, none of whom served a full term in office. They were Meredith M. Marmaduke (1844), John S. Marmaduke (1844-1847), and Claiborn F. Jackson (1860-1861). It was also the home of the artist, George Caleb Bingham, Dr. John Sappington of medical fame, and General Thomas A. Smith, an agriculturist.

Arrow Rock began to diminish in importance and population after the Civil War. By 1873, the population was 600. Major fires scarred the town in 1873, and again in 1901. The fire in 1873 was believed to have been the work of three young arsonists, who were reportedly lynched by mobs. By 1901, Arrow Rock was considered very old and something of a relic.

The death knell for Arrow Rock was sounded in 1923, when a bridge across the Missouri River was constructed at Glasgow instead of Arrow Rock. Thus the irony of Arrow Rock is complete — it rose to importance because of its location along the major transportation route to the frontier and declined in importance when bypassed by more modern transportation routes.

The past continues to live in Arrow Rock. Stroll down Main Street for a walk through the Nineteenth Century. The village has a working blacksmith shop, a circa 1872 church that houses the Lyceum Theatre, George Caleb Bingham's home, a gunsmith shop dating back to the 1840s, an old newspaper office with antique presses, the old jail, courthouse and of course the Arrow Rock Tavern.

In 1964, the National Park Service, Department of the Interior, designated the Village of Arrow Rock a National Historic Landmark, because of its association with the beginning of the Santa Fe Trail.

Today, Arrow Rock and the 150-acre State Historic Site adjoining the town are on display as a living history of our frontier past.

There are several nice antique shops in Arrow Rock. One, *C. Frederick Breitwiess Antiques* is located at #6 Public Square on the Boardwalk. (660) 837-3777. When I visited here, I saw a barley twish drop leaf table, a circa 1850 Windsor chair, a pine blanket chest, an 1890's maple wash stand, a pine meal bin, a set of four Hitchcock chairs, an English Mahogany armoire, a circa 1886 parlor table, a 19th century grandfather clock, a mahogany two drawer table, a tilt-top table, a circa 1820 English drop front desk, and a set of four rush seat ladder back chairs. There was also a set of eight pieces of 1860's iron garden set. Smaller pieces included baskets, pictures, Alfred Meakin Royal Ironstone, coin and sterling flatware from 1817 to 1850. There were some nice antique hinged porcelain lidded boxes, a pair of Staffordshire dogs, plates and platters, cut glass, pitcher and bowl sets, and candle sticks.

EVERGREEN RESTAURANT
Arrow Rock

I very much enjoy old buildings and the older they are, the more I enjoy them. The building that houses the Evergreen Restaurant is certainly old. This Italianate Revival home was built of stone during the 1840s. Fully restored, it is very much the way it was almost 160 years ago.

My daughter, my grandson and I ate here. The ambiance was great, the food was excellent and the service was outstanding.

Shrimp salad with poached shrimp, artichoke hearts, tomato, mixed greens and remoulade sauce, seafood quiche and ginger beef were some of the luncheon fare.

Dinner selections included roast prime rib served with natural Au jus, grilled lamb chops, brochette of pork, stuffed chicken breast and shrimp New Orleans style.

We all thought this a nice place to eat, and I'm sure you will think so too.

EVERGREEN RESTAURANT: Hwy. 41, one block north of Main Street, P.O. Box 125, Arrow Rock, 65320. (660) 837-3251. Hours: September - May, weekends only by advance reservation. June through August, Wednesday through Sunday for lunch and dinner. Bob and Chris Rappold, owners.

OLD ARROW ROCK TAVERN
Arrow Rock

In 1834, Joseph Huston, a former Virginian noticing the swelling numbers of immigrants to Arrow Rock from the East, decided a need existed for a tavern. Slaves were put to work cutting down huge walnut trees, baking bricks and quarrying stone for the building. In the 1840s, a two room addition was used for Huston's grocery store and for a ballroom and meeting hall. A dining room and kitchen were on the first floor. It soon became the most important structure in town. The State of Missouri acquired the building in 1923 and restored the tavern.

Today, one of the oldest inns west of the Mississippi River stands renewed as a reminder of those days when the Nation was young and is once again offering home cooked meals in a setting of 160 years ago. Clay Marsh and Chet Breitweitser are the proprietors.

The Old Arrow Rock Tavern offers a complete menu including my favorite, fried chicken. Other entrees are catfish and country ham, all accompanied by fresh vegetables, desserts and beverage. Desserts include bread pudding with rum sauce, chess pie and blackberry cobbler.

OLD ARROW ROCK TAVERN: Main Street, Arrow Rock, 65320. (660) 837-3200. Open April 1st through December 31. June, July and August open 11 to 2 on Tuesday and Sunday. Wednesday-Saturday 11 to 2 and 5 to 8. April, May, September through December weekends only. Call for hours. Bunny Thomas, general manager.

BORGMAN'S BED & BREAKFAST
Arrow Rock

Captain George Bingham, a relative of the great artist George Caleb Bingham, built this house sometime between 1850 and 1860. It is a classically simple farmhouse with a two-story porch across the front. Captain Bingham served in the local militia during the Civil War and afterward came back to Arrow Rock and put a second floor addition on the house. The house has remained a private residence ever since.

In 1982, Helen Borgman purchased the house, and along with her daughter Kathy, remodeled and decorated the entire home. The old place still retains all of its charm. The plank floors and woodwork throughout are original. Kathy designed the stenciled wall borders that adorn each of the guestroom ceilings.

The wide pine floors in the entry hall are covered with area rugs. It is wallpapered and has an antique hanging lamp that hangs from the ceiling. Look in the old trunk here. You might just see the hand-crafted gift you've been hoping to find.

The family/living room is available for guests. It is nicely furnished with sofa and chairs. Wind up the old Victrola for a song, choose a game or puzzle, read or just sit awhile.

The kitchen is furnished with beautiful antiques including an oak pedestal table and matching chairs. There is also an early oak cupboard.

The breakfast is continental plus! It's a family style breakfast with all you can eat cinnamon rolls, juice, fruit, freshly baked bread, jelly and coffee or tea. The bread is a house specialty.

A first floor guestroom (Kathy's Room), has a three piece, solid walnut bedroom suite that features a large four poster bed. Old quilts cover it. There is also an upholstered arm chair, a gateleg table, and a rocking chair. The windows have lace curtains.

On the second floor, a large carpeted sitting room is furnished with antique rocking chairs and a television. The hall opens onto the porch overlooking the historic town.

Three guestrooms are on the second floor. They are all large, cheerful rooms furnished with family heirlooms. Minnie's Room has two antique, full-size beds, an antique dresser, an upholstered rocker, an arm chair and a table.

Anna's Room has an antique, full-size Eastlake bed, an antique cradle, a rocking chair, washstand, dresser, and an early platform rocker. These two rooms are named for Kathy's grandmothers.

Helen's Room is furnished with an antique full-size bed, an antique dresser and a rocking chair. All of the guestrooms are decorated with small antiques, prints, pictures and hurricane lamps. There are lace curtains at the windows and braided or throw rugs on the floor.

Kathy works for The Friends of Arrow Rock, Inc. and will tell you all about the little village and what it has to offer. She can recommend restaurants and also a tour guide for the town.

Some of the attractions you don't want to miss are the fine repertory theatre, the Lyceum, antique shops and the old country store. Marilynne Bradley, a top-notch artist, holds a watercolor workshop in Arrow Rock each year in July.

BORGMAN'S B & B: Arrow Rock 65320. (660) 837-3350. Open all year. A four guestroom, pre-Civil War home in a town that is a national landmark. Children welcome. No smoking. No pets. Close to all the historic sites. Helen and Kathy Borgman, hosts.

DIRECTIONS: From Kansas City or St. Louis, Take I-70 to Hwy. 41 (four miles west of Boonville). Go North on Hwy. 41. It is 13 miles to Arrow Rock. Turn right on Van Buren (first street into town). One blocks to the inn.

LADY GOLDENROD INN BED & BREAKFAST
Boonville

The home which is now Lady Goldenrod Inn B & B was built at the turn of the century by John Bell and is listed on the National Register of Historic Places. It is a Queen Anne style with a wide veranda, bay windows and some gingerbread trim. Another owner, Thomas Hogan who designed and built the unusual staircase leading to the front porch, also built the town's first brick street and originated the waterworks and sewage system. George and Lica Ruselowski, the present owners, have preserved the home's historic integrity. All of the woodwork, staircase, windows and doors are original.

Entering the home by the wide wraparound porch, you are in an entry hall. A highly carved stairway leads to the second floor guestrooms. At the first landing, there is a large stained glass window. The entry hall has an antique love seat, a Victorian parlor table and an antique drop front secretary. A pocket door leads to the parlor.

The parlor is furnished with a Victorian love seat, a pair of matching Eastlake chairs, an old wind-up Victrola, a secretary desk, a bookcase and an early, upholstered open arm rocking chair. A tile fireplace has a very unusual carved mantelpiece.

The dining room also has pocket doors and a tiled fireplace with a columned mantelpiece. A large bay window has lace curtains. The room is furnished with an oval ball and claw foot table, eight matching oak, high back chairs, and a kitchen cupboard. There is a very nice antique quarter sawn oak sideboard and an oval oak china cabinet that holds a collection of carnival glass, plates and antique clocks. A crystal chandelier is over the table.

A home cooked, full breakfast is served in the dining room with such fare as juices, fresh fruit in season, homemade muffins, bread and apple butter, eggs, sausage or bacon and biscuits with gravy. The coffee is freshly ground in an antique coffee grinder.

At the top of the stairs, a wide hallway has a small sitting room with several wicker chairs, a tea cart, an etagere and a reading lamp. The hall itself has a small settee, a pair of late 19th century chairs and a Victorian table. The bath, shared by the hosts and guests, has the original claw foot tub.

There are two guestrooms. One is furnished with a queen-size brass bed with a handmade quilt, an antique marble top dresser with candle stands, a Victorian rocker, a marble top Victorian parlor table for a night stand and a wicker doll buggy. Several items of children's vintage clothing are displayed. The other guestroom has twin Jenny Lind beds, an antique oak dresser and a pair of white wicker arm chairs. There are two ornate metal base tables; one with a reading lamp and one between the twin beds. The beds have pink spreads, the windows have lace curtains and swags at the bay window. A pink and blue floral print paper in on the walls.

LADY GOLDENROD INN B & B: 629 East Spring Street, Boonville, 65233. (660) 882-5764. Open all year. No pets. (Resident dog and three cats.) Children welcome. Smoking in designated places. High chair, crib and roll away are available. Just a few minutes to the Katy Trail, antique shops and restaurants. George & Lica Ruselowski, innkeepers.

DIRECTIONS: From I-70, take Hwy. 5 exit north to Spring Avenue. Turn right on Spring. House is on the corner of 7th and Spring.

SWEETBRIAR BED & BREAKFAST
Fayette

Located directly across from Central Methodist College in Fayette, Sweetbriar is a circa 1890 home that offers quiet enjoyment of small town country life.

A nice front porch is an ideal place to sit and watch the younger generation, as they head for college classes. For seating, there is a church pew and wicker chairs. There is also an ice cream table and chairs.

When you enter the house, you are in an entry hall that is nicely wallpapered in an early print pattern. There is an antique desk, a willow bent chair and house plants.

A carpeted front parlor is furnished with a sofa upholstered in a crewel pattern, an antique walnut pie safe, a cherry drop leaf table, an upholstered arm chair and an antique coffee bin. The room is decorated with plants and craft items, mostly from Missouri artisans.

A living room has an antique sofa in front of a fireplace that has a 150 year old mantelpiece. There is also a blue plaid wing chair, an antique Amish wardrobe and a grandfather clock.

The dining room also has a fireplace. There is a long trestle table with bow-back chairs, an antique jelly cupboard and an antique cupboard from a farm in Maine. A porcelain and brass chandelier hangs over the table.

Each of the guestrooms have central air, ceiling fans, and cable television. The Blue Room is furnished with a full-size bed covered with a handmade quilt, an antique washstand with towel bar, a rush seat rocking chair and a lamp table with a reading lamp. The room is decorated with quilts and nice pictures. Blue curtains are at the windows, which have stained glass inserts.

The Garden Room is furnished with a queen-size short poster bed and a roll-away for a third person. There is an upholstered arm chair, a mirror stand and an antique dresser. White curtains with floral swags are the windows and area rugs cover the floor.

The Uncle Sam Room has a full-size antique iron bed, a 1930s vanity and a rocker from a farmhouse in Iowa. The shuttered windows have swags.

A large bathroom with both tub and shower is shared. Guests are furnished with robes during their stay.

Breakfast is served in either the dining room, or on the screened-in porch, weather permitting. Carolyn's breakfast consists of juice, fresh fruit in season or fresh thawed fruit in winter. One of her guests' favorite dishes is creamed eggs with cheddar cheese on an English muffin served with ham or bacon and onions. Another favorite is ham, egg and mushroom pie. There are homemade blueberry muffins, caramel rolls, jams, jellies, coffee or tea.

Mints are always placed in the rooms, and coffee is available in your room before breakfast.

Maison on Main is a circa 1870 home that has been recently been put on the National Historic Register. It is one of eight original brick streets in Fayette. It is decorated in a French Country theme with a yellow, blue and rose color scheme. There are two large bedrooms with private baths. The Rose Room and The LeFleur Room. Both rooms have queen-size beds, cable TV and ceiling fans. The sitting room has a sleeper sofa and is a comfortable room to gather for games, TV or conversation. There is a dining room and kitchen plus two porches. A continental breakfast with rolls, muffins, bagels, cereal, juice and coffee is available for your breakfast. Reservations are made by calling the Sweets at (660) 248-1117. The key can be picked up at Sweetbriar B & B.

SWEETBRIAR B & B: 506 N. Church, Fayette, 65248. (660) 248-1117. Open all year. A three room B & B with shared bath. Close to Columbia and Rocheport, Katy Trail and Historic Arrow Rock. No pets. Smoking on porches. MC/Visa accepted. Carolyn and George Sweet, innkeepers.

DIRECTIONS: Sweetbriar is twenty-two miles west of Columbia, 120 miles east of Kansas City, and 145 miles west of St. Louis. From St. Louis take I-70 to the Fayette exit at Hwy. 40 and 240, just past Columbia. Take Hwy. 240 straight into Fayette. The inn is located on the Highway across from the College. From Kansas City, take the Hwy. 5 exit north through Boonville and New Franklin to Fayette. Turn right at the junction of 5 and 240 and go about two blocks. The inn is on the right.

LEXINGTON

Thisarea along the Missouri River had been regarded as an attractive place of residence long before the European settlers arrived. Numerous burial grounds, thousands of arrow heads, spear points, stone knives and innumerable fragments of pottery tell an eloquent story of the Indian villages that dotted these green hillsides before the coming of the white man.

Lexington is one of the oldest cities in Missouri. The first white men to travel around or near the area that is now Lexington are believed to have been Lewis and Clark. They ascended the Missouri River, passing these same bluffs in 1803, and were followed by trappers and traders in increasing numbers.

Founded in 1822 by settlers from Lexington, Kentucky, the early population was primarily a mixture of prosperous merchants from all parts of the Southern states of Kentucky and Virginia, along with groups of gamblers, slave traders, and speculators. In 1823 it was named the county seat.

During the middle of the 19th century, Lexington was one of the main river ports on the Missouri River. At times, there were as many as a dozen boats in port at once. In addition to the river trade, one of the reasons for the importance of the town was its agricultural richness. Early farmers profited greatly from hemp, cattle and tobacco. The area still enjoys that richness today, and is the largest producer of apples in the state. The Waverly-Lexington area produces almost thirty percent of the State's output, or almost twice as much as the second largest producing area.

Lexington became a strategic point in early 1861, just prior to the Civil War. The Union army was ordered to hold the important river port at all costs in order to keep the Confederate forces north of the Missouri River from joining the Missouri State Guard under Gen. Sterling Price's command. Lexington is the site of a three day battle during the war, and the scars of the major battle are still visible on the 105 acre Battle of Lexington State Historical Site.

Another place you don't want to miss seeing, is the most beautiful courthouse in the state. It is listed on the National Register of Historic Places. Built in 1847, this classical temple form brick structure of handsome colonial design with a tall clock tower and massive stone columns is on of the oldest continuously used courthouses in the State. A cannonball, fired during the siege of Lexington, hit the courthouse and is still embedded in one of the columns. Be sure to see the Lexington Historical Museum, the circa 1848 Christ Church Episcopal, with its pews of solid walnut, and the Elks Lodge Building, built in 1846.

An interesting sidelight to the historical aspects of Lexington is cited in three names. The county, Lafayette, is synonymous with liberty (Lafayette was the gallant Frenchman, who helped youthful America win her independence from England during the Revolutionary War). The first county seat, Mount Vernon, was named for the home and last resting place of the Nation's first president The present county seat bears the name of the first battle of the Revolutionary War and the site of the "shot heard round the world," Lexington, Massachusetts.

Riley's Irish Pub, at 913 Main Street, is located in what was once the infamous "Block 42," a saloon block, which women and children avoided. Legend has it that there were 42 saloons and one church on this block... but really "Block 42" refers to the block number on the plat map. The pub was built in 1890. It is 18 feet wide and 80 feet long. The front stained glass window, pressed tin ceiling, tile floor, and back bar are original to the building.

Today the pub is open to all. The pub serves quality foods and drinks. The menu features a grilled (not breaded) tenderloin, salmon steak, and beef steaks. A children's menu is also available. You can't go wrong here.

The proud history of this quiet, warm and friendly town in the western part of the State includes having been the home of five colleges, including the first Masonic college in the world; and the headquarters of the famous westward freighting firm that founded the Pony Express.

Today, Lexington, with its 100 plus antebellum homes, is well worth a few days of anyone's time. Visitors can wander through museums, tour the old homes, dine and shop, or just walk down tree lined streets and experience the gracious living of the past.

GRAYSTONE PARK
Lexington

The first portion of this 10-room Greek Revival mansion called Graystone Park was built in 1833 by Dr. Matthew Flournoy, a dentist. It consists of two first floor rooms and two second floor rooms with a central chimney. As his practice flourished, he added the front portion in 1850. It was built of slave-made bricks with the tone for the window sills of native gray limestone, hence the name Graystone. The house stands today, as it did 165 years ago. Five of the eight fireplaces, the 11-foot ceilings, walnut staircase, woodwork and doors are all original to the house. During restoration by previous owners, documents dating back to the 1840s, 50s and 60s were found in the attic. They are on display throughout the house. Allen Brauninger and Judith Pitcher, the owners, have decorated and furnished the house with their antiques.

An oriental carpet covers the front entry hall floors. A crystal chandelier hangs from the ceiling. There is an antique huntboard and large table.

Two parlors are on the first floor, both furnished with mid-1800s pieces. The first parlor has a fireplace which is cast iron and hand grained to resemble marble. The walls have a burgundy Victorian Jacquard pattern paper. Ecru drapes are at the windows. An oriental carpet is on the floors. It is furnished with a circa 1840 chickering square grand piano, an upholstered Empire sofa, a gateleg drop leaf table, a pair of etageres, two bookcases and a lamp table and lamp. There is also an upholstered sofa and a marble top parlor table.

The second parlor, across the hall, also has an oriental carpet and a Rococo style chandelier hands from the ceiling. A Victorian pattern wallpaper covers the walls that have family pictures. It is furnished with an upholstered camel-back sofa, a Queen Anne style coffee table, two upholstered barrel back chairs, a stereo and a television. Two built in cupboards are original.

A Queen Anne style table, 12 feet long, eight matching chairs, a circa 1840 carved china cabinet, a marble top sideboard from 1840, an etagere and a library table are part of the furnishings in the dining room. Bay windows have lace curtains. Victorian floral print paper is on the walls along with an 1880s Waterbury clock.

The three guestrooms are on the second floor along with a nursery. An antique rolltop desk is on the second floor landing.

The Yellow Room is furnished with a circa 1856 burled walnut high back bed, a matching marble top dresser and wash stand. There is a pair of upholstered Victorian arm chairs also. The original gas chandelier hangs from the ceiling. The walls are painted yellow and there are area carpets on the floor. Lace curtains are at the windows. One of the original fireplaces is in this room.

The Pink Room also has one of the original fireplaces. It is furnished with an antique full-size high back bed, a stack bookcase, and the antique wardrobe that once belonged to Col. Ryland Todhunter, who was an officer in the Confederate Army. He lived in the house from 1901 until 1945. Antique oriental rosewood wishbone chairs are on either side of a large brass table. Lace curtains are at the windows, the walls are painted pink. A brass chandelier hangs from the ceiling.

Overlooking the front portion of the property, a smaller third guestroom has an oriental style carpet. The walls are papered with a yellow and grey floral stripe paper. It has a single bed and a long bookcase. There is a small balcony.

The nursery has a brass day bed, a rocker and a chest. Allen found an antique iron crib, had it repaired and painted and it is also in this room.

A brass chandelier hangs from the hall ceiling. A full bath with a tub and shower are off this hall.

Juice, a fresh fruit compote in season, homemade muffins and pastries, coffee, tea or milk are offered at breakfast.

GRAYSTONE B & B: 324 South 25th Street, Lexington, 64067. (660) 259-7775 or 7017 for information. E-mail: graystonellc@sprintmail.com. Children welcome. Pets within reason. Smoking on porch. An historical home where once the Union Army marched across the lawns to the Battle of Lexington. Allen Brauninger and Judith Pitcher, innkeepers.

DIRECTIONS: From I-70 east or west, exit at Hwy. 13 north (exit 49). Go 13 miles to Lexington. At the first stop light, go straight on 20th Street to South Street. Turn right on South Street to 25th Street. Turn right one block. Graystone is on your left.

THE VICTORIANNE BED & BREAKFAST
Lexington

The year was 1885 when banker, Robert Taubman, built a Queen Ann Victorian house in Lexington, Missouri. Mr. Taubman wanted his house to be the largest in town, and the story is told that he went out in the night to measure other homes to be sure that his was the largest being built. The house is brick with a foundation of stone three feet thick. The curved turrets of the house and the oriels give it the appearance of a castle. A beautiful brick driveway and the iron fence surround the front and side yard.

Today this house is the home of Victorianne Mystiques, bed and breakfast and antique shop, owned by Mary Ault and Shirley Childs.

Inside the front door is a beautiful oak staircase with spelter figurines on the newel posts, all original to the house. Overhead is a "thousand eyes" chandelier, due to the pattern it makes on the ceiling when illuminated.

There are ten fireplaces adorned with Italian tile. The fireplaces were originally coal burning and have now been converted to gas. The tiles of fireplace in the foyer carry out the theme of the spelter figurines.

Pocket doors separate two of the three parlors. It is interesting to note that on one side the pocket door is oak, which matches the woodwork in the hall and on the other side of the pocket door cherry wood, matches the trim and fireplace mantle in the other parlor.

A baby grand piano is located in the front parlor. The fireplace there is carved cherry. Black lusters are on the piano. Pictures in the room include 1800's silk pictures, a Maxfield Parrish print, and Bernard Martin remarked pictures, and a vase from the time of Marie Antoinette. One window is of decorative stained glass.

In the center parlor there is also an antique grandfather clock. There is a cherry fireplace with carved lions heads, above which is a Maxfield Parrish print. A curio cabinet in the room has many interesting collectibles including Goebels and a Llardro. Early French vases and a Phoenix glass lamp, and other old lamps, a love seat, and an antique French table are also in this parlor.

The third parlor contains a large Remington bronze and art work reflecting various cities of the world. The basket-weave tile of the fireplace is surrounded by cherry wood.

The dining room with its tin ceiling, oak fireplace and beautiful stained glass window, is the site where guests are treated to breakfast while at the Victorianne. The guests are seated at a beautiful Queen Anne style table. On the buffet is a cut glass punch bowl and epergnes. Throughout the downstairs there are showcases displaying many items of interest.

The Victorianne has the carriage house, and two bedrooms in the main house for guest usage. The carriage house is self-contained, much like an apartment. There is a sitting area, a TV, a dining area, an antique armoire, bed, dresser and chest of drawers. For your comfort there is also a small refrigerator stocked with soda. This accommodation has private bath.

In the main house two bedrooms are available – the Red Room and the Green Room.

Guests in the main house share a bathroom with an old fashioned tub including a brass ring holding the shower curtain. The bath has a beautiful hand-painted prismed light fixture.

The Red Room has a queen-size bed of period style with a fainting couch located at the foot of the bed. The room has three windows, which makes it seem very light and airy. Appropriate pictures for the period adorn the walls. The tile on the fireplace is a subdued red complemented by a red carpet.

The Green Room has a full-size bed and includes the usual bedroom furniture, and a desk.

A gazebo houses the hot tub in which a guest can relax before retiring. Guests are served a "continental plus" breakfast. Mary, known for her fresh ground gourmet coffee sees that the guests get a good start for their day.

THE VICTORIANNE B & B: 1522 South Street, Lexington, 64067. (660) 259-2868 or (660) 259-6691. E-mail: Msrg@land.net. A wonderful Victorian Queen Anne home. Two guestrooms and a suite in the carriage house. No children. No pets. No smoking in the house. Mary Ault and Shirley Childs, innkeepers.

DIRECTIONS: From Kansas City go I-70 to the Lexington exit (Route O). Go north on Route O to Hwy. 13. Continue north on Hwy. 13 until you come to a stop sign. At the corner of South Street turn right. Go three blocks east and you will see the Christian Church – to the left you will see the brick driveway of the Victorianne.

OLIVER HOMESTEAD BED & BREAKFAST
Marshall

The Oliver Homestead was established under the 1820 Homestead Act of Congress. William Oliver was granted the original 300 acres in 1836, which now encompasses the "old residential area" of Marshall. Mr. Oliver went on to establish the Rockland Mills on the Salt Fork River, six miles from Arrow Rock.

The stately old brick home was built in several stages, beginning in the 1840s and completed before the turn of the century. The home is in the Federal Style with some Victorian cottage influences. The handmade brick is believed to have been made on site by slave labor. The walls are three bricks thick.

You enter the house from a two story porch that has a balcony on the second floor and find yourself in an entry hall furnished with an antique hall stand and a Victorian table. Throw rugs are on the original floors. The staircase is also the original.

A large brass hanging lamp with glass globe and prisms hangs from the ten foot ceiling in the parlor. A floral patterned carpet is on the floor. Lace curtains with swags are at the windows and the painted walls have a 18 inch wide ceiling border. The room is furnished with an antique walnut roll top secretary, a Victorian marble top lamp table, an upholstered open arm wing chair, a camel back sofa, a barley twist table and an antique organ. A tile fireplace has a white mantelpiece.

A second parlor is furnished with a large Victorian two door bookcase with lots of books. A three-piece turn of the century sofa, arm chair and a rocking chair. An antique spinning wheel, a Lincoln desk and a lamp table with lamp make up the rest of the furnishings.

A large billiard room contains an antique billiard table, a church pew, armoire and a small kitchen cupboard. A built-in cupboard displays a miniature village.

A glassed in porch with pieces of wicker and primitives overlooks a garden and a patio that has wrought iron furniture. Huge old trees and shrubs surround the house.

An antique table and six cane bottom chairs, a corner cupboard, a marble top carved sideboard, an antique jelly cupboard and a tea cart make up the furnishings in the dining room. A brass chandelier hangs over the table. Lace curtains are at the windows and walls have a chair rail and a picture rail.

A full country breakfast is served at Oliver Homestead. Pam varies her menu. Always there is juice, fresh seasonal fruit, homemade breads, cinnamon rolls and coffee, tea or milk. Eggs, sausage, ham, or bacon with fried potatoes, or biscuits and sausage gravy are served. On the lighter side there is quiche with muffins.

In second floor hall is a grandfather clock and a small table with a lamp. A door opens onto a front balcony which has an old porch swing. Two guestrooms are on the second floor.

One room is furnished with a Victorian full-size bed and a matching marble top dresser with glove boxes and candle stands, an antique love seat and an antique desk., and a Victorian lamp table used as a night stand. The room is carpeted with oriental throw rugs. White curtains are at the window. An unusual bird patterned wallpaper is on the walls. The private bath is in the room.

The other guestroom has a matching three piece Victorian bedroom set that includes a full-size bed, dresser with a marble insert, glove boxes and candle stands, an antique lamp table and cane seat chair. The bath is on the first floor with an old-fashioned claw foot tub. Guests are provided with robes.

This is a very nice place and I'm sure you will enjoy touring this house with its period antiques and family heirlooms.

OLIVER HOMESTEAD B & B: 424 East Arrow, Marshall, 65430. (660) 886-5725. Open all year. Not suited for children. However, a crib is furnished for infants. No pets. Smoking on porch. Pam and Paul Jensen, innkeepers.

DIRECTIONS: From I-70, take Hwy. 65 north ten miles.

LA PAZ BED & BREAKFAST
Mexico

The Italianate La Paz B & B, with over 4,000 square feet of living space, was built in 1923 by John D. O'Rear, the Consular of the American Embassy in La Paz, Bolivia. It is now the home of Tom and Linda Hylas.

The mammoth entry parlor contains the most beautiful woodwork I have ever seen. You won't believe the arches, carvings, and paneling. A magnificent staircase has molded scrollwork all the way to the upper floor. It is done in the harvest pattern shaded in gray to highlight the architecture. A large mantel is full of scrollwork and cherubs in bas-relief. The first floor windows are beautifully preserved leaded glass. A love seat, several upholstered chairs and a large table are at one end of the parlor.

A sofa and love seat, a wing chair and cherry tables surround yet another antique fireplace in the living room. The paneled walls are shaded gray. The carpeting throughout the house is a matching gray.

Just off the living room, French doors lead into the dining room that has a double pedestal table, eight chairs and a matching china cabinet. An antique brass and crystal chandelier hangs over the table. A three sides bump out added to this lovely room is done in 14th century architecture. There is a delarobia archway over a winged buffet table in the recess.

A family room has television, VCR, and a stereo system. It is furnished with a sofa and a pair of recliner rockers. Sliding glass doors lead onto a covered patio that has two umbrella tables and seating for eighteen people.

A full breakfast is served between 7 a.m. and 10 a.m. It begins with fresh fruit, juice, and freshly ground coffee. Belgian waffles, French toast or eggs supreme are offered along with croissants, English muffins, homemade coffeecake and several varieties of jellies and jams. Breakfast can be served on the patio under a canopy of flowers, or in the elegant dining room with candlelight service, china, crystal and silver.

Rooms have electronically filtered air, smoke alarms and other safety devices. All of the guestrooms have clock radios, telephones, cable television, decorative house plants and flowers, books, magazines and touch lamps Complementary robes are provided during your stay.

At the top of the winding staircase is the Charleston Suite done in a burgundy and blue decor with a queen-size bed. An adjoining library/reading/entertainment room is off the French doors and small balcony. There is a large private hall bath with shower.

The newly decorated Atlanta Room is furnished with a queen-size bed, dresser and a wing back chair. The quilt and drapes are done in shades of beige, blue and green. The room is papered in a color-coordinated print. There is a private bath with tub and shower.

The New Orleans Suite has blue carpeting with a queen-size bed, double dresser, and a pair of round cherry tables with touch lamps. French doors open onto a nicely carpeted atrium furnished with an upholstered rattan sofa and a rattan glass top coffee table, end tables and bookcases with a collection of movies and books. A carpeted balcony bordered with flower boxes has a lounge chairs and a chaise lounge. The suite has a private bath with tub and shower.

Cat lovers will enjoy our Molly, featured in the 1995-96 calendar by Hallmark: Cats, Cats, Cats. Our other feline is Smokey, an English gray. Both cats have the run of the house.

LA PAZ B & B: 811 S. Jefferson, Mexico, 65265. (573) 581-2011. Two guestrooms and one suite with private baths. Open all year. Tennis courts across the street. Ten minute walk to town square for eating, antique shops. Concert hall nearby. Quiet area, excellent for walking, bicycle riding. Children over 10 welcome. No pets. Smoking on patio, deck or porch only. Visa/MC accepted. Member of BBIM. Tom and Ginni Trembley, innkeepers.

DIRECTIONS: From I-70 take Hwy. 54 north from Kingdom City exit fifteen miles to Mexico. Call for reservations and directions.

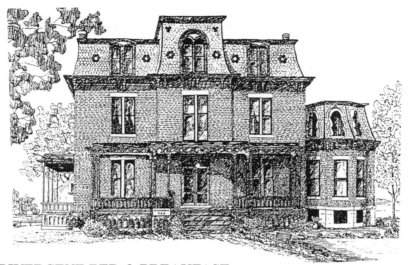

RIVERCENE BED & BREAKFAST
New Franklin

River towns have their own special charms. In New Franklin, one of them is Rivercene, the 15 room mansion built by the riverboat baron, Captain Joseph Kinney. On the National Register of Historic Places, the Captain began building Rivercene in 1864 with. materials shipped from all over the world: imported Italian marble for nine fireplaces, black walnut for the front doors, hand carved mahogany for the grand staircase.

The Captain lived here until his death in 1892, and the home remained in the family until 1992, when it was purchased by Jody and Ron Lenz.

Massive doors ten feet high, give entry to rooms with twelve foot ceilings. A mahogany staircase leads to the second floor. The hall has a carved library table, a Victorian sofa, a china cupboard and a huntboard.

An oriental carpet covers the floor of a large parlor off the hallway. It is furnished with a circa 1860 chickering piano, a three piece antique parlor set and a large antique lamp table. One of the marble fireplace mantels is here and an eighteen inch frieze of painted flowers circles the room.

A second parlor has been changed into a dining room. There are floral patterned carpets, an antique brass chandelier and another fireplace. The room is furnished with a long antique table that seats fourteen. Other pieces include two drop leaf tables and an antique sideboard.

Breakfast is served in the dining room or a breakfast room that has a fireplace, floral patterned carpets and a glass chandelier. An oak table, six matching chairs and a built-in cupboard are part of the furnishings.

For breakfast it may be Finnish pancakes, quiche, or crepes with sauteed vegetables and hollandaise sauce served with juice, fresh fruit in season, muffins or coffeecake and coffee, tea or hot chocolate.

Rivercene offers nine beautifully decorated rooms, five with marble fireplaces. There are eight private baths. The shared bath is rented only to a group traveling together. The honeymoon suite has a jacuzzi.

Off the entry hall on the first floor a front room is furnished with a queen-size bed, an antique dresser and a 1920s three piece parlor set.

Down a private hall off the entry, a guest room has a queen-size antique reproduction bed, two wing back chairs, an antique sofa, and a lyre base drop leaf table. An ornately carved archway leads to a dressing room.

There are four guestrooms on the second floor. A front room, with a white marble fireplace, has an oak high poster bed, an antique bachelor wardrobe, an antique marble top Eastlake dresser, a pair of upholstered chairs, a coffee table, night table and a floor lamp.

Across the hall a room with another white marble mantel, has a 1930s queen-size bed, an antique wishbone dresser, a lamp table and reading lamp and two Martha Washington arm chairs.

The next guestroom is furnished with a queen-size small poster bed, two Queen Anne wing chairs and an antique sideboard. The fourth room has a queen-size brass bed and a single bed, two rocking chairs, and art deco wardrobe and an end table.

The three guestrooms on the third floor have great views of the property and the huge trees that surround the seven acres of lawn. At the top of the stairs, a guestroom is furnished with a full-size poster bed, a mahogany chest and dresser, a twin bed, an upholstered sofa, a dressing table, and an art deco wardrobe. The private bath has a tub and shower.

Down the hall, a second guestroom has a queen size brass bed, a pair of upholstered chairs and a table and chair. A hooked rug is on the floor. A private bath has a tub with shower.

Across the hall, the third guestroom is carpeted and is furnished with a queen-size brass bed, a bedside table, an antique dressing table, an upholstered sofa, sofa table, a table and two chairs, coffee table and an antique linen press. The private bath has a shower and a whirlpool tub.

RIVERCENE B & B: 127 County Road 463, New Franklin, 65274. (800) 531-0862, or (660) 848-2497. Open all year. A 15 room mansion with seven guestrooms and suites with private baths. Major credit cards. Well behaved children welcome. No pets. Outdoor or porch smoking. Ron and Jody Lenz, innkeepers.

DIRECTIONS: From I-70, take exit 103. Go north through Boonville. Cross the Missouri River bridge. Turn right at first road (County Road 463). Rivercene is located 1/4 mile east.

J. D.'S BED & BREAKFAST
Pilot Grove

This home, built in 1886, was at one time the rectory for the Methodist Episcopal Church. As you enter the house, you are in a small entry hall with a carpeted living room on the left. The wall are papered in a green floral print, with a chair rail border. The lighting fixtures are antique and all of the woodwork is original. The room is furnished with an antique love seat and a pair of wing back chairs. An antique parlor table displays a most unusual metal lamp. There is also an antique hall tree, a lamp table with a "Gone with the Wind" lamp, an matching antique chair and chaise lounge and a table and lamp combination for reading. There are nice prints and pictures on the walls.

French doors open into a carpeted dining room that has a green and mauve stripe paper on the walls. It is furnished with an antique oak dining table with a lace tablecloth. There are eight oak chairs. An antique chandelier hangs over the table. There is a sideboard, a small oak table for serving, and seating for six or more persons. A mahogany broken pediment breakfront holds antique dinnerware and various other pieces. Plates, mirrors and pictures decorate the walls.

Joyce's breakfast consists of juice, fresh fruit in season, eggs, sausage, biscuits and gravy and coffeecake or muffins, coffee, tea or milk. A lighter continental breakfast provides juice, fruit, cereal, muffins and beverage.

A first floor guestroom is furnished all in oak, with a full-size bed, a washstand with a lamp, a rocking chair, dresser and a small hall tree that was redesigned to make a seat. The room is carpeted and newly wallpapered. A hall bath has a shower.

A fully equipped kitchen has a microwave, toaster, refrigerator and stove and table and chairs for guests to use.

Off the kitchen, a small room holds a washer and dryer, a baby crib, a high chair and a day bed that can be placed in a guestroom for added sleeping space.

The guestroom at the top of the stairs is carpeted and holds twin beds, a 1930s vanity and matching chest, a desk and lamp and an antique rocking chair. Pictures decorate the mauve painted walls. A bath has both tub and shower.

At the end of the hall, another carpeted guestroom is furnished with an antique iron bed, a low-boy dresser, an antique rocker, an antique iron baby bed and a lamp table with lamp. A one hundred year old christening dress is on display. The room is wallpapered in a small print with blue curtains at the windows.

Across the hall a third guestroom has a circa 1857 walnut full-size bed, a walnut dresser with glove boxes, a Victorian lamp table with a lamp by the bed, an antique washstand, an antique chair and a small table. White curtains with green swags are at the windows. A dark green print wallpaper is below a chair rail with a striped patterned paper above. There are many wall decorations.

You will find candy or cookies waiting in your room.

J. D. 'S B & B: 211 Roe Street, Pilot Grove, 65276. (660) 834-5100 or 834-4630. Open all year. Well behaved children welcome. No pets. Smoking on patio. Close to several antique shops, Boonville and Arrow Rock. Twenty-five miles to Columbia. Just 1 1/2 blocks to the Katy Trail. Trail bikes can be locked in a shed on the property. Joyce Day, innkeeper.

DIRECTIONS: Call for reservations and directions.

ROCHEPORT

A ferry was established at Rocheport in 1821 and a warehouse was erected in the same year. Lots in the town were sold during the 1820s. The town was platted in 1832 and was incorporated in 1836. Rocheport, after its founding, became an important landing place and ferry crossing of the Boonslick country. The town, located on the Boonslick Road, served in later years as a ferry crossing on the National Old Trails Road. As early as 1827, Congress established a post road connecting Fulton, Columbia, Rocheport, Boonville and Independence. Accessible by both land and water, Rocheport was considered by the State Senate in 1835 as the site of the State university. It was also chosen as the location for the Whig Convention of 1840. Several thousand delegates from various parts of Missouri came by steamboat, wagon, carriage, and on horseback to attend the meeting held here.

The growth of Rocheport paralleled the development of steamboat transportation on the Missouri River. In the 1850s, as the steamboat trade increased, Rocheport became the largest shipping point between St. Louis and St. Joseph.

During the Civil War, the town became infamous and bore the title of the "Outlaw Capitol" when "Bloody Bill" Anderson's guerillas made their headquarters here. The Civil War found Rocheport in sympathy with the Confederate cause and the community was visited regularly by the not too friendly Federals and Bushwhackers. The close of the war left Rocheport scarred and blackened.

In 1865 business was reviving in the town and the hope was expressed that the town would rise phoenix-like from the ashes of the burned out district. The next year nineteen men were again engaged in business and new business buildings replaced those which had burned.

Before the turn of the century businesses thrived, banks were organized, newspapers were published and Rocheport became a prosperous business center during the 1880s and 1890s. The ferry, in later years a double-decker boat, carried passengers until the 1920s.

A gradual decline in population became significant by the early 1900s. Disastrous fires in 1892 and 1922, the development of modern highways and the automobile contributed to the decline of the town. The ferry was no longer needed as a river crossing and boats no longer stopped at the landing. The halcyon days when Rocheport was a shipping point on the Missouri are now only memories.

Today the complete town of Rocheport is listed on the National Register of Historic Places and is an attractive historic site with many charming, restored 19th century homes and buildings. People, live, work and raise their families here as they have for more than 160 years.

Rocheport has a well deserved national reputation for its quality antique shops, craft shops and restaurants. A visitor can easily spend the entire day exploring the area's superb and diverse shops.

One of these shops is the *Whitehorse Antiques,* located in the Historic circa 1840 Waddell House at 3rd and Clark Streets. (573)698-2088. This is really a great shop. They specialize in 18th and 19th century formal and country antique furniture, pewter, primitives, early quilts, stoneware, and decorative accessories. When I was there, I saw a 1850 jelly cupboard in the original mustard paint, a rare grain-painted chest, an early hutch table, an early New England settle bench, a pine pewter cupboard, an early 1800 tiger maple chest, a mid-1800's plantation desk, a 19th century set of four windsor chairs, a circa 1820 Boston work table in mahogany and a great early hanging corner cupboard from New England. There was also a New England blanket box, circa 1865 corner cupboard, a twelve tin pie café, spinning wheel, and a pine chest of drawers with square nails. There were plenty of crocks, quilts, baskets, coin silver flatware, pewter, clocks, decoys, oil paintings and many more nice pieces.

One of the oldest brick homes in Boone County, the Dr. George Wilcox home was built in 1837. Now, as *Richard Saunders Antiques,* it is both residence and an antique shop owned by Richard Saunders. It has been featured in *Country Living* and *Country Gardens* magazines. Pine country furniture and unusual accessories are featured. There was a marble top wash stand, a circa 1890 solid brass and copper samovar, several sizes of coffee mills and a circa 1925 toy steam engine from Germany (it works). There was also a New England pine and tiger maple linen press. Located at 21 E. Second Street. (573) 698-3765.

Located in the lower level of the Schoolhouse B&B at 3rd and Clark, *B. Caldwell Booksellers* has thousands of books of every description. There are books on war, Missouri history, crafts, cooking, Americana, American Heritage, and British History. There are also books on Mark Twain and Harry Truman plus Eric Sloan books, childrens books, books on nature, old maps and many rare books. (573) 698-BOOK (2665).

KATY O'NEIL BED & BIKEFEST
Rocheport

You can't get much closer to the Katy Trail than Rodney O'Neil's Katy O'Neil Bed and Bikefest. About forty feet. In fact, it borders his property. It's a nice house, built in about 1880. Four rooms are offered, since a converted railroad box car was added. Rodney, himself has made twelve bicycle tours, visiting all forty eight contiguous states as well as Canada and Mexico, since 1975. So, if you want to talk bicycle, he's been there.

An outdoor hot tub is available to all guests. Guests also have access to the living room, kitchen, television, telephone, refrigerator and laundry. Rodney has a collection of almost 1500 films, most on laserdisc or DVD to choose from. Guests also have free use of an assortment of bicycles, including tandems.

In the main house, a living room is furnished with a baby grand piano, a Jenny Lind type day bed, an upholstered Danish sofa, and a 32 inch television. Rodney's grandfather's antique toolbox from his days with the MK&T Railroad is now an end table. The shiny pine floor has an area carpet and the windows have paisley swags.

Off the living room, a guestroom is furnished with a circa 1880s double bed with an early Irish handmade quilt. There is also a desk, a vintage steamer trunk and two bookcases holding laserdisc movies and CDs. Floral swags are on the windows and a braided rug is on the floor. This is a great room for children and adults alike. On the walls are old movie posters and all kinds of paper memorabilia, including Mark McGuire. Some antique toys and other interesting things are displayed.

On the second floor, a 17 x 25 family suite has a queen-size mission type bed covered with a colorful quilt. There is also a futon, a mission library table, a bookcase, an unusual blanket chest, a bedside table, a wardrobe and a steamer trunk. There is a private bath. The entire suite is under the eaves.

The Santa Fe Railroad boxcar was purchased by Rodney and moved to the present location and the way it has been redone, it contains a small kitchen with a sink, refrigerator and a coffee maker at one end of the car. The other end contains a sleeping area with an antique brass bed and two bedside tables with lamps. Rodney installed a ceiling over part of this area and has a ladder that takes you up to a loft which has a futon. He tells me kids love it. The center area has an oak L-shaped booth and table that partially shields the sleeping area. It is furnished with an upholstered sofa with dual recliners, a cable television, and a DVD player (you get your movies at the main house). There are all sorts of railroad items displayed here and in the house. The two large doors of the boxcar now have two glass doors. It is fully air conditioned, fully carpeted and you have complete privacy.

Above the garage there is a large rustic room with a sloping ceiling. It has a full-size iron bed and a full-size metal spindle bed, both with hand made quilts. There's a bedside table, two benches, a small chest, a futon and an upholstered sofa. It can sleep six and serves as a bunkhouse for cost conscious travelers.

A huge cottonwood tree shades part of the area which has a patio with an umbrella table and chairs and a picnic table. The hot tub looks awfully good to bikers and hikers just off the Katy Trail.

Rodney has a simple way to fix breakfast. At check-in, he gives his guests a menu. You check what you would like. There are 10 different cold cereals, 3 hot cereals, orange juice, coffee, toast, waffles with or without walnuts, pancakes with or without walnuts or bacon and eggs.

Katy O'Neil Bed & Bikefest is ideal for the bicycle traveler. It is adjacent to the Katy Trail between the depot and the tunnel at Katy Trail mile 178.5. Rodney offers cold drinks, hot showers and laundry facilities.

KATY O'NEIL BED & BIKEFEST: 101 Lewis, Rocheport, 65279. (573) 698-BIKE. Open all year. Four different sleeping choices. Children welcome. No smoking indoors. Pets must be kept in carriers or outside. Telephone in living room is available to guests for local or calling card calls. Rodney O'Neil, owner.

SCHOOL HOUSE BED & BREAKFAST INN
Rocheport

School was not one of my favorite places as a child. I was, however, afraid to skip, knowing what the penalties would be. So I begrudgingly walked the seven blocks to the Bryan Mullanphy School in south St. Louis. Those few years seemed like an eternity. Now I know they were fleeting. I recalled some pleasant memories, when I walked into the School House B & B. I was reminded of the cloak room, the long halls, the principal's office (not that I ever had to go there, mind you), and best of all recess.

The Rocheport School was built in 1914 and served the town until 1972. John and Vicki Ott purchased the building in 1987, installed central heat, air-conditioning and replaced the plumbing and electrical service.

The School House B & B has ten guestrooms, all with private baths, two with two person Jacuzzi. The rooms, with thirteen-foot ceilings, are spacious, airy and bright. The large schoolhouse windows, covered with lacy handmade curtains, let in plenty of light. Most of the rooms have ceiling fans, beautiful hardwood floors and plantation shutters on the windows.

On the first floor, the Honor Roll Room has a queen-size, antique brass bed, an oak dresser, love seat, drop leaf table and lamp, a night stand and an oriental carpet. The white woodwork sets off the deep cherry walls.

Dick and Jane's Room has a four poster rice bed with a canopy, a Victorian marble top dresser, a painted armoire, a wing chair, and a Victorian marble top lamp table with a brass oil lamp. An area carpet covers the hardwood floors. A his and hers shower is found in its bathroom.

The Graduate's Room is furnished with a cherry, Queen Ann four poster, queen-size bed, an antique armoire, a black and white sleeper sofa and a night stand with reading lamp. There is a fireplace mantel. The walls are lilac color.

The Spelling Bee Room has a handmade, four pencil-post queen-size bed, a walnut armoire, a table with two ladder back chairs and a skirted night stand to match the bed linens. The walls are pale yellow.

Papered in a pink and green cabbage rose design, the Prose Room is furnished with a queen-size brass bed, a white iron day bed, a massive mirrored armoire which compliments the high ceilings and skirted night stands with matching brass lamps.

On the second floor, The School Marm Room has a white queen-size iron and brass bed, an oak armoire and washstand and two bedside tables with matching candlestick lamps. The walls are papered in a pink floral print on navy background. Enjoy the old-fashioned claw-footed tub in this whimsical room.

In the School Master Room use steps to climb into the queen-size rice carved plantation bed. An original blackboard still graces the deep sage colored walls of this stately room along with a circa 1926 radio, a birds-eye maple armoire and a table and lamp next to a reading chair.

The Show and Tell Room is furnished with a queen-size bed, an upholstered chair, a pair of night stands with lamps and a unique European oak corner armoire. A heart-shaped Jacuzzi is featured in this room with fabric covered walls in a yellow and hunter green Waverly print.

Miss Edna's Room, done in taupe and shades of blue, is a cozy room on the third floor under the eaves. It has an antique white iron double bed, a wing chair, Victorian dresser, built-in bookcases and a skylight.

The spacious Teacher's Pet Suite features a king-size bed, two skylights and a two-person Jacuzzi. There is an antique oak dresser and a sofa, rocker and end tables all in white wicker. The walls and carpet are pale heather rose. On the second floor, where breakfast is served, is a common sitting area with comfortable furnishings and an entertainment center. A sample breakfast would consist of brewed coffees and assorted teas, chilled juice, seasonal fruit, homemade blueberry muffins and a freshly made egg, cheese and vegetable frittata. Penny's special touches include warm cookies on check-in, fresh flowers, ironed bed linens and your name on the blackboard.

SCHOOL HOUSE B & B: Third & Clark Sts., Rocheport, 65279. (573) 698-2022. Website: www.schoolhousebandb.com. E-mail: inkeeper@schoolhousebandb.com. Open all year, except Christmas. Children over five welcome. No pets. No smoking inside. John and Vicki Ott & Penny Province, owners.

DIRECTIONS: Rocheport is located about 10 miles west of Columbia on I-70. Then north 2 miles on Rt. BB. Call for reservations.

YATES HOUSE BED & BREAKFAST
Rocheport

The Yates House B & B is a wonderful new home adapted from a circa 1850 roadside inn. And if it affects you as it did me, you will be looking for someone like Patrick Henry or Samuel Adams as you walk through this home. It is an elegantly simple home whose high ceilings and spacious design will charm you. Hardwood floors throughout with beautiful oriental rugs compliment the Colonial Williamsburg colors and wallpapers.

The Keeping Room overlooks the large back porch and patio herb and flower gardens. Seating is provided by a large leather sofa and floral tapestry loveseat and side chair. Two antique benches serve as a coffee table and a plant and pottery display. Antique brass floor lamps and stained glass table lamps provide warm lighting.

The antique wardrobes provide storage, one contains the TV/VCR and stereo systems. The walls are decorated with several antique shelves and old clocks.

A library has a wall of floor-to-ceiling bookcases with books and family momentos. A piano is available for guests to enjoy. A Lincoln library table, sofa and pair of wing chairs, along with two mission style rockers furnish this room that beckoning for a fire in the fireplace. The walls are teal green as is the fireplace trim. A large area carpet is on the hardwood floor and floral drapes are at the six over six windows.

The dining room is furnished with a large oak table with antique arrow back chairs, a beautiful walnut corner cupboard, a circa 1850 pegged kitchen cupboard and a hunt board. A brass eight-arm chandelier hangs over the table. A chair rail has mauve striped wallpaper below and a floral print paper above. An Oriental rug is on the floor and matching drapes are at the four six over six windows. There is a large fireplace that is always glowing during breakfast – weather permitting of course. There are small antiques, hand-painted dishes and paintings on the walls. Visualize having breakfast here on a cold day in front of the fireplace. You'll love it.

Dixie's gourmet kitchen is well known as the source of many culinary delights. The freshest ingredients she can find, including locally grown seasonal produce, are used to create a sumptuous leisurely breakfast you will never forget. The kitchen is furnished with some really great antiques. There is a screened porch off the kitchen with wrought iron seating. Breakfast can be eaten here in spring or summer.

Two guestrooms are on the second floor. Both are large and airy, furnished comfortably in antiques and have a private full bathroom. Both offer a wonderful view of the National Historic District of old Rocheport.

The Tasha Tudor Room has a 1920s era bedroom set with a queen-size bed, dresser and an upholstered arm chair. Conrad's great grandmother pieced the old quilt blocks that were made into the quilts. The room is papered in a blue print wallpaper below a chair rail and a floral stripe pattern above. Oriental throw rugs are on the floor, Belgium lace was used to make the shades and white lace curtains that cover the six over six windows. There are nice pictures on the walls and pieces of porcelain are displayed about the room. The bath has a reproduction sink, tub and shower.

The Valentine Room is furnished with a queen-size antique iron bed, an antique oak dresser and a corner walnut cabinet. An antique table is used for a night stand and a floor lamp is next to a rocking chair. Pink and blue floral wallpaper covers the walls, area carpets are on the floor and white lace curtains are at the six over six windows.

The Historic Rocheport Suite is located on lower lever. The entire suite is filled with lovely antebellum furnishings. Its bedroom features an exquisite cherry Queen-size bed. The private sitting room is perfectly suited to intimate conversation and has its own television set. The private bath has a shower and a pedestal sink.

YATES HOUSE B & B: 305 Second Street, Rocheport, 65279. (573) 698-2129. Open all year. No smoking. Not suitable for children. In the heart of Historic Rocheport. Website: http://rocheport.missouri.org/yateshouse. Conrad and Dixie Yates, innkeepers.

DIRECTIONS: Rocheport is located off I-70 on Hwy. BB. Call for reservations and directions.

YATES GARDEN HOUSE
Rocheport

The Yates Garden House, unlike its sister house next door, is a 150-year old home that was built in 1840, and stands much like it did when it was built, except for the garage and a small room in the back of the house. These two additions were probably added on in the 1970's, when the previous owner renovated the complete house. All of the woodwork, floors, and windows are mostly original. Even the old brick outhouse and brick summer kitchen are original.

Conrad and Dixie Yates, who just purchased this house, also own the Yates House B & B next door. They have been putting their finishing touches to it. Now, both houses make up Conrad and Dixie's bed and breakfast.

Upon entering, you are in a hallway leading back to a kitchen and breakfast area. A long runner is on the parquet floors. The walls are wallpapered in several shades of brown grass paper. A small table and lamp are here. There is a stained glass window at the foot of the staircase. The woodwork and cove moulding are painted in a taupe color.

To the right of the entry, double doors open to the Wildflower Guestroom. It is furnished with a queen-size, pine high-back bed with matching bed linens, an antique white wicker rocker, a night table and lamp. An armoire holds a television. The four windows have eggshell colored tie-back drapes over accordian shades. The walls are painted jade green and have a pair of unusual wall sconces. The woodwork is painted white and the refinished floors have a large, floral patterned area rug. A fireplace (non-workable) has a large gilt mirror over it. A washstand in the room has a sink in it. The private bath has a walk-in shower.

Down the hall, the three room Garden House Suite consists of a living room, bedroom, kitchen and bathroom. The living room has an upholstered sofa, a Shaker-type lamp table and brass lamp, a large bookcase, coffee table, an antique parlor table, a pair of Shaker Chairs and an armoire housing a television. A wall-to-wall floral patterned carpet covers the floor. An arch leads into a bedroom that has a queen-size, carved, four poster rice bed, two bedside tables with brass reading lamps, a Shaker style table and a pair of chairs. The walls are paneled with wide boards painted a taupe color. Five windows with 10 panes of glass in each, cover almost one wall. A stained glass window is on one wall, with a door leading into the garden area. The bedroom floor has the same kind of carpet as the living room.

The kitchen is fully furnished and has a breakfast area. The private bath has a walk-in shower and a whirlpool tub.

A dining room has a large bay window with floral drapes. The original fireplace, now with gas logs, has an ornate mantle piece. A built in bookcase on one side of the fireplace holds stoneware and other pottery. A wrought iron, tile top table and six antique chairs rest on an oriental carpet. The room is paneled with wide boards painted taupe and has two wall sconces.

Carpeted stairs lead to the Rose Room. It is a large room furnished with a queen-size, wrought iron bed and matching bed linens, an antique open arm chair, an armoire with a television, an antique Morris recliner, a small table and chair, an antique rocker and an antique work table with brass lamps act as bedside tables. A black and white patterned paper covers the walls, the woodwork is painted an eggshell color, and fringed curtains are at the windows. A large private bath has a tub and shower. It is wallpapered in a pink and green floral pattern on a black background. The window has a fringed café curtain and a valance.

Dixie varies her breakfast menu. A typical menu would be: juice, coffee or tea, fresh fruit dish in season, homemade bread and scones. Omelets using farm fresh eggs, as frittatas, or a fresh vegetable entrée with a breakfast meat. All entrees include oven roasted potatoes. Breakfast is served in the Yates House B&B, weather permitting or in the Yates Garden House dining room.

At the rear of the house a large brick patio has large trees, flower beds, a gazebo and ground cover. An antique iron fence surrounds a good part of the property. But, the neatest thing is the original brick outhouse and summer kitchen buildings.

YATES GARDEN HOUSE B & B: Second Street, Rocheport, MO 65279. (573) 698-2129. Two guestrooms and a three room suite all with private baths. No pets. Outside smoking. No amenities for children. In the heart of Historic Rocheport and on the Katy Trail. Website: http:// rocheport.missouri.org/yateshouse. Conrad and Dixie Yates, innkeepers.

DIRECTIONS: Same as Yates House B & B. Please see previous B&B profile.

THE INN AT PATRICK PLACE
Sweet Springs

Built in 1899 by Dr. James Jarves for his family, this charming Victorian bungalow sits graciously amid beautiful gardens, on a large corner lot in Historic Sweet Springs. The good doctor kept a hand written list of the costs he incurred in building his house. The total cost was $1,720.00 and that included furniture and drapes. The home has the late 1800s Victorian flair of fish scales combined with a turret, accented by the 1900s architectural bungalow style with a mission feel.

I was supposed to meet Carol Levy, who, with her husband Bob, owns the inn, at 11:30 a.m. one day. I drove from my home in St. Louis in plenty of time for the 200 mile drive, and made such good time, (without speeding), that I arrived half an hour early and Carol hadn't arrived yet. I got out of my car and went up on the long, wide front porch which goes across the entire front of the house. The ceiling is of beaded boards. At both ends, there are seating areas with wicker tables, chairs, plant stands, porch swings and one area has a hammock. There are lots of plants and flowers. Behind a stone wall that went from the house to the edge of their property, there's a brick walk, a gazebo and a bench. Landscaped areas had flowers, shrubs, tall trees and a wonderful rose garden. I don't think I was ever so satisfied waiting for anyone. Even better, she was a little late.

The front entry foyer has a pair of upholstered wing chairs, a piano, an antique fainting couch, a walnut desk and a child's bench.

To the left in the turret library room, there is an antique library table, an upholstered sofa and a sofa table with a lamp, a Murphy bed, bookcase, television and a pair of upholstered chairs. The walls are hunter green and the floor has area carpets.

The dining room is furnished with a carved, antique oak table with a collection of candles on it. There's an antique oak chest, an oak buffet, an antique china cupboard holding antique glassware, a pair of Victorian side chairs, a caned seat Lincoln rocking chair and an antique two door cupboard.

The inn has two guestrooms on the first floor. The Blackwell-Tremmel Room, named for the first paying guest, is furnished with an antique walnut Eastlake full-size bed, with a 3 inch feather bed on a mattress. There is also an antique drop leaf table with a lamp used as a night stand, an antique wardrobe, a very small trunk, an upholstered blue and white chair, and an antique trunk at the foot of the bed.

The private bath has a walk-in shower. The walls are a dark blue. White lace curtains with blue and white floral swags and drapes are at the windows.

The Violet Room, located on the southwest corner is a bright, cheery room, furnished with an antique full-size brass and white iron bed, a white chest, an upholstered chair, a bird cage, an antique sewing machine base is used for a table and a chest is at the foot of the bed. The walls are pale lavender, and the woodwork and café curtains are white. Area carpets are on the original floors. A private bath with tub and shower is in the hall. Fluffy Turkish robes are in each of the guestrooms.

A second floor guestroom features a private apartment complete with a studio kitchen and private bath. An antique full-size walnut bed and a twin bed tucked away in a delightful little alcove make for great family accommodations.

For large groups, the library has a hide-a-bed and an unusual ¾ Murphy bed.

A large country kitchen has beamed ceilings. There is an antique table and chairs and a bakers rack. Take a peek at Carol's Back Porch Gift Shop.

Carol gives you your choice of a gourmet breakfast. Among the entrees would be Belgian waffles, pancakes, French toast with red raspberry, blueberry or lemon ginger syrup, Carol's homemade granola, bacon and eggs or biscuits and gravy. It's all served with juice, fruit, freshly made flax bread with assorted fresh fruit jams, jellies or local honey. Fresh coffee, tea or milk.

THE INN AT PATRICK PLACE: 600 Patrick Place, Sweet Springs, 65351. (660) 335-4241 or (660) 335-6623. Open all year. Children welcome. Smoking on porch. No pets. Two bikes and helmets available. Sit back and sip lemonade on a wonderful porch. E-mail: candb@juno.com. Bob and Carol Levy, innkeepers.

DIRECTIONS: From I-70 north or south, exit #66 (Hwy. 27) south. Take 27 past Main Street to Ray Street. Turn right at Patrick Place.

Section Ten

MARK TWAIN REGION

Bethel
Bethel Colony B & B

Clarksville
Retreat at Aberdeen
Daniel Douglas House
Meadowlark at Fieldstone Farm
Rosemont Farm B & B

Ethel
Recess Inn

Hannibal
Fifth Street Mansion
Garth Woodside Mansion

Louisiana
Applegate B & B
Louisiana Guesthouse
Meadowcrest B & B
Orthwein Mansion
Serandos B & B
Thousand Acre Farm

Macon
St. Agnes Hall B & B
Stagecoach Inn

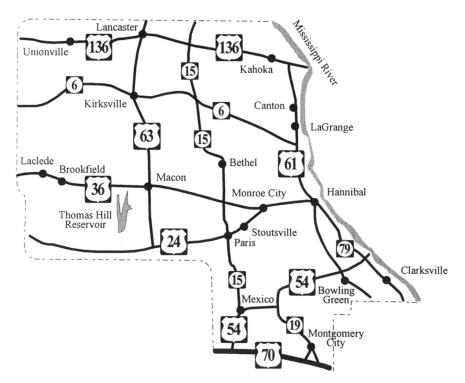

From the Mississippi River on the east to Highway 65 on the west, and from the Iowa border on the north, to Highway 24 on the south, the Mark Twain Region of northeast Missouri is a land of waterways, hills, and history. Mark Twain's birthplace and the town where he grew up are highlights of an area, which abound with reminders of the great author and humorist. Born in Florida, Missouri, Samuel Clemens brought fame and honor to his home state writing as "Mark Twain." Today, you can begin where he began, at the little cabin where he was born. It is now preserved in the 1,192 acre Mark twain State Park. It is Hannibal, however, that is most closely associated with Twain.

Travel through this region and you'll find much more than memories of Mark Twain. Rivers crisscross the area. Many are tributaries of the Mississippi. There are lakes for water fun. There's theatre to enjoy in an old ice house, an outdoor amphitheater, or on a land locked riverboat. You can visit the "world's wild goose capital," take a ride on the Mississippi, and see the home of a six star general. Dine at quaint restaurants in restored, grand old buildings throughout the area. Covered bridges at Paris and Laclede, museums and state parks all add to the special appeal and fun awaiting you in the Mark Twain Region.

On the western side, there are many more places to see. In the area's second largest city, Kirksville, take a look at the historical displays at the E.M. Violette Museum on the campus of Northeast Missouri State University. Also the first school of osteopathic medicine in America was founded here in 1892.

Famous men have left their imprint on this region. Two noted military men were John J. Pershing and Sterling Price. Pershing, who led American forces in Europe during World War I, was born at Laclede, and his home there remains a popular tourist stop. A state park in the area also honors Pershing. In Kirksville, the Sterling Price Monument honors a former governor of Missouri who served as a general for the Confederacy during the Civil War.

Honor paid to these great soldiers does not detract from the memory of another famous man of this area. A modern day Missourian, whose achievements were of a sort that rarely go together. He created a successful business empire and became one of the world's best loved men. Walt Disney, who spent his boyhood in Marceline, has probably had more impact on America's youth than any other man of his generation.

There's much more to the Mark Twain Region. It is tops for recreation. There are fine state parks including Wakonda near LaGrange, Thousand Hills at Kirksville, and Graham Cave near Montgomery City.

Outdoorsmen are right at home in this region. The Swan Lake and Fountain Grove Wildlife Areas near Sumner, provide excellent waterfowl hunting. Over a hundred thousand Canadian geese and many species of ducks pause here during their spring and fall migration.

In the wild goose capital of Sumner, look for the famous 40-foot tall wild goose statue. The world's largest, it has become a favorite with photographers.

Area rivers and community lakes offer more water fun, led by three large lakes: Long Branch and Thomas Hill, both near Macon, and the 18,600 acre Mark Twain Lake, the largest lake in northern Missouri. It is located southwest of Hannibal at the Clarence Cannon Dam. At Macon, stop and see the second oldest continually used courthouse in the State. St. Agnes Hall B & B and the Stagecoach Inn are in Macon.

At Bethel, virtually the entire town is a museum, with thirty buildings remaining from a communal colony founded there in 1844. The Bethel Colony B & B is here.

The northernmost Civil War Battle in Missouri was fought at Athens just a few miles from the Iowa Border. Today, the site is remembered at The Battle of Athens State Park.

Highway 61 follows the Mississippi River from Canada to the Gulf of Mexico. In Missouri, it begins at Alexandria. Further south is the town of Canton, a 150 year old city where you can enjoy dinner theatre on the land locked Golden Eagle Riverboat.

Nearby, St. Patrick is the only town so named in the United States with a shrine to its namesake. Continue south on Highway 61 to Palmyra. In 1860, it was called the handsomest city in northern Missouri. However, during the Civil War, President Abraham Lincoln referred to one day in Palmrya's history as the blackest day of the Civil War, when he learned ten Confederate prisoners had been executed in retaliation for the Confederacy's refusal to release a northern sympathizer.

At New London, stop and see the beautiful Ralls County Courthouse, built in 1858. It has been preserved in its original state. It was here that Mark Twain was sworn into the Confederate Army.

Highway 79, commonly called the "Great River Road" in Missouri, parallels the Mississippi River from Hannibal to St. Peters. With its high hills, bluffs, panoramic vistas of farmlands, forests and the magnificent river, it is truly one of the State's most beautiful drives. It is especially memorable in the fall when the leaves are a profusion of color. Several scenic overlooks have been provided along the highway to allow views of the river, shoreline and the many islands dotting the Mississippi. Note how blue the river is in some places. Small river towns such as Old Monroe, Winfield, Foley, Elsberry, and Annada are all towns settled many years ago. At Elsberry, stop by Vaughn's Hallmark Shop at 401 Broadway for the best chocolate malted milk you'll ever taste. Arline Vaughn uses hand-dipped ice cream. I've taken many a one in a "to go" glass. Notice the old time soda fountain.

All along the highway, you'll find a blend of old and new, stately homes, locks and dams shuttling traffic on the river, scenic vistas of the "camel hump" terrain to the east and the bluffs arising from the rivers edge. At Clarksville, the highest bluffs on the Mississippi overlook miles of countryside. The Clarksville skylift offers easy access to the top. The Daniel-Douglas House is in Clarksville and the Aberdeen Retreat, Meadowlark Inn and Rosemont Farm B & B are all just a few miles from Clarksville.

About ten miles north is the grand old town of Louisiana, home of Stark Brothers Nursery, the largest in the world and the oldest in America. The town is full of antique shops. The Applegate B & B, Louisiana Guest House, Meadowcrest B & B, Orthwein Mansion B & B, Serando's B & B and Thousand Acres Farm B & B are all in Louisiana.

Next comes the most popular town for visitors, Hannibal, home of Mark Twain. You'll find plenty to see and do here and it's a great place to eat. Fifth Street B & B and Garth Woodside Mansion B & B are in Hannibal.

For those of you interested in antiques, you will find many shops to browse through in this area. One of the largest is *Feed Store Antiques* located in Eolia, just off Highway 61. Betty Martin and Mildred Hunter have over 13,000 square feet of space filled with thousands of items. They are open seven days a week from 10 a.m. to 5 p.m. You could probably find anything you want here. When I was here, I saw a game table with twisted barley legs, several Jenny Lind bed, a pine dresser, a walnut corner cupboard, a dry sink, an oak china cupboard, trunks, an ornate iron baby bed, an opossum belly cupboard and a pair of large oak corner cupboards. There were also a lot of crocks, oil lamps, framed pictures, kitchen utensils, quilts and much more. Phone (573) 485-7000.

BETHEL

H idden away in secluded corners throughout the country are America's 19th century communal colonies, each intended to be a Utopia. There is New Harmony, Indiana; Shakertown, Kentucky; Bishop Hill, Illinois and the Amana Colonies in Iowa. All living examples of century old communal religious societies.

Bethel is Missouri's example of that hoped for Utopia. In the late 1840s, William Keil, a religious leader born in Germany, and his followers settled in northeast Missouri. They founded one of the oldest communal groups west of the Mississippi River. He attracted some 700 adherents to Bethel, where members shared property and worked for each other's welfare.

In 1855, Keil, fearing that the colony had become too worldly, led 198 of his followers west to establish a new settlement. Keil never returned to Bethel, but the remaining members continued the colony until Keil's death in 1877, when the colony was disbanded and the property divided among the members.

The village is little changed from that time 150 years ago. Today, thirty structures from that period remain, including the Bair house, the wheelwright, the Bauer house, home of the druggist, and Der Schneider Laden, the tailor shop which made clothing for the men and boys. This complex also includes a communal barn and smokehouse. Keil's stately home Elim, is a mile east of town.

Historic Bethel German Colony, on the National Register of Historic Places, offers the pleasures of a simple world. You'll find Bethel a warm and friendly place, reflecting the slower pace of a time past. Don't snack on your way. It's best to arrive here hungry.

The Colony Restaurant serves wholesome plain food and lots of it. Generous pies will remind you of Grandmother's Sunday dinner and the prices are almost as good as the food.

You are welcome to sit on a bench or watch the sheep dogs work during the World Sheep Fest. Tap your foot to the sound of the German Band practicing time honored polkas. Smell the apple butter bubbling in the copper kettles during Harvest Fest. At Christmas enjoy fiddlers, jigging, scarecrows and the Black Santa.

Bethel is located on Highway 15 about thirteen miles north of Shelbina and twenty-five miles south of Edina. From Hannibal, take Highway 36 to Shelbina and turn north through Shelbyville. From Kirksville, take Highway 6 to Edina and then south on Highway 15.

BETHEL COLONY BED & BREAKFAST
Bethel

The building that houses the Bethel Colony B & B was one of the first structures built after the Bethel Colony disbanded. Erected in 1878, a grocery store and dry goods store was on the first floor, with a clothing and harness making shop on the second. Today, the Bethel Colony Communal Restaurant is on the first floor, with the bed and breakfast on the second.

Don't look for ornate or fancy here, because you won't find it. You can, however, step back into a communal life of 150 years ago and see how people lived then. I would highly recommend a visit.

A rather steep flight of stairs leads to a wide hallway that runs the length of the building. The old original floors are painted gray and are covered with scatter rugs. The walls are painted white and are very plain and undecorated. Several nice pieces of antique furniture include a pierced tin pie safe and an old wooden coffee bin. It is my understanding they were made in the early days of the colony.

There are five guestrooms which open off the hallway. A shared bath is located at the end of the hall The rooms are furnished in the style of the commune - plain and simple, but with handsome pieces of handmade early colony furniture. In one room there is an immense, four poster bed with an antique quilt and a large dresser. In another, an iron bed has an old coverlet on it. A low, two door cupboard with drawers was fashioned in the early days.

All the guestrooms are furnished with iron or antique wooden beds, handmade quilts and a few other early pieces of furniture. Six additional double rooms are available at two other Bethel Colony B & Bs just down the street.

Breakfast is included in the room rate, which is very nominal. I've never eaten breakfast here, but I've had lunch on several occasions and the food is very good and there is plenty of it. The home baked bread is delicious, as is the apple butter. If you eat here, be sure to order pie and cobbler early. They run out rather fast!

This is a most interesting place to visit. An unusual town with exceptionally friendly people.

BETHEL COLONY B & B: Box 127, Bethel, 63434 (660) 284-6493. Open all year. Children Welcome. No pets. No smoking. Cindy Baker, manager. Call Cindy for information and reservations.

CLARKSVILLE

L egend has it that Clarksville was named to honor William Clark of Lewis and Clark fame. However, many years before Lewis and Clark, the area was the site of a Sac and Fox Indian Village.

The earliest settlers came here from Kentucky in 1808, and in 1818 the town was platted and the first lots were sold. With the arrival of the steamboat in 1825, Clarksville's first business boom was underway. By the 1840s the town had grown to about 300 residents. Between 1840 and 1880, many large brick homes and businesses were built in town and in the surrounding hills. Many of these homes still stand, attracting visitors, historians, and building enthusiasts. To get a good look at Clarksville and save wear and tear on your feet, take Tony and Fran Caradonna's open air shuttle and really see the town's Greek Revival, Italianate and Gothic houses. The shuttle is open for tours Thursday through Sunday, from mid-April through October. 11:00 a.m. – 5:00 p.m. Phone (573) 242-9874.

Today, Clarksville, with a population of about 500, is the same as it was in 1860. It has several interesting attractions. The sky lift will take you to Lookout Point six hundred feet above the Mississippi River for an eight hundred square mile view of beautiful scenery and the glacier formations of Missouri and Illinois. Lock and Dam No. 24 has an observation platform to watch the barge traffic maneuver through the locks. Watch for bald eagles in the winter months.

Clarksville has excellent places in which to shop for antiques and gifts, all within walking distance of each other. *D.A. Rinedollar Blacksmith Shop* is in the building that was the original blacksmith shop. Darold forges beautiful and quality items that are perfect for your home, or to give as gifts. He has fireplace sets, ram's head door knockers, candle stands, floor lamps, unusual coffee and dining tables, fences, gates and planter boxes. Lois Rinedollar has an antique shop in the same building and specializes in selected antiques as well as antique garden and patio furniture. Located on Highway 79 and Lewis Street in the heart of downtown Clarksville. (573) 242-3323.

Howard Hughes Antiques is located at 108 S. 2nd St. (573) 242-3376. When I visited here there was an upholstered Victorian folding chair, a circa 1860 upholstered Lincoln rocker, an oak wash stand, a circa 1840 gentleman's chest, a circa 1900 Arts & Crafts mission oak hall tree, a pair of caned Victorian chairs, a rustic twig fern stand, an upholstered Victorian sofa, several drop leaf tables, various wall shelves, a Victorian easel and an original Thonet 1850's cane bottom chair. There were oil lamps, depression dishes in cobalt blue, a full set of blue willow dishes, and hand-painted plates and bowls.

The Mississippi Glassworks, Inc. is at 108 Howard Street, (573) 242-3858. Deborah showed me a opossum belly cupboard, an antique loom, a walnut entry table, a circa 1880 pine dresser with a wishbone mirror, a domed trunk, a pie crust table, a circa 1870 bird's eye maple serpentine front wash stand, a pine drop leaf table, and an English display case. Deborah belongs to the North America Butterfly Association and the Lepidopterisis Society. She buys some of the most beautiful butterflies from around the world, then mounts and frames them. They are absolutely outstanding. If nothing else, stop by and look at them.

As far as antiques go, Vernon Hughes and Ralph Huesing have filled the century old *Clifford-Wirick House* with really nice pieces of porcelain and earthenware including Limoges, Royal Doulton, flow blue, Fiesta, tea leaf luster and white ironstone. There is a large selection of oriental vases, old Nippon, Depression and Elegant glassware, Victorian pattern glass and oil lamps. Pottery items include Weller, Roseville and Hull. They also have many antique framed prints and pictures. Be sure to note the stained glass objects which they make themselves. Located at 105 So. 2nd (Highway 79). Phone: (573) 242-3376.

If you want to see artistry in wood, stop off at Mike Greenwell's *Clarksville Furniture Shop* at 110A South Second Street. (Highway 79). Mike specializes in custom-made furniture and accessories in walnut, cherry and oak. Some of the pieces on display included farm tables, washstands, cupboards and breakfronts. He had a beautiful butternut standing desk. Smaller pieces included tie and coat racks, fern stands and wall shelves.

Another fine furniture craftsman is Brent Tucker of *Brentwood Furniture* located at 302 Kentucky St. (573) 242-3800. Brent offers a new concept in classic furniture: Shaker and Country French designs. Each piece is painstakingly designed, crafted and finished by hand, one piece at a time. Brent also offers a limited edition collection of exclusive original pieces that are numbered and signed by the craftsman.

There are two restaurants in Clarksville. *The Apple Basket* is located at 117 Howard St., owner Cheryl Cooper has a special each day. She also serves ham, turkey or roast beef on your choice of bread; white, sourdough, rye or croissant. There are soups, salads, quiche, combos and desserts. (573) 242-3332.

Then there's *The Pine Point fine Food and Cocktails*, located on scenic Hwy. 79, overlooking the majestic Mississippi River. Jim and Nicole Watry offer breakfast, lunch and dinner served daily from 6:00 a.m. the traditional American menu features catfish, salmon, prime rib, liver and onions, as well as sandwiches and pastas. Homemade pies are great for dessert or an excellent mid-day snack. *Pine Point Pub* features a full service bar, with Missouri wines and from around the world. Jim also does banquets and catering and has patio dining and to go items. Phone: (573) 242-3223.

DANIEL DOUGLAS HOUSE BED & BREAKFAST
Clarksville

Built in 1859 by Daniel Douglas, this house has changed very little since the day it was erected. All of the floors, woodwork, doors and a lot of the less noticeable handwork are just as they were over one hundred forty years ago. Careful and extensive restoration has enhanced many of the fine architectural details. Note the dentil molding under the wide eaves and the lintels over the second floor windows. It also has a nice wraparound porch.

Entering the home, you are in a hallway. On the left side, through French doors, a small sitting room is furnished with an antique desk and chair, an upholstered love seat, a rocker and a small table and lamp. A door leads to a bath with tub and shower.

The front parlor has floor to ceiling windows. All of the ceilings are ten feet high. There is a built-in bookcase and a faux marbled fireplace. The room is furnished with a Tennessee rush seated wagon bench, a corner cupboard, an upholstered floral pattern chair, an antique drop leaf table, several rush seated chairs, a folk art primitive cupboard, a pair of Victorian side chairs and a bench with a giant-size chess set on it. Folk art is displayed throughout the house, and this room is no exception. An oriental carpet is on the floor. A rose stripe wallpaper covers the walls.

The dining room has a fireplace and a brass chandelier. An oriental carpet is on the floor. There is a hand-made round table and eight Windsor chairs made by a fifth generation folk art chair maker. A hand-made primitive cupboard holds pottery pieces, while a hand-made hutch has a collection of various wooden items and pottery. There is a nice small mission style hunt board. Pale rose wallpaper is below a chair rail and a rose print paper above. Breakfast is usually served here.

Three guestrooms are reached by ascending the walnut hand-made staircase in the front hallway. An antique dresser is in the second floor hall.

The Cabbage Rose Room is furnished with a queen-size, white iron and brass bed, red, green and yellow floral spread, an antique dresser with carved fruit pulls, a twig rocker and a twig night table with a pottery lamp. There is also a quilt rack with quilts and a twig bench is at the foot of the bed. All of the twig furniture in the house is Amish made. Oriental area rugs are on the painted floors, the walls are yellow and the same pattern bedspread is on the four windows. It is a bright and airy room. It also has a non-working fireplace.

The Noah's Ark Room is carpeted wall-to-wall. It has a brass bed with a red and white quilt on it. A small Amish style bedside table and lamp, an antique rocker, a narrow seven-drawer chest and a long wall shelf with pegs. The walls have a gold and burgundy stripe wallpaper with a Chinese motif, lace curtains over blinds at the window and white woodwork.

The Homestead Room has an antique, full-size ornate iron bed, a twig rocker, an Amish night table and a chest. A wall light is by the bed. The room is papered in a pink, green and white print. Hooked throw rugs are on the floor and lace curtains are at the six over six paned windows.

The second floor bathroom has a vintage bathtub for guest use, and those that prefer a shower, the first floor bathroom is also available.

A full breakfast is offered at the Daniel-Douglas House between 8:00 and 9:30 a.m. Sandy serves orange juice, an egg, sausage and potato casserole, muffins, fresh fruit in season, jams and jellies and coffee, tea, milk or cocoa.

DANIEL DOUGLAS HOUSE: 103 S. Second Street, Clarksville, 63336. (573) 242-3939. Open all year. A three guestroom home with shared bath, that has been completely restored. No pets. No smoking in guestrooms. Within walking distance of everything, especially the local antique shops. Susan and Charles Sluka, innkeepers.

DIRECTIONS: From I-70 at St. Peters, take Highway 79 north about forty-three miles. Hwy. 79 become Second street in Clarksville.

MEADOWLARK HOUSE AT FIELDSTONE FARM
Elsberry

When I first met Bill Thompson, he was the owner/editor of a nationally known horse magazine, Saddle and Bridle. I had not seen Bill for many years. That is, until I heard he owned a farm in beautiful Lincoln County, and just a short distance from Clarksville, where my artist, Jamie McIlroy lives. Needless to say, I phoned him when I found out he was about to open a bed and breakfast.

Bill has fifty six acres of pasture and woods with a three acre lake. You can fish the lake and hike the woods. Or, if you want to bring your horse, you can ride the trails or ride from the farm to the Mississippi River. A great stable is available with a fee.

Bill's love of horses is very plain as he uses his farm mainly as a retirement home for older show horses. They are truly great horses, some being national champions. There are great views of the surrounding countryside from anyplace on the property.

The house, a three story brick, with walls 14 inches thick, was built in 1933 by the Waltke Family from St. Louis, as a place they could go to for safety, if need be, during the depression.

You enter the front door from a 12 x 50 foot L-shaped screened-in porch that overlooks the lake, woods and meadows. At one end is a seating arrangement of a wicker table and wicker chairs. At the other end is a wood table and chairs, and more wicker seating. There are plenty of live plants.

The porch leads you to a 30 foot living room which has a stone fireplace. It is furnished with an upholstered sofa, two antique wash stands, each with an antique brass and marble double globe lamp, a butlers tray, coffee table, a pair of light green upholstered Victorian arm chairs, a pair of plaid upholstered arm chairs, a tripod table with a reading lamp and a baby grand piano. There are great pictures on the wall, and other decorative pieces. Five six over six windows offer a great view.

Off the living room, a dining room has an antique armoire, and a country French refactory dining table with six upholstered armless chairs. There is also an antique step back cupboard and a hanging cupboard is over a small two drawer hunt board. A large live ficus plant along with a live buckhorn plant green up the room. There are beautiful oriental carpets throughout the first floor. Six over six windows look out on the front porch and the countryside.

Guests have access to the kitchen and an early cup of coffee, especially if you want to talk horses to Bill.

Off the kitchen there is a glassed-in breakfast porch with a tiled floor. A Vermont gas stove is great on chilly mornings for drinking coffee as you look out at the horse pasture. I love to watch these old beauties run. Its furnished with a round walnut table and four rush seated walnut French country chairs. A real antique coal oil lamp hangs over the table. There is a dry sink, a floor lamp and several large plants.

Just off the hall from the living room is a den. It is furnished with an upholstered sofa, an antique step back cupboard, a music cabinet, a dough box on legs and an antique school master's desk that belonged to Bill's grandfather. A table holds a large sailboat model that can be sailed on the lake. There is plenty of reading material, great pictures and a view of the lake from the two six over six windows.

Further down the hall is a family room. There is a multi-colored sofa upholstered in a stripe pattern, a blue leather wing back chair, an upholstered recliner, antique end table, a pine chest, an antique carpenters tool box, a wrought iron floor lamp, and a nice entertainment center with a television. There is also a walnut table and four Hitchcock chairs. There are some nice framed equestrian prints, Vanity Fair and original art on the walls. Persian carpets are on the floor. French doors open onto a terrace with a wrought iron umbrella table and chairs, and a wrought iron fence crafted by a local blacksmith. This is one of several places in the house, ideal for a quiet cup of coffee.

A wide staircase leads to the guestrooms on the second floor. At the landing, there is an upholstered love seat with end tables, each with antique brass lamps, a Victorian chair and a copper weather vane can be seen outside the window. The area is decorated with quilts, plants, pictures and a pair of brass wall sconces.

A hall at the top of the stairs leads to the guestrooms. There is an antique console with a lamp and an oval gold mirror on the wall. A tiled pink has a tub and shower.

The Green Room is furnished with a full-size maple bed covered with a floral spread, a matching chest and dresser. An antique, one drawer work table is used as a bedside table with a lamp. Another holds a television. There are live plants, framed prints are on the jade green walls, and two windows, one with four over four panes and one with six over six panes, give a view of the lake, huge trees and open fields.

The Purple Room has an antique full-size brass bed with plaid bed linens. An antique table and lamp are by the bed. There is an antique chest, a pair of upholstered armless chairs, and a walnut top table. Two six over six paned windows offer a great view.

The Yellow Room is furnished with twin Jenny Lind beds, a marble top Victorian parlor table and lamp, an antique chest and an upholstered arm chair. Original art is on the yellow walls. The six over six paned windows offer a view of the lake and fields.

The Blue Room offers an antique full-size short poster bed, an antique chest, a table with an antique lamp, an open arm chair and ottoman. Area carpets are on the floor. A view of the lake and huge trees can be seen through the six over six and eight over eight paned windows.

The Red Room is furnished with a full-size oak headboard and a matching chest and a dresser. A pair of bedside tables have brass lamps. Area carpets are on the floors, a quilt is on the bed and pictures are on the walls. A view of the wooded hillside is seen from the six over six paned windows.

A full breakfast is served at Meadowlark House. Juice, in season fruit, then the entrée which will vary. A typical breakfast would be an egg dish, breakfast meat, American fried potatoes, hot rolls, jelly and jams, and coffee, tea or milk. Or, maybe buttermilk pancakes with sausage and American fried potatoes. But, you won't go away hungry.

MEADOWLARK HOUSE AT FIELDSTONE FARM: 198 Mad River Lane, Elsberry, 63433. (573) 898-3245. Open all year. No smoking in house. No pets. Well behaved children welcome. A five guestroom house on a 56-acre farm. William Thompson and Ken Wilson, innkeepers.

DIRECTIONS: From I-70 and Hwy 79, go north on Hwy 79 approximately 30 miles to Elsberry. Three miles north of Elsberry, turn left on Dameron Road. Go one mile to Mad River Lane. Turn right to Meadowlark House.

RETREAT AT ABERDEEN
Clarksville

Of all the bed and breakfast homes I have visited in the past 10 years that I have written about (more than 400), I don't think any can compare as to the history, beautiful grounds and buildings as Aberdeen Farm. For years I have driven by this jewel of a place. Many times, I've pulled off to the side of the road just to take in the white fences, the limestone bottom creek, huge barns, towering trees and the wonderful, white house. So one might imagine how I felt when I heard Aberdeen was to become a bed and breakfast retreat.

I have never been more excited in all my drives as I was the day I drove through the stone entrance, crossed the creek and up the drive to the house.

John Bruere, the owner, answered my knock on the door, invited me in and after a few moments of self introduction, walked me through the house, giving me historical data on it. We sat down in the kitchen and he proceeded to tell me the fascinating story of Aberdeen. I would like to share a bit of it with you.

In 1833, a group of Meriwethers and Lewises, along with their families and slaves, left their homes in Virginia, came to Missouri in covered wagons, and settled in Pike County, near Clarksville, to grow tobacco.

The first portion of this house was a frame room with an attic over it and then attached to the frame part, a one-story brick room. The last addition of brick was two and one-half stories high, built into the side of a hill, so that the second story opened onto the hillside. Everything that went into its construction was homemade. The weather boards of black walnut were beaded, the joists were of oak and the bricks were made on the place. Over the years, a few additions were made, and today comprise 7,000 square feet of living area. The first two portions of the house along with these additions are now covered with wood siding and the whole house is painted white. One of the children who was born and raised on Aberdeen in the 1800s had such fond memories that he wrote a book about Aberdeen entitled "Days of Long Ago." John has several original copies and is going to expand and reprint it. It is a fascinating look at family farm life in the 1800s.

Entering the front door, you are standing in a wide hall running the depth of the house. The walls have a panel chair rail and woodwork painted Williamsburg gray. Two large 16-arm brass chandeliers hang from the ceiling. An oriental carpet is on the floor and up the staircase. It is furnished with an ornate carved Persian two door cabinet, pier mirror, a circa 1870 rolltop walnut secretary, bookcase, an upholstered Victorian sofa and a pair of Victorian chairs.

A pocket door to the right of the entry leads to a 38-foot long parlor. It has a huge fireplace and a bay window at the end of the room. It is fully carpeted and has a large crystal chandelier. It is furnished with an upholstered sofa, an antique china cabinet, an 8-leg spool table with a floral arrangement, a pair of upholstered wing chairs, a marble table top, an antique ladies rocker, a coffee table and a piano. The door leads into the dining room/library.

The dining room/library is a beauty. It is tongue and groove paneling painted gray. Built-in bookcases are on one wall, part of another, and over two doors—full of fine books. A fireplace has a great mantle piece. There is a long, double pedestal French country table and eight chairs, and an antique open arm chair. An oriental carpet is on the floor. In an alcove, windows have burgundy drapes. Five antique wall clocks and pictures decorate the walls. The exit door opens onto a 15 x 30 foot porch. Two sides are framed and two are screened in. It is furnished with a round rattan table, four chairs and a couch. There is a wicker porch swing, a four piece wicker set with an arm chair, rocker, table and a foot stool. The door opens onto a great open porch, some 40 feet long with a brick floor, four huge columns and a view of fences, trees and a lake.

Another door in the hall opens to the den or family room. The walls are the original walls of the 2 and one-half story addition. They are of exposed brick, 16 inches thick. There is a fireplace with a walnut mantle, and the oak beamed ceilings have a brass chandelier. It is furnished with a pair of leather chairs, a leather ottoman, a drop leaf table, an antique corner cupboard, a drop leaf tea cart, and an antique jelly cupboard. A huge brass apple butter kettle is among the decorations. A door leads to a small, brick floor and screened in breakfast porch with a wrought iron table and chairs. Another door from the room leads to the large commercial kitchen.

From the entry hall, the staircase takes you to the second floor guest rooms. An oriental runner is on the floor of the hall. There is an antique walnut dresser with fruit pulls, a pair of Victorian upholstered chairs and a grandfather clock. The paneled walls, chair rail high, are painted Williamsburg gray, as is the woodwork.

French doors lead into another hall, which is decorated with an oriental rug. Four guestrooms are off this hall, which John offers as two suites with private baths, or as four rooms with two sharing baths. One is furnished with a high back carved oak bed, an oak highboy chest, a carved blanket chest, an oak two door wardrobe and an oak stand with a lamp. A view from the windows overlooks the farm buildings.

Another guestroom is a large room with four windows that look out on the lake and white fences. It is furnished with a queen size brass and white iron bed, a pair of wicker rockers, a wicker bedside table with a lamp, an antique treadle sewing machine, a cane rocker, an antique walnut dresser, and an antique burled walnut wardrobe.

A large hall bath has wainscoting painted gray. An old-fashioned tub has a brass shower.

Missouri's former governor, Lloyd Stark, lived here at Aberdeen for thirty years. A guestroom, named for him, is furnished with a full size walnut poster bed. Two upholstered wing chairs face a wood-burning fireplace. Floral patterned wallpaper covers the walls. Four windows overlook the landscape. A private bath has a walk-in shower.

John offers several packages. Package A is a stay from Friday evening through Sunday to 3 p.m., with two breakfasts served in your room. Package B is the same as A, except a Saturday night dinner is served. Package C is Package B with a Sunday brunch instead of breakfast in your room.

Also available at an extra charge would be a picnic lunch for either Saturday or Sunday. A typical in-room breakfast includes juice, hot drink, fresh bread or muffins, omelet or hot cereal. A typical dinner might feature ceasar salad, carrot soup, fresh vegetable in season, garlic potatoes, and herbal salmon or chicken bolognese with a pecan bourbon tart for dessert.

Beginning in the spring, other packages on specific dates are offered for health, healing and stress-free retreats, which include a format for a person to discover the relationship of mind, body and spirituality. Body energy facilitation (sometimes called therapeutic touch or non-touch) is available by a resident facilitator. Therapeutic massage, reflexology, herbal treatments and sources of information about complementary medicine will be available on special dates.

RETREAT AT ABERDEEN B&B: 21307 Hwy D, Eolia, 63344. (573) 485-6122. Open all year. Two two-room suites with private baths. No smoking. No pets. A great way to really enjoy a weekend. This is one of my favorite places. John Bruere, innkeeper.

DIRECTIONS: From Hwy 61, north or south, exit at Eolia exit. It will be Route D. Turn left, go through Eolia and about three miles to Aberdeen, on the right side.

ROSEMONT FARM BED & BREAKFAST
Clarksville

Thomas Trundel III was born in Maryland in 1787. He moved to Kentucky with his widowed mother. In 1815 he married Pricilla Bowen, moved to Missouri and settled in Pike County. He was deeded this property in 1824 by President James Monroe. Pricilla died in 1838 and Thomas in 1858. The current home was built by William Trundel, Thomas' son, in 1854. It was named Rosemont for Alexander and Mary Rose who were slaves that seemed to have stayed at the farm as hired workers after the Civil War.

Today, Rosemont is a 160-acre historic farm with a two-story, ten room, brick home, nestled in the rolling hills a few miles from Clarksville. All of the woodwork, floors and windows are original, including some of the windowpanes.

The original entry has antique plant stands on each side of the door. It has a small drop leaf table and two chairs and a mirror with candle sconces. The staircase has the original walnut handrail and spindles.

Enter into one of two parlors. The first thing I noticed was the smell of the wood burning stove. The floor has a large hooked area carpet and white lace curtains are at the windows. Green walls are decorated with pictures and craft items. The furnishings include a pair of upholstered wing chairs, two bookcases, a rocking chair and a small chest with a TV/VCR.

The second parlor has a blue, pink and white hooked carpet, lace curtains, and there is also a wood burning stove. The walls have pictures and sconces.

It is furnished with a pair of burgundy, Victorian chairs with wood trim, an upholstered Victorian sofa with wooden trim, an antique pump organ, a marble top Victorian table, an antique lamp table and a brass planter.

The dining room has a ball and claw-foot, double pedestal table with six chairs, an antique high chair, and a breakfront with a dinner service of Royal Doulton china. A wood burning stove has the original mantle piece and tall windows have lace curtains. Dark green wallpaper has a Chinese motif of bird in tree branches. Framed prints and a large gold-leaf mirror decorate the walls. A crystal chandelier with hurricane globes hangs over the dining table.

The Bettie Bell Smith Room, named after the third mistress of the house, is located on the first floor. It is sunny and bright with a small pattern wallpaper in yellows, blues and pinks. It is furnished with a short four poster bed with a feather mattress over the regular mattress and covered with a colorful quilt. There is a night table with a lamp, and a dresser. The room has a large private bath with a walk-in shower.

Two guestrooms are on the second floor. In the hall there is a roll-top desk, an antique treadle sewing machine and a quilt rack with quilts. A door opens to a balcony over the front porch. There is also a sitting room furnished with an upholstered recline, a wooden rocker, a stack bookcase and a round table. Sheer curtains are on three tall windows.

The Emily Trundel Room, named for William Trundel's wife, Emily, is furnished with a tall poster headboard, with a floral spread, an arts and crafts library table, a pair of round night tables with lamps, an upholstered open arm rocking chair, a pair of bookcases, a quilt rack, cedar chest and a cheval mirror. Pink and white curtains are on the windows. A door opens onto a balcony where you can get a great view of fields and woods.

The Martha Turner Room is named for the wife of John Turner who purchased the farm in 1865. It has an antique, full-size, white iron bed, a pair of barrel-back upholstered chairs, an antique oak chest, dresser and a wardrobe-chest combination. Tan floors have area carpets, the walls have a floral print wallpaper and the windows have white lace curtains.

Breakfast is served in the dining room. After an early cup of coffee and juice, there is a fruit dish of some sort, then an egg dish, sausage, bacon or ham, gravy and biscuits, hash browns or fried apples. Another choice is Belgian waffles with fruit, syrup and whipped cream with sausage, bacon or ham. There are always coffee, tea or milk. Lunch and supper are also available.

ROSEMONT FARM B & B: 29328 Hwy. H, Box 9A, Clarksville, 63336. (573) 847-2219 or (888)812-3391. E-Mail: rosemontfarm@inweb.net. An antebellum home on 160 acres. Great views, peace and quiet. No smoking. No pets. Children welcome. Terry and Linda Lewis, innkeeper.

DIRECTIONS: Take Hwy. 40-61-64 north 12 miles past Troy. Take Eolia exit. Hwy. D to Hwy. H, 4 ½ miles to farm. Or Hwy. 79 north from I-70, 35 miles to Annada. The Hwy. H, 7 ½ miles to farm.

RECESS INN BED & BREAKFAST
Ethel

The town of Ethel was just twenty-one years old when they built the school building, that is now the Recess Inn. Ethel had used a two-room frame school building from 1890 until the brick school was opened in 1910. It was used continuously until December, 1980. It is now home to Ralph and Sandy Clark and the three "r's" here are rest, relaxation and a little reminiscing. I think people always like to reminisce about school days, even if your favorite class was recess.

The entry is protected by a large arch as you enter the building. A foyer has a drop leaf table, a flower cart, house plants, an old school desk and an antique gas lamp.

A gathering room has a raised brick hearth with a wood burning Franklin stove. The room is furnished with a sofa and matching love seat, a teacher's school desk, a book rack with children's antique books, a vintage floor model art deco radio and a wooden rocking chair. An original blackboard is on one wall and a burgundy wallpaper is below a floral patterned chair rail border. A large area rug is on the floor. There are old maps, a world globe and a collection lunch boxes.

The dining room is furnished with a country French table with six high-back caned chairs, an oak buffet, an antique piano and an antique cupboard. A teal carpet fully covers the floor. Note the lace curtains at the windows and the brass light fixture with a green globe. There are pictures relating to school days of yore.

Enjoy a hearty old-fashioned country breakfast served "grandma" style. Sandy serves juice, fresh fruit, sausage and eggs, biscuits and gravy. Quiche is also served as a entree variation. There are homemade cinnamon rolls, homemade muffins and banana bread, jams and jellies, coffee or tea.

Three large comfortable rooms with twelve-foot ceilings are decorated with antiques and quilts. They each have a private bath.

The first guestroom has a queen-size, antique iron bed covered with a beautiful quilt, an oak chest, an antique oak rocker, a bedside table with lamp and a child's school desk. Lace curtains cover the eight-foot windows. Three walls are painted tan and a schoolhouse pattern wallpaper in on the fourth.

Another guestroom has a full-size ornate iron bed and green on green plaid bed linens. There is an old beaded corner cupboard, a child's antique metal bed, an upholstered chair, a floor lamp, an antique rocker and a small desk and mirror. Three walls are painted tan and the fourth has a paper in a green stripe.

A honeymoon suite contains a king-size poster bed with a tester, an antique pine washstand with a towel bar, a roll-top desk, a lamp table with lamp and a 1930s platform rocker. Pale teal walls have a ceiling border.

Plenty of fun can be had at the two major lakes near Macon, just a short distance away. There is hiking, fishing, bicycling and occasional hayrides.

Enjoy a picnic lunch at a nearby lake. Your hosts will prepare and pack it for you. Or just take a stroll along the quiet country roads.

Ralph and Sandy Clark along with Donald and Linda Souther, also offer Hunter's Inn Bed & Breakfast, a quaint two-story hideaway, on a hill overlooking the town of Ethel. It's a great place for guests to watch the comings and goings of the many trains that pass through the town. It's also in the heart of wonderful hunting country. A full country breakfast is brought to you from the Recess Inn. You can contact them by calling the Recess Inn or direct to Hunter's Inn at (660) 486-3404.

RECESS INN B & B: 203 S Main, Ethel, 63539. (660) 486-3328 or (800) 628-5003. Website: www.bbonline.com/mo/recessinn/. Open all year. Children Welcome. No pets. No smoking. Ralph and Sandy Clark, proprietors.

DIRECTIONS: From I-70 and Hwy. 63, go north to Hwy. 36. Left on 36 to Hwy. 149. North to Ethel.

FIFTH STREET MANSION BED & BREAKFAST
Hannibal

T his three story home is one of the remnants of "millionaire's Row," an impressive block of grand homes built and owned by some of Hannibal's wealthiest and most influential citizens. It was built in 1858 by Brison Stillwell, three time Mayor of the city.

After the Civil War, the mansion became the townhouse of John and Helen Garth. Both the Garths were childhood chums of young Sam Clemens and remained lifelong friends. It was in this house the Mark Twain dined with Mrs. Garth and Laura Hawkins Frazer (his Becky Thatcher) on his last visit to Hannibal in 1902.

The Italianate architecture of the exterior was designed to look like an Italian country villa. The style is characterized by extended eaves that emphasize cornices set with heavy brackets, slender floor to ceiling windows, and a cupola topping the house and providing a view of Hannibal and the Mississippi River.

When you step inside the home of Mike and Donalene Andreotti, the owners, you'll enter a world of crystal chandeliers, polished brass, and stained and leaded glass. There are eight fireplaces done in ceramic tiles with walnut and oak mantels, each one unique. The original chandeliers and brass gasoliers have been retained throughout the house. One of the most striking features is a six by eight-foot Tiffany window on the first floor landing. The twenty-room home is decorated in period furnishings.

A large front parlor with twelve-foot ceilings has a hanging brass chandelier and a fireplace. The period furnishings include an Empire sofa with matching chair and a lady's desk. The walls are done in yellow and there is a sculptured floral carpet.

Huge double parlor doors open into the dining room. A tile and carved fireplace, a hanging gas chandelier, Victorian wallpaper and an oriental carpet create an atmosphere of the turn of the century. There are half a dozen tables where guests are served breakfast.

The library is also open for guests to enjoy and is furnished with a French provincial sofa and love seat, a television and bookshelves, with numerous books to choose from. The paneling in this room is a fine example of hand grained walnut. Wall to wall carpet is on the floor. Wander in and sample a glass of Missouri wine on your arrival, find the tales of Huck Finn or Tom Sawyer, and curl up and enjoy Hannibal's past.

Mike and Donalene like to give their guests a good start to their day, so they serve a full breakfast consisting of juice, a generous fruit plate and either breakfast meats and eggs, French toast, an egg casserole, or blueberry pancakes, along with an assortment of breads and rolls, and coffee or tea.

There are seven guestrooms, each with a private bath. Each room is tastefully decorated and offer both elegance and comfort. Several of them have four poster beds; some have high-back or brass beds. The furnishings are a combination of French and Victorian and include armoires, dressers, sofas and chairs, leather wing chairs, and rocking chairs.

Some of the guestrooms have fireplaces and most have oriental carpeting. Mike and Donalene have created an authentic Victorian milieu with beautiful floral print wallpapers, lace curtains and many antique pictures.

A family suite on the third floor consists of two rooms and a private bath. Both rooms have brass beds, easy chairs and tables.

There are two wraparound porches that provide inviting spots for conversation, reading, or just doing nothing. So, for whatever kind of visit you choose, a get away from it all or a tour of the historic spots in this city, you will find Fifth Street Mansion offers a perfect blend of Victorian charm and contemporary comforts with plenty of old fashioned hospitality.

FIFTH STREET MANSION B & B: 213 South Fifth Street, Hannibal, 63401. (573) 221-0445. Reservations: (800) 874-5661. FAX (573) 221-3335. Website: hanmo.com/fifthstreetmansion. A 20-room mansion featuring seven guestrooms with private baths. No pets. Smoking limited. Open all year. Mike and Donalene Andreotti, innkeepers.

DIRECTIONS: Call for reservations and directions.

GARTH WOODSIDE MANSION
Hannibal

"I spent many nights with John and Helen Garth in their spacious beautiful home. They were children with me and afterwards schoolmates." So said Samuel Clemens on a return trip to Hannibal in 1882.

There is always a glow in the faces of couples who have traveled from afar to stay at this award-winning inn. This private, Victorian estate is nestled on 33 acres of rolling meadows, tall woodlands, and flowered gardens. A must stop, the inn focuses on the warmth and simple beauty provided by nature. A national "American Home Award" winner and voted by bed and breakfast travelers as the "#1 Bed and Breakfast in Missouri," Garth Mansion is memorable for all the right reasons.

The mansion is now the home of Julie and John Rolsen, who purchased the Inn in 1999 and will continue operating it as a bed and breakfast. As you enter the home through a large double door entrance, you will see the most significant feature of the mansion, a magnificent flying staircase made of walnut that spirals up all three levels.

A formal parlor, off the hall on the right, features a seven piece Eastlake cherry parlor set, that once belonged to the Garth family. A white marble mantel with carved lion's head motif, and the ornate plaster-ceiling medallion are original to the house. There is also an antique cylinder secretary and an antique etagere holding a collection of Victorian pottery.

The focal point of the dining room is a pedestal walnut table which extends to seat twenty-four. Irv and Diane's collection of pressed and cut glass is displayed in an antique Renaissance Revival three cupboard breakfront of carved walnut.

To the left of the entry hall, a library features another collection. Hundreds of books that belonged to the Garths are displayed in their original Empire style bookcases. An unusual rosewood and red velvet reclining chair and a huge Victorian sofa are antique pieces. Here comfortable furnishings, a fireplace, and an informal atmosphere are conducive to conversation and are a part of Garth Mansion's charm.

The family parlor on the first floor is a cozy room that has an antique bookcase, a Victorian upholstered chair and a matching rocker, a nice large ice cream table and four chairs. A huge bay window overlooks the grounds.

The second and third floors house eight guestrooms that blend history with modern amenities. All of the rooms are large, air-conditioned and have private baths. They are furnished in Victorian splendor with original Garth pieces. Each room provides the comfort of home with many personal touches including turndown service and night shirts.

The most sought after guestroom is the one in which Mark Twain slept, The Clemen's Room. It is furnished with a huge antique queen-size half tester bed, a marble top dresser with candle stands, an antique marble top washstand, Victorian table and an antique platform rocker. An oriental carpet in on the floor. There is a private bath with shower.

Throughout the hallways you will find special collections and personal items that belonged to the Garths.

The Rolsens feature a full sit down breakfast elegantly served in the dining room. Fresh fruit with lemon cream sauce, juice, homemade carrot muffins, and coffee or tea. Entrees differ each day and could be such delights as french toast with peach sauce, or crepes with a quiche filling of eggs, sausage and cheese.

Afternoon tea is served on the huge wraparound veranda while guests gaze at magnificent vistas with the smell of the garden flowers lingering in the air. A lifetime of memories that belonged to John and Helen Garth still remain at the Garth Woodside Mansion, and John and Julie wish to share them with their guests.

GARTH WOODSIDE MANSION: 11069 New London Road, Hannibal, 63401. (888) 427-8409 and (573) 221-2789. An eight guestroom country inn reflecting the lifestyles of the 1870s. Open all year. Children over 12 welcome. No pets. Smoking is allowed on the veranda and balcony areas. Julie and John (Col. USAF, retired) Rolsen, innkeepers.

DIRECTIONS: From Hwy. 61 in Hannibal, go south to the first road south of the Holiday Inn (Warren Barrett Drive). Turn east and follow signs. Reservations preferred.

Notes:

_____

_____

_____

_____

_____

_____

_____

_____

_____

_____

_____

_____

_____

LOUISIANA

Wedged among the majestic Mississippi River hills and bluffs, Louisiana, founded in 1818, is a lively old river town well worth visiting if history and architecture are of interest to you. It has been labeled "one of the best kept secrets in the Midwest." Descendants of settler, who obtained land grants from the Spanish in 1812, still live here.

At one time, it was a tobacco and river port. There are dozens of beautiful antebellum and Victorian "gingerbread" homes along the quiet, tree-lined streets. The century old, downtown buildings are being renovated and now hold great antique shops and other enterprises. In fact, seven blocks on both sides of Historic Georgia Street remain virtually unchanged by time, with street scenes reminiscent of the mid to late 1800s. Other antique shops are in huge old mansions, just a block or so from the downtown area, which incidentally, is on the National Register of Historic Places.

Jeanne's House of Antiques is located in one of these old homes at 400 North Main. (573) 754-6836. Twenty rooms are packed full of nice pieces, and just about anything you would want is probably here or downstairs on a lower level at her daughter Clarissa's. Jeanne specializes in glass, china and good, early walnut furniture. The first thing I noticed was a circa 1850s Solianware (a forerunner of Coalport) dinner set. There was a circa 1860 chest, an antique set of wicker that included a couch, table, chairs, and a lamp table. Other pieces included a pair of lawyer's stack bookcases, a chest of drawers, a Victorian love seat, a teachers desk, a marble top Eastlake dresser with glove boxes and candle stands, a nice old wooded coffee bin, a circa 1840 two door corner cupboard in cherry, a mission library table and several wooden trunks. There was also a yarn winder, a marble top chest and matching wash stand, a Victorian parlor table, a circa 1850 step-back cupboard from Quebec, a cherry dropleaf two drawer table, a brass bed, a blanket box, an oak clawfoot round table, a walnut jelly cupboard, a walnut dresser with fruit pulls, and a step-back cupboard from Bethel, Missouri. Some of the smaller pieces included a coffee grinder, fish lures, Royal Doulton mugs, a pitcher and bowl set, hanging lamps, Buffalo pottery, tureens, framed prints and pictures, hand painted bowls and plates, jewelry, and a Celestina with paper rolls (quite rare).

You can spend a couple of delightful days browsing the many shops in this historic town and have enough places you had to skip, to beckon you back for another visit.

APPLEGATE BED & BREAKFAST
Louisiana

Over one hundred years ago, Highway 79 was a plank road and also a toll road. Horse races were held on Sundays around the town of Louisiana and the toll was paid at a toll house that sat where Applegate B & B's driveway connects to the highway. In fact, the stone foundation is still there. At that time, the house on the property was a brick home, built in 1843. Today, it is covered with frame siding and is the home of Ron and Judy Allely and the Applegate Bed and Breakfast. It is comprised of 66 acres with board fences, outbuildings, a barn and an apple orchard.

Just at the outskirts of Louisiana, a winding drive from Hwy. 79 takes you up to the house. A stone wall is partially around a patio. A door leads into the paneled family room. It is carpeted wall to wall with Berber carpeting. It is furnished with a suede upholstered love seat and sofa, end tables and lamps, an upholstered glider love seat, a desk, coffee table, bookcases, an upholstered rocker recliner and a television. A fireplace with an insert stove has a long shelf above it, filled with decoys, arts and crafts, old churns and other collectibles.

Part of a large L-shaped room has a pool table for your use, a park bench, a real vintage Wurlitzer juke box and a curio cabinet with a collection of miniature houses. The room is paneled below a chair rail. There is an entrance to the outside that guests may use. The other part of the room has a large wood burning fireplace, area carpets on the floor, and four six over six paned windows have lace curtains. It is furnished with an upholstered sofa with wood trim and an antique carpenter's chest is used for a coffee table. There is an end table with brass lamp, a wicker chair, a cushioned oak rocker, and a reproduction icebox holds a television.

The dining room has wall-to-wall carpeting, a fireplace with an insert stove, a built in cupboard holds Franciscan china, a long bay window has a floral valance. It is furnished with a long maple table and four Windsor chairs, an antique oak kitchen chair and a plate rack with more Franciscan dishes. There's a good view of the property.

Upstairs on the second floor, there are three guestrooms. One, The Mackintosh Room, has wall-to-wall blue sculptured carpet, white walls and white criss-cross curtains. It has a full-size brass bed with a handmade colorful coverlet, a bedside table and lamp, a wicker arm chair, chest and a table and lamp. There is a view of the winding drive, the barn, huge trees and the hills. A private bath just outside the door has a walk-in shower. It also has a double sink and tile walls and floors.

The Johnathan Room is furnished with twin beds with handmade quilts in the wedding ring pattern, a chest, a desk and a small table with a reading lamp. The floor has wall-to-wall blue sculptured carpet, blue curtains and white woodwork. The view of the woods is seen from the windows.

The Winesap Room has a full-size brass bed with handmade quilts, a white wicker chair, a chest with a white wicker framed mirror and a bedside table with a lamp. The windows have blue curtains, white woodwork and a sculptured blue carpet.

A sitting area between the rooms has a white wicker love seat and a wicker coffee table.

For breakfast, Judy serves juice, fresh fruit in season, and Applegate French toast, which is made with French bread with apples, cinnamon, brown sugar and butter and Kayro syrup served with sausage or bacon. Or, there is quiche, a breakfast meat of some kind, muffins, jam and jellies and coffee, tea or milk.

Upon arrival, Judy offers her guests cheese and crackers and wine or ice tea or lemonade in the summer and hot cocoa or cider in the winter. She always places some chocolate kisses on your pillow. There's also a lot to do here. If you want to go to antique shops, Louisiana has some nice ones, but for me, a long walk in the woods and apple orchard, bird watching and hoping to spot some wildlife would be my thing (although I like antiques).

APPLEGATE B & B: 738 Frankford Road, Louisiana, 63353. (573) 754-4322. Open all year. Three nice clean rooms. A 66-acre farm and apple orchard, and a 150-year-old house. Judy and Ron Allely, innkeepers.

DIRECTIONS: From St. Louis, take I-70 to Hwy. 79 just west of St. Charles. Stay on Hwy. 79 until you get to Louisiana. Go approximately 1.7 miles past town to Frankford Road. Turn left.

LOUISIANA GUESTHOUSE
Louisiana

Louisiana Guesthouse is a lovely two story Cape Cod set back among large old trees in one of the residential areas of the town, with great antique shops just a few blocks away. The home dates back to the late 1800s and is classically furnished with antiques throughout the house. The owners, Mett and Betty Jo Bryant, will make you feel very welcome. Upon arrival, hors d'oeuvres and beverages are offered, served in antique goblets and on antique china. In your room are freshly cut flowers, usually from their own cutting gardens.

Betty Jo serves a full breakfast for her guests, using china patterns to compliment the room where you are served. It can be served in the living room in front of the fireplace, or in the comfort of her blue and white kitchen. Entree vary according to your preference and the menu will accommodate both your taste and diet restrictions. Choices include eggs Benedict, or French toast stuffed with pecans and apricots, or even a country breakfast with homemade biscuits and gravy.

Upstairs, under the eaves, is a very cozy bedroom with hardwood floors and furnished with family heirlooms, antique quilts, and children's board games from the twenties and thirties. Antique rocking chairs in front of a dormer window and handmade braided rugs complete the warm feeling of this room.

A larger bedroom features a custom made antique queen-size bed with antique quilts and furniture to coordinate with the cobalt blues and pinks in the oriental rug covering the floor.

The bedrooms have private baths with claw foot tubs, individual soaps, shampoo and bathrobes.

While you're here, be sure to visit the many beautiful antebellum homes and visit the nearby Amish country.

LOUISIANA GUESTHOUSE: 1311 Georgia Street, 63353. (573) 754-6366 or call toll free (888)753-6366. A two bedroom guest house with private baths. Just a few blocks from most of the antique shops and a view of the Mississippi River. Open all year. No smoking. Gift certificates available. Member BBIM. Mett and Betty Jo Bryant, hosts.

DIRECTIONS: From St. Louis, take Hwy. 61 north to Eolia. Turn right on Rt. D and go 15 miles to Hwy. 79. Turn left into Louisiana and proceed to Georgia Street, Left on Georgia to 1311. Or take the scenic route. From I-70 go to Hwy. 79 and head north. It is about 50 miles to Louisiana.

MEADOWCREST BED & BREAKFAST
Louisiana

Tucked away in a tranquil country setting, is the one story traditional brick home of John and Karen Stoeckley. John is a well-known Missouri historical artist and his pen and ink drawings are nationally recognized. Meadowcrest has twelve acres of meadows and woods to hike or stroll with an abundance of wildlife and song birds.

The entry hall has gray slate tile with an oriental area rug, a pair of bookcases and a long low table. The walls are papered.

A large family room has a beamed ceiling with a fireplace on a built up hearth. A long couch is positioned at each end of the room with a classic billiards table between them. There is an upholstered arm chair, a rush seat rocking chair and an entertainment center with stereo. A wicker trunk is now a lamp table. Area carpets and runners cover the floor. There are many pictures and a very nice collection of ducks. This room overlooks a patio that has several seating pieces and an umbrella table.

The house is brimming with fine art by renown artists from around the country.

The living room has a fireplace and is furnished with a sofa and love seat, a pair of wing chairs, a Queen Anne style end table and coffee table, an antique drop leaf table, an antique slant front desk, an antique blue print cabinet and a ball and claw foot Chippendale chair. At the windows are sheer curtains with beige drapes. There are several floral arrangements. There is a light blue carpet here, as well as in the dining room.

An antique Queen Anne style table with eight chairs, a long library table, a china cupboard, a server and a liquor cabinet are in the dining room. Curtains and drapes match the living room. There is a brass five arm chandelier over the table.

Karen has studied the culinary arts both here and in Europe and her guests are the beneficiaries. She is also the Food Editor for *Missouri Life Magazine*. You can enjoy breakfast in the pavilion, on the patio, or an a lower deck overlooking a pastoral setting, weather permitting. Otherwise, breakfast is served in the dining room and offers a full complement of delicious main dishes, juices, fruit, homemade muffins, coffee and tea. Picnic lunch baskets and evening meals can be arranged at the time you make your reservations.

A beige carpeting is in the hall and continues into the two guestrooms. One is furnished with an antique four poster bed, a dressing table, a dresser from Germany, an antique table for a night stand and pair of 1920s red maple side chairs. The walls are done in a blue, pink and green floral print on one wall, and repeated in miniature on the other three. Sheer curtains with blue and white swags are at the windows. Pictures and a collection of blue plates are on the walls.

The second guestroom is furnished with a traditional queen-size bed, an armoire, a dresser with a double mirror, night tables and lamps and another red maple chair. Off white walls are below a chair rail and dark green above. There are matching drapes and bedspread. Sheer curtains are at the windows. Three pieces of John's work hang in this room.

Off the hall, a large bath with tub and shower is shared. It is very attractively decorated and you will find a basket of toiletries, in case you've forgotten some of your own.

Located in the old stagecoach depot in Louisiana is the main studio and gallery of Missouri Historian artist, John Stoeckley. Here you can take a trip back through time and view over 100 pen and ink and watercolor drawings of notable Missouri sites and landmarks, including covered bridges, barns, mills and college campus buildings. Open Tuesday through Saturday, *Reflections of Missouri Gallery* offers framed art and hand thrown pottery art of other Missouri artist, as well as interesting art objects and décor from other countries. For special occasions, you may book the gallery for private dining for eight to 18 people, enjoying gourmet meals designed just for you and your friends. Located on South 9th street in Louisiana, Missouri.

MEADOWCREST B & B: 15282 Hwy. NN, Louisiana, 63353. (573) 754-6594. Open all year. No smoking inside. No pets inside. John and Karen Stoeckley, innkeepers.

DIRECTIONS: Call John or Karen for directions and reservations.

ORTHWEIN MANSION BED & BREAKFAST
Louisiana

Built by a member of the Anheuser-Busch Brewing Company in 1905, this baronial style mansion is the scene for pampered hospitality. It is owned by Dottie Brown, the third family to reside here.

The house, which has been featured in Mid-West Living and St. Louis Magazine, sits on four acres on historic Georgia Street. The property is beautifully landscaped and has a winding driveway leading to the carriage entrance to the house.

An extravagant and magnificent brick, three story home with pillars across the front porch, it has twenty rooms with dark oak and cherry woodwork, stained glass windows and carved mantelpieces of excellent quality and workmanship. Two of the most outstanding features of the house are the paneled and beamed ceiling in the dining room and an unbelievable hand-carved cherry staircase. At the landing is a stained glass window of beautiful colors and design. The massive dining room table, and the matching chairs were custom carved from quarter sawn oak made specifically for this room. There is seating for twenty-four people.

The living room has a Queen Anne style sofa facing the fireplace. A pair of wing chairs are placed in front of a leaded glass bay window. An oriental carpet is on the floor and there is a brass chandelier.

On the second floor, guests will find a fresh flower arrangement in their room. The suite is one wing of the second floor.

It is furnished with a full-size four poster brass bed, a love seat, a chest, butler's tray table, an antique pie safe, a wardrobe and a television. Floral dust ruffles on the bed match the drapes. An original brass chandelier and lace covered pillows add to the charm of this room.

A country basket is left at your door in the morning. The menu varies but it is all freshly prepared and delicious.

Dottie has a respect for privacy. After an initial introduction and an exchange of pleasantries about the charming 19th century town of Louisiana, Dottie gives her guests the utmost privacy. They are left alone to discover the many comforts prepared for them. A tray of wine, and cheese awaits you when you arrive. Despite the grandiose air of this house, it is very comfortable and friendly. Dottie has a wonderful "live and let live" attitude you will appreciate.

ORTHWEIN MANSION B & B: 2000 Georgia Street, Louisiana, 63353. (573) 754-5449. Open all year. A one suite baronial mansion with private bath. No children or pets. Smoking permitted. Reservations in advance. Dottie Brown, host.

DIRECTIONS: From I-70 at St. Peters, take Hwy. 79 (The Great River Road) north to Louisiana (53 miles). Left on Georgia Street. Or take Hwy. 61 at I-70, north to Hwy. 54. East to Louisiana.

SERANDOS HOUSE BED & BREAKFAST
Louisiana

The earliest portion of this early Victorian home was built around 1876 with additions added on over the years. The house is old enough to be distinctive, and modern enough to be comfortable. Tom and Jeannie Serandos have spent a great deal of time on the renovation and redecorating of their home. They have retained the stained glass windows, oak and yellow pine woodwork and many of the original fixtures. Take note of the unusual paneling in the front hall and stairwell with its deeply embossed landscape scenes.

Guests are free to make use of the first floor. The living room is paneled and fully carpeted with a fireplace and a small built-in bookcase. The room contains a sofa and pair of matching chairs, a comfortable recliner-rocker, and a TV/VCR with a selection of movies.

A large bay window in the paneled dining room is filled with house plants. The room is furnished with a large dining table and ten chairs, breakfront, server, and a grandfather clock.

The Family Room is fully carpeted with a fireplace and a small built-in bookcase. Contains a sofa, recliner, swivel chair, a roll top desk, TV/VCR and a stereo.

The two guestrooms on the second floor are fully carpeted, have ceiling fans, air-conditioner, and each has a new TV/VCR. The rooms share an extra large bathroom with tub and shower.

The first room has a covered balcony. This room is furnished with a queen-size bed, chest, triple dresser and two small night tables. Jeannie has matched the drapes, curtains and bedspreads and hung attractive prints and pictures on the paneled walls. There are many houseplants about the room.

A large, sunny second guestroom is furnished with a queen-size bed, chest, writing desk, an armoire and a dresser. The wall are papered in a pleasing print pattern.

The Serando's believe breakfast is the most important meal of the day and it shows. There is ham, sausage or bacon and eggs any style, biscuits and gravy or pancakes with hot maple syrup, homemade bread, toast, jelly and jam, juice, fresh fruit in season, coffee, tea or milk. Breakfast is served in the dining room, dinette or on the patio.

With advance notice, and at an additional charge, the Serando's will prepare a delicious dinner for their guests, or small groups. Entree choices are steak, rib eye, barbecued chicken or pork. A salad, two vegetables, dessert, coffee or tea accompany your entree.

At the rear of the house, Tom has built a large private patio. It is furnished with redwood and metal furniture, with plenty of chairs, lounges and umbrella tables. In one section of the patio is a leisure room with an eight foot spa available for guests year round enjoyment.

SERANDOS HOUSE B & B: 918 Georgia Street, Louisiana, 63353. P.O. Box 205-63353. (573) 754-4067. (800) 754-4067 for reservations. A two guestroom home with shared bath. Off street parking. Closed from Thanksgiving to mid-February. No pets. Children can be accommodated. No smoking in guestrooms. Most of the antique shops in Louisiana are within walking distance of the house. Jeannie Serandos, hosts.

DIRECTIONS: From I-270 in St. Louis, take Hwy. 61 north to Hwy. 54. East on Hwy. 54 to Hwy. 79 in Louisiana. Turn right on 79 and go to Georgia Street. Turn right to home. Or take Hwy. 79 from 1-70 to Louisiana and turn left on Georgia Street to home.

THOUSAND ACRES FARM GUEST HOUSE
Louisiana

Thousand Acres Farm is dedicated to those that are seeking pampered luxury, and Rich Arenson provides just that, so bring along a great sense of expectancy when you visit here.

There are three special features at Thousand Acres. The first is the setting, the second is your host and the third is the quality of the food.

The setting is idyllic - peaceful, relaxing and comfortable. It has a panoramic view of hills and fields, where deer and turkey abound and where you may occasionally spot a bald eagle or a falcon. This view can be enjoyed from any one of three large decks on two sides of the house. In spring and summer, dozens of huge clay pots are filled with zinnia, petunia and geranium making a wall of flowers. In fall colorful chrysanthemums take their place. Rich grows all of his flowers from seed.

Your host, is most gracious and will make you feel at home from your first moment. He is attentive to all your needs and provides his guests with all the ingredients for a special visit: a quiet atmosphere, fine food, comfortable setting and beautiful surroundings.

The Torra gate is the entrance to the large herb and flower garden leading to the house. The guest house was designed by Rich, who was inspired by the Frank Lloyd Wright school of architecture. The house is extremely contemporary, built of rough sawn cedar and glass. The living/dining room is one large area looking out on nature. The plush, carpeted living room is very intimate with a wood burning fireplace. The luxurious furniture includes a couch on one side of the fireplace and two easy chairs opposite. The distinctive tables and lamps are of superb quality. A collection of antique laboratory bottles are displayed in a recess.

In the dining area is a round glass top table and four yellow leather chairs with antique morocco grill work. One wall is of smoked glass mirrors, while another has bookcases filled with books on gardening and cooking. The third wall is glass with sliding doors leading to a sun deck. There are wooden tables and seating for six or eight. A perfect place for breakfast in nice weather. A shaded deck is an outdoor living room in the summer, furnished with comfortable outdoor furniture.

Two guestrooms share a bath with tub and shower. Rich prefers to accommodate a group traveling together or just one couple. Both guestrooms have king-size beds and television sets. The windows overlook the rolling hills.

Rich not only grows his own herbs for seasoning, but has a vegetable garden where he gathers the ingredients for mouth-watering salads and side dishes. The food is all prepared in a professional cook's kitchen on the premises. Rich lives in the main house on the farm, but comes to the guest house, at an appointed time, to prepare breakfast or dinner. On arrival guests are offered a tray of handmade hors d'oeuvres and wine.

Among the many dinner entrees you may select from are freshly dressed rock Cornish hens stuffed with a pecan dressing, basted in cognac, and baked to a golden brown. Fresh salad with homemade dressing, fresh vegetables accompany the entree and are followed by a special dessert.

Breakfast selections would include breakfast meats, eggs, souffles, waffles with strawberries, fresh peaches on creamed French bread, or eggs benedict. All served with coffee, tea or milk.

Guests staying two nights are greeted with a huge appetizer assortment including potato salad wrapped in fresh country ham and Swiss cheese, Mexican deviled eggs, and olive wraps. There is also wine and dessert. It's really a dinner. The second breakfast is a San Francisco brunch served later in the morning. Dinner that evening is prepared from a choice of two entrees: Fresh fillet of lemon sole roulade or 1 1/2 inch T-bone steak. They are served with salad, vegetable and dessert.

THOUSAND ACRES FARM GUEST HOUSE: P.O. Box 123, Louisiana, 63353. (573) 754-5245. A secluded guest house in rolling hills near Louisiana. No children. No pets. Smoking permitted. Open all year. Call for reservations and directions. Member Bed & Breakfast of Greater St. Louis Reservation Service. Richard Arenson, host.

ST. AGNES HALL BED & BREAKFAST
Macon

This stately, old brick home has been considered one of the most interesting historical landmarks in Old Macon. It was built in the late 1840's by James A. Terrell on land acquired by an original land patent from the State of Missouri. During the Civil War years, the house was commandeered for use as Union Headquarters. It was believed to have been used as a "safe House" for slaves going north, before the war. In 1884, the property was converted to St. Agnes Hall, a boarding and day school for girls and young ladies. Following the close of the school in 1895, the house was extensively remodeled and turned back into a private home. It was then the family home of U.S. Senator James P. Kem until 1929. Beginning in 1944, it was used as apartments until Scott and Carol Phillips purchased the house and turned it into a bed and breakfast home. They have done an excellent job of renovating this interesting house and restoring the period gardens.

The entry hall is all oak with a huge stairway. The hall is furnished with antique furniture and small antiques, which Scott and Carol have collected. Many of the pieces are family heirlooms handed down through the generations. This includes a quilt from Carol's great, great, great grandmother.

The living room has a unique corner fireplace and a cherry beamed ceiling. There is a sofa and two wing chairs, a leather wing chair, an antique desk, television and a Victorian parlor table in front of the sofa. As in all of the rooms, there are many house plants, artwork and paintings.

Pocket doors lead into the dining room which has leaded glass windows overlooking a garden area. The room has an antique buffet, a Victorian table, rush seated chairs and a gateleg table.

Breakfast is served in the garden, on the veranda, in the dining room, or in your own room. A full breakfast is served and consists of juice, bacon, sausage or ham, homemade biscuits and gravy, and scrambled eggs. There are also homemade sweet rolls, homemade jams and jellies and coffee or tea.

There are three guestrooms and a suite at St. Agnes Hall, all with private baths. The Balcony Room, on the second floor is furnished with a king-size poster bed, upholstered chairs, an antique oak gentlemen's dresser, a vintage ice cream table with two chairs and a blanket chest. A beautiful cherry wood fireplace has curved green tiling. A door opens out on a balcony, which overlooks the garden.

The West Room is thirty feet long. At one end there is a queen-size four poster bed and at the other a full-size brass bed. In between there is a round oak table and four matching chair and a television. A Victorian love seat and matching chair is at the foot of the poster bed.

The South Room is furnished with a queen-size high-back bed, a Victorian table, chess table and chairs. The room has a bay window.

A two room suite on the third floor consists of a sitting area furnished with rattan chairs and a lamp table, rock and an antique tin tub (for show). Off one side of the sitting area is a room with a circa 1936, matched hard rock maple bedroom set: a queen-size Jenny Lind bed, a chest and vanity. There is a wicker chair and a corner table with lamp by the bed. Off the opposite side of the sitting room is a second bedroom with a queen-size broken pediment poster headboard bed, a chest, and a lamp table with lamp. This is a cozy retreat up under the eaves. The private bath has a six foot tub.

ST. AGNES HALL B & B: 502 Jackson Street, Macon, 63552. (660) 385-2774. Fax: (660) 385-4436. Three guestrooms with private bath on the second floor and a two bedroom suite with private bath on the third. Open all year. Children welcome. Smoking outside only. Scott and Carol Phillips, hosts.

DIRECTIONS: Located three blocks west of Hwy. 63 at the corner of Walnut and Jackson. From I-70 at Columbia, take Hwy. 63 north sixty miles to Macon, or from Hannibal take Hwy. 36 sixty miles west. Macon is at the crossroads of 63 and 36.

STAGECOACH INN
Macon

T he Stagecoach Inn not only has the distinction of being Macon's oldest standing structure, first post office and stagecoach station, but it also has deep family ties that link the town with the family who built the house.

Scott and Carol Phillips, the owners, purchased the house and restored it to look as it did in the 1890s. They have preserved the original craftsmanship, that makes it unique. The Phillips also own the St. Agnes Hall B & B up the street.

Entering the house from the original entrance you are in a small hallway with a coat rack and a table. The woodwork is painted a dark teal green color and has a high chair rail with a striped pattern paper below and a floral print above in colors of wine and green.

A carpeted gathering room is furnished with a sofa, rocking chair, a Victorian coffee table, captain's chair, a television and a corner cupboard. The room has off white walls with dark teal green woodwork and lace curtains at the windows.

A double door leads into the dining room, where guests usually play table games. The carpet, walls and woodwork are the same as the gathering room. A large brick fireplace has an antique cover. Two oak tables, each with four chairs, an antique oak sideboard and a library table complete the furnishings. Off this room is a half bath.

In the entry hall, a curved staircase takes you to guestrooms which both have a very cozy atmosphere as they are under the eaves. The front room has twin four poster beds, a night table with a reading lamp, a wicker sofa and chairs, a marble top dresser and a television. It is papered in a floral print. There is a private bath with tub and shower.

The other guestroom is furnished with a queen-size, antique iron bed, a two drawer chest, an antique bedside table and lamp, an antique chiffonier, dressing table and a rocker. A private bath has tub and shower.

A door from the dining room opens to a hall with stairs leading to a another second floor guestroom, which also has an outside entrance off the balcony, leading to the parking area. The room is furnished with a king-size bed, an ice cream table with two chairs, an antique Eastlake dresser, an upholstered chair and a bedside night table with a reading lamp. There is wallpaper in a floral and stripe design. A curtained off, private bath has a claw foot tub.

With a private entrance in the first floor addition, a suite has a carpeted sitting room furnished with a sofa and arm chair, a recliner, an ornate armoire, a rush seated chair, television, library table, a table with lamp, a floor lamp and an etagere. Three walls are off white, the fourth is paper in a crewel design. The woodwork is painted a plum color. A bedroom has a queen-size, high-back oak bed, an antique oak dresser, an ornate mirrored wardrobe and six leg tables with lamps by the bed. One wall is off white and the others are papers in a floral and stripe pattern. There is a private bath with tub and shower.

A fully equipped kitchen is available to guests. It is accessible to all three separate guest areas. Breakfast is served to guests at St. Agnes Hall Bed & Breakfast just up the street.

STAGECOACH INN: 309 Vine Street, Macon, 63552. (660) 385-2774. Fax: (660) 385-4436. Open all year. A three guestroom and one suite all with private baths. Children welcome. Smoking on porch only. Scott and Carol Phillips, innkeepers.

DIRECTIONS: Located west of Hwy. 63 at the corner of Vine and Jackson. From I-70 at Columbia, take Hwy. 63 north sixty miles to Macon. From Hannibal, take Hwy. 36 sixty miles west. Macon is the crossroads for Hwy. 63 and Hwy. 36.

Alphabetical Index of Inns

The Show Me Missouri Series

A to Z Missouri—A dictionary-style book of Missouri place name origins Abo to Zwanzig! Includes history for each town, pronunciations, population, county, post office dates and more. 220 pages. By Margot Ford McMillen. $14.95. ISBN: 0-9646625-4-X

The Complete Katy Trail Guidebook—U.S.'s Longest Rail-to-Trail The definitive guide to services, towns, people, places and history along Missouri's 200-mile Katy Trail. This completely revised and updated fifth edition covers the cross-state hiking and biking trail from Clinton to St. Charles. Includes maps, 80 photos and more. 224 pages. By Brett Dufur. $14.95. ISBN: 0-9646625-0-7

Daytrip Illinois—The tour guide standard for Illinois Covers daytrips around the state, including annual events, travel tips, 60 photos and 20 maps. Daytrips to help you enjoy the best of the Land of Lincoln. Exhaustively researched. 420 pages. By Lee N. Godley and Patricia Murphy O'Rourke. $16.95. ISBN: 0-9651340-0-6

Daytrip Missouri—The tour guide standard for Missouri Covers daytrips around the state, including annual events, travel tips, 60 photos and 20 maps. 224 pages. By Lee N. Godley and Patricia Murphy O'Rourke. $14.95. ISBN: 0-9651340-0-8

Exploring Columbia
Guide to hidden highlights, galleries, museums, towns, people and history in Columbia, Rocheport, Centralia and Boone County. Full of fun daytrips and inexpensive outings. Most trips are free or under $10. Includes maps and photos. 168 pages. By Pamela Watson. $14.95. ISBN: 0-9646625-2-3

Exploring Missouri Wine Country
This guidebook to Missouri wine country profiles wineries, including how to get there, their histories, wine tips, home-brew recipes, dictionary of wine terms and more. Also lists nearby bed & breakfasts, services and state parks. 208 pages. By Brett Dufur. $14.95. ISBN: 0-9646625-6-6

Forgotten Missourians Who Made History
A book of short stories and humorous comic-style illustrations of more than 35 Missourians who made a contribution to the state or nation yet are largely forgotten by subsequent generations. 168 pages. Compiled by Jim Borwick and Brett Dufur. $14.95. ISBN: 0-9646625-8-2

The Show Me Missouri Series

Guide to Cycling Kansas City

Seasoned cyclist's advice, maps & route information for more than 85 routes throughout Kansas City. Road routes, trails and more. 168 pages. By Steve Katz. $15.95. ISBN: 0-9632730-3-5

Guide to Cycling St. Louis: Second Edition

All new for 1998. The definitive cycling guide to St. Louis for road and mountain bikers. 192 pages. By Margo Carroll. $15.95. ISBN: 1-891708-01-5

Katy Trail Nature Guide—River Valley Companion

A nice balance between nature, science and fun. This easy-to-use, richly illustrated four-season guide identifies commonly seen trees, flowers, birds, animals, insects, rocks, fossils, clouds, reptiles, footprints and more. Features the Missouri River valley's most outstanding sites and nature daytrips. 256 pages. Compiled by Brian Beatte and Brett Dufur. $14.95. ISBN: 0-9646625-1-5

Missouri Ghosts—Spirits, Haunts and Related Lore

A lifetime collection of spirits, haunts and folklore. Highlights more than a century of Missouri's most spine-chilling and unexplainable phenomena. Fully illustrated. 230 pages. By Joan Gilbert. $14.95. ISBN: 0-9646625-7-4

Show Me Mountain Biking

Comprehensive, all-new guide to 50 of the best, most scenic single track adventures in the state. Great maps, photos and just the information we've all been waiting for. For beginners to advanced riders. 256 pages. By Brett Dufur. $16.95. ISBN: 1-891708-02-3

Show Me Romance

A new book highlighting romantic daytrips and adventures with ideas and places to go all around Missouri. Chapters include the frugal romantic, the adventurous romantic, the sports romantic, the romantic connoisseur and more! This book certainly has something for everyone. 220 pages. By Kate Kogut. $14.95.

Wit and Wisdom of Missouri's Country Editors

More than 600 pithy sayings from pioneer Missouri papers. Many of these quotes and quips date to the 19th century yet remain timely for today's readers. Richly illustrated and fully indexed to help you find that perfect quote. 168 pages. By William Taft. $14.95. ISBN: 0-9646625-3-1

S how Me Missouri books are available at many local bookstores. They can also be ordered directly from the publisher, using this form, or ordered by phone, fax or over the Internet.

Pebble Publishing also distributes 100 other books of regional interest, Rails-to-Trails, Missouri history, heritage, nature, recreation and more. These are available through our online bookstore and mail-order catalog.

Visit our online bookstore, *Trailside Books,* on the Internet at www.trailsidebooks.com. If you would like to receive our catalog, please fill out and mail the form on this page.

Pebble Publishing

P.O. Box 2 ❖ Rocheport, MO 65279
1 (800) 576-7322 ❖ Fax: (573) 698-3108

Quantity   Book Title   x Unit Price =   Total

- -
- -
- -
- -

Mo. residents add 6.725% sales tax = - - - - - - - - - - - -
Shipping ($3.20 first book, $1 each additional title) = - - - - - - - - - - - -
Total = - - - - - - - - - - - -

Name:_____

E-mail Address:_____

Address:_____ Apt._____

City, State, Zip_____

Phone: (_____) _____

Credit Card # _____

Expiration Date _____/_____/_____   Please send catalog _____

Visit online at http://www.pebblepublishing.com